Programming Social Applications

Programming Social Applications

Jonathan LeBlanc

O'REILLY®

Beijing · Cambridge · Farnham · Köln · Sebastopol · Tokyo

Programming Social Applications

by Jonathan LeBlanc

Published by O'Reilly Media, Inc., 1005 Gravenstein Highway North, Sebastopol, CA 95472.

O'Reilly books may be purchased for educational, business, or sales promotional use. Online editions are also available for most titles (*http://my.safaribooksonline.com*). For more information, contact our corporate/institutional sales department: (800) 998-9938 or *corporate@oreilly.com*.

Editor: Mary Treseler	**Indexer:** Lucie Haskins
Production Editor: Holly Bauer	**Cover Designer:** Karen Montgomery
Copyeditor: Rachel Monaghan	**Interior Designer:** David Futato
Proofreader: Jennifer Knight	**Illustrator:** Robert Romano

Printing History:

August 2011:   First Edition.

ISBN: 978-1-449-39491-2

[LSI]

1313169636

*To my amazing wife, Heather, and our little
miracle, Scarlett*

Table of Contents

Preface

I first began developing social applications when Facebook opened up its developer platform in 2007, giving people like me a taste of the extensive social data that an application can use to improve growth and target personalization settings. At the time, I was building social fantasy sports applications for *CBSSports.com*, pulling user information to enrich that fantasy sports data into a highly personalized state.

It wasn't until 2008, when I joined the partner integrations team in the Yahoo! Developer Network, that I got my first peek at an open source approach to social application development through OpenSocial. What attracted me to OpenSocial was not the fact that you could build an application once and deploy to numerous OpenSocial containers (which proved to be a faulty notion), but rather that through an open source approach I could build social applications on a container and understand how these platforms worked from a core level. I developed a deep drive to explore how the relationships that people form on the Web can enrich and personalize their online lives. This was the starting point of my career advocating open source social technologies.

OpenSocial was the gateway specification for me, leading me to explore the Shindig OpenSocial container, OpenID and OAuth (for authentication and authorization, respectively), the third-party code security technologies Caja and ADSafe, and newer distributed web framework specifications like Activity Streams, PubSubHubbub, and the Open Graph protocol. I quickly came to realize that there was a wide range of open source technologies to enable the construction of rich social frameworks. These technologies and specifications built rich layers of functionality in a simple way using very open methodologies.

These social technologies and specifications are what this book is about. Each chapter uncovers a new layer in the construction of highly viral social applications and platforms. We start by exploring the concepts behind social applications and containers, and then dive into the technologies used to build them. With the application basics down, we look at technologies to secure third-party code on a container, and follow with a discussion of how to secure user information and develop a standard login architecture for platforms. After exposing all of those complex layers, we take an in-depth look at distributed web frameworks that showcase standardization techniques for syndicating activities, discovering rich web and user data from sites and email addresses. And finally, we explore some wonderful upcoming standards in the social application world.

The content of this book comes from years of direct partner integration work emphasizing the power and features behind open source technologies while collaborating with other developers and companies to create rich social integrations with Yahoo!. This book is a labor of love, as I have both taught and learned from seeing firsthand how social integration technologies are applied to real-world applications and interactions.

Audience

Since this book touches on many different areas of social web application development, container specifications, architecture, and standards, the audience that it will appeal to includes a wide breadth of fields and proficiencies, including (but not limited to):

- Social web application developers who are building applications for Facebook, iGoogle, Orkut, YAP, or any other social networking site that hosts third-party applications
- Application platform architects and server-side engineers who are building products to host a socialized experience
- Frontend engineers who wish to leverage the customization and direct targeting afforded by the massive social graph derived from these technologies
- Hackers and part-time developers who are building small-scale personal projects off of the social web
- Followers of open source technology who want to understand how these technologies are being used to promote social sharing and standards
- Web developers and company teams who wish to develop membership systems and authentication security
- Security gurus and engineers who want to learn about security within online social experiences

Contents of This Book

This book covers many technologies and tools for working with the social web, from container and application development to building highly engaging social graphs.

Each chapter builds on the fundamentals you've learned in the preceding chapters' social explorations. Here are the overarching topics covered throughout the book, broken down by chapter:

Chapter 1

Takes you through an overview of applications, systems, and open source fundamentals to give you a good foundation for implementing the technologies in the remainder of the book.

Chapter 2

Explores the concepts behind the social graph, breaking it down into its fundamental properties.

Chapter 3

This chapter forms the base of our social application development, walking you through the construction of a social container to host third-party applications.

Chapter 4

Examines extensions and features built into the OpenSocial JavaScript libraries.

Chapters 5 and 6

These chapters offer a deeper exploration of the OpenSocial specification. We will look at the core social aspects of a social platform, from the social graph implementation to the data architecture model.

Chapter 7

Our final OpenSocial chapter will dive into advanced OpenSocial topics such as templating, data pipelining methods, and the future of OpenSocial.

Chapter 8

Covers third-party code security models and how a container can protect itself and its users against malicious code using frontend security systems.

Chapter 9

Explores user and application authorization through OAuth, diving into both OAuth 1 and the newer OAuth 2 specification.

Chapter 10

Details experimental and new technologies being developed for constructing social graphs, activities, and distributed web frameworks.

Chapters 11 and 12 (Chapter 12 available online)

These final chapters look at user authentication and authentication security through the use of OpenID and the OpenID OAuth hybrid extension.

Chapter 12, the Glossary, and the Appendix are available on this book's website (*http://www.oreilly.com/catalog/9781449394912*).

Using an Open Source Technology Stack

Since this book's major focus is teaching the fundamentals of social application, container, and graph development using an open source stack, it is only prudent that I outline the technologies we will examine.

The major set of open source technologies we will explore in this book includes:

- OpenSocial for exploring the social graph and application development
- Shindig and Partuza as container implementations using OpenSocial
- OAuth for secure application and user authorization
- OpenID for user authentication, including the hybrid OpenID OAuth extension
- Caja and ADsafe for securing frontend code
- The Open Graph protocol to explore social web entities
- Activity Streams as a foundation for delivering activity content
- WebFinger as a means of discovering public user data using email addresses
- OExchange as a means of sharing any URL with any other web service on the Web
- PubSubHubbub as a means of syndicating user conversations from a root provider to multiple subscribers
- The Salmon protocol for taking the foundation of PubSubHubbub and unifying conversations between publishers and subscribers

As we explore this open stack, we will compare the technologies with many of the current proprietary standards used in the industry today. This will give you a good overview of both the potential and the implications of using open source fundamentals.

Conventions Used in This Book

The following typographical conventions are used in this book:

Plain text
> Indicates menu titles, menu options, menu buttons, and keyboard accelerators (such as Alt and Ctrl).

Italic
> Indicates new terms, URLs, email addresses, filenames, file extensions, pathnames, directories, and Unix utilities.

`Constant width`
> Indicates commands, options, switches, variables, attributes, keys, functions, types, classes, namespaces, methods, modules, properties, parameters, values, objects, events, event handlers, XML tags, HTML tags, macros, the contents of files, or the output from commands.

`Constant width bold`
> Shows commands or other text that should be typed literally by the user.

`Constant width italic`
> Shows text that should be replaced with user-supplied values.

This icon signifies a tip, suggestion, or general note.

 This icon indicates a warning or caution.

Using Code Examples

This book is here to help you get your job done. In general, you may use the code in this book in your programs and documentation. You do not need to contact us for permission unless you're reproducing a significant portion of the code. For example, writing a program that uses several chunks of code from this book does not require permission. Selling or distributing a CD-ROM of examples from O'Reilly books does require permission. Answering a question by citing this book and quoting example code does not require permission. Incorporating a significant amount of example code from this book into your product's documentation does require permission.

We appreciate, but do not require, attribution. An attribution usually includes the title, author, publisher, and ISBN. For example: "*Programming Social Applications* by Jonathan LeBlanc (O'Reilly). Copyright 2011 Yahoo! Inc., 978-1-449-39491-2."

If you feel your use of code examples falls outside fair use or the permission given above, feel free to contact us at *permissions@oreilly.com*.

Safari® Books Online

Safari Books Online is an on-demand digital library that lets you easily search over 7,500 technology and creative reference books and videos to find the answers you need quickly.

With a subscription, you can read any page and watch any video from our library online. Read books on your cell phone and mobile devices. Access new titles before they are available for print, and get exclusive access to manuscripts in development and post feedback for the authors. Copy and paste code samples, organize your favorites, download chapters, bookmark key sections, create notes, print out pages, and benefit from tons of other time-saving features.

O'Reilly Media has uploaded this book to the Safari Books Online service. To have full digital access to this book and others on similar topics from O'Reilly and other publishers, sign up for free at *http://my.safaribooksonline.com*.

How to Contact Us

Please address comments and questions concerning this book to the publisher:

O'Reilly Media, Inc.
1005 Gravenstein Highway North
Sebastopol, CA 95472
800-998-9938 (in the United States or Canada)
707-829-0515 (international or local)
707-829-0104 (fax)

We have a web page for this book, where we list errata, examples, and any additional information. You can access this page at:

http://www.oreilly.com/catalog/9781449394912

To comment or ask technical questions about this book, send email to:

bookquestions@oreilly.com

For more information about our books, courses, conferences, and news, see our website at *http://www.oreilly.com*.

Find us on Facebook: *http://facebook.com/oreilly*

Follow us on Twitter: *http://twitter.com/oreillymedia*

Watch us on YouTube: *http://www.youtube.com/oreillymedia*

Acknowledgments

First and foremost, my heartfelt thanks go out to my wife, Heather, for "putting up with me" throughout these many months of obsession and late nights, and for the constant support she has given me.

Thank you also to Mary Treseler of O'Reilly for being a sounding board for my many questions and for helping to guide me through this process.

To Rachel Monaghan, the copyeditor for this book, I am grateful for the wonderful tone and flow that you have provided in these chapters.

Next, I want to express my gratitude to all of the reviewers of this book: Matthew Russell, Bill Day, Henry Saputra, Mark Weitzel, and Joseph Catera. Thank you all for catching issues before they became immortalized in print, for suggesting wonderful improvements to this text, and for calling me out on content that was simply not good enough to be a part of this book.

My appreciation goes out to my parents and sister for always standing by me and for teaching me that with hard work I can accomplish anything.

A final big thanks goes out to Havi Hoffman, who runs the Yahoo! Press program at Yahoo!. Without her help and support, this book could have never happened.

CHAPTER 1

Social Application Container Core Concepts

As we can see from the rise of social networking sites like Facebook, LinkedIn, My-Space, the Yahoo! Application Platform (YAP), and hundreds of others around the world, there's a major shift taking place in how humans interact with the Web and how the Web in turn interacts with them. The static web is an artifact of the past, having been replaced by the idea that sites or applications should, as a standard practice, provide their users with an experience customized to their preferences. The Internet has quickly become a vast community of people who find relevance in their online social experiences and interactions. Just as with our real lives, our online lives contain different communication buckets, such as interacting with friends or networking with other professionals. Humans instinctively build these categories of social engagement, deriving value from the people with whom they choose to interact in a particular space.

This is where application development on the social web comes in. Social application developers can help drive the relevance of the interaction that a user chooses to have on the Web. Traditionally, developers have had to build their product, launch it, and then try to adopt users. The social web has given developers the ability to increase the adoption rates of their applications by starting in a space that already has a rich social graph and user base. This space is the *social application container*.

In this chapter, we will explore a number of topics and attempt to answer the following questions:

- What are social application containers and their features?
- What are the differences between open and proprietary standards?
- What are the different types of application development environments, and what are the security issues to be aware of?
- What does the user interface of an application consist of?
- What are application permissions, and what are they used for?

- What are some real-world examples of mistakes you should avoid making when building your applications?
- What are some real-world application models that have worked in the past?
- What are some quick tips that you can use to get started?

Let's begin our exploration with a look at what an application container is.

This book includes numerous sample gadgets, applications, and programs. For your convenience, I've added all the major code examples to the following Github repository so that you can easily integrate and deploy them: *https://github.com/jcleblanc/programming-social-applications*.

What Is a Social Application Container?

Social networking sites are a very familiar part of our daily lives; for example, we use Facebook to connect with friends and family, and LinkedIn to network or interact with colleagues. These sites have become deeply ingrained in our daily online habits. As social networking sites attempt to increase participation among their user base, they may begin allowing third parties to build applications that reside within them.

At a base level, such applications can provide the social networking site with integral functionality for users, delivering valuable features where none existed previously. In some cases, these applications may have even been planned integration points for the site.

A site that hosts a third-party application, thus providing a means by which the application can leverage the social data of its user base, is a *container*. The relationship between the container and an application is mutually beneficial:

- The container builds more value for its users by providing new content that can tap into the profile information or connections they already have, thereby increasing their amount of time on site.
- The application gains a new outlet for promoting its content. In addition, it immediately inherits the benefit of the social graph built out by the container. The application can use this graph to drive new users back to its root site or build additional users for its service.

Jive Software is one example of an enterprise social networking container. Jive could have created a feature to provide survey functionality, but because it allows third-party developers to construct applications on top of it, the SurveyGizmo app supplies this functionality instead. Both companies benefit from this relationship.

A social networking container typically consists of at least three categories of user-based social information that an application can take advantage of:

The user profile
    Information the user has provided about himself

Friends and connections
    The user's social graph, comprising a rich web of interconnected, relevant contacts

Activity stream
    The user's news feed, which provides an aggregated view of the activities around the network and updates from his friends and connections

Each piece helps to build the relevance of a social container. More importantly, it offers an instant starting point from which application developers can reach a large new audience for their products and applications, where otherwise they might have had to host a site to display the information and build up their own social graph.

The User Profile

A user's profile (Figure 1-1) consists of personal information, such as name, birthday, websites, interests, photos, location, and a host of other details that he chooses to provide for friends (or the whole world, depending on the privacy settings specified) to see.

Basics		Edit
Full name	Jonathan LeBlanc	Visible to connections only
Display name	Jonathan LeBlanc	Visible to everyone
Gender	Male	Visible to everyone
Birthday	December 06, 1980	Visible to connections only
Location	Livermore, California	Visible to everyone

Figure 1-1. Basic user profile

From a development perspective, the user profile is a gold mine of information the developer can use to construct applications that provide a highly targeted and personalized user experience. Many users of social networking containers want to provide as much information about themselves as possible. They want to create their own little corner of the Web, where they can communicate with friends, store photos, or perform any other social networking actions they wish. In addition, many containers provide statistics on how complete a profile is, prompting users to complete their entire profile and engage with the container as much as they can. For containers, this feature helps them develop an engaged user base and increase their daily active users, which in turn benefits application developers as they attempt to personalize applications for each user.

User Friends and Connections

User friendships and connections form the basis for a social graph within the social networking container. People who build a profile will add to their network their friends, family, coworkers, and a host of other people who have some sort of social relevance in their lives, online or offline. Figure 1-2 shows a visualization of a user's social connections.

Figure 1-2. Social profile friendships

As people build relationships within their online world, they sort those relationships into buckets, such as friends, family, or coworkers. When you develop applications, understanding the concept of these buckets will help you identify the best targeting methods for content you produce through the application.

The User Activity Stream

One of the major interaction points of a social networking site is the user's activity stream, or news feed. This feed (shown in Figure 1-3) shows users an aggregated view of their own activities and status updates, as well as the application activities of their connections and friends.

Figure 1-3. A user's social activity stream

Often, applications within a container are not promoted in that container's prime real-estate locations. This means that in order to drive traffic back to their applications, developers need to take advantage of features that put their applications front and center for the users.

Because it is the major interaction point for users, the activity stream is the prime outlet for doing just that. Being able to push out application-promoting activities to the user's stream allows developers to reach an entirely new audience—the user's friends and connections—and drive traffic to their applications.

Implementing Proprietary Versus Open Standards

As social sites continue competing for dominance over the online world, you'll inevitably face the question of whether to implement proprietary or open standards when creating a container. Do you implement a custom solution for all aspects of the social container, or do you go with a specification that includes contributors from many of the major technology companies in the space?

Both implementation methods have their benefits and drawbacks, as described next.

Proprietary Implementation

It may not always be appropriate for a container to have an open-ended specification that caters to many different locales and requirements. In this case, building custom software to fit your needs can be a good approach. Doing so has a number of definite benefits for container implementers:

- The software will be highly targeted for your container's specific needs and requirements, thereby reducing code bloat and unneeded features.
- The code base is divorced from the requirements of an open specification. This means that if a change is needed in the code that conflicts with the initial development specification, you can make that change without having to contribute it back to the open specification (and working to get it standardized in future versions) or having to maintain the code differences from the specification when you upgrade to new versions.

These are definitely powerful drivers for many development shops. You are building a project that exists within a silo, separate from the rest of the world. However, there are also a number of drawbacks to this approach:

- You have to develop all code in-house or for the container itself. Since this is a proprietary code base, you'll have to devote engineering time for all upgrades and new features.

- The company must offer support mechanisms for developers building on top of the platform. The community of integration specialists on the particular platform will not include other companies or developers who have implemented a solution based on the same specification.

Facebook is one container that has a lot of its implementation built around proprietary technology developed specifically for its needs. We can see from its example that the proprietary approach can be very successful, but it takes a lot of effort, engineering, and development time.

In recent years, Facebook has begun integrating certain open source initiatives into its proprietary stack, such as the new OAuth 2.0 standard and the Open Graph Protocol, both of which we will cover in later chapters.

Open Source Implementation

Small development shops, or any developers who want to take advantage of the vast community of engineers and knowledge in the social container and application development space, will find a lot of value in the open standard approach. Leveraging a community comprising some of the greatest minds in the space helps developers create powerful tools and specifications for any social container or application.

This approach has many benefits, including:

- The specifications and tools built within open source communities usually have numerous contributors, all of whom have different perspectives on the software. This approach lends itself well to building comprehensive solutions for a lot of the normal problems that would otherwise have to be custom developed through a proprietary approach.

- Open specifications are constantly in development. Unless your company is actively engaged in developing these specifications and tools, the upgrades and features are added independently of your company or product. This means that you do not need to devote engineering resources to upgrading the product with new features. When a new version is developed, the teams implementing the product simply need to revise their tools based on the requirements set forth by the specification. Even though you do have to allow for some development time in this approach, the issues related to security, features, and upgrades have already been solved and outlined within the specifications.

- The supporting community and documentation for open source software is often extensive, providing many supporting samples and use cases.

With all of that in mind, we can see that the benefit of open source initiatives is really about the community interaction with the specifications. As with the proprietary approach, though, open source standards have a few drawbacks as well:

- The solutions are not custom built for any one container. Even though specifications like OpenSocial define methods for integrating only the portions of the specifications that you require for a particular implementation, these pieces still encompass a lot of use cases that you may not have needed for a custom container or application solution.
- The specification upgrades are usually bound by community voting procedures, where everyone has a voice and can vote on which upgrades they see as the best features. This process can be a benefit at times, but it can also mean that not all the requested features make it back into the core specification.

Even with these considerations, many containers build upon open source initiatives, including companies with open container approaches such as Yahoo!, Google, Hi5, and LinkedIn, as well as enterprise vendors such as Jive, IBM, Atlassian, and many others.

Why This Book Covers Open Standards

When it came down to it, this book had to target one approach—either open source initiatives or a single proprietary container implementation. The reason this book covers the open standards approach for social application containers and development is because it is not tied to any one container. I didn't want to limit the scope of this text to a single proprietary platform that could change on a whim and may contain a shallow view of the social web.

My main goals are to provide an overview of the creation and use of a social application container and how applications are built on top of those containers. The concepts behind open source projects are solidly based in the state of the social web, regardless of whether any single container implements all of the features included within a particular open source project.

The Embedded Application: Building in a Black Box

One of the most important things to remember when you're developing applications on top of a social container is that you are not building within a traditional application environment, where you just have to ensure that your application is loading and your server uptime is high. Those are all variables that we as developers can account for and adjust if necessary.

Figure 1-4 displays the difference between a traditional application development environment (right) and the black box environment of a social application container (left). This is a very base-level comparison, as each layer may also contain a number of processing, filtering, and serving mechanisms.

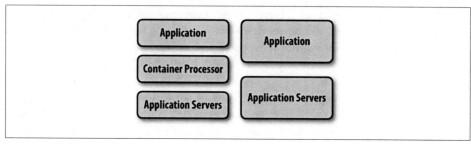

Figure 1-4. Loading an application in a container (left) versus a traditional server environment (right)

The difference is the middle tier of the social container environment. When building social applications within a container, you are building on top of the infrastructure that the container defines. Instead of the application servers providing the code and functionality for the application directly, they provide content to the container for processing. The container may then filter the content for malicious code, unsupported features, or any number of other elements before returning the sanitized content back to the application.

What this means is that you are now relying on a third-party source to serve your application, so any changes to its processes will directly affect the communication between your server and the container, or the data processing for the application itself. The container issues that will affect you the most are:

Container upgrades
> Upgrades can be the bane of any developer's existence when he's working in a black-box environment. They may reveal new bugs or produce issues with backward compatibility.

Uptime of the container
> If the container goes down, your application goes down.

Changes in support
> Containers may change the features that they support, which may affect your application. For example, when Twitter removed support for Simple Authorization (username/password) in 2010, applications built on the Twitter platform had to upgrade to use Open Authorization (OAuth) for authentication instead.

Broken features
> Some of the container's features that you may be using (e.g., custom tags, REST endpoints, etc.) can break on occasion.

When working in these environments, you can do a lot to make sure that you are not blindsided by container changes or issues:

Follow container blogs, mailing lists, Twitter feeds, and communication channels
> When a container upgrades its platform, that release usually coincides with a blog entry and release notes. If you follow those channels, you can check functionality

when the release comes out—or even before, if the container provides early release announcements (usually via the container mailing lists) to make developers aware of changes. Lastly, many containers now use Twitter to provide up-to-the-minute announcements of downtime, upgrades, or bugs, so those feeds should be your first resource if you notice platform issues.

Be aware of the container's bug-reporting structure

Some containers use open bug-tracking systems, while others use forums to report and track bugs within the system. If the usual communication channels don't provide the information you need on an issue, then you should invoke the bug-reporting tools.

Build appropriate feature testing tools

Many containers do not provide an externally available, automated test suite to ensure that all platform features are functional and running. Building your application with test-driven development practices in mind can give you full end-to-end tests to check feature availability easily and quickly when platform changes occur.

While black-box development can be more challenging than traditional methods, its benefits are also worth mentioning. In a traditional development environment, you would create or integrate all the functionality needed to run the application's social features from your own servers. With the black-box environment, however, you are building on top of an ever-upgrading container; the container itself takes care of development to ensure that features are up to date, as well as appropriate QA and end-to-end testing. This means that application developers don't need to worry about development and can instead allocate their time to different aspects of the application.

Embedded Application Security

Social applications running on top of a container pose a major security risk for that container. To host the applications, containers essentially need to run third-party code within their pages. This raises the question of how to host applications without introducing a security risk to the users of the social networking container.

There have been numerous efforts to mitigate this concern. Some containers encourage developers to build their applications using a secured subset of HTML and JavaScript functionality, giving the containers assurance that the code they host is safe from potential security problems. Other approaches include the implementation of frontend code rewriters like Caja or ADSafe, which allow the container to rewrite an application's code to a secured subset of functionality, stripping out any tags or functionality that could be used maliciously. We will explore these technologies more in the upcoming section "Securing Applications" on page 11, and in Chapter 8, which covers secure application development methods.

Despite the number of methods that have been employed to secure applications, iframes remain the most popular for the vast majority of containers. The benefits to using iframes are quite clear: they are easy for containers to implement, and they give application developers maximum functionality with minimal restrictions.

On the other hand, though, the limited restrictions imposed on developers who build their application content within an iframe are also the main drawback to this method. Malicious developers can take advantage of this freedom through a number of well-known iframe exploits, described in the following sections.

Cross-Site Scripting

Cross-site scripting (XSS) is a prevalent security concern in untamed web applications, especially those within the confines of a container. XSS is the most widely used vulnerability attack in this space. An attacker can use XSS to inject client-side scripts into the pages viewed by other users. Once on the page, these scripts can be used to bypass access controls like the same-origin policy.

The consequences of working with a site that is running XSS can range from simple annoyance all the way up to a serious security vulnerability that allows the attacker to capture login details, credit card information, the user's personal profile data, or any number of other private interactions that take place online.

A simple example of XSS is the implementation of advertising on a web application, which allows the third-party advertiser to run some frontend code within the site. Advertising is a form of self-inflicted XSS, but in most cases the website can trust that the advertiser won't do anything malicious.

Even though this is a standard security vulnerability with web applications, it reinforces the need for some measure of application control when third-party code and applications are running within a social networking container.

Same-Origin Policy and Older Browsers

The *same-origin policy* is a very important security concept in terms of user interaction within a website or application. Without the implementation of the same-origin policy, arbitrary sites loaded within an iframe would not only be able to access the DOM of the parent site, but also its cookies and form data.

Modern browsers do a good job of implementing the same-origin policy to prevent this from happening in social application development, but some older browsers do not take adequate measures to restrict sites from violating the policy.

While these older browsers are by no means a large majority of those currently in use, these insecurities should still be noted.

Drive-by Downloads

Drive-by downloads are the processes by which a malicious site can download content to the user's computer without that user having any knowledge that it is happening. This is not a problem exclusive to iframe security, but since using an iframe to secure an application allows the application developer to run any frontend code she wishes, the potential for drive-by downloads is magnified.

Drive-by downloads may mimic the functionality of a pop-up window. When attempting to dismiss the pop up, the user may inadvertently download spyware, malware, or viruses onto his system. These pop-up windows may appear as error reports, advertising, or any other deceptively common message. Since the user's action initiates the attack, he is considered to have given consent to download the malicious package.

This is just one of the methods that a malicious developer may employ. Drive-by downloads take many forms and can be a prevalent problem when third-party code is allowed to run unchecked within an application container.

Securing Applications

Many methods are accepted as appropriate solutions for securing third-party application code within a container host. Two of these, Caja and ADSafe, accomplish this task in particularly unique ways.

Caja is a JavaScript compiler that rewrites any frontend code that is to be loaded into the container. During this rewrite process, insecure functionality will be stripped out and all code will be rewritten as "Caja-safe" code. When working in a Caja-defined container, the underlying application will have indirect access to the DOM of the parent container page, thereby allowing any requests to be secured as needed.

ADSafe does not rewrite the application code, but rather works by stripping out any JavaScript functionality that is deemed to be insecure. This approach is not as painful to work with as Caja's complete rewriter, but it also doesn't provide the extensive security approach that Caja does.

We will discuss both of these topics in more depth in Chapter 8.

The External Application: Integrating Social Data Outside the Container

The main focus of our discussion thus far has been on the construction of applications to exist within the container itself. But this isn't the only context in which social networking applications can exist.

Most containers offer access to their social and container data through a series of URI endpoints. For on-container application development, these endpoints are generally wrapped within an easier-to-use method, such as OpenSocial JavaScript requests or container-specific tags that allow secure access to users' social data and are processed when the application is rendered. In the context of off-container application development, however, these endpoints provide a means by which developers can leverage the container's social data to enhance their websites and applications without needing to build them on the container itself.

To provide this access layer safely and protect their users' social data from attacks, many containers use security implementations such as OAuth. Many of the most popular social networking containers—including Facebook, YAP, iGoogle, Orkut, MySpace, and others—currently implement OAuth in some capacity.

Leveraging a container's social features can help developers extend their reach far beyond the silo of the container itself and build out a rich social graph for their web applications or sites immediately, instead of having to build their own custom relevant graph during their website's inception.

In addition to being able to capture social information from a container off-site, developers can use other technologies to allow users to sign in to a website using the username and password login structure of the container. One open source technology that allows developers to implement such a login structure is called OpenID (Open Identification). By not requiring users to create a new login for your particular site, you can help further socialize your web-based application and decrease the amount of drop-off during the registration process. Once a user logs in using OpenID, the site can then implement a facility to allow users to customize their profiles.

Combining these two technologies (OpenID and OAuth) into a sort of hybrid authorization process, developers can construct a login structure to prevent drop-off during registration (OpenID) and then use the container's social URI endpoints to prepopulate a user's profile and leverage whatever rich social data the container provides (OAuth).

We will discuss the implementations of OAuth and OpenID in the context of an off-site application or website in later chapters.

Application Views

Views allow an application to interact with a user on a social container. The container may have one or more views that an application developer can build content for, enabling the user to view and interact with the application throughout different pages in the container.

Generally speaking, all views will fall under one of two types:

Small view

> A view that is usually restricted in size and functionality. Small views usually appear on the user's profile or her personalized home view, which only she can interact

with. There may be many small views present on a page, depending on how many applications the user has installed.

Large view

A view that usually delivers a fully immersive user experience. This view is seldom overly restricted and will provide most of the same functionality you'd find when developing an application on an external website that you have complete control over. Large views generally have only one application on the page, meaning that users on that view will be engaged only with the application itself.

On most of the current social networking containers, iframes are used to cordon off all views from the rest of the container. While this might provide a small measure of security for the container and its users, it's far from a secure environment. In many cases, applications will load only after the full container has loaded to prevent performance degradation on pages where multiple applications are attempting to load.

The Home View (Small View)

An application's *home view* is generally a small view that provides personal aggregated content specific to a user. In other words, the home view cannot be accessed by any of the user's friends or connections. For the most part, this type of view is the main interaction that the user has with the particular container, providing an aggregate feed of the activities of his connections, upcoming events, pictures, etc. Depending on the container that hosts this type of view, numerous applications may be displayed to the user in this view. Figure 1-5 shows its placement within the container.

Figure 1-5. The application home view

The home view also typically offers a small window view into the full application. Quite often, the container imposes restrictions on this view, such as limiting the markup that may be used to HTML, CSS, and some secure, container-defined tags that provide access to social information like invite drop-down lists, user data, etc. Many containers highly regulate the use of JavaScript and Flash due to performance and security concerns.

Since this view is often the user's first interaction with your application in the container, it is vitally important that it provide as much functionality as possible to draw a user in to one of the more extensive application views. If a small view contains a number of the aforementioned restrictions, many developers will mostly ignore it, opting to devote the majority of their time and attention to the fully featured view. In a vast number of cases, this means that the small view becomes an afterthought and usually just contains a number of calls to action for users to go to the canvas view, without adding any incentive for them to actually do so.

Any view that helps form a user's first impression of your application should warrant as much of your attention as the full feature set of the application. I can't stress this point enough: devoting proper attention to a small view can increase daily active use of your application, drive engagement, and ultimately add users and increase monetization potential.

Any application small view should provide compelling and engaging content (e.g., new activities that users can do in the application), should never be a direct copy of the canvas view, and should provide enough base-level functionality that users do not have to fully engage with the application to get some value.

The Profile View (Small View)

The *profile view* is the publicly available profile that the user exposes to the outside world, and can be accessed by anyone the user allows. In some containers, the profile view may reveal applications that the user has added to anyone viewing his profile. Applications such as those that display gifts sent and received or provide information about the user, or wall-type applications with ping abilities, are all popular within this space because they allow interaction between an outside party and an application that the original user has installed. Figure 1-6 shows the placement of this view within the container.

Figure 1-6. The application profile view

It's less common for containers to have this view in addition to just a standard small view (home view) and a large view (canvas view), but if available, the profile view has a great number of benefits. Unlike with the home view, the direct audience for this small view is anyone viewing the user's profile. This audience will see your application load with some content attempting to draw them into using it. Because you are reaching out to an audience that is relevant to the user in some way, you have a real opportunity here to drive new user installations of your application. You can provide new methods by which that person can reach out to the original user beyond what would normally be available from the social container itself. Such interaction methods might be providing free gifts to the two users, helping them out in games, or comparing maps of where they have been in the world. When the new person interacts with your application to do something like this, she will be prompted to add it to her own profile, gaining you a user.

Since this view is essentially a small view that allows outside interaction, development for it usually contains the same restrictions as those for the home view. Working with all available views to provide a comprehensive user experience that allows users to interact with whatever view of the application they wish is probably the most vital thing we'll talk about here. Users will never use your application in exactly the way that you intend, so plan accordingly and provide them with as much application depth as you can in every view.

The Canvas View (Large View)

The *canvas*, or large, view is considered the fully featured view for your application. Most containers do not impose restrictions on the use of JavaScript or Flash within this view, and it offers the greatest amount of functionality for providing content and tools to end users. This view is the meat of your application, providing the bulk of the functionality and features that the application is capable of.

Unlike the small view of an application, the canvas view is not displayed with other applications in the same view; rather, it generally encompasses the majority of the social container view, delivering a high pixel count for the available height and width, as shown in Figure 1-7. What this means for developers is that when users interact with this view, they have already engaged with the application by either visiting it directly or by being interested enough in one of the small views to follow a call to action to see the larger view. In the vast majority of cases, if a user comes to this view, he is already invested in your application.

Figure 1-7. The application canvas view

The most important thing to remember here is that this view is the best interaction the user will have with your application. Overcomplicating his experience, abusing his social information (e.g., pushing too many messages to his activity stream), or failing to provide a means by which he can engage with it as he wishes are all sure-fire ways to have him stop using your application.

Some of the best applications not only provide a rich experience in this view, but they also offer an appropriate link between the smaller views and this large view. For example, if the user is interacting with the small view of the application, provides some information on a form, and then clicks Submit to go to the canvas view, the application should respond with exactly the application state the user expects, such as a processed form request.

The other vital piece of information here is that you are still within a social container and have the ability to access the user's profile and friends. If your application requires user information such as interests, name, or ID, you can obtain these details via the personal information that the user has already entered about herself in her profile. Requiring the user to enter account information to register for a service without pre-populating the fields with the information already available to you is a recipe for user drop-off.

The Default View (Any View)

The last view that is generally available within many social containers is not actually a view at all, but more of a view state. The *default*, or *preview*, view of an application displays content to users who have not already installed the application or to individuals who are currently logged out of the social network. This view is in public view space, and therefore, may not have direct access to much of a user's profile information, similar to how the public badge provided through the user profile provides only a small subset of information about her.

This view state can emerge within any traditional view, including the profile and canvas view. The home view, however, is generally a personal profile for a logged-in user, so it is unlikely that the default state would emerge in that view. In the case of a signed-out user, you will not be able to take advantage of any personal information because it's unknown. If this state emerges in a small view, it may simply be a case of someone trying to view a user's profile; although your application will render, this event does not necessarily indicate a user who is engaged with it. If this state emerges within the application's canvas view, though, you most likely have a user who is interested and wants to learn more.

For cases where this state emerges in the smaller views of an application, you should be providing a method to try to immediately drive the viewer to your application's canvas view to install the application, or provide a method to engage with her and then drive her to the canvas view. Since the user has never interacted with the application and thus will not have entered personal information that you can leverage, it's difficult to personalize this state. An engaging small view is important even in these cases, but your ultimate goal for the default view is to drive the user toward an install state and engage her.

When this state emerges in the larger canvas view, it's likely that users are looking to see what the application is before committing to installing it. In this case, you should try to provide them with as much interaction with the application as possible while still pushing them to log in and install. Coupling the install state of the container with the functionality of the application is a good way to seamlessly add a new user. If the user begins interacting with the application's controls and customizations, you can bring her to the container install state and walk her through installation to begin working with the application.

Application Permission Concepts

Applications within a social application container do not automatically have access to a user's social profiles, activity streams, and friendships—that would be a major security concern. Containers usually require that the application define the *permission scopes* it needs access to. As shown in Figure 1-8, these scopes will be requests that a user must agree to when installing the application.

Figure 1-8. An application permission screen

Typically, *social scopes* are defined as major pieces of social information about a user, such as his:

- Profile
- Activity stream
- Friendships

Each container may define different scopes or even include a number of nonsocial scopes that a container may gain access to. Once the user accepts the scopes, the container can do things on his behalf. For the three aforementioned social scopes, these things may respectively include:

- Allowing the application to capture all information within the user's profile.
- Allowing the application to obtain any activities in the user's activity stream and to push new activities to this stream on the user's behalf.
- Allowing the application to obtain the profiles for all of the user's friends. Although those friends have not necessarily added the application, once a user declares that someone is his friend, it establishes a trust relationship, and applications capitalize on this. Essentially, the user trusts that friend with his personal information. When that friend in turn trusts an application with her information, there exists a trust "bridge" between the application and the friends. Some containers impose restrictions on how much social information can be obtained with these predefined trust relationships.

These scopes are usually secured through authorization mechanisms such as OAuth, which require that a user sign in through the container when he grants permissions to an application.

Client-Side Versus Server-Side Applications

As you begin developing applications on a social network, you'll inevitably have questions about the best method for serving an application's content. Should you use a client-side approach, taking advantage of many of the client tools a container usually makes available? Or should you use a mainly server-side approach to provide a scalable, high-performance user experience? In other words, what are the best tools for the job? These are some of the questions that we need to answer before building an application.

Before we begin development, we should look at a few factors that can help you build an application that is scalable and offers good overall performance.

Using Template Systems for the Markup Layer

Although some template systems require additional development time to integrate, using them can provide noticeable results when you're attempting to scale an application environment. Simply put, templates allow developers to separate out their programming logic from the visual layer of the application. This makes application development easier, allows for multideveloper collaboration, provides an easier means for debugging the environment, and enables you to scale the product as needed.

There's no doubt that some template systems can add a large amount of unnecessary heft to application code, but the question comes down to what systems you really need for the specific application you're developing. Small applications will not get a lot of mileage out of fully developed template systems, which are built for large-scale development projects; on the flipside, large application projects would require a lot of development effort to create a custom template solution.

Again, the real question comes down to need. As we explore the different open source techniques for application development in this book, we will look into a few excellent template solutions offered through the OpenSocial application framework.

Using a Blended Server and Client Environment

As mentioned earlier, when beginning a new application project, developers usually face questions about the proper methods for building its programming logic. Developers tend to use an approach that is comfortable to them, sometimes ignoring other good options that are available because of their ingrained habits.

When it comes to developing an application, is a heavy client-side system better than a heavy server-side implementation, or vice versa? The short answer is that both approaches provide different benefits that add to the performance, functionality, or development ease of an application.

Most containers that currently allow applications to be developed on their platforms offer a series of secure tags from which the developer can create quick visualizations of user social data without actually having to make any server calls. This provides an obvious boon to frontend development, as the container can take care of processing social data without actually requiring the user to grant the application permission to access her personal information. Secure tags are just one benefit available to developers who are building out a frontend system, but having the container manage the frontend processing of social data is usually the critical piece that allows developers to build highly social applications.

Exploring the alternate side of the fence, a server-side approach has obvious benefits for developers. First of all, server processing doesn't have to account for browser quirks like JavaScript does. The server environment will be consistent no matter which browser the user views the application in, and will not be affected by a user's browser settings, such as having custom JavaScript disabled. In addition, server processing allows the developer to cache data results and thus provide quicker responses to data requests from the application.

So when should we use a server-side approach versus a client-side implementation? Data processing is more efficient from the server side and offers caching mechanisms that speed up data requests. The client side, on the other hand, allows for custom tags and access to other container-specific social data by enabling the container to efficiently parse and display a user's personal information without requiring the application to request access to it. The short answer is that a blended client/server environment is the most efficient and offers the largest opportunity for taking advantage of container-specific tools and utilities.

Deferring the Loading of Noncritical Content

When a social networking container imposes strict security measures on the content being loaded to it, applications with large amounts of content tend to load much slower and might time out if the container expects all the application content to load within a specific time. This problem can be compounded if the application being built loads its content from a single server request, which in turn performs an extensive amount of processing before returning the complete application markup. Processing an entire application from a single request can certainly reduce the number of HTTP requests that are being made from the application and can help with performance. So, for many smaller applications, this may make sense. But in the case of applications with heavy content loads, this approach can be detrimental to the point that it sometimes prevents the application from loading within the container at all.

Using a deferred loading approach can easily mitigate this issue. Since most containers load applications on a page only after the container and page content have finished loading, there is usually precious little time for an application to capture the user's attention. An application that stays in a loading state for eight seconds while all of its markup loads will usually miss this window, as the user moves on to doing other tasks within his profile.

If you load the most important content of the application within the first HTTP request, returning data such as core user customizations or pertinent application information like scores or statuses, you can grab the user's attention. Once you have that attention, the application can continue to make HTTP requests to the server to gather additional, less important content, loading once that's completed.

By using this technique to engage with users as soon as possible, you can increase the number of daily active users.

When Good Applications Go Bad

Even with the developer's best intentions, sometimes a good application can fail because of improper architecture, not having enough room to scale, or by not leveraging the social tools available to it. But with a little bit of planning before the development actually begins, developers can build an application core that can scale, makes use of available social hooks to drive traffic, and will make money in the long run.

Before beginning an application project, developers should ask themselves a series of questions:

- What is our intended audience? Do we plan to expand to additional audiences or languages?
- How are we planning to scale the server backbone to handle traffic spikes if the application becomes popular?
- What social features of the container can we use in the application to drive traffic and new user installs?
- How can we monetize the application?

These are just some of the basic questions that we should ask and answer before development even begins. It's important to lay a good foundation and plan for the future.

With that in mind, let's take a look at a few use cases that have some inherent issues in their development practices.

The Portable Flash Application

Quick turnaround time and portability between containers is a major selling point for many development shops. Having a complete application process that consists of taking a new container platform, slapping in an iframe that points to the developer servers, and loading a Flash movie can seem like a great advantage during development, but this type of development practice has some serious ramifications in the social realm.

As mentioned previously, many social networking containers impose limits, sometimes including Flash and JavaScript restrictions, on the content that is served from the small views of an application. For a developer who has embedded his application's sole content in Flash, this means that his small view is often a glorified ad trying to forward the user on to the large view or developer site, or it'll end up having little relevance to the actual application. It certainly won't provide similar functionality to the large view.

Next, let's explore the social features. Portability is not the only aspect that you should consider when developing an application for cross-container functionality. All too often, Flash-based applications silo themselves from the container's root social features, including activity hooks to push out updates to users, friendship graphs to promote application growth, or even simple messaging systems to drive additional traffic and installs. Such applications usually have a very shallow user following. They have a high turnover and eventually fizzle as new user growth areas become harder to find. Without social hooks and relevant views, the application does not go far enough to keep users engaged.

Cross-container development should mean that developers spend time building an abstraction layer that sits between the container and an application. This allows the developer to build a single, highly social application and then just plug in the social and data hooks of any new container that is integrated into the architecture.

The Underdeveloped View

I've mentioned the fact that having relevant small views can help to promote user growth and engagement, but the same is also true for the larger views. Some development shops wish to work only with the larger views; likewise, some want to work only with the small views since that is the first thing the user sees in most circumstances.

Let's look at an application's small views first. We've already talked about how some containers impose restrictions on the small view that may prevent JavaScript and Flash integration, and these restrictions are usually the chief reason why developers don't develop a rich and compelling small view. Since it is the user's first interaction with your application, a compelling small view will promote application growth. Once the user has been regularly interacting with your application, you should change the small view to incentivize him to continue on to the large view. For a game, this incentive might be current statistics, stats of friends for comparison, or new items that the user can earn by performing some action. For productivity applications, it might include reminders for upcoming tasks, a comparison of his actions against those of his friends, or some simple functionality for interacting with the application.

Moving on to the large view, the main reason why some developers don't develop this view is that they create applications containing functionality that's so simple it is not impeded by any small view restrictions. This is a very shallow way to think about a social application and basically means that you don't think your users will need or want any further functionality other than the basic data you're providing. Most containers do not offer a way to turn off a view, so they show a blank page for views that are not defined. This means that the developer has to go through the task of attempting to hide the means for users to switch between views, which may actually require some development effort, depending on how containers have implemented their view-switching mechanisms. The bottom line is that such a developer basically restricts users to views that are smaller and contain fewer features because she doesn't want to make the effort to build a compelling application that leverages the container's existing features.

Users quickly catch on to applications that try to deliver them content without any extensive depth or those that expect them to use the application from only a single place.

The Copycat View Application

We all know how tempting it can be to copy our view code in each view instance. We want to provide our user base with as much functionality (and as many different views) as possible without expending a lot of engineering resources. Cloning that view for every portal that's visible to the user can seem like a no-brainer at times.

The simple fact is that users will see right through this technique, and will view your application poorly, if they switch between a small view and a large view only to be presented with exactly the same thing they just saw. This can create a lack of trust once the users see something amiss in the application. After all, if the developer has not put in the time and effort to fully build out the application, how can they trust that application with their social information?

Let's explore the trust relationship of this scenario first. If you're building an application that will attempt to either monetize the user experience or drive traffic back to a source, the last thing you want is for a user not to trust that application. When a user actively migrates to a different view and is presented with the same screen and functionality that he just saw, he will believe there's something wrong with the application—something happened that shouldn't have. He'll remember this when you try to monetize that experience. Essentially, you're establishing a trust relationship in order to get some sort of return on investment from your users.

Next, let's look at the view differences. If you copy your small view to your large view (or vice versa), you will face one of two visible issues:

- If you built the application to a specific width instead of making the size fluid, the application will either look too small or too large for the view. If it's too large for the view, it will also require the user to scroll to view the content. In either case, this makes for an unpleasant user experience.

- If you built the application using fluid width techniques, allowing the content to drop down to the next line if it needs to, then you have mitigated against many of the previous option's concerns. But the issue of too much versus too little content still comes into play here. If you build an extensive amount of content, the small view looks excessively large and bloated; likewise, if you integrate too little content, the large view looks too sparse.

No matter which use case you are developing, the amount of effort you'll expend to fully answer and develop solutions for the aforementioned issues can nearly equal that of creating a second view in the first place.

The Oversharing Application

The next use case we'll look at is an application that abuses the user's activity stream. Shamelessly pushing every action the user takes within it, the "oversharing" application promotes itself relentlessly through the news feed, where it's visible to all of the user's friends. Those of us who have used applications within a social networking container have undoubtedly come across such an example.

The problem here really occurs in the news feed items that are displayed to the user's friends. What do we all do when we encounter continuous updates from an application that we have never seen before? Well, most users disable updates from that application (if that functionality is available) or from the user completely. In either case, this disables the application's communication channel to a relevant user base, making it more difficult to reach new users. There are precious few channels available for application developers to reach potential users, so having a major one disabled can be detrimental to the application's longevity.

Later in this book, we will talk about different sharing methods to help developers choose a solution that is right for them without overtaxing the user's activity stream.

The Unmonetized Application

One of the saddest things in the application world is seeing a great idea poorly executed. Time and time again, developers build highly successful applications without ever giving any thought as to how they will make money from the user experience. Unless you're banking on selling your application to one of the top application development companies in the space, you need to be able to pay for the expenses that the server traffic will incur.

Even if you don't implement all of the monetization techniques you'd like in an application, plan to upgrade from the beginning. It's important to understand the key areas of your application that can produce some sort of return on investment. Setting clear goals about when and how you'll integrate the monetization effort is part of a good long-term strategy for the application. For instance, you might plan to develop an in-app marketplace when you hit a certain number of users or daily active users.

As important as monetizing is, *how* you go about it is just as important. Essentially, you want the act of requesting additional money to convince users that the application will get much better if they purchase something, whether that's upgrades or new content. You still want the application to be functional for those users who don't put down much or any money, but you want to make it known that their experience can be much improved with additional features—with a premium account, if you would.

There are numerous methods that an application developer can use to monetize the user experience, including:

- An in-game marketplace that offers new content or features to enhance the application's user experience. These are virtual offerings, not tangible.
- Social networking application advertising platforms. There are a number of advertising platforms that are built to work well in applications running within a container.
- A product marketplace that presents the user with tangible sale items that may be based on the application or related to the user's social information (i.e., targeted social sales).

These techniques are widely employed by many of the most successful applications in the more popular social networking containers. If used tactfully and with proper consideration for how the sales techniques flow with the application logic, monetization techniques do not need to be imposing or irritating to your user base.

The Feed Application

The last application type we'll look at is used quite often by publishers trying to syndicate their feed out to a different source, such as an application in a social networking container. Many times, publishers just want to take an XML or RSS feed of their news content, apply a stylesheet, and link every story back to its originating source—most often, their website. This application model certainly provides easy and fast integration, but easy is not always good.

The reasons why publishers choose to implement such applications are usually fairly simple. Either they don't wish to devote much engineering effort to the application until they see a return on investment (i.e., an increased number of active users), or they don't want to provide all of their content on another site since they don't have all of their same tracking and marketing mechanisms within the application context.

First of all, publishers who use this method tend to either not integrate all application views, or populate each view with exactly the same content. We discussed the reasons why this type of application model tends to fail in the earlier section "The Copycat View Application" on page 23, so I won't reiterate those points here.

Besides the view issue, the major drawback to this application model is simply that the implementation is shallow and doesn't provide any value for a user. In this instance, the only difference between using this application and reading through an RSS feed of the same content is the styling. In addition, having each link within the application jump the user from the social networking container over to the publisher site is jarring. People use applications to get all of their content in one place; they don't want to have their viewing experience terminated just to look at the content of a story.

Feed applications are truly a shame, because most of the time they have real users who want to consume their information from their favorite source. It was proven long ago that a closed application development model—not providing your technology or data outside of your company—doesn't work. Opening up your data and sources helps you reach entirely new audiences. If nurtured correctly, these users can become loyal readers, which can in turn translate into monetization benefits.

Fortunately, it's easy to adjust this model into something that delivers a clear benefit to users. First, publishers don't need to provide the entire content of their stories within the application context. Most of the time, users look through an application's synopsis and title to see if they are interested in reading more; publishers should support that use case by providing a paragraph or two of content inside the application to pique user interest. Below that content, they can provide a link to the full story on their website. This small change to the application can make a world of difference.

Next, in the large view of the application, developers can integrate additional configuration options to allow users to consume only the data that they are interested in. This configuration panel will provide users with an additional layer of functionality that helps them get relevant information from the application, driving more daily activity.

All in all, this application model is one of the easiest to change. Thinking of an application less as a feed outlet and more like an interactive object can help increase application growth, the number of unique users, and the overall amount of traffic that returns to the originating website.

Application Model Case Studies

Now that we've examined some application models that do not work and why they don't, let's take a brief tour of three different application models that *do* work, looking at specific companies that are implementing these models today.

The case-study models we'll cover are:

- Friendship-based social gaming applications
- Product sales applications
- Location-based applications

This section should give us a good overview of some business models that work in the application, mobile, and social spaces.

Case Study: Friendship-Based Social Gaming

Our first case is a social gaming application whose infrastructure is built off of social interactions between two-way, or reciprocated, connections (friendships). Building upon the real-life relationships that people have with their friends, family, coworkers, and everyone else in their stream is a great method for developing an extensive relevant graph within the social game as well.

Let's take as an example one of the biggest players in the social gaming space: Zynga. Zynga has built its core business from creating highly addictive social games that are some of the most played in the social gaming space. Love it or hate it, Zynga is one of the most successful social gaming companies in the business, developing titles such as *FarmVille*, *CityVille*, and *Mafia Wars*. Companies like Zynga use several tactics to build highly viral, lucrative games.

Even though we are speaking specifically about social gaming applications in this case study, you can apply these principles to any social-based application that makes use of someone's social graph.

Understanding user targeting

Understanding the appropriate audience (i.e., which demographics you should be targeting) should be one of the first steps for any social application developer. Simply understanding who makes up your existing audience is not enough anymore, though. For instance, if you build a great social game targeting an audience that is completely saturated with other great social games, you are not going to see the same return on investment as you would by targeting another niche group.

This is an area Zynga has navigated incredibly well. Traditionally, online games were targeted to specific demographics, such as males between the ages of 14 and 25, and were created for noncasual users. Zynga changed the state of online gaming by targeting the casual gaming market, drawing in many users who were younger, older, and of a different gender than the stereotypical online game audience. The company developed an entire market for social-based casual gaming.

Building a relevant graph in the game

Even if the social graph of the platform on which you're building your social game is vastly irrelevant (i.e., users have few two-way connections and of those that they do have, many have no real-life significance to the users), that should not prevent the social graph within the application from being vastly relevant to the game.

Zynga has proven this case as it has moved from different platforms, even those that had just emerged as a social network, such as the YAP. No matter what the state of the user-based connections within a platform, the game environment offers you the chance to build up a social graph to the level of relevance required for a viral application.

You can take advantage of this by developing comprehensive invitation flows within your application so that a user may send notifications to any connections asking them to join her in the game. This process needs to also have some sort of benefit to the user, though, or it will not be effective. For instance, Zynga builds an invitation flow into its applications' gameplay; *Mafia Wars* players gain power by adding new connections to their mafia, and *FarmVille* players get help with their farms. Earning a few core benefits from adding users will motivate players to search out new connections who have a shared interest in the game in order to build themselves up in the game. While these connections may not know each other personally, they are relevant to the game because they share an interest and mutually benefit from remaining connected.

Allowing connections to interact with one another in the game

Expanding upon an earlier point, it's important to offer some benefit for users to interact with one another. While the previous case had to do with increasing the relevance of the social graph, it's equally crucial to present in-game opportunities for social interactions in order to help increase the number of daily active users who play your game.

To showcase this point, let's go back to our Zynga *Mafia Wars* example. If you are playing the game with friends, you can take advantage of a few mechanisms Zynga has built in to allow you to work directly with the social graph you have built in the game, such as:

- Starting missions where your friends can help you
- Asking your connections for items in the game (gifts)

Gift giving is a very popular aspect of these games. Having options where users can give and request free gifts from one another every day allows them to improve their in-game personas while also increasing their activity.

In short, once you have the channels to draw users in to your game, you also need the mechanisms in place for keeping them there.

Providing clear benefits for actions taken in a game

Another aspect of vital importance in this case study is providing a clear incentive for people who are already using your application to continue using it. In other words, you need to create opportunities for growth within the game or application itself.

There are several different mechanisms you can employ to retain the user's long-term interest. Just to name a few:

- Offering increased power levels within the games based on the amount of time played and the number of game actions the user performs.
- Providing character-based level progression so that users associate the amount of time they invest with the progression of their avatar in the game.
- Delivering real-time growth mechanisms. Making the acts of, say, building new facilities or growing crops time-based will keep players coming back within certain timeframes. You can take this a step further by providing a time window where a user must do something after the building process (e.g., harvest crops before they

wither) or she'll lose what she's built. This will dramatically increase the use of your application within those time periods.

Providing such benefits will help to increase the number of daily game players, which in turn gives you more time to monetize their use.

Integrating social channels through email, notifications, and activities

Application platforms usually provide numerous viral channels for developers to communicate with users or invite other people to the game. Although these channels are one of the most important features to promote growth in your application, for most developers, they're often secondary to feature enhancements to the product.

Let's look at Zynga, for instance. If you monitor the activities that the company pushes from its applications, you will see that it makes subtle changes to the update's static text on a regular basis. This is because the language you use in an activity can vastly increase the number of new users you obtain from the update. The user's activity stream is a direct pipeline to his regular news feed, which is the same data that he consumes on a regular basis to see what his friends are doing.

Application platforms usually have alternate contact methods for application developers to leverage, such as direct email correspondence (initiated by the user) or action-item notifications that the user must accept or decline. Instead of using the user's activity stream as a passive delivery device for increasing application use or obtaining new users, emails and notifications require the user to take some action in order to dismiss them. This action can either be deleting the message or acting upon it, but in either event, you get the user's direct attention.

 Do not overuse communication channels to send many messages to users. No one likes a spammy application, and doing so will negatively impact your application's growth.

At the end of the day, you should be constructing an application that leverages every single viral and communication channel that the platform has available. Plan the application architecture to embed opportunities where you can communicate with users, and don't overproduce updates to them. Be conscientious of your application users.

Monetizing through the sale of virtual goods

One of the best milestones you can reach in the monetization arena is offering a product that costs you nothing to produce. This is exactly what many of the top-grossing games in the business are doing.

Let's look at the Zynga *Mafia Wars* game example again. Within the game, the user can purchase reward points (as shown in Figure 1-9), which can be considered virtual currency. Players can use this virtual currency to buy equipment and bonuses in the game to put them ahead of their competition. Zynga collects money by providing something that isn't even tangible, so the production cost of that item really doesn't exist (though of course, the company is still responsible for server costs, employee salaries, and the like).

Figure 1-9. Zynga's Mafia Wars Marketplace

Increasing the amount of money that comes in from the game can be as easy as creating new items for users to purchase in the virtual store, and is only limited by the imaginations of the application engineers and designers.

Case Study: Product Sales Applications

For our second case study, we will look at an application type that is quite different from the social gaming examples we just discussed.

Arriving on the scene in the past few years, companies like Groupon and Living Social (as well as many others) have built large empires around the idea of offering goods and services to users at a heavily discounted price.

We'll explore the experiences that these companies deliver in the following sections, looking at the components that make these "daily deal" applications so successful.

It's not all about games

Many of us have probably seen an oversaturation of games on the social networking sites we frequent, but it needs to be said: *it's not all about the games*. In fact, numerous productivity and product sales applications have raised millions in funding for their companies. These applications, which are inherently social and make users' day-to-day lives easier, can be just as popular as those in the gaming space. They succeed by providing:

- A solution to a problem in users' lives
- A way for users to get answers about something that they can't get elsewhere (i.e., shared social experiences)
- A product that improves the way that users normally do something

These are just a few of the reasons why people use productivity and sales applications.

Taking an old idea and making it new

What makes Groupon such a wonderful product is that it takes a very old, embedded societal invention—coupons—and updates it for today's social and mobile world. Rather than simply taking the old way of doing things and adding some social and mobile features, however, Groupon has entirely rewritten the concept of a coupon.

 If you're unfamiliar with Groupon, think of it as a small daily dose of Black Friday or Boxing Day sales.

This is one of the most important things you can do if you are building an application that includes a sales aspect. People don't want yet another method for doing the exact same thing; they need a compelling reason for using your application, and that reason is *innovation*. Your product has to provide a new way of doing something, a custom spin on the thing that you are trying to sell or do.

Groupon not only gives people a way to find the goods and services that they already enjoy at a discounted price, but it also exposes them to new products or experiences that they may have never encountered otherwise. Many users enjoy Groupon most for that reason—it provides them with things to do that they wouldn't normally do.

These factors are what make Groupon such a great product.

Opening up discussions to get and provide feedback

One of Groupon's other advantages is the fact that each available product or service represents an opportunity for potential buyers to discuss the product not only with each other, but also with Groupon staff and, many times, with the business that is offering it.

A discussion area like this delivers numerous benefits, including:

- Pushing users who are on the fence into buying the product or service simply by being able to address their concerns about the product directly.
- Placing the application business, its users, and the business selling the product at the same level, in a single discussion thread. This goes a long way toward making buyers more comfortable with the process.

Using methods such as discussion areas may take some time and effort from the customer service angle—and from the people who understand the product well—but you gain the benefit of building a quick FAQ for the product or service and closing more deals by addressing potential buyers' concerns upfront.

Gifting a service

Productivity and sales applications can take their core concept a step further and draw in additional sales by offering users their products as gifts for someone else.

As you can see in Figure 1-10, Groupon implements this concept very well. While the offered product may not appeal to the user, it might to someone she knows, or she might have an upcoming event that she needs a unique gift for. By simply providing users with another option for consuming what you are selling, you can increase sales significantly.

Figure 1-10. Groupon's "Buy it for a friend!" gifting option

Case Study: Location-Based Applications

In this case study, we will explore an application type that has gained a lot of popularity over the past few years: the location-based application.

Applications like Gowalla, FourSquare, or even Facebook Places demonstrate the current capabilities of these types of services. We'll use these services as a jumping-off point for exploring the ways that location-based applications can gain new users, increase levels of daily active use, and deliver highly customized monetization experiences.

Meeting friends

One of the greatest benefits to location-based applications is being able to see where your friends are. At some point, we've probably all thought to ourselves, *I wonder what so-and-so is doing*, or *I wonder if any of my friends are someplace interesting where I can join them*. With location-based applications, users no longer have to wonder. Providing functionality for people to follow one another and see the places their friends check in to allows them to socialize more.

 When users want to join friends at a location that they have checked in to, one issue they might face is that their friends might not actually be at that location anymore. Although these services offer a check-in option, they do not offer a check-out option.

Giving users a location-based way to interact with their friends allows them to use your service for something way beyond its original intent, and in doing so, motivates them to find new and innovative methods for deriving more relevance from (and thus spending more time in) your application.

Providing badges and points

One of the methods for driving user activity within a location-based application is to reward them with virtual goods when they take certain actions in the application. This method keeps users engaged with the product, and it requires only a minimal amount of effort from the application developer to implement.

For example, Gowalla has included a feature within its application that gives users badges and items based on the places that they have checked in to. With each new place that a user visits, he is given a badge to signify that he was there. He may also obtain multiple badges if he is checking in to a new state or country. Sometimes he may be lucky enough to pick up a new item when he checks in to a new place, and he can add such items to his official collection to more easily see everything he's collected over time.

Gowalla also shows the user any items that he is missing, as shown in Figure 1-11. A "fear of loss" is often enough to push people to check in at more places in the hopes of obtaining the elusive items they need for their collections.

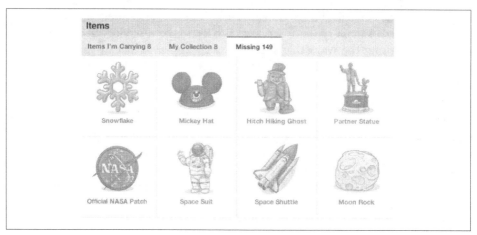

Figure 1-11. Missing items on Gowalla

In contrast to social gaming applications, location-based applications tend to use virtual goods to boost user engagement as opposed to monetizing the application.

Offering competition (mayorships and leaderboards)

What's wrong with a little healthy competition? When it comes to location-based applications, nothing at all.

Gowalla introduced a leaderboard (Figure 1-12) within its application that displays a ranked list of users for a specific location based on the number of times that they have checked in. Similarly, FourSquare built a mayor list to promote a single user to the status of "mayor" for a given location.

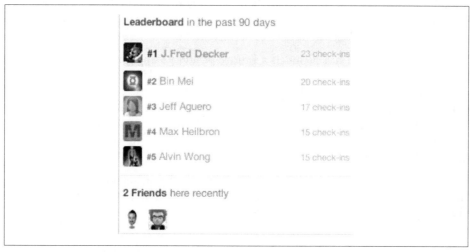

Figure 1-12. The leaderboard on Gowalla

Such utilities encourage people to use the application more to try to gain the top spot at a given location (although they have also prompted some false checkins from users hoping to promote their status). Providing a means for users to compete against one another by using the service more is a great way to keep users engaged on a daily basis.

Location- and profile-based ad targeting

What is one of the biggest benefits to knowing where a person is when she uses your service? Knowing what's around her. When you combine this knowledge with the information you have obtained about her and her habits, you have a perfect formula for serving up content that is much more targeted toward her specific tastes and interests.

Let's say we have our own check-in application like Gowalla or FourSquare, and we maintain a history of the locations where a user has checked in. Now, from those spots we can determine some of her interests, such as foods she likes (based on restaurant trends), general area of interest (based on density of checkins in a specific location), and general consumption times (based on the check-in times). By combining all of this information, we can start serving up ads for local businesses that match these criteria or are in the same family of businesses as the trends we have discovered. We can also shuffle these ads on a timely basis depending on when the user generally checks in.

Now we'll take this a little bit further. Let's say that the user is using the location-based application, so we know where she is and which neighborhoods she likes. When she searches for restaurants, the application can suggest places based on her tastes, such as promoted businesses around the area in which the user is checking in.

While this is a very specific example, you can easily see how the physical location and location history that you obtain from such an application can help you serve up content that is targeted toward one user. When you tailor advertising or suggestions to an individual user's habits, you increase the likelihood of her accepting the offer. Working with local businesses and advertisers is a very effective strategy for providing suggestions geared toward a specific user's habits and trends.

Offering promotions through local businesses

Now let's look at a different angle on monetization of location-based applications: partnerships with local businesses.

If your application is based on the user's physical location in the real world, you have a great opportunity to build partnerships with local businesses that might mutually benefit from offering discounts or benefits to your application's users.

Let's take FourSquare as an example. Back in May 2010, the company partnered with Starbucks to provide the mayors of local Starbucks shops with a discount on one of its new drinks, as shown in Figure 1-13. For Starbucks, it was a way to promote its new drink offering within a large group of users, while FourSquare benefited from like promotion,* increased user activity in specific locations, and a general sense that its service was not just for "fun and games," but in fact had some real-world benefit.

Figure 1-13. FourSquare's Starbucks mayor offer

When it comes to location-based applications, the benefits reside in the fact that you can play in both the virtual and real worlds, showing people that their online actions have a direct correlation to their real-world lives.

Quick-Start Tips

Building applications can be a tricky business, especially when you are under pressure to see a return on your investment. Before beginning the development process, you need to answer a number of practical questions, specifically around how the processes will be developed.

Understand Your Audience

The most important question that any business should answer is, "who is my audience?" The same is true for social application developers—you must understand the

---

* The term *like promotion* draws from services such as the Facebook Like button, where a person viewing a page or product "likes" it, thereby promoting it to other users through social media channels.

core users you're trying to target with your application. Once you understand this, you can structure the application discovery mechanisms, gallery placement, and promotion methods around this information.

Build Social Integration Points Early

One of the biggest pitfalls for a lot of applications being developed within social containers is failing to account for the fact that a social application is not a traditional closed application. Building a simple service that doesn't include any social hooks, promotional mechanisms through the user activity stream, or a means of interacting with the social graph is not enough. These social elements are critical for the application's longevity and user growth.

When first specifying how the application should run, you must understand how social information will play into the overall application structure. Specifically, you should thoroughly explore how to promote your application through the user's activities, interact with the user's social graph to invite new application users, and leverage profile information to personalize your application.

Build with Monetization in Mind

Another application developer failure point is not knowing how to monetize a good idea. As you develop your applications, you must have a clear understanding of how they will eventually make money. If it's through advertising, you must make sure to set aside the appropriate space for the ads.

If advertising is not your preferred monetization method, there is a host of other methods available to you. Adding content upgrades to enrich the user experience can be an excellent way to keep users happy and give them the freedom to use the application how they wish.

Another effective method is integrating monetization into the application's flow. For example, some game companies will provide a small amount of powerful enhancement points that players can use to speed up production of something, give them better stats, or add any number of other upgrades. Most players will just use the free points as they are slowly allotted, but some will purchase additional amounts to get an advantage over their peers.

No matter which method you use, it's essential to form a strategy for how your application will make money prior to the start of development.

Create Comprehensive Views That Play Off One Another

We've discussed the importance of views when you're building out social applications. The best current social applications utilize all possible views to the maximum degree possible. Don't simply provide all your content in every view, but rather, use the different views to complement one another.

For example, use the canvas view to configure the content of the smaller views. Offering dynamic views that a user can customize to suit his viewing needs will go a long way toward building an active user base for your application.

CHAPTER 2

Mapping User Relationships with the Social Graph

Relationships, between both people and things, are the root of a user's social graph. The links in this graph are a rich source of information about a person—his hobbies, preferences, purchasing habits, and many other details that an application developer can use to build a user experience geared specifically to an individual.

A relevant social graph is an application developer's single most important tool. It is the means by which you engage a new, relevant user base, grow your social application's audience, and target a set of users based on their social profile details and preferences.

This chapter explores some of the concepts behind the social graph, how you can manipulate it, and how you can extend the social links between users with entity objects that they may interact with. We'll conclude with an exploration of the Facebook social graph, which is a practical implementation of the graph concepts covered in this chapter, and the OpenLike widget, which can help you promote your product to multiple sources in one easy step.

The Online Social Graph

We no longer live in a time where our offline lives are divorced from our online lives, where a user can interact anonymously with the Web without worrying about the implications it may have on her life.

Today, any social web interaction we participate in, site we log on to, or online merchant we purchase from leaves a virtual footprint that someone can track to enhance ad targeting, provide alternative options for our future purchases, or identify individuals in our social circles who have a higher likelihood of using or purchasing something if someone they know has already done so.

As citizens of the social web, we typically have a multitude of different social graphs depending on which social services we use, what information we have provided to them, and how they interact with other social services. Although we might share different information on these services, the concept of the social graph applies to all of them.

 Our social graphs differ depending on how we use the service. For instance, we may have one professional social graph for colleagues and professional contacts on LinkedIn, another for friends and family on Facebook, and yet another for technically minded peers on Github.

There is an adage relating to the concept of a free web: *if you are using a service for free, you are not the customer—you're the product being sold.* What this means is that companies like ad agencies use your online footprint, social relationships, and interaction history to target their ads appropriately. A user is more likely to click on these targeted ads because they are served based on her social interactions within a site, and are thus more relevant to her. In other words, these companies leverage the concept of a social graph, where user relationships are mapped into a set of logical social groupings (Figure 2-1).

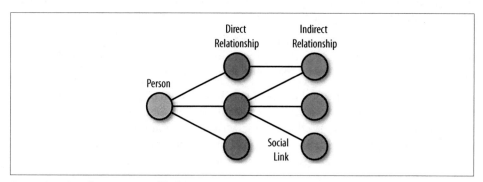

Figure 2-1. Social groupings and links

On the social web, a user interacts with other people who may or may not be related to her outside the virtual web construct. These people may be friends, family, coworkers, or any number of other logical groupings. Social links to people we know are referred to as *direct relationships*. Direct relationships contain the highest degree of social relevance to a user, which means that targeting them is more likely to produce successful returns. As we branch further away from the root user (e.g., friends of the user's friends), we enter the realm of *indirect relationships*. These relationships map back to the root user through another user. Indirect links still provide some social relevance since they have a common association, but that relevance is greatly diminished compared to that of a direct relationship.

All relationships can be categorized in relevance tiers. A direct relationship is the first tier, providing the greatest social link. A first-level indirect relationship is the second tier, and so on. As we expand outward into a user's social links, relevance to the root user exponentially decreases.

Because direct relationships produce the greatest return on investment for a company or application developer, it is important to capitalize on those links between two users, building a construct known as a *one-to-few cluster*. To illustrate this concept, consider the difference between having a cluster containing the root user and her immediate family (parents, siblings, children) and having one containing all her family members (immediate family, cousins, second cousins, and the entire extended family relationships). In many cases, communication and relationships between a person and her immediate family will be stronger, so if we can develop behavioral profiles for how that user interacts with those small clusters, we reach a holy grail of relevance. In simpler terms, we're hoping to achieve incredibly detailed targeting of a user, her behaviors, habits, likes, and dislikes—essentially, her online DNA.

Applying the Real-Life Social Graph Online

There's a stark contrast between the social graphs we have in real life and those we build online. To comprehend the difference, we need look no further than our own day-to-day interactions with the people around us, minus the computer, mobile device, or any other tool that connects us to the online world.

Our online social graph is a deeply interconnected web of relationships, where the majority of our conversations involve people spanning many different social groups, including our family, friends, peers, etc. The graph generated from these types of interactions doesn't include the concept of *clustering*.

This is where the real-life social graph differs. In our day-to-day interactions, we consciously form clusters for the people in our lives, interacting with each group in different ways and through various methods. We develop social boundaries for these clusters, sharing different pieces of ourselves with each group. For instance, you may be more candid with your friends about a physical relationship you are involved in than you are with your immediate family members.

Unfortunately, user clustering is one area where the online social graph is lacking. Since different criteria—anything from physical location to topics of interest—determine a person's status in a cluster, it is incredibly difficult to programmatically categorize his relationship to someone else and maintain any level of privacy or security.

Clustering Users Automatically

It's easy enough for an online service to start clustering people into like groups based on physical location, topics of interest, family status, or any number of other factors that a site may take into account within its profile system. However, it gets much more difficult when the site allows you to manually cluster connections instead of doing it automatically. The fact is that the majority of people will not participate in this type of tedious exercise just to gain some simple communications benefit for interacting with a specific group. In addition, users may cluster only some of their connections, leaving a large portion in a group "void." The real task here is finding a method to automate this more meaningful type of user clustering.

Privacy and Security

One particular challenge with user clustering involves privacy and security, and developers should keep both concepts foremost in their minds when exploring this area.

Simply clustering users does not advance your goal of engaging them. It may be an interesting metrics technique, but in the end you must apply clustering *purposefully* to maximize user engagement, increase time on site, target advertising, and build revenue. You do this by automatically targeting conversations between clusters, sharing information with certain clusters and not others (much like we do in our real lives). In this way, you protect user privacy and help to build a trust relationship between users and the social sites that they are using.

Let's look at a practical example of a use case that was a failure point for previous services that endeavored down this path, and which you should avoid at all costs. Let's say you are using clustering to identify the people a user communicates with the most to give them privileged access to more information about one another, such as feeds from other services they use. This sounds like a good clustering target since these are the people a user has chosen to interact with the most; the logic is fairly sound. The problem here is that relationships (and thus the clusters) change with each interaction (or lack of interaction); for example, a husband and wife (in the family cluster) might go through a particularly bad breakup. The service is now broadcasting privileged information about those users to each other when they may not want it anymore.

This is a flaw of automatic clustering and can have some serious implications for a person's physical security. What if our previous example involved one party who was violent and abusive? And what if our privileged information included the user's location and contact information? You can easily see how physical security can become a concern.

Establishing Trust

While the concepts underlying user clustering can lead to innovative, highly engaging products, developers should not tread this path lightly. As described in the preceding section, privacy and security should be paramount in any clustering system. If you have to sacrifice features to protect your users, then so be it. Within any social service, the trust relationship between the service and the users determines the product's success. If implementers of these services don't care about their users' privacy and security, they should at least understand that their indifference has a cost. If a user doesn't trust you, his interaction with your service—which might come in the form of additional profile information or social data that could be monetized through ad targeting or other sales mechanisms—will diminish or disappear completely.

Sharing Private User Data: Opt-in Versus Opt-out

Most of us probably share a lot of our private data with applications or containers that we interact with on a regular basis. Whether this is Facebook or another social network that maintains a complete user profile on us, or services like Gowalla and Foursquare that track our locations, it's crucial to understand how our information is being shared with others.

Let's face it: the true value in a social network or application is the opportunity it gives us to interact and share information or ideas with others, so we're unlikely to stop putting that data out there. Even though this is the case, we should still be aware of the different models the majority of containers use to share our personal information with others.

The Opt-in Sharing Model

The *opt-in sharing model* has a simple premise. By default, an application with this model will not share information about the user publicly or with other users that he may be connected to. To begin sharing information, the user has to manually enable that feature through the application.

> A good example of this type of model is a location-based application. Before using your physical location, the application will request that you allow it to do so. If you allow the application to track your location, you are *opting in*.

The opt-in sharing model is a clear benefit for the user, not the application or network requesting the information. The user will need to either modify his sharing settings manually or enable them through prompts that the service provides. This protects the user by forcing him to understand exactly what he'll be sharing through the application before he commits.

A social service's life-blood is having that sharing mechanism enabled. It increases user interaction, time on site, and adoption through community awareness. But since many users do not enable the full gamut of social sharing features, the service's reach is often limited and growth occurs at a slower rate.

Many services that implement this model prompt the user to allow the service to use and share his information, because some users never venture into the service's privacy and sharing settings. By prompting the user, the service forces him to make a choice one way or another.

The Opt-out Sharing Model

In complete contrast to the opt-in sharing model, with the *opt-out model*, any user of the service will share everything by default. The amount of data that is shared, and with whom, depends on the needs of the service in question.

 If you are not sure whether a social network or application that you are using (and have provided personal information to) uses an opt-in or opt-out model, it is best to assume that it uses an opt-out model. You should check the privacy and sharing settings of any online tool that you use to ensure that you are sharing only the information you wish to.

The benefits of this type of model definitely favor the service, not the user. Many users will never bother to view and edit their privacy and sharing settings on a service, blissfully ignorant of what the service may be doing with their information. The one benefit to the user here is that sharing more information may, and often does, make the service that she is using more valuable and useful.

Using an opt-out sharing model, the service can instantly capture and share all of the information that it needs from the user without having to prompt her or wait for her to enable the appropriate setting. This approach increases the service's adoption rates, since more information is being shared and interaction between users will likely ramp up.

Understanding Relationship Models

As we delve further into the core concepts underlying a user's relationships with people and objects, and how applications can use that information, we need to understand the basic types of relationships that users have on the different social networks.

We will explore these three relationship models, which represent some of the most popular social sites available today:

Follower model
    The user interacts with many other people at once.
Connection model
    The user interacts with one other person at a time.
Group model
    The user interacts with small groups of people.

Each model has its own reach and complexities. In the sections that follow, we'll explore them in more depth to see what they are all about.

The Follower Model

In the *follower model*, the user is always interacting with the majority or all of her following. When you post something on a network developed around a follower model, your potential reach is the number of followers you have.

This model's focus on reach comes at the expense of privacy and deep relationship links. Unless you're taking the extra step to protect your messages (meaning that people who wish to follow you must get your permission), you don't get to choose who is part of your social circle or to whom you broadcast messages. People will follow you based on shared interests, the appeal or relevance of your messages, or any number of other reasons.

Social relationships formed within this type of model tend to be limited and shallow. The focus here is more on the "what" (messages and updates that are posted) and less on the "who" (the person posting them). Implementers of this model tend to limit the amount of information that can be posted in a single message or update, and may provide only a very limited amount of social information about the individual. This means that you will not get the same depth of social relationships that you might from a more relationship-centric model.

Example

As you might have guessed, Twitter is a prime example of the follower model. Through Twitter, users post messages ("tweets") that reach their followers. Followers may in turn retweet those posts (in most cases, giving the original user proper attribution) to *their* followers, thus increasing global reach.

If a user doesn't protect his tweets, individuals other than his followers will also be able to see his tweets by going to his Twitter page.

Although Twitter provides mechanisms for direct messaging between users or mentions between groups of followers, it's built around the action of a user posting updates to all of his followers. At its core, it's a mechanism for quick dissemination of information among many users.

Privacy

Unless you are taking advantage of the more extreme option to protect your tweets (to stick with our Twitter example) or to protect your data on another service that uses the follower model, then the vast majority of your content will be fully visible to friends, followers, and people you've never met. In the case of Twitter, it has partnered with popular search engines that can conduct real-time searches of its content, meaning that your tweets are also displayed within search results.

Removing the Twitter example from the equation, the follower model type is rife with privacy concerns because your interaction with the service using it is fairly global. You should assume that any data that you share on sites with this model will be seen by everyone—including people you may want to hide it from.

The Connection Model

Taking a 180-degree turn from the follower model, the *connection model* focuses on personal, singular interactions with other people or objects. To this end, implementers typically allow users to generate highly detailed and rich profile systems and tie them to other groups, organizations, and movements.

This model focuses on shared social experiences rather than the quick dissemination of information to large groups. Users of this model tend to share many of the most important events of their lives—both good and bad—with their friends via text, photos, and videos.

Example

Facebook is an ideal example of this model type. The meat of the site is constructed around its users' social profiles, which allows individuals to reach out and share pieces of information with one another and interact on a very personal level.

Although the Facebook news feed acts as a global push mechanism to share information with all of your friends, the true advantage for most active users is on the personal level. When you post items to your Wall, your friends may comment, providing a shared social experience. People who do not use Facebook simply as a feed mechanism for cross-posting between multiple services (such as Twitter) can use the site to develop highly engaging social experiences with friends, family, coworkers, or even strangers.

Between constructs such as direct messaging, status comments, groups, pages, applications, and more, Facebook offers users the opportunity to build a comprehensive profile and interact with people on a personal level.

People who are actively engaged in Facebook are looking for different things from the service than they would from Twitter, and in fact, casual Facebook users often comment that they "don't get" Twitter. This is because the two services reach their audiences in very different ways.

Privacy

Since a connection model usually contains a vastly complex and detailed amount of user information and personalization settings, privacy is often one of the most important priorities for implementers. Normal implementations tend to include layered privacy settings that allow users to display different pieces of information to different people, or to hide some data altogether by setting it to private. In addition, users generally have the option to hide the majority of their profiles from people they have not included in their circle of friends.

While sites built on this model usually have a strict security policy in place, it's still very difficult to secure social data and shared information. This is especially true if you have an embedded application environment where third-party developers can build an application that accesses the profile information of users who have added it.

Another issue is that privacy settings within this type of model can become convoluted, especially when the application offers a high degree of customization. For example, Facebook has a number of security pages, like those shown in Figure 2-2, which are just a small portion of the full security features that are actually available on the site. With this kind of complexity, users can quickly become confused and misunderstand settings, making it easy for them to inadvertently allow unwanted parties to obtain access to their privileged data.

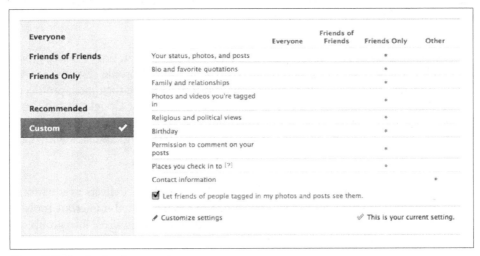

Figure 2-2. Facebook privacy settings

The Group Model

The last model we'll look at, the *group model*, is based upon the interactions and shared experiences of a group of like-minded individuals or people with similar interests, backgrounds, or situations. You can think of this much like hanging out with a group of friends—you have things in common that make you want to spend time together, sharing experiences and learning from one another. The same is true for the group model. You are interacting with a micrograph, a small portion of your entire social graph. There may be one or many groups in your graph, and some may overlap when there are people who bridge the gaps between multiple areas of interest.

Now let's explore the simple and complex iterations of this type of graph.

Simple group model: User-defined groups

At a very basic level, you can establish the group model by simply providing predefined methods for users to manually add themselves (and others) to communication clusters such as groups, pages, or initiatives. The onus is on the user to define the group relationships and then manage those groups when relationships change.

If your entire service is built on such a model, clustering comes naturally. The problem here lies in segmenting a large relevant social graph into pieces when you want to offer a service that is not just focused on group relationships, but also on the individual, her profile, and close interactions with other users.

Example. There are many examples of this type of model, since allowing users to group themselves is a simple matter of defining the space, security, and communication tools and methods. These examples include:

Yahoo!/Google groups
> These are an example of the simple group model at its purest. Both of these group products have overarching companies with standardized profile systems, as well as users who may have many connections and contacts from their mail, profile, or application systems. Each group uses the user's Yahoo! or Google account as a base but allows individuals with similar interests to section themselves off in a small communications bubble, where they can speak and interact with like-minded users.

Facebook
> Even though the main driver behind a lot of what Facebook delivers as a platform lies within its connection model, the company has integrated numerous tools—such as Groups and Pages—to allow users to organize themselves into groups of like-minded individuals.

Many other products and services integrate this type of grouping system because it gives people the freedom to interact with the service and with other users in exactly the ways they wish.

Privacy. The simple one-to-few clustering examples are some of the easier to secure. Users build their own groups or pages and then usually define a series of privacy and visibility settings; for instance:

- How communications are sent (email digest, SMS, etc.)
- Whether someone outside the group can view group messages
- Whether administrators have to approve messages before posting
- Whether people requesting access to the group have to be accepted by the administrator(s) prior to being added

Users can manually tune these security and privacy controls to create a very closed group environment or open it up so that the entire world can join in and view the comments.

Complex group model: Automatic clustering

Now that we have explored the simple version of the group model, let's look at a more complex iteration. It's no secret that we naturally form clusters and groups for the people that we choose to or need to interact with; we've already covered this in great detail. We do this automatically in our real lives, placing people into different groups and accordingly adapting the methods and approaches we use to interact with them.

This is the core concept behind the complex group model: automatic clustering of users into communication channels where each group is shown different content depending on the nature of that content and the group's privileges. For instance, if you are posting photos of a New Year's Eve event at which you drank a little too much, you may want to expose those photos only to your close friends—not to your boss.

When done right, automatic clustering can provide online users with a great deal of privacy, security, and peace of mind. The tricky part is implementing it correctly and erring on the side of caution when a message's content is in dispute.

Example. Before we began our discussion of models, we explored the real-life social graph and the ways in which it relates to our online social graphs. When it comes to the complex group model, the real-life social graph is the best example we have.

Even though companies such as Facebook and Google have attempted to build the complex model into their graphs and users' interactions, there's currently no true, complete representation of it in the sense of automatic, secure, private clustering that allows users to interact with others in groups. A system would have to be smart enough to recognize the intricacies of social relationships and the context of each user update to correctly categorize them into an appropriate group or range of groups. Facebook is definitely leading this charge with its privacy settings, Pages, and Groups—all of which allow a user to manually define his own user clusters—but we're still a long way from being able to develop this type of interface.

Privacy. Of all the models we have examined in these last few sections, this group model contains the highest degree of complexity when automatic clustering is put in place, meaning that it has the trickiest set of privacy settings in a (most likely) layered approach. In the past, companies have attempted to autocluster users based on communication frequency, where those users you speak with most frequently receive the highest level of viewing privileges. This would be fine if the people you talk to most often are the people you wish to share everything with (e.g., your boss). The problem is that communication frequency alone is not the only determining factor for privileges. Other considerations include:

- Location
- Relationship
- Political affiliation

- Place of work
- Shared interests

And the list goes on; there is an infinite amount of methods for clustering users. The real challenge is finding methods for defining clusters without sacrificing user privacy and security. With the complex group model, implementing privacy and security measures can be truly tricky and should not be attempted without a solid plan in place. Breaking the trust relationships with your users by accidentally leaking some of their supposedly secure information to the wrong source can be an application killer.

Relationships Versus Entities

As we explore the concept of user relationships on the Web, we realize that a user's social graph extends far beyond her connections to other people and groups. A user may interact with many more common interest sources on the Web, moving far beyond a person-to-person relationship cluster. This is where the concept of *entity relationships* comes into play.

Entities consist of any links to a root user's behaviors, such as searches she conducts, websites she visits, or online purchases she makes. We can map a user to these entities with the intention of grouping her into additional targeted clusters. In doing so, we extend the traditional model of the social graph into a rich, interwoven online personality, thereby helping companies and applications personalize a user's web experience through highly funneled advertising or specially targeted products.

Let's break down the entity and relationship links into a practical example. Suppose we host an application on a social network that provides content and ads targeted to each user. Suppose also that this social network provides web search capabilities, tracks the searches that a user makes, and has a social graph providing links to her family and friends. If we look at the user's search history, we see that she searches for fishing and camping equipment often. We now know that our user has some interest in fishing and camping. If we then correlate that hobby with her relationships to find any linked users who also like fishing or camping, we now have a highly targeted cluster that we can drive content for. This is an extremely personalized state developed just for that one user, all built without her ever knowing that her online habits and connections have allowed the application to target her in a very singular way.

Regardless of whether all of these facilities are available to an application developer, building a successful social application relies heavily on the developer's understanding of how to create a relevant social graph for a user. Developers can also take advantage of information that users have entered within their social profiles by mapping the levels of communications between a group of users or harnessing any number of other social indices.

A one-size-fits-all approach to online experiences no longer applies on the social web. Content has always been promoted as king, but without any relevance to the user, it may fall on deaf ears.

Building Social Relevance: Exploring the Facebook Social Graph

Now that we have a good core understanding of many aspects of working with a social platform and what makes up a user's social interactions on it, let's take a look at one that has had quite a lot of success at developing the social web: Facebook. As a major player in the social platform space, Facebook has a vastly relevant, rich social graph that extends far beyond the confines of its site.

Even though Facebook has a lot of proprietary implementations on its platform, it also supports and implements a wide array of open source initiatives, including (but by no means limited to):

- OAuth 2
- The Open Graph Protocol
- Hadoop

The company has also contributed several projects to the community, including HipHop for PHP, which transforms base PHP into highly optimized C++.

Facebook is the largest social network in the space, with a successful infrastructure built around bringing an online presence to the real lives of its users. Therefore, it would be neglectful of this book to not explore a few of the basic precepts behind how this platform works to connect people, companies, and entities.

Building Upon Real Identity

One of the most important concepts to understand about the social graph on Facebook is *real identity*. Facebook strongly believes in having its users build their profiles upon their true, real-life identities.

Unlike many social networking sites, which allow a person to refer to himself using an alias and withhold his personal information from the outside world, Facebook delivers an experience that is actually enriched as users share more of their real identities.

During the signup process, Facebook does a good job of enforcing this core concept, rejecting names that it suspects are aliases (Figure 2-3). Requiring users to input their sex and birthday also reflects the site's emphasis on delivering a real-world experience to its user base.

Real identity is also a good concept to keep in mind when you're building systems on social networking containers. It is in your best interest to stick with leveraging profile

Figure 2-3. Facebook signup screen, preventing an invalid user from creating an account

systems that include information that can be traced back to an actual person, because this is what allows you to not only target an application to a specific person, but also to make it incredibly relevant for her.

Understanding the Viral Channels

When you're building out applications that have their social features tied to a specific social network, understanding that platform's *viral channels* will help you increase your user base and the number of engaged users.

A social networking container's viral channels are those services that are available to a developer to help you promote the application, message or invite users, and generally put yourself front and center to people using the service.

Facebook uses many such channels for reaching out to people on the network, and application developers can take advantage of them to build up their services and grow their applications. These include:

- Pushing new activities (updates) to a user's news feed to show an action that a user has taken and attempt to enlist new users

- Promoting through the notification system to encourage a user to interact with the application or service and with other users, thereby increasing his overall engagement and time on site

Understanding and taking advantage of a platform's available channels for growing your application and increasing user engagement is an important component to developing a successful, high-quality application.

Building User Groups

Since our current social networks don't yet allow for the autogeneration of user clusters based on real-world relationships, providing users with a method to cluster themselves based on shared interests or backgrounds will help them connect with others as they wish.

Two main channels that Facebook uses for this purpose are Pages and Groups. These mechanisms allow people to follow (or *like*) companies or topics that they are interested in, as well as have a central discussion space to interact with people that share the same interest.

Capitalizing on these group relationships is also a very important aspect of application development. Groups and Pages, which are displayed as "entities" within the user's social profile, give a developer a wealth of knowledge about a person beyond what her profile can tell you. This information will allow you to build a relevant social graph within the application or site that you are constructing.

Avoiding Irrelevant Social Graphs

One major issue you might face with a social platform hosting applications that leverage a user's social profiles, friendships, and activities has to do with the nature of the social graph these applications are building.

As a social platform creator, you want your users to add friends or connections that have some relationship significance to them. In other words, you want to be able to use a user's relationships and connections to grow the platform; for example, by:

- Increasing the number of actionable activities that a person posts
- Increasing the number of group interactions through activities
- Promoting features or items through user relationships (i.e., word of mouth)

Basically, you want to gain as much as possible from a user's simple interactions with his friends and with the platform itself.

Now, if you don't have these relationships to begin with and you start introducing social games that require players to add friends to progress, then you get into a particular predicament. A user who lacks the existing relevant connections will seek out other people who play the game but may otherwise have no shared interests or relationship to the user. This creates a graph that's relevant within the game itself (since the users have direct interactions in one way or another every time they play) but almost entirely unusable for the rest of the platform.

To complicate matters, it's difficult for a user to move from an irrelevant graph to a relevant one by adding friends and connections, because his profile is already filled with people he doesn't really know on a personal level. For many people (not all, of course), this prospect would make them hesitant to interact socially and share information about themselves with perfect strangers.

Facebook is one example that has succeeded in building relevance in its social graphs while introducing social applications to its users. The important thing to remember here is that Facebook became known as a social engagement platform long before it served applications. Building up your user base *prior* to launching social applications— thus focusing your attention on social engagements—can greatly improve the relevance of the social graph that users construct on your platform.

Defining Entity Likes and Dislikes Through the OpenLike Protocol

Now that we have a good understanding of entities, let's look at a practical open tool that allows us to implement them: OpenLike.

The OpenLike protocol gives us a quick way to attach entities to our existing social profiles. It is similar to the Facebook Like utility, but integrates a number of different sharable sources within a small, easy-to-assemble package. By defining a standard way for users to flesh out their social graphs with like and dislike preferences, OpenLike expands the user/entity relationships on the Web.

We've already explored entities and relationships in depth, and how important they are to the future of social interactions, so let's get right into what the OpenLike protocol comprises.

Integrating the OpenLike Widget

Now that we understand what OpenLike is and how you can use it, let's take a look at how to integrate the widget on your own sites. The process is quick and painless, and at a base level, involves only three elements:

- An HTML page title
- The script include
- A JavaScript initialization call

Here's what the code looks like:

```
<!DOCTYPE HTML PUBLIC "-//W3C//DTD HTML 4.01//EN"
    "http://www.w3.org/TR/html4/strict.dtd">
<html xmlns="http://www.w3.org/1999/xhtml" xml:lang="en-us" lang="en-us">
<head>
<title>OpenLike Widget Example</title>
</head>
<body>
<!-- include the OpenLike JavaScript -->
<script type="text/javascript" src="http://openlike.org/v1/openlike.js"></script>

<!-- initialize the widget -->
<script type="text/javascript">OPENLIKE.Widget();</script>
<body>
</html>
```

Basically, we have a simple HTML page that includes the title that we want to use for the like event as the shell. Next, we have the script include that introduces the OpenLike library to the page. The source of the library should be *http://openlike.org/ v1/openlike.js*. Finally, we simply make a call to OPENLIKE.Widget() wherever we want to render the widget.

Once you've installed the OpenLike widget, the user can "like" your page through a number of different web sources. Figure 2-4 displays a simple implementation of numerous different sharing mechanisms for the associated sites.

Figure 2-4. How the OpenLike widget renders

How the Shared Likes Appear

Once the user interacts with a site including the OpenLike widget and shares some content by "liking" it, that action will be posted out to the appropriate source.

For instance, if you "like" the example implementation page shown in Figure 2-4 using the Facebook option, your Facebook profile will display a new like notification (Figure 2-5).

Figure 2-5. An OpenLike activity event on Facebook

The process is that simple. OpenLike is a base widget that builds upon any single sharing or like functionality to allow users to push out notifications to whatever source they choose.

Conclusion

Integrating social interactions on the Web, whether through a platform itself or an application built on it, boils down to a few core concepts around how people interact with one another in real life and online.

In a perfect world, we could interact with social features on the Web in the same way that we do in our real lives, but online social interactions work differently depending on the product or container in which they take place.

In this chapter, we've explored many features of a social container and how we interact online. We've looked at the biggest player in the social container space, Facebook, and have seen how one open source initiative, OpenLike, can help developers promote their sites or services to many different sharing mechanisms and increase user growth.

Now that we understand these basic concepts, we can move on to practical social container implementations and see how a container can be built from open source initiatives.

CHAPTER 3

Constructing the Foundation of a Social Application Platform

Once you understand the core concepts behind an application platform, the next step is to define the skeleton for your application and platform. Apache Shindig is a widely accepted standard for creating the container infrastructure for hosting OpenSocial gadgets. This infrastructure allows developers to use a simplified gadgets XML spec file to mark up their gadgets.

What You'll Learn

This chapter will focus on building the foundation of a social networking container. In the following sections, we will explore several root technologies and concepts, including:

- Using Apache Shindig to render gadgets
- Setting up a sample social networking website using Partuza
- Building and running a custom OpenSocial gadget using Shindig

At the end of the chapter, we will use the Shindig installation we've set up to build our first OpenSocial gadget, applying the lessons we will learn in the following sections.

Apache Shindig

Shindig is an open source Apache project that functions as an OpenSocial container. It allows developers to quickly and easily host OpenSocial gadgets by providing the code to render gadgets and proxy requests, and to handle REST and RPC requests.

Shindig's architecture is split into four separate parts, as shown in Figure 3-1 and described in the list that follows it.

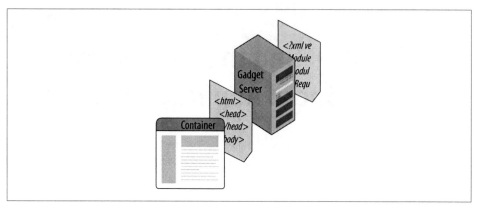

Figure 3-1. Shindig's architectural layers

Gadget container JavaScript
> The handler for managing an OpenSocial gadget's security, communication, and UI and JavaScript features

Gadget rendering server
> Renders the gadget XML document (the definition for a gadget) into HTML and JavaScript for the container JavaScript to expose

OpenSocial container JavaScript
> The JavaScript environment that sits on top of the gadget container JavaScript to provide OpenSocial API functionality

OpenSocial data server
> Provides a mapping implementation of the container to the server interface so developers can implement their own data syncs

Shindig has a couple of core goals:

- To allow new sites to develop a mechanism for hosting gadgets with very minimal effort.
- To become a language-neutral platform in which the container is provided in many different languages. Currently, only container versions in PHP and Java are available and supported.

Setting Up Shindig

Before we begin setting up applications, using personal information from a container, or syndicating social activities and notifications, we have to lay the foundation for running applications on a server.

This process will guide you through setting up Apache Shindig on localhost (running locally on your computer). There are prerequisites for installing Shindig in either language.

PHP:

- Apache web server with mod_rewrite enabled
- PHP 5.2.x with the JSON, simplexml, mcrypt, and curl extensions enabled

Java:

- Servlet container supporting Web Application 2.3 or above and JDK 1.5 or above

We will be implementing the PHP version of the Shindig environment, so the following steps assume that the Apache web server is installed and PHP 5.2.x is available. We will cover how to customize them both to meet the minimum requirements.

Installing Shindig on Mac OS X (Leopard)

This section guides you through installing Shindig on a local Apache server on Mac OS X (Leopard). This installation will allow you to run OpenSocial gadgets using the URL structure *http://shindig/gadgets/ifr?url=gadget_url*.

Requirements

This installation guide requires that you have the following server and program environments installed on your machine:

- Apache HTTP Server (see the section "Installing Apache HTTP" Server in the Appendix [available online, see Preface for details] for installation instructions)
- PHP 5.2.x (see the section "Setting Up Your PHP Environment" in the Appendix for installation instructions)

First, we need to create a directory to house the Apache Shindig code base. This directory structure should be set up at the root of the localhost directory. In most instances, Apache comes preinstalled on Mac OS X, and the localhost directory is */Library/WebServer/Documents*.

Once we've created the directory and we cd into it, we can check out the Shindig source code from the Subversion (SVN) repository. Load Terminal and run the following commands:

```
mkdir /Library/WebServer/Documents/shindig
cd /Library/WebServer/Documents
svn co http://svn.apache.org/repos/asf/shindig/branches/2.0.x/ shindig
```

In this example, we are checking out the 2.0.x branch of Shindig rather than trunk, since I used the 2.0.x branch to document this setup. If you would like to download the most recent version of Shindig from the trunk instead, use the following SVN checkout command:

```
svn co http://svn.apache.org/repos/asf/shindig/trunk/ .
```

Next, we have to add a hostname entry for Shindig in our *hosts* file, which Apache can use to identify our new Shindig URL. This allows us to use *http://shindig/* as the root of our Shindig container instead of hijacking *http://localhost* for the task.

Our *hosts* file is located at */etc/hosts*. Since it is also a system file, we need to use sudo vi to edit it:

```
sudo vi /etc/hosts
```

Once the *hosts* file loads, there should already be an entry for localhost, such as:

```
127.0.0.1  localhost
```

We need to add the Shindig reference to this entry so we can reference our new *shindig* directory. Your revised entry should look like this:

```
127.0.0.1  localhost shindig
```

Save your *hosts* file and exit. Next, we need to enable virtual hosts in Apache to allow us to point to *http://shindig/* and have it reference the *shindig* directory we set up in our localhost directory. In addition, we will enable mod_rewrite (one of Shindig's requirements) since this will be under the same file. Enabling mod_rewrite allows Shindig to dynamically rewrite portions of a URL structure to point to other files within the Shindig code base, without the developer having to worry about it.

sudo vi into your Apache *httpd.conf* file to get started:

```
sudo vi /etc/apache2/httpd.conf
```

A short distance into the file, you'll see a list of LoadModule calls. Search for the reference to rewrite_module in this list; it should look like this:

```
#LoadModule rewrite_module libexec/apache2/mod_rewrite.so
```

The # symbol at the beginning of the line is commenting out the mod_rewrite module within Apache. Remove that # symbol to enable this functionality. The line should now look like this:

```
LoadModule rewrite_module libexec/apache2/mod_rewrite.so
```

Next, we need to enable virtual hosts to be able to specify where *http://shindig/* will point. Look for the following line near the end of the same *httpd.conf* file:

```
#Include /private/etc/apache2/extra/httpd-vhosts.conf
```

As before, this line is commented out. Remove the # comment so that the line looks like this:

```
Include /private/etc/apache2/extra/httpd-vhosts.conf
```

Save and close the *httpd.conf* file. Now that our virtual host file is available, we can add in the entries for the folder that *http://shindig/* will point to. Within the Apache directory is an "extra" folder that houses the virtual hosts file. sudo vi into this file:

```
sudo vi /etc/apache2/extra/httpd-vhosts.conf
```

Unless you have previously edited this file, there will be a few example hosts in the file after the following line:

```
NameVirtualHost *:80
```

These examples will prevent Apache from starting up, so remove every host reference after that line (but not the line itself).

Now that we have a clean file, we need to add two new entries, one for localhost and one for Shindig. We are adding in a reference for localhost because if a hostname typed in a browser does not have an entry available (e.g., *http://example/*), Apache automatically uses the first entry, which defaults to localhost. Add the following entries to the bottom of the file, substituting the */Library/WebServer/Documents* lines with the location of your localhost public directory (if it's not */Library/WebServer/Documents*):

```
<VirtualHost *:80>
  ServerName localhost
  DocumentRoot /Library/WebServer/Documents
</VirtualHost>

<VirtualHost *:80>
  ServerName shindig
  DocumentRoot /Library/WebServer/Documents/shindig/php
  <Directory /Library/WebServer/Documents/shindig/php>
    AllowOverride All
  </Directory>
</VirtualHost>
```

Save and close the *httpd-vhosts.conf* file. Now that all of our Apache configurations are in place, we need to satisfy PHP's requirements—namely, by enabling the JSON, simplexml, mcrypt, and curl extensions. JSON and simpleXML should already be active in PHP, so we'll just need to activate curl and mcrypt. While we're at it, sudo vi into the location housing your *php.ini* file (in the following example, */etc/php.ini*):

```
sudo vi /etc/php.ini
```

We're looking for two lines in the *php.ini* file, both preceded with semicolons. For convenience, I've stacked them here, though they don't appear this way in the file:

```
;extension=php_curl.dll
;extension=php_mcrypt.dll
```

Enable both lines by removing the semicolon at the beginning:

```
extension=php_curl.dll
extension=php_mcrypt.dll
```

Now that our required extensions are available, we need to check, and adjust as necessary, a few last PHP configuration settings.

Search for the following lines within the *php.ini* file (as with the previous example, they do not actually appear consecutively, and their values may be different).

```
always_populate_raw_post_data = Off
short_open_tag = Off
magic_quotes_gpc = On
```

If any of your values match those in the preceding lines, you'll need to change them to their opposite values as follows:

```
always_populate_raw_post_data = On
short_open_tag = On
magic_quotes_gpc Off
```

Save and close *php.ini*. For all of our Apache and PHP changes to take effect, we'll need to restart our Apache server with the `apache restart` command:

```
sudo apachectl restart
```

Installing Shindig on Windows

This section guides you through installing Shindig on a local Apache server on Windows, allowing you to run OpenSocial gadgets from *http://shindig/gadgets/ifr?url= gadget_url*.

Requirements

This installation guide requires that you have the following server and program environments installed on your machine:

- Apache HTTP Server (see the section "Installing Apache HTTP Server" in the Appendix [available online; see Preface for details] for installation instructions)
- PHP 5.2.x (see the section "Setting Up Your PHP Environment" in the Appendix for installation instructions)

These installation instructions assume that Apache and PHP are installed to the following installation directories:

- PHP: *C:\php*
- Apache: *C:\Program Files\Apache Software Foundation\Apache*

If your installation paths are different, swap all paths to files in these directories with your own paths when proceeding through the following steps.

To begin the Shindig installation, we first need to obtain the source code for the project from the Shindig trunk. Go into your localhost *htdocs* directory (by default, Apache sets this to a path such as *C:\Program Files\Apache Software Foundation\Apache \htdocs*), create a directory for Shindig, and check out the code using Subversion. Open up a command shell and type in the following:

```
mkdir C:\Program Files\Apache Software Foundation\Apache\htdocs\shindig
cd C:\Program Files\Apache Software Foundation\Apache\htdocs\shindig
svn co http://svn.apache.org/repos/asf/shindig/trunk/ .
```

The source code will now download into your *shindig* directory.

If you don't have Subversion installed on your Windows machine, refer to the Appendix for installation instructions.

Our next task is to configure Apache correctly to meet Shindig's requirements. Load the Apache *config* file at *C:\Program Files\Apache Software Foundation\Apache\conf \httpd.conf*.

Search for the reference to rewrite_module in this list. The line should look like this:

```
#LoadModule rewrite_module modules/mod_rewrite.so
```

The # symbol at the beginning of the line is commenting out the mod_rewrite module within Apache. Remove that # symbol to enable this functionality. The line should now look like this:

```
LoadModule rewrite_module modules/mod_rewrite.so
```

Next, we need to enable virtual hosts so we can specify where *http://shindig/* will point. Look for the following line near the end of the same *httpd.conf* file:

```
#Include conf/extra/httpd-vhosts.conf
```

As before, this line is commented out. Remove the # comment so that the line looks like this:

```
Include conf/extra/httpd-vhosts.conf
```

Save and close *httpd.conf*. Within the same *conf* folder under your Apache directory is another folder for "extra." Load the *httpd-vhosts.conf* file in that folder at *C:\Program Files\Apache Software Foundation\Apache\conf\extra\httpd-vhosts.conf*.

Unless you have previously edited this file, there will be a few example hosts in the file after the following line:

```
NameVirtualHost *:80
```

These examples will prevent Apache from starting up, so remove every host reference after that line (but not the line itself).

Now that we have a clean file, we need to add two new entries, one for localhost and one for Shindig. We are adding in a reference for localhost because if a hostname typed in a browser does not have an entry available (e.g., *http://example/*), Apache automatically uses the first entry, which defaults to localhost. Add the following entries to the bottom of the file, substituting the *C:\Program Files\Apache Software Foundation \Apache\htdocs* lines with the location of your localhost public directory (if it's not *C:\Program Files\Apache Software Foundation\Apache\htdocs*):

```
<VirtualHost *:80>
  ServerName localhost
  DocumentRoot "C:\Program Files\Apache Software
        Foundation\Apache\htdocs"
```

```
    </VirtualHost>

    <VirtualHost *:80>
      ServerName shindig
      DocumentRoot "C:\Program Files\Apache Software
              Foundation\Apache\htdocs\shindig\php"
      <Directory>
        AllowOverride All
      </Directory>
    </VirtualHost>
```

Save and close the *httpd-vhosts.conf* file. Now that the virtual host references are in place, we can add the hosts reference to tell Windows that there is a virtual host reference available for *http://shindig/*. Open your Windows hosts file at *C:\Windows \System32\drivers\etc\hosts*.

Once the hosts file loads, there should already be an entry for localhost, such as:

```
    127.0.0.1  localhost
```

We need to add the Shindig reference to this entry so we can reference our new *shindig* directory. Your new entry should look like this:

```
    127.0.0.1  localhost shindig
```

Save and close the hosts file. Our next step is to make our modifications to PHP to enable Shindig's required features. Load your *php.ini* file, located at *C:\php\php.ini*.

Search for the following extensions within the file. If any of the lines begin with a semicolon, remove the semicolon to enable to extension:

```
    extension=php_curl.dll
    extension=php_mcrypt.dll
    extension=php_openssl.dll
```

Now that our required extensions are available, we need to check, and adjust as necessary, a few last PHP configuration settings.

Search for the following lines within the *php.ini* file (in the actual file, they are not consecutive and their values may be different):

```
    always_populate_raw_post_data = Off
    short_open_tag = Off
    magic_quotes_gpc = On
```

If any of your values match those in the preceding lines, you'll need to change them to their opposite values as follows:

```
    always_populate_raw_post_data = On
    short_open_tag = On
    magic_quotes_gpc Off
```

Save and close *php.ini*. For all of our Apache and PHP changes to take effect, we'll need to restart our Apache server with the `apache restart` command. Open a command prompt and enter the following (substituting the Apache path with your own):

```
"C:\Program Files\Apache Software Foundation\Apache\bin\httpd.exe" -w -n
    "Apache" -k restart
```

Testing Your Shindig Installation

No matter which installation method you used, your Shindig implementation should now be viewable using your new *http://shindig/* virtual host. This host points to the *shindig/php* directory created with the Shindig source code.

To display OpenSocial gadgets, we will point to *http://shindig/gadgets/ifr* within the Shindig code base. An Apache `RewriteRule` loads the appropriate gadget parsing code by accepting a `GET` parameter for the URL to the gadget to be parsed.

Now that we have installed and set up Shindig, we can test out the installation by pointing our browser to:

> *http://shindig/gadgets/ifr?url=http://www.labpixies.com/campaigns/todo/todo.xml*

You should see an OpenSocial gadget similar to Figure 3-2.

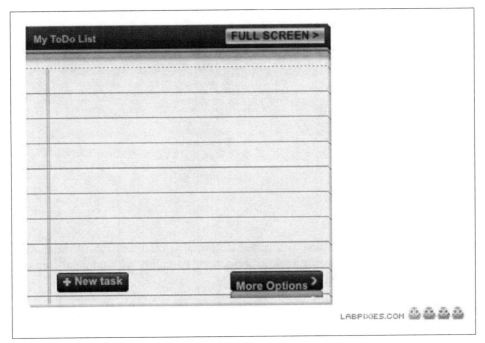

Figure 3-2. Sample OpenSocial gadget, running on Shindig

You can load any gadget this way by replacing the source of the URL with any valid OpenSocial XML gadget file.

With our Shindig installation up and running, we can load gadgets directly into the browser. The Shindig installation is the backbone we'll use to build and test all of the OpenSocial application development features in the next few chapters.

Partuza

Now that we are able to load OpenSocial gadgets, what's next? At this point, we are still a long way from developing a fully featured social networking website; to do that, we would need a user management system, registration, login, and a proper method to load and display our new gadgets. Instead of going through the intricacies of social networking application container development, let's take a giant leap forward and build out an example container with Partuza.

Partuza, shown in Figure 3-3, is an example OpenSocial social networking container that works with Shindig. This example container has an abstraction layer for Shindig built in, which allows users to seamlessly interact with OpenSocial gadgets by entering in a URL to the gadget. The word "partuza" is Spanish slang for "party," just as "shindig" is American slang for the same.

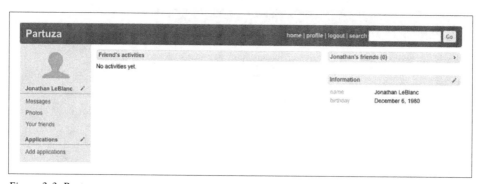

Figure 3-3. Partuza

Installing Partuza will give you an immediate jumping-off point for working with OpenSocial gadgets and creating a social networking container with minimal configuration and engineering effort.

Requirements

This installation guide requires that you have the following server and program environments installed on your machine:

- Apache HTTP Server
- PHP 5.2.x
  - Apache Shindig

See the Appendix (available online; see Preface for details) for installation instructions for the preceding requirements.

Installing Partuza on Mac OS X (Leopard)

This section will guide you through installing Partuza on a local Apache server on Mac OS X (Leopard), which allows you to host the sample OpenSocial social networking container at *http://partuza/*.

The first step is to obtain and configure the Partuza container code base. To obtain the source code for Partuza, open Terminal and enter the following commands:

```
mkdir /Library/WebServer/Documents/partuza
cd /Library/WebServer/Documents/partuza
svn checkout http://partuza.googlecode.com/svn/trunk/ .
```

Once the checkout has completed, we need to change the permissions of the *people* images directory. The web server runs under a different username and set of permissions, so taking this step will allow it to write thumbnails to that directory:

```
chmod 777 partuza/html/images/people
```

Now we need to add the host entry so that the system can relate a virtual host entry with localhost. Edit your *hosts* file to add this entry:

```
sudo vi /etc/hosts
```

There should be an existing entry for localhost and shindig, such as:

```
127.0.0.1  localhost shindig
```

We need to add the Partuza reference to this entry so we can reference our new *shindig* directory. Your new entry should look like this:

```
127.0.0.1  localhost shindig partuza
```

Save and close this file. Now that the host entry is in place, we need to change the configuration settings for *http://partuza/* to our virtual hosts configuration file. Load the virtual hosts file.

```
sudo vi /etc/apache2/extra/httpd-vhosts.conf
```

The entries for localhost and shindig should already exist in this file. After those two entries, at the end of the file, add the following entry for Partuza:

```
<VirtualHost *:80>
 ServerName partuza
 DocumentRoot /Library/WebServer/Documents/partuza/html
 <Directory /Library/WebServer/Documents/partuza/html>
  AllowOverride All
 </Directory>
</VirtualHost>
```

Save and close that file. Now we'll edit our PHP configuration to add in the extensions and settings needed for Partuza. Load your *php.ini* file to begin adding them:

```
sudo vi /etc/php.ini
```

Search for "short_open_tag" and ensure that the value is set to On. Once you've verified this, save and close the *php.ini* file.

Our next setup task is to download and configure MySQL on the system. If you already have MySQL installed, you can skip this step. Go to *http://www.mysql.com/downloads/mysql/* and download the MySQL *.dmg* image for your system. Once it's downloaded, double-click the *.dmg* file to mount the image and view its contents.

Run the installer by double-clicking the *mysql-5.1.50.osx10.5-x86_64.pkg* file (or whatever package name you downloaded). Go through the installation with the default settings.

Once the installation has completed, double-click the *MySQL.prefPane* item in the mounted image to add the MySQL preference pane to the system preferences panel. Select the "Automatically Start MySQL on Startup" option and then click Start MySQL Server.

To be able to execute MySQL commands from the Terminal, we need to add the MySQL directory to our global system profile. From the Terminal, load the system profile:

```
sudo vi /etc/profile
```

At the bottom of the file, add:

```
PATH=$PATH:/usr/local/mysql/bin
export PATH
```

Save and close the file, and then close and reopen the Terminal for the changes to take effect. Our MySQL installation should now be complete. To test it out, type **mysql** on the command line.

You will be presented with the MySQL Terminal interface, which allows you to edit and configure your databases. To see the current databases on the system, type **show databases;** after the mysql> prompt.

Once you press Enter, you will be presented with the current databases on your system, which should look similar to this:

```
mysql> show databases;
+--------------------+
| Database           |
+--------------------+
| information_schema |
| mysql              |
+--------------------+
2 rows in set (0.00 sec)
```

If everything was successful, type **exit** to leave the MySQL Terminal interface. We can now create a database for Partuza to store user profile and social information. Within the *partuza* folder is a file called *partuza.sql*, which we will use to import default settings for the database. To accomplish this, we just need to run a few commands:

```
cd /Library/WebServer/Documents/partuza/
sudo mysqladmin create partuza
sudo mysql partuza < partuza.sql
```

The partuza database has now been created on your system. To access this database in the future, run the following command:

```
sudo mysql partuza
```

We now need to configure Shindig to use the Partuza data handler. To do this, add a new configuration file to the *shindig* directory as follows:

```
cd /Library/WebServer/Documents/shindig/php/config
vi local.php
```

Within the new *local.php* file, add the following PHP code:

```
<?php
$shindigConfig = array(
    'person_service' => 'PartuzaService',
    'activity_service' => 'PartuzaService',
    'app_data_service' => 'PartuzaService',
    'messages_service' => 'PartuzaService',
    'oauth_lookup_service' => 'PartuzaOAuthLookupService',
    'extension_class_paths' => '/Library/WebServer/Documents/partuza/Shindig'
);
```

Save and close the file, and then restart Apache. The values entered into *local.php* will override those in *container.php*, allowing you to keep the SVN repository files intact.

Shindig is now fully set up and configured for you to use.

Installing Partuza on Windows

This section will guide you through installing Partuza on a local Apache server on Windows, which allows you to host the sample OpenSocial social networking container at *http://partuza/*.

Partuza requires a MySQL database installation, which is used to store all social and user information for the container. Since this is the storage backbone for Partuza, this is where we will start. If MySQL is already installed on your computer, you may skip this step.

Go to *http://www.mysql.com/downloads/mysql/* to download the recommended MySQL MSI installer (either 32-bit or 64-bit, depending on your Windows version). Once the download is complete, double-click the *.msi* file to begin the installation. On the first screen that appears, click Next, which will take you to another screen where you can select a configuration type. Select Standard Configuration from the options and click Next; the installer will now create a general-purpose configuration, which you can fine-tune later as needed.

Next, you will be presented with a screen where you set Windows options for the installation. Select both "Install As Windows Service" and "Include Bin Directory in Windows PATH." The second option allows us to work with the MySQL instance through the command line. Your configuration settings should look like Figure 3-4.

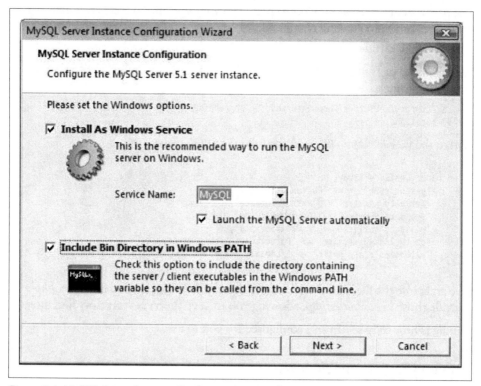

Figure 3-4. MySQL Server Instance Configuration Wizard

Once you've selected these options, click Next. The next screen presents security options for the MySQL installation. Make sure that Modify Security Settings is selected, and enter in a new root password. There is no need to create an anonymous account for this installation, so leave that option unchecked. Click Next and then click Execute to finalize the installation.

MySQL is now installed, and your Start menu should include a MySQL directory. Within that directory is an executable called MySQL Command Line Client, which allows you to work with your MySQL databases through the command line. To test the installation, load this program. You'll be asked for the password you entered as the root password during the installation. You should now be presented with the `mysql>`

prompt, from which you can enter SQL commands. View your current databases by entering **show databases;**.

Once you press Enter, you will be presented with a list of the current databases on your system, which should look similar to this:

```
mysql> show databases;
+--------------------+
| Database           |
+--------------------+
| information_schema |
| mysql              |
+--------------------+
2 rows in set (0.00 sec)
```

Now that you've verified the installation, you can close the MySQL command-line utility.

The next step is optional but very much recommended for users who are not familiar or comfortable with working in a command-line SQL environment, or for those who prefer a richer set of tools. We will install a visualization utility called phpMyAdmin on top of the MySQL installation; this utility will allow us to work quickly with databases and tables, import database configuration settings, and explore a host of other features. The next steps for installing Partuza will assume that phpMyAdmin has been installed on the system.

Go to the phpMyAdmin download site at *http://www.phpmyadmin.net/* and click the option to download the most recent version of the tool (click the Download text instead of the *.zip/.gz* text). This presents you with a number of download options for phpMyAdmin. Download the *.zip* packages for all languages or just English. Once you've downloaded the file, unzip it.

The content of the zip file is a folder containing all of the source and configurations needed to run phpMyAdmin. Copy the folder over to the root of your localhost directory and rename the folder to *phpmyadmin* to make it easier to load from localhost.

phpMyAdmin has several core requirements for the PHP installation on the host it runs on, including:

- PHP version 5.2.0 or newer with session support and the standard PHP library (SPL) extension.
- zip extension to support uploading zip files.
- mbstring and type extensions to support multibyte strings (UTF-8, which is currently the default).
- gd2 extension to display inline thumbnails of JPEGs ("image/jpeg: inline") with their original aspect ratio.
- mcrypt extension if using the "cookie" authentication method. mcrypt is also strongly suggested for most users and is required in 64-bit machines. In addition, not using mcrypt will cause phpMyAdmin to load pages significantly slower.

Now that we have our requirements down, let's make the necessary adjustments to get phpMyAdmin working. Load your *php.ini* file (e.g., *C:\php\php.ini*) for editing.

Search for the following lines and make sure they are enabled (i.e., remove any leading semicolons from each line):

```
extension=php_bz2.dll
extension=php_mbstring.dll
extension=php_zip.dll
extension=php_mcrypt.dll
```

In addition, search for "short_open_tag" and ensure that its value is set to On. Close the *php.ini* file and restart Apache.

We now meet the requirements for running phpMyAdmin, so let's go ahead and configure our database connections. Create a directory called "config" under the *phpadmin* folder within localhost and make sure that it is *not* read-only (right-click it and select Properties for details). This is a manual security step that will be used to output the required database and system configuration settings.

In a browser, load *http://localhost/phpmyadmin/setup/index.php* to begin the visual configuration of phpMyAdmin. On the page that loads, you will see that no servers have been configured yet. Click New Server to add one. This new page provides you with basic configuration settings for the server. Configure the server with the following settings, leaving blank anything not listed:

• Server hostname: localhost
• Connection type: tcp
• PHP extension to use: mysqli (make sure the extension is turned on)
• Authentication type: cookie
• User for config auth: root
• Password for config auth: enter the password you used for the MySQL root account

Click Save to return to the previous screen, and click Save at the bottom of that screen as well. Your *config* file will now be created in the *config* directory we set up earlier. Move the *config* file from *phpmyadmin/config/config.inc.php* to *phpmyadmin/config.inc.php* so that phpMyAdmin can use it. Once you've moved the file, delete the *config* directory.

phpMyAdmin should now be configured to work with your database. To test the installation, go to *http://localhost/phpmyadmin/index.php* in a browser (make sure you have cookies enabled). To view the panel, log in with root and the password you entered earlier. You should see something similar to Figure 3-5.

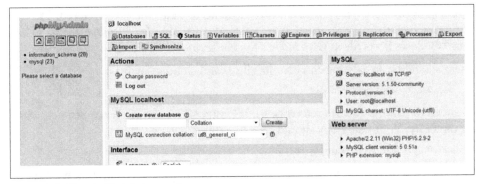

Figure 3-5. The phpMyAdmin panel

Under "Create new database" below the "MySQL localhost" heading, enter **partuza** (case sensitive). Click the drop-down box to the right of the input field, select "utf8_unicode_ci" from the bottom of the list, and then click Create to create the database that Partuza will use.

Once the database has been created, the database screen will come up. At the top of the page, click the Import tab. At the top of the new screen, you'll see a button to "Browse" for a file to import. Click that button and select the *partuza.sql* file in your *partuza* directory at *C:\Program Files\Apache Software Foundation\Apache\htdocs \partuza*. Finally, click Go at the bottom right of the screen. This will import all the tables Partuza requires into the new database. You should see a success message once the import is complete.

Now that all the prerequisites are in place for Partuza, we can download and set up the project on top of Shindig. We need to create a new directory within localhost for Partuza and then download the source code to that directory. Open a command prompt and input the following (substituting localhost paths for your own):

```
mkdir C:\Program Files\Apache Software Foundation\Apache\htdocs\partuza
cd C:\Program Files\Apache Software Foundation\Apache\htdocs\partuza
svn co http://partuza.googlecode.com/svn/trunk/ .
```

The code required to run Partuza will now download to the current directory. Once it has completed, close the command prompt. Next, we have to add a virtual host entry for Partuza to allow us to load it from *http://partuza/*. Edit the Apache virtual host file at *C:\Program Files\Apache Software Foundation\Apache\conf\extra\httpd-vhosts.conf* and add the following entry to the bottom of the file:

```
<VirtualHost *:80>
 ServerName partuza
 DocumentRoot "C:\Program Files\Apache Software
     Foundation\Apache\htdocs\partuza\html"
 <Directory>
  AllowOverride All
 </Directory>
</VirtualHost>
```

Save and close the *httpd-vhosts.conf* file. Now we can add the hosts reference to tell Windows that there is a virtual host reference available for *http://partuza/*. Open your Windows hosts file at *C:\Windows\System32\drivers\etc\hosts*.

There should be an existing entry for localhost and shindig, such as:

```
127.0.0.1  localhost shindig
```

We need to add the Partuza reference to this entry so we can reference our new *shindig* directory. Your new entry should look like this:

```
127.0.0.1  localhost shindig partuza
```

Save and close that file. There are a few Partuza configuration settings that we need to adjust to get it working on localhost.

Within the downloaded Partuza files, edit *partuza/html/index.php*. Search for the following line:

```
$uri = $_SERVER["REQUEST_URI"];
```

And change it to:

```
$uri = PartuzaConfig::get('library_root') . $_SERVER["REQUEST_URI"];
```

This change enables Partuza to load files from the right path on your local machine. Next, edit *partuza/html/config.php*. Search for the following line:

```
'db_passwd' => ''
```

and add your MySQL database password as the value. Now Partuza can connect to the MySQL partuza database.

The final step is to configure Shindig to use Partuza. Navigate to your *C:\Program Files \Apache Software Foundation\Apache\htdocs\shindig\php\config* directory and create a new file called "local.php." Edit this file and input the following code block:

```php
<?php
$shindigConfig = array(
    'person_service' => 'PartuzaService',
    'activity_service' => 'PartuzaService',
    'app_data_service' => 'PartuzaService',
    'messages_service' => 'PartuzaService',
    'oauth_lookup_service' => 'PartuzaOAuthLookupService',
    'extension_class_paths' => 'C:\Program Files\Apache Software
                               Foundation\Apache\htdocs\partuza\Shindig'
);
```

Save and close the file, and then restart Apache to have the settings take effect. This new file will override the default Shindig configuration variables, which allows Partuza and Shindig to play nicely together and work as one cohesive unit.

Partuza should now be configured to work with Shindig and MySQL.

Testing the Partuza Installation

To try out your new social networking container, open a browser and navigate to *http://partuza/*. Once the container loads, click the Register link at the top of the page. Enter some sample user data and click Register. If everything succeeded, you will now be presented with the new user profile, which should look similar to Figure 3-6.

Figure 3-6. The Partuza test container

The OpenSocial Gadget XML Specification

While Shindig and Partuza are tools for building an OpenSocial container, the gadget XML specification is a tool for building application gadgets to run within a container. This XML specification file contains a series of configuration settings and data that allows the container to load the application content and information.

A gadget XML file contains a few main nodes (or elements). The root `Module` node contains three child nodes, `ModulePrefs`, `UserPref`, and a series of `Content` nodes. `ModulePrefsk` defines the characteristics (metadata) about the application, `UserPref` allows gadgets to define user-specific data, and the `Content` nodes contain the code for the gadget views.

This is the standard format of a gadget XML file:

```
<?xml version="1.0" encoding="utf-8"?>
<Module>
    <ModulePrefs ... />
    <UserPref ... />
    <Content ...>
        Gadget Content
    </Content>
</Module>
```

In the sections that follow, we'll explore the content of each node and the possible configurations for building out a gadget.

Configuring Your Application with ModulePrefs

The ModulePrefs node allows a developer to not only define metadata about a gadget (such as a title and author), but also features and processing rules. This is core information defined by a gadget developer, and it cannot be modified by gadget users.

ModulePrefs contains a number of attribute strings, all of which are elements that containers are required to support, but which are optional for developers to specify. These attributes are listed in Table 3-1.

Table 3-1. ModulePrefs attributes

Attribute	Description
author	The author of the gadget.
author_email	A working email address for the gadget's author. Since gadgets for public social networking containers are also public, there is potential for spam, so this should be a dedicated gadget email account, not a personal one.
description	A description of the application.
screenshot	A publicly accessible URL that provides a screenshot of the application. This field is generally used in gadget galleries or for invitations to applications.
thumbnail	A publicly accessible URL that provides a thumbnail image for a gadget. This field is generally used in conjunction with the title to display brief information for a gadget.
title	The title of the application.
title_url	A URL, such as a website or forum, linked from the title of the application.

A fully qualified ModulePrefs node can take the following form:

```
<ModulePrefs author="John Smith"
             author_email="john@smith.com"
             description="My application does all sorts of cool things"
             screenshot="http://www.myimage.com/ss.png"
             thumbnail="http://www.myimage.com/thumb.png"
             title="My Application"
             title_url="http://www.mysite.com">
```

Under ModulePrefs, there are a number of subnodes that provide additional configuration settings for your gadget. Let's explore them now.

Require/Optional

The Require (must include) and Optional (may include if available) elements denote feature dependencies to be made available to a gadget. Both tags have a single attribute available, feature, whose value denotes the feature that should be included. Within the confines of an OpenSocial gadget, the Require and Optional statements are typically used to indicate feature dependencies such as the OpenSocial version to use (e.g., opensocial-1.0) or library-specific methods like the OpenSocial lightweight JavaScript APIs (e.g., osapi).

Following are some sample `Require` or `Optional` elements within the `ModulePrefs` node:

```
<ModulePrefs>
    <Require feature="opensocial-0.9"/>
    <Require feature="osapi"/>
    <Require feature="dynamic-height"/>
    <Optional feature="shareable-prefs"/>
</ModulePrefs>
```

Preload

The `Preload` element is a great resource for improving your application's performance and load time by preloading external content prior to loading it through HTTP requests. Including a `Preload` element instructs the container to fetch data from an external source while the gadget is being rendered.

This element is used in conjunction with the OpenSocial JavaScript API method `gadgets.io.makeRequest`, which fetches data from external sources. When used with `Preload`, the `gadgets.io.makeRequest` method request will return the content instantly.

For example, if the gadget will be making a request to *http://www.test.com* and we want to preload the content, we'd set up the `Preload` element in the following way:

```
<ModulePrefs>
    <Preload href="http://www.test.com" authz="signed" />
</ModulePrefs>
```

`Preload` has a few available attributes, listed in Table 3-2, that allow further levels of customization.

Table 3-2. Preload attributes

Attribute	Description
href	The URL for the content that the container is to preload. This field is required.
authz	The authorization type to use when requesting the content. This field is used in conjunction with the authorization field of the `gadgets.io.makeRequest` method. The values for this field are none (default), signed, or oauth. This field is optional.

Icon

The `Icon` element allows the developer to specify a 16×16-pixel thumbnail to be associated with the gadget. Icons usually appear beside the gadget's title in the context of a gadget gallery. The content of the `Icon` element can be either a URL to a web-based image or inline base64-encoded image data.

Icon may take the following form:

```
<ModulePrefs>
    <Icon>http://www.mysite.com/favicon.ico</Icon>
</ModulePrefs>
```

Table 3-3 lists the attributes available to you when specifying an Icon. Both are optional.

Table 3-3. Icon attributes

Attribute	Description
mode	The encoding you use for the image when embedding it. Only base64 is currently supported.
type	The MIME type of the embedded icon text.

Locale

The Locale element specifies the locales, or regional language types, supported within your gadget. There may be many Locale nodes within a single gadget if it supports many international countries and languages.

Locale may take the following form:

```
<ModulePrefs>
    <Locale lang="en" country="us" />
</ModulePrefs>
```

In addition to basic locale identifiers, a number of attributes may be tied in with a Locale node, as shown in Table 3-4.

Table 3-4. Locale attributes

Attribute	Description
country	The country associated with the locale supported. Countries are specified as two-digit codes based on ISO 3166-1 standards; for more details, see *http://en.wikipedia.org/wiki/ISO_3166-1*.
lang	The language associated with the locale. This is an optional field, but one of either country or lang must be present in a Locale node. Languages are specified as Alpha-2 codes based on ISO 639-1 standards; for more details, see *http://en.wikipedia.org/wiki/List_of_ISO_639-1_codes*.
language_direction	The text-reading direction that the language dictates. The values for this field can be either ltr (left to right) or rtl (right to left). This is an optional field with a default value of ltr. For multidirection support, there are several substitution variables you can use with rtl or ltf: __BIDI_START_EDGE__ If the gadget is in left-to-right mode, the value is left; if it's in right-to-left mode, the value is right. __BIDI_END_EDGE__ If the gadget is in left-to-right mode, the value is right; if it's in right-to-left mode, the value is left.

Attribute	Description
	`__BIDI_DIR__` If the gadget is in left-to-right mode, the value is `ltr`; if it's in right-to-left mode, the value is `rtl`.
	`__BIDI_REVERSE_DIR__` If the gadget is in left-to-right mode, the value is `rtl`; if it's in right-to-left mode, the value is `ltr`.
`messages`	A URL to an XML message bundle that contains translation strings for a given locale.

Even though you're only required to specify one of either `country` or `lang` within a `Locale` node, if you don't include both, it's assumed that the default value of an omitted tag is * (ALL). In other words, if you specify a country but no language, it is assumed that you support all languages associated with that country. Likewise, if you specify a language but no country, it is assumed that you support all countries associated with that language.

For Chinese characters, there are two exceptions to the language rules:

Simplified Chinese
> The `lang` code is `zh-cn` and is typically used with a `country` code of `cn` (China).

Traditional Chinese
> The `lang` code is `zh-tw` and is typically used with a `country` code of `tw` (Taiwan) or `hk` (Hong Kong).

`Locale` is extremely important when you want to support multiple languages within your gadget. It allows you to provide a direct line to your intended audience and may be used by a container to filter an application gallery for specific regions and languages.

Link

The `Link` element allows a developer to take advantage of application life-cycle events defined by a container. Such events might be application installs or uninstalls, or any other event in the day-to-day life of a social application. The container supports these features by sending relevant query parameters denoting the event to a URL endpoint specified within the `Link` node.

A `Link` node may take the following form under the `ModulePrefs` element:

```
<ModulePrefs>
    <Link rel="event" href="http://www.mysite.com/ping.php" method="POST" />
    <Link rel="event.addapp" href="http://www.mysite.com/add_app.php" />
    <Link rel="event.removeapp" href="http://www.mysite.com/remove_app.php" />
</ModulePrefs>
```

As you can see in the preceding example, the `Link` node has several associated attributes. They are listed in Table 3-5.

Table 3-5. Link attributes

Attribute	Description
rel	The string value that denotes the event being triggered. This value is required.
href	The URL to make a request to once the event has been triggered. This value is required.
method	The HTTP request method, either GET or POST, to use when making a request to the URL supplied in the href attribute. The default request method is GET. This is an optional attribute.

If a Link node is specified with a rel of *opensocialevent* (e.g., rel="event"), then any undefined life-cycle event types will be sent through to that href value by default. If there are one or more Link nodes with a rel of *opensocialevent.type* (e.g., rel ="event.addapp"), then any container life-cycle event with a matching type will be forwarded on to the href value specified in that node.

As shown in Table 3-6, there are currently four event types defined within the Open-Social specification, which developers can use to handle life-cycle events.

Table 3-6. OpenSocial event types

Event	Description
addapp	Event triggered when one or more users install the application. The parameters attached with the event are:
	id
	Unique ID that identifies the users who have installed the application.
	from
	Identifies how the users installed the application. Defined values are invite, gallery, or external. This parameter is optional.
remov eapp	Event triggered when one or more users uninstall the application. The parameters attached with the event are:
	id
	Unique ID that identifies the users who have uninstalled the application.
app	Event triggered when the developer or container changes the application state. The parameters attached with the event are:
	action
	The action performed on the application to change its state. Defined values are enabled, disabled, or approved.
	reason
	The reason that the action was taken. Defined values are policy, quota, or maintenance. This parameter is optional.
invite	Event triggered when someone has invited other users to install the application. The parameters attached with the event are:
	id
	Unique ID that identifies the users who have been invited to the application.
	from_id
	Unique ID that identifies the user who sent the application invitation.

The value of supporting life-cycle event notifications through tools such as Link nodes cannot be stressed enough. Having an up-to-date database of user records and links that is in sync with the actual application use on the container is vital for maintaining a high-performance, targeted service. This is a low-cost measure for containers, but even more importantly, both the container and the gadget developer reap the benefits of offering applications with a greater degree of user control, making this a win-win situation.

Defining User Preferences

You may need to save user preference variables persistently within an application's OpenSocial gadget. This is where the UserPref element comes into play. It allows you to configure which variables you would like to store for a user. These configuration variables, along with JavaScript features we will talk about in later sections, provide simple key/value storage without requiring you to set up a database.

UserPref contains a number of configurable attributes, listed in Table 3-7.

Table 3-7. UserPref attributes

Attribute	Description
datatype	An optional string that denotes the date type present within the user preference variable. The value may be string (default value), bool, enum, hidden (not visible or user-editable), or list (dynamic array generated from user input).
default_value	An optional string that stores a default value for a user preference in the event that the user does not specify a variable configuration.
display_name	An optional string that represents the user preference during editing. This value must be unique.
name	The name of the user preference. This value is required and must be a unique value.
required	An optional Boolean value (true/false) indicating whether the user preference variable is required or not. The default value is false (not required).
urlparam	If a Content section within an XML gadget has the type set to url, signifying a separate file from which to load data, this optional parameter is passed along to that file as well if these preferences are set.

A UserPref element may take this form:

```
<UserPref name="zip_code",
          display_name="Zip Code"
          datatype="string"
          default_value="90210">
```

For practical examples of how to leverage these elements from the JavaScript layer, see the section "Saving State with User Preferences" on page 108 in Chapter 4.

Enum Data Types

With the enum data type, a developer can include a number of user-specified values within a single UserPref element. You can think of this type as an HTML drop-down list that allows the user to select a value from several different choices.

For example, let's say we're building a movie-rating widget and want to allow users to store movie ratings from 1–5 (with 0 meaning the user did not rate the movie). We could increase the base UserPref node with our additional EnumValue nodes:

```
<UserPref name="rating" display_name="Rating" datatype="enum" default_value="0">
    <EnumValue value="1" display_value="Worst Movie Ever"/>
    <EnumValue value="2" display_value="I just wasted 2 hours of my life"/>
    <EnumValue value="3" display_value="Meh"/>
    <EnumValue value="4" display_value="That was pretty entertaining"/>
    <EnumValue value="5" display_value="Epic"/>
</UserPref>
```

We specify enum as our data type, and within the UserPref node we define the Enum Value nodes for each rating value the user can choose from. Each node has a display value that the user sees (e.g., "Epic") and a value that the developer uses to denote the chosen option (e.g., "5").

Application Content

Content sections allow developers to define the content to be loaded for the different views of a gadget. As described in Chapter 1, most containers include different views, such as a small or large view, and Content sections are where those views are defined.

Content sections have several attributes available to them, all of which are optional (Table 3-8).

Table 3-8. Content attributes

Attribute	Description
href	A destination URL for the content to be loaded. This is a proxied content-loading approach to defining your gadget sections.
prefer red_height	The initial height of the gadget in pixels.
prefer red_width	The initial width of the gadget in pixels.
type	The type of content to be loaded. The values can be either html (default) for content within the gadget, or url for an external content URL specified with the href attribute.
view	The view for which the content is to be loaded. Containers may offer multiple views, which can be defined through these Content sections. Multiple view names are specified as comma-delimited values (e.g., home, profile).

Defining Content Views

The concept of views may be completely foreign to many application developers, but it's a critical one to understand when you're developing gadgets for social networking containers.

Having a cohesive view architecture is vital to an application's success. There are countless instances where an application with a good concept fails because its developer expects people to use it from a specific view, so he neglects the other views by simply putting an image of, or call to action to load, the larger view (or vice versa, if he develops a small view but ignores the large).

The most important point here is that a user will never use your products in exactly the way that you intended them to be used. For this reason, you must spend equal time thinking about all of the views and how they interact, rather than focusing 99% of your attention on a single view and leaving the others as an afterthought. Some users may want to interact only with the subset of functionality defined in a small view, while others want to use all of the views depending on the particular tasks they want to complete at a given time. With this in mind, let's explore view functionality in the context of an application gadget.

Each container defines its own views and variations depending on its use for gadgets (e.g., whether the container is inherently social in nature or geared to business applications). Table 3-9 outlines the view types that can be used in many of the available containers.

Table 3-9. View types

View name	Description
default	Renders on any view that does not have a Content section currently associated with it.
profile	Renders on the user's profile. profile is visible to individuals viewing the user's profile, even if they don't have the gadget installed. This view can be used as a call to action for a viewer to install the application.
home	Renders within a smaller view, which is visible to the user only. This view is indicative of a gadget window and usually contains numerous gadgets installed by the user.
canvas	Renders within a larger "full" view. This view is typically used in conjunction with the smaller views (profile and home) and generally comprises a more extensive and fully featured version of the smaller views.

Many of the current containers implementing the OpenSocial standard are listed on the OpenSocial wiki at *http://wiki.opensocial.org/index.php?title=Containers*. If you click the links to view details, you'll find some more container-specific information, including the supported view names.

Now that you understand the container views, we'll explore the numerous methods for defining the views that you would like the gadget to build upon.

Creating a Content section

 If you are using inline markup within the Content nodes of your gadget instead of loading markup from an external file, you should always wrap the content in <![CDATA[... Content ...]] tags. This will prevent the markup from being rendered as part of the gadget XML file—that is, as gadget-specific tags—when it loads.

A base-level Content section within a gadget includes a few items. Within the Module Prefs element, if you want to be able to work with views through the gadget JavaScript layer, you will need to require the views feature by using the Require element. Following that, you can define a Content element with the view you want to load the content for. If you wish to inline your HTML, CSS, and JavaScript within the gadget, you should wrap the code within the Content section in CDATA tags. This will prevent your HTML elements from being treated as if they were part of the gadgets XML spec.

```
<Module>
    <ModulePrefs>
        <Require feature="views" />
    </ModulePrefs>
    <Content view="canvas">
        <![CDATA[
        This text will show up in my larger canvas gadget
view
        ]]>
    </Content>
</Module>
```

Creating multiple Content sections

We can build upon our definition of a single Content section by defining additional sections the same way; we simply define a new Content element with another view. These new Content elements may include either inline or proxied content and will be treated in the same way as the original section.

```
<Module>
    <ModulePrefs>
        <Require feature="views" />
    </ModulePrefs>
    <Content view="canvas">
        <![CDATA[
        This text will show up in my larger canvas gadget view
        ]]>
    </Content>
    <Content view="home"
            type="url"
            href="http://www.site.com/index.php"
    />
</Module>
```

Creating one Content section with multiple views

If you want one `Content` section to define the content for multiple sections, you may define multiple comma-separated view names within the `view` attribute. This technique is especially useful when you have multiple small views within a container (such as `home` and `profile`) and wish to serve up the same content in each.

```
<Module>
    <ModulePrefs>
        <Require feature="views" />
    </ModulePrefs>
    <Content view="home, profile">
        <![CDATA[
        This text will show up in my home and profile gadget views
        ]]>
    </Content>
</Module>
```

Creating cascading Content sections

There may be instances where you have pieces of content, such as a header, that should appear in multiple views. Instead of repeating the same code within each `Content` section for each view, you can create multiple `Content` sections with redundant views; when the gadget is rendered, the `Content` sections are concatenated together into a single code base for each section.

```
<Module>
    <ModulePrefs>
        <Require feature="views" />
    </ModulePrefs>
    <Content view="canvas">
        <![CDATA[
        <div>This is the content of my larger canvas view</div>
        ]]>
    </Content>
    <Content view="canvas, profile">
        <![CDATA[
        This is my footer
        ]]>
    </Content>
</Module>
```

If we load the preceding example in a container's profile view, it produces the following:

    This is my footer

If we load the example in the canvas view, however, the two sections are concatenated and give us the following:

    This is the content of my larger canvas view
    This is my footer

Navigating between views

In a social networking gadget container, Content sections are strictly tied to specific pages on the site. For instance, if I had a profile on a site and a gadget loaded on that profile, I would expect the Content section with the view attribute set to profile to load in that view. This is how containers are able to delegate locations for each section of a gadget. But this is not the only method for loading different Content sections—there are also JavaScript methods available within your gadget to push users through from one view to the next while keeping them in the context of your application. You enable these JavaScript functions by adding a Require element for the views feature.

This following example defines two views, profile and canvas, and uses an onclick handler to include a button within each view. These onclick handlers invoke the OpenSocial JavaScript gadgets view method requestNavigateTo to forward the user browser to the view specified as the function's parameter:

```
<Module>
  <ModulePrefs>
    <Require feature="views" />
  </ModulePrefs>
  <Content view="profile">
    <![CDATA[
    <button onclick="gadgets.views.requestNavigateTo('canvas'); ">
      Click to navigate to the canvas view
    </button>
    ]]>
  </Content>
  <Content view="canvas">
  <![CDATA[
    <button onclick="gadgets.views.requestNavigateTo('profile'); ">
      Click to navigate to the profile view
    </button>
  ]]>
  </Content>
</Module>
```

 The full code for this sample is available at *https://github.com/jcleblanc/ programming-social-applications/blob/master/chapter_3/navigating_be tween_views.xml*.

This functionality allows you to control the view flow for your application. You could define a subset of functionality on the profile view, for instance, and include a call to action for the user to click a button to go to the canvas view, where she can see the full range of functionality for the application.

Passing data between views

While the navigation functionality is a valuable asset for controlling the flow of your application, you may need to pass data between the views during the navigation process. If the user were to set temporary state details in the profile view and then navigate to the canvas view, for example, you would want to pass that state information to the canvas view for processing.

You can pass information this way by extending the requestNavigateTo(...) parameter list to include a second parameter. This second parameter is a string containing all of the information to be passed to the next view:

```
<Module>
   <ModulePrefs>
      <Require feature="views" />
   </ModulePrefs>
   <Content view="profile">
      <![CDATA[
      <script type="text/javascript">
      function loadCanvas(postData){
         gadgets.views.requestNavigateTo('canvas', postData);
      }
      </script>
      <button onclick="loadCanvas('user123');">
         Click to navigate to the canvas view
      </button>
      ]]>
   </Content>
   <Content view="canvas">
      <![CDATA[
      <div id="postData"></div>
      <script type="text/javascript">
         var postVal = gadgets.views.getParams();
         document.getElementById('postData').innerHTML = postVal;
      </script>
      ]]>
   </Content>
</Module>
```

 The full code for this sample is available at *https://github.com/jcleblanc/ programming-social-applications/blob/master/chapter_3/passing_data _between_views.xml*.

Our profile view button will call a function, passing in a string representing a user variable. This variable is passed as the second parameter to our requestNavi gateTo(...) method. The browser will then forward the user to the canvas view. Once the canvas view content loads, we capture the data passed to the view with the gadgets.views.getParams(...) method and insert it into a div in the view.

Creating and working with subviews

Subviews are a way to define different content pages (or slates) for a single view. They allow the developer to switch the content of a particular view without having to control that content flow with JavaScript. The developer will need JavaScript only to navigate from a main view to the subview.

To define a subview, you create a Content section as you did previously, but you name the view using the convention *view.subviewname*. For instance, if I want to create a subview named "sub" that resides on the canvas view, I would set the view attribute to canvas.sub. We can navigate to the subview by making a request to requestNavigate To(...), as we've done before, and insert *view.subviewname* (e.g., canvas.sub) as the first parameter:

```
<Module>
    <ModulePrefs>
        <Require feature="views" />
    </ModulePrefs>
    <Content view="canvas">
        <![CDATA[
        <button onclick="gadgets.views.requestNavigateTo('canvas.sub');">
            Click to navigate to the canvas sub page
        </button>
        ]]>
    </Content>
    <Content view="canvas.sub">
        <![CDATA[
        This is the content of my subpage
        ]]>
    </Content>
</Module>
```

 The full code for this sample is available at *https://github.com/jcleblanc/ programming-social-applications/blob/master/chapter_3/working_with _subviews.xml*.

When the preceding code runs and the user is viewing the canvas view, she will see a button asking her to click to navigate to the canvas subview. When she clicks this button, the content of the canvas view will be replaced with the content defined in the Content section with the view of canvas.sub.

Defining error view states

If you are implementing views that use a proxied content approach (i.e., that link to an external file via the href attribute), the OpenSocial specification defines standard methods for handling HTTP error states automatically within a gadget. Containers should process these content views, but at the very least they should display meaningful error messages to the user.

You should integrate an error view into your gadgets wherever possible. In an ideal world, your code will always work and your servers will have 100% uptime, but this is the real world—things break. An error fallback view, where you can display a pleasant "something went wrong" message with relevant links or instructions, is always better than an impersonal HTTP error message.

If containers encounter an error while trying to retrieve the proxied content, they should obtain the error message from a view with a name of *viewname.error*. So, for example, if the container gets a 404 Not Found error message when trying to retrieve the content for the canvas view, it should display an error message from content obtained from a view named `canvas.error`:

```
<Module>
    <ModulePrefs>
        <Require feature="views" />
    </ModulePrefs>
    <Content view="canvas" href="http://www.mysite.com/canvas.php" />
    <Content type="html" view="canvas.error">
        <![CDATA[
        An error occurred, please refresh the application window.
        ]]>
    </Content>
</Module>
```

 The full code for this sample is available at *https://github.com/jcleblanc/ programming-social-applications/blob/master/chapter_3/defining_error _view_states.xml*.

In the preceding example, should a request to *http://www.mysite.com/canvas.php* fail, the container should display the message "An error occurred, please refresh the application window" to the user instead of something like "HTTP 404 Error: Resource Not Found."

When a container supports these error views, they should be defined for each Con tent section that uses a proxied content approach.

Inline Versus Proxy Content

As you have seen, the Content section may contain either inline content—including HTML, CSS, and JavaScript—or you may use a proxy file to load the content. This proxy file, which is the URL value of the href attribute, needs to be a file of type HTML, XHTML, PHP, or any other server-side language. The proxy cannot be, for instance, a link to a *.swf* Flash file, an image, or a *.mov* QuickTime movie. To embed these items, you must wrap them in an HTML document and serve them via that file.

"Is it better to inline your content or have a proxy?" is usually one of the first questions that comes up when developers start building their applications. As far as the accessibility of container-specific features, there are really no differences between the two methods. When a gadget is rendered, all Content sections are concatenated together in a similar fashion. Choosing one method over another really comes down to maintainability, number of server requests, and load time.

Most containers internally cache the gadget XML files that are uploaded to their systems so they can serve up gadgets quickly. Once you make edits to a gadget XML file, these containers will require you to reupload or update their cache by syncing the XML file. This can be a tedious task depending on how the container handles caching, and if you inline your content inside the gadget XML file, you will have to do it each time you wish to view edits.

On the other hand, if you proxy your content using the href attribute, you will not need to update the gadget XML spec file when you update that Content section. This significantly improves the efficiency of your gadget-engineering practices and allows you to work independently of the gadget architecture.

Another issue emerges when we look at how data is obtained for a proxy Content section. Proxied content will mainly be fetched at the time of gadget rendering, when a user is using your application. This means that a request to your server has to be made each time the gadget loads if the container lacks a caching mechanism for proxied content. If there isn't a caching mechanism in place for storing Content section data, this could result in a much higher server load. In this case, gadget implementers should integrate a data-caching layer on their servers to decrease processing load.

Finally, you need to consider the speed at which the gadget will load. If you are serving the gadget inline from a cached state, the gadget will render almost immediately. This is the ideal situation. Under normal circumstances, having to make a server request for data and wait for that response would make the proxied content method the clear loser. But while we can't prevent the server request, we can certainly control when the content starts being fetched. If we specify the same proxy URL in a Preload element in the gadget XML file, the data fetch begins immediately. This means that when processing begins for the Content sections, the response should have already completed and the gadget will render as though it were cached.

Table 3-10 summarizes the features and benefits for each request type.

Table 3-10. Inlined versus proxied content

	Inlined content	Proxied content
Can work independently of the gadget XML file		✓
Takes advantage of container caching	✓	
Quick rendering time	✓	✓

It appears that we have a tie, but if we look closely at what each option *does not* do, we can figure out which is the best approach for any gadget.

If you are developing a small-scale gadget that will have minimal server load, the best approach may be to choose engineering and editing efficiency rather than taking advantage of the container's caching mechanisms. Let's face it, though: in 99% of cases, we will be developing applications that we believe will succeed and obtain a large number of users, so we should plan for scale here. This means choosing inline content to reduce server load allows you to serve more users at any given time.

To take advantage of both categories, we should ideally have two gadgets: a development gadget and a production gadget. The development gadget should use proxied content to allow us to work independently of the production-level gadget without having to worry about it taking down the application. The production gadget should embed those proxied scripts directly in the gadget, so that it may be served up as efficiently as possible.

Putting It All Together

 The full code for the samples in this section is available at *https://github.com/jcleblanc/programming-social-applications/blob/master/chapter_3/chapter_final.xml*.

In this chapter, we have examined several core concepts surrounding OpenSocial application gadgets, including:

- Building an environment to host OpenSocial gadgets
- Expanding on that environment by applying a full social network on top of the gadget host
- Having multiple gadget views, working with subviews, passing data between views, and building error states into the views
- Comparing inline and proxied content within an OpenSocial gadget

Using the lessons we've learned from the previous sections, we will now build a base-level gadget with the features usually implemented within an application and allowed by a container. We will implement a `ModulePrefs` node to define the gadget's metadata, as well as some locality and link-based information, and then include a number of `Content` sections to define the application's content. We will create a `Content` section that displays only the canvas view content; define a second `Content` section that will act as a standard footer for the gadget in the canvas, home, and profile views; and then define a final `Content` section to display an error fallback view should there be a problem with any of our content:

```
<?xml version="1.0" encoding="utf-8"?>
<Module>
    <ModulePrefs title="Chapter 3 rollup example"
                 title_url="http://www.jcleblanc.com"
                 description="Displays the concepts of viewes and module preferences"
                 author="Jonathan LeBlanc">
```

```
<Require feature="opensocial-0.9"/>
<Require feature="views" />
<Preload href="http://www.mysite.com/small.php" />
<Locale lang="en" country="us" />
<Link rel="event.addapp" href="http://www.mysite.com/add_app.php" />
<Link rel="event.removeapp" href="http://www.mysite.com/remove_app.php" />
</ModulePrefs>
```

Our first task is to define all of the module preferences that we need to use the application, and any markup that we wish to include to document the application. Within the `ModulePrefs` node, we define a title for a gadget, a URL to link the title to that provides more details about the author or application, a description of what the gadget does, and the gadget author info.

Now we need to define the OpenSocial JavaScript library features that we will need when using the application. First, we define the OpenSocial version that we will be working with. Since OpenSocial 0.9 is nearly identical in functionality to 1.0, and since Shindig supports versions up to OpenSocial 0.9, we'll specify version 0.9 of the spec. In addition, since we'll be working with navigating between views in the gadget, we want to include support for views.

This gadget will use a mix of inline (within the gadget) and proxied (linked to a remote source) content. To reduce the load time for the views using proxied content (in this case, the profile and home views), we add a `Preload` tag, which will begin loading the content right away instead of when the view begins loading.

We then specify the language/text support that we will be integrating into this application. In this case, we support US English.

The final piece of the module preferences is the application life-cycle events. We specify two `Link` nodes that will be triggered when the application is added or removed. Once the `Link` nodes are triggered, the `href` associated with each event type will also be triggered, allowing us to maintain personal statistics about the application's current user base.

With our module preferences out of the way, we can define our application's different views through multiple `Content` sections:

```
<Content type="url" view="home, profile" href="http://www.mysite.com/small.php" />
<Content type="html" view="canvas">
   <![CDATA[
   This is my standard large view
   ]]>
</Content>
<Content type="html" view="canvas, home, profle">
   <![CDATA[
   <!-- Standard footer for all content views -->
   <div id="footer">
      Navigation Options:
      <a onclick="gadgets.views.requestNavigateTo('home');">Home</a> |
      <a onclick="gadgets.views.requestNavigateTo('profile');">Profile</a> |
      <a onclick="gadgets.views.requestNavigateTo('canvas');">Canvas</a>
```

```
            </div>

            <style type="text/css">
            div.contentWrap, div#footer{ font:11px arial,helvetica,sans-serif; }
            div#footer{ font-size:10px;
                        font-weight:bold;
                        margin-top:10px;
                        padding:10px;
                        border-top:1px solid #e3e3e3; }
            div#footer a{ cursor:pointer; }
            </style>
            ]]>
        </Content>
        <Content type="html" view="canvas.error, profile.error, home.error">
            The application could not be loaded at the current time.
        </Content>
    </Module>
```

The first `Content` section we specify is for our home and profile views. These views will contain the same proxied content that is loaded from a remote source.

Our next `Content` section specifies the information that will be displayed in the larger, canvas view of the container. This content is loaded inline within the gadget.

The third section specifies additional content for all three of our currently defined views. As we talked about earlier, when the gadget is rendered, any `Content` sections with the same view name will be merged together. Within this section, we define a global footer for the application that allows the user to cycle through the different views. To cycle through the views, we use the `gadgets.views.requestNavigateTo('view')` JavaScript method. Note that views such as home or profile usually refer to part of the user profile that has applications embedded in the page content, but the application is only a small piece of the overall structure of the page.

Our last content section defines an error state view for all of our views. If supported within a container, this section will be used if an error occurs within the application flow.

What we've built in this complete example is the core architecture for a gadget. We used the `Content` sections to reduce redundancy in our code, define methods for tracking install and uninstall events, and build an error state into the gadget's flow to handle unforeseen issues.

Now that we understand the fundamentals of a container and gadget, we are ready to move on to more advanced features, visualizations, and functionality. Using the base we've developed here as a starting point, Chapter 4 will explore how to expand our gadgets into fully scalable projects.

Defining Features with OpenSocial JavaScript References

Within the confines of an application, the OpenSocial specification defines a large number of features that are available for containers to implement. Some of the OpenSocial specification's more useful features are JavaScript libraries that contain helper functions to aid developers with the construction of their applications—whether by saving simple key/value pairs of data for a user without a database, or displaying messages that aren't dismissed by pop-up blockers.

What You'll Learn

This chapter focuses on the core features of the JavaScript libraries that may be included within OpenSocial. We will explore how to use these to:

- Dynamically adjust the height of your application to remove whitespace.
- Insert Flash movies into your gadgets where restrictions are present.
- Display different types of messages to the user.
- Create and save simple state information for a user without a database.
- Set the title of the application dynamically.
- Build a tabbed gadget.
- Create your own JavaScript features.

The knowledge we gain throughout the chapter will allow us to build a rich client-side feature set into our gadget in such a way that it will not only migrate between different containers easily, but will also provide multibrowser support.

Including the OpenSocial Feature JavaScript Libraries

There is a series of JavaScript-based features available in the gadgets JavaScript specification to help you build out your application. The functionality these features offer ranges from embedding Flash movies to creating simple tabs.

These JavaScript features include those that are built for server communication (e.g., content-rewrite) as well as for client communication (e.g., dynamic-height). This means that your gadget can use these features to communicate directly with the hosting server and to create client-based functionality.

As shown in the following example, you can include a specific feature by adding a Require element in the gadget XML spec file. Once initialized, the feature may be rendered via spec-defined JavaScript initialization calls that you include in a Content section:

```
<ModulePrefs>
    <Require feature="tabs" />
</ModulePrefs>
```

A number of JavaScript features are currently available through the gadgets spec; these are listed in Table 4-1.

Table 4-1. JavaScript features

Attribute	Description
dynamic-height	Gives a gadget the ability to resize itself automatically. This is useful if you're inserting or replacing content via AJAX requests and the height of your gadget changes.
flash	Embeds a *.swf* Flash movie in your gadget.
minimessage	Displays within your gadget a small message window, which can be dismissed by the user.
setprefs	Allows you to programmatically save key/value pair state information for a user.
settitle	Allows you to set the gadget's title programmatically. You can use this to personalize the state of the gadget for each user.
tabs	Allows you to create a tabbed interface in your applications.

Let's explore some of these features in more depth and see how they can help personalize the gadget experience.

Dynamically Setting the Height of a Gadget View

The JavaScript definitions for setting a dynamic height allow the gadget developer to automatically resize the user's current view. Many social networking containers that host gadgets define a maximum gadget height by default and do not automatically resize it once the content in the view has changed. This can lead to excessive whitespace or cropped content, frustrating developers and users alike. The Content sections of a gadget XML file do provide a parameter for preferred_height, which the developer can use to specify the initial height in pixels of the particular view, but that parameter does not allow for dynamic resizing of the view when content changes.

There are two steps for executing a call to dynamically resize the current view's height to the current height of the application content:

1. Within the `ModulePrefs` node of the gadget spec file, add a `Require` element to enable the `dynamic-height` JavaScript library.
   - Include: `<Require feature="dynamic-height"/>`
2. When you wish to dynamically resize the height of the current view, call the `adjustHeight()` method of the `gadgets.window` object.
   - Method call: `gadgets.window.adjustHeight();`

It is important that you call this method immediately after the application content has changed, such as right after making an AJAX request for new content and embedding it into the page:

```
<Module title="Module to make AJAX request and dynamically resize view">
    <ModulePrefs>
        <Require feature="dynamic-height" />
    </ModulePrefs>
    <Content view="canvas" preferred_height="300px">
        <![CDATA[
        <div id="updateNode">This is my initial content to be updated</div>
        <button onclick="makeRequest();">Update Page Content</button>

        <script type="text/javascript">
        function makeRequest(){
            //make AJAX request to get new page content using OpenSocial AJAX methods
            osapi.http.get({'href':'http://example.com/sendResp.php'}).execute(function
            (result){

                //update div with new content obtained from request
                document.getElementById('updateNode').innerHTML = result.content;

                //dynamically resize the view height to the new content height
                gadgets.window.adjustHeight();
            });
        }
        </script>
        ]]>
    </Content>
</Module>
```

 The full code for this sample is available at *https://github.com/jcleblanc/ programming-social-applications/blob/master/chapter_4/setting_gadget _height.xml*.

In the preceding example, we start with the `Require` statement in `ModulePrefs`, which indicates that we would like to enable the functionality for dynamically resizing the gadget height. This is followed by a `Content` section, in which we set the canvas view's starting height to 300px. The `Content` section has a `div` node with some starting content and a button with a click event to initiate the data fetch and resize. When a user clicks that button, the `makeRequest` function will initiate. The first thing the `makeRequest` function will do is perform an AJAX get request to fetch data from *http://example.com/sendResp.php*. In this example, that URL returns new HTML content to be embedded within the canvas view. Once that AJAX request completes and returns the `result` object, we set the `innerHTML` of the default `div` to the new content returned, and then immediately make a request to `gadgets.window.adjustHeight()` to resize the canvas view's height to the height of the new content. If we didn't execute the `adjustHeight` method call, the canvas height would have remained at the 300px that we initially set it to, and our new content would be cropped at that point.

Inserting Flash Movies in Your Gadget

The JavaScript feature libraries also offer you the capability to embed a *.swf* Flash video into your gadget. Doing so allows you to quickly, and with minimal code, include a standards-compliant Flash movie.

To integrate this feature, you need to take the following steps:

1. Within the `ModulePrefs` node of the gadget spec file, add a `Require` element to enable the JavaScript `flash` library.
   - Include: `<Require feature="flash"/>`
2. When you wish to insert a new Flash movie into your gadget, call the `embedFlash()` method of the `gadgets.flash` object.
   - Method call: `gadgets.flash.embedFlash(...);`

The `flash` library also includes several methods under `gadgets.flash` for working with and displaying Flash movies, listed in Table 4-2.

Table 4-2. Methods included under gadgets.flash

Method	Description
embedFlash	Embeds a *.swf* Flash movie, loaded from a provided URL, into a specified DOM node within the gadget. Parameters include:
	url *(string)*
	A URL to a *.swf* flash movie
	container *(string)*
	The ID of the container in which to insert the Flash movie
	params *(object)*
	Returns `true` if successful; `false` if unsuccessful

Method	Description
embedCachedFlash	Embeds a cached Flash movie into the specified DOM node. Parameters and return type are the same as embedFlash.
getMajorVersion()	Returns the major version of the Flash player or 0 if not available.

```
<Module>
    <ModulePrefs>
        <Require feature="flash" />
    </ModulePrefs>
    <Content view="canvas">
        <![CDATA[
        <div id="insertFlash">Loading Flash Movie ...</div>

        <script type="text/javascript">
        if (gadgets.flash.getMajorVersion() === 0){
            //flash player not available
            var msg = "Flash player check failed - please download flash player";
            document.getElementById('insertFlash').innerHTML = msg;
        } else {
            //flash player available
            var flashURL =
                "http://developer.yahoo.com/yui/examples/swf/assets/SWFExampleSimple.swf";
            gadgets.flash.embedFlash(flashURL, "insertFlash", {
                swf_version: 9,
                id: "flashObj",
                width: 400,
                height: 350
            });
        }
        </script>
        ]]>
    </Content>
</Module>
```

The full code for this sample is available at *https://github.com/jcleblanc/ programming-social-applications/blob/master/chapter_4/inserting_flash _in_gadget.xml*.

In this example, we include the `Require` node to load the `flash` library for us to use. The `Content` section contains a default `div` node in which we will attempt to insert the Flash movie. We then check to see if Flash player is currently available on the user's system. If not, we insert a "Please download Flash" message; if so, we embed a Flash movie into the `div` node.

Displaying Messages to Your Users

The `minimessage` library enables the developer to display a message window to a user. This is a valuable feature when you're trying to obtain user input or display status messages to a user that autodismiss after a short interval.

To integrate this feature, take the following steps:

1. Within the `ModulePrefs` node of the gadget spec file, add a `Require` element to enable the `minimessage` JavaScript library.
   - Include: `<Require feature="minimessage"/>`
2. Within the gadget JavaScript layer, insert an initialization function for the minimessage features.
   - Method call: `var message = new gadgets.MiniMessage(__MODULE_ID__);`
3. When you wish to create a new message window, call one of three message window request methods.
   - Dismissible message: `message.createDismissibleMessage("My Message", call back);`
   - Static message: `message.createStaticMessage("My Message");`
   - Timer message: `message.createTimerMessage("My Message", 3, callback);`

As noted in step 3, there are three different message types that a gadget implementer may specify:

Dismissible message
  Remains visible until the user manually closes the window.

Static message
  Remains visible until the code-specified event occurs. This message may be dismissed only via the gadget code.

Timer message
  Remains visible until a predefined timeout occurs. These messages will autoclose when the allotted time expires.

Moving from basic concepts into functional examples, next we'll explore how to build and customize message windows using the available JavaScript library methods.

Creating a Message

As we just discussed, there are three different message types that we can create within a gadget, each of which has its own specific expiration criteria. Let's go over them in more depth.

Dismissible messages

The dismissible message window is a standard alert that, if it's not programmatically set to close, requires the user to interact with the window dismiss controls (generally an "x" in the top-right corner) to close it. These messages are generally developed to alert the user of changes within the gadget—such as new messages for her, or profile detail changes requesting an accept or cancel action from her.

We can create a dismissible mini-message simply by following the requirements described previously:

```
<Module title="Gadget to display a mini-message">
   <ModulePrefs>
      <Require feature="minimessage" />
   </ModulePrefs>
   <Content view="canvas">
      <![CDATA[
      <div id="msgDisplay"></div>

      <script type="text/javascript">
      //message dismissal callback
      function msgCallback(){
         document.getElementById("msgDisplay").innerHTML = "Message window closed";
      }

      //create new dismissible mini-message
      var message = new gadgets.MiniMessage(__MODULE_ID__);
      message.createDismissibleMessage("My dismissible mini-message", msgCallback);
      </script>
      ]]>
   </Content>
</Module>
```

 The full code for this sample is available at *https://github.com/jcleblanc/ programming-social-applications/blob/master/chapter_4/creating_mes sage_dismissible.xml.*

We add in our `Require` element to enable the `minimessage` JavaScript library; then, within the `Content` section that will load the message, we add the required JavaScript to create a new `MiniMessage` gadget object and initialize the message. The message creation method has an optional second parameter, a callback function reference. When the message window is dismissed, this callback function will be executed and display a message to the user.

Static messages

Like the dismissible message window, the static message is displayed to the user, but it differs in that it can only be dismissed programmatically, allowing the developer to dictate under what circumstances the window will be closed. Dismissing the message

window requires a call to the `minimessage` library method `gadgets.MiniMessage.dis`
`missMessage(...)`. Static messages are valuable when the user's input is required for
him to continue using the application, as with a username and password. They take
the form of a modal background overlay, which prevents background application interaction and displays the message window in the front.

Using the preceding dismissible message gadget code, we can replace the scripts within
the Content section to give us a dismissible message with a link to close the window:

```
<Content view="canvas">
  <![CDATA[
  <button onclick="dismissWindow();">Close Window</button>

  <script type="text/javascript">
  //create new dismissible mini-message
  var message = new gadgets.MiniMessage(__MODULE_ID__);

  //dismiss window function
  function dismissWindow(){
      gadgets.MiniMessage.dismissMessage(message);
  }

  //create new static message window
  message.createStaticMessage("This is my static mini-message");
  </script>
  ]]>
</Content>
```

 The full code for this sample is available at *https://github.com/jcleblanc/*
programming-social-applications/blob/master/chapter_4/creating_mes
sage_static.xml.

In this code sample, we have generated a static message. In addition, we've included a
button on the page that will call the `dismissWindow()` function, which in turn will close
the window by calling the `gadgets.MiniMessage.dismissMessage()` method.

Timer messages

The timer message is the final message type available for displaying a user prompt. It
is a message window with a `setTimeout` applied to the window close event, so after the
specified interval, the window will automatically close; no user or developer action is
required to dismiss it. These types of messages are very handy when you want to alert
a user that his actions had a particular effect, such as confirming that a message was
sent out from the gadget.

If we take the core gadget we generated for the dismissible message example and replace
the Content section, we can set up a timer message:

```
<Content view="canvas">
  <![CDATA[
```

```
<div id="msgDisplay"></div>

<script type="text/javascript">
//create new timer message window
var message = new gadgets.MiniMessage(__MODULE_ID__);
message.createTimerMessage("This is my timer mini-message", 3, function(){
    document.getElementById("msgDisplay").innerHTML = "Message Dismissed");
});
</script>
]]>
</Content>
```

 The full code for this sample is available at *https://github.com/jcleblanc/ programming-social-applications/blob/master/chapter_4/creating_mes sage_timer.xml*.

As with the previous examples, we first start by creating a new `MiniMessage` object. To initialize the timer message, we call the `createTimerMessage` message, passing in the message string to display as the first parameter, and the number of seconds before the window automatically closes as the second parameter. As the optional third parameter, the callback will be executed once that close event happens, displaying the text "Message Dismissed" within the gadget.

Positioning the Message Windows

Displaying a message to your gadget users is a great way to inform them of pertinent changes, upsell items for in-app purchases, and more. Many times, you'll want to position those windows in a specific spot in your application to prevent the default pop-up location from being used and supplemental content from being covered.

There are a few methods available for positioning single windows or all windows at once.

Positioning a single message

If you have multiple mini-message windows that you want to position at different locations, or if you only have a single message in the gadget that you would like to position, then it may be easiest to position one window at a time.

In addition to allowing plain text for the content of a message window, the `createDis missibleMessage()` method also accepts a DOM node reference that denotes the window's HTML-based content.

Again taking the dismissible message gadget sample as our foundation, we can change the `Content` section to dictate the position on the page that a message window should be displayed, based on where the DOM node is placed:

```
<Content view="canvas">
  <![CDATA[
  <style type="text/css">
  #msgWindow{ width:200px; float:right; }
  </style>

  <div id="msgWindow">
     <b>This is my message header</b><br />
     Visit <a href="http://www.mysite.com">my site</a> for more details.
  </div>

  <script type="text/javascript">
  //create new mini-message object
  var message = new gadgets.MiniMessage(__MODULE_ID__);

  //get the message node and create a new dismissible mini-message
  var msgWindow = document.getElementById("msgWindow");
  message.createDismissibleMessage(msgWindow);
  </script>
  ]]>
</Content>
```

 The full code for this sample is available at *https://github.com/jcleblanc/ programming-social-applications/blob/master/chapter_4/position_single _message.xml*.

In the preceding example, we create a message context node with an `id` of `msgWindow`. This `div` contains our message window's content and has style constraints to position it. The window is floated to the right of the canvas view and is constrained to 200 pixels wide.

In the `script` block below that, we start by creating our `MiniMessage` object. We then get the message window content by obtaining the DOM node reference for the HTML we created. Finally, we create a new dismissible mini-message window from that content; it will be displayed at the same location as the `msgWindow` node.

Positioning all messages

In your gadget, you might have a series of messages that will be displayed to a user at different points, but you want them all displayed in the same location, such as a messaging box construct.

This type of implementation requires a slightly different approach than the single positioning flow. Instead of using the content of a DOM node as the HTML displayed in the message window, we use a DOM node for just the box positioning:

```
<Content view="canvas">
  <![CDATA[
  <div id="msgWindow"></div>
```

```
<script type="text/javascript">
//call mini-message constructor with DOM node to position messages to
var msgWindow = document.getElementById("msgWindow");
var message = new gadgets.MiniMessage(__MODULE_ID__, msgWindow);

//create a new dismissible mini-message
message.createDismissibleMessage("First Message");
message.createDismissibleMessage("Second Message");
</script>
]]>
</Content>
```

The full code for this sample is available at *https://github.com/jcleblanc/programming-social-applications/blob/master/chapter_4/position_all _messages.xml*.

In the preceding sample, we create a `div` to act as our positioning node. When we call the mini-message constructor we pass in, as a second parameter, the DOM node reference to that positioning `div`. When we then create our dismissible message windows, they will be inserted into the `div` that we specified. Messages will be displayed in the order in which they were added.

Styling the Message and Window

We've explored how to create message windows using simple text constructs to populate their content, but if this messaging system is to have any real value, we need to be able to customize it as we see fit. So, next we'll cover ways to apply custom styling to the message window's content as well as the message window itself.

Styling message content

In addition to plain text, a message window accepts an HTML DOM node structure as its content. Since the message window will not exist in the DOM, the new node will be appended to the window.

Using our dismissible message gadget as our base, we can revise the Content section to use a DOM node we create instead of the text message specified:

```
<Content view="canvas">
  <![CDATA[
  <script type="text/javascript">
  //create div node for message
  var msgNode = document.createElement("div");
  msgNode.innerHTML = "See <a href='http://mysite.com'>My Site</a> for more details";

  //set mouse events on message content
  msgNode.onmouseover = function(obj){ obj.style.color = "#da1d1d";  }
  msgNode.onmouseout = function(obj){ obj.style.color = "#000";  }
```

```
//create new dismissible mini-message
var message = new gadgets.MiniMessage(__MODULE_ID__);
message.createDismissibleMessage(msgNode);
</script>
]]>
</Content>
```

The full code for this sample is available at *https://github.com/jcleblanc/ programming-social-applications/blob/master/chapter_4/style_message _content.xml.*

We first create the DOM node, a `div`, which will house our message. We insert the content of the `div` and a few mouseover events to change the text color. When we create a new dismissible message window, instead of passing in the text of the message content, we pass the DOM node we created. This will create the message window with the `div` as the appended content.

Styling a single message window

Not only can you style the content of a message window, you can also style each message as it is being created, giving you a lot of design control over the window itself.

You can do this by using the return value of our message window creation functions, such as `createDismissibleMessage()`. The return value of these functions is an HTML element, meaning that we can use the return value as we would any other DOM node we create.

Working from our dismissible gadget, we can explore how to do this with some new Content JavaScript:

```
<Content view="canvas">
  <![CDATA[
  <script type="text/javascript">
  //create new dismissible mini-message and capture returned node
  var message = new gadgets.MiniMessage(__MODULE_ID__);
  var msgObj = message.createDismissibleMessage("My message content");

  //style the message window
  msgObj.style.color = "#da1d1d";
  msgObj.style.backgroundColor = "#c0c0c0";
  </script>
  ]]>
</Content>
```

The full code for this sample is available at *https://github.com/jcleblanc/ programming-social-applications/blob/master/chapter_4/style_single _message_window.xml.*

We create the message window just as we have before, but this time when we make a call to `createDismissibleMessage()`, we capture the return value—an HTML element—in a variable. Using that variable, we adjust the window's font color and background color.

This is a simple method for customizing the message windows in your gadgets on a one-off basis. Next, we'll go over how to style all the windows in your gadget simultaneously.

Styling all displayed message windows

Editing each generated message window individually makes sense if you want to customize every one with different styles, but in many instances, you may just want to set the styles to personalize all the messages at once. To this end, there are a few classes that you apply to the message window content. These include:

mmlib_table
> The root class for the message window itself. Child nodes underneath may be targeted using this class.

mmlib_xlink
> Class applied to the "x" link on a dismissible message window only.

Using this information, we can apply a few global styles to override the standard message window classes:

```
<Content view="canxvas">
  <![CDATA[
  <style type="text/css">
  .mmlib_table{
      font: bold 11px arial,helvetica,sans-serif;
      background-color: #000;
      color: #fff;
  }
  .mmlib_xlink{
      font-weight: bold;
      color: #da1d1d;
      cursor: pointer;
  }
  </style>

  <script type="text/javascript">
  //create new dismissible mini-message and capture returned node
  var message = new gadgets.MiniMessage(__MODULE_ID__);
  var msgObj = message.createDismissibleMessage("My message content");
  </script>
  ]]>
</Content>
```

The full code for this sample is available at *https://github.com/jcleblanc/programming-social-applications/blob/master/chapter_4/style_all_message_windows.xml*.

In the preceding example, we create our standard dismissible message window as we have previously. The main difference is in the style block right before the scripts. We define the mmlib_table style for the window to change the font specifications, background color, and font color. Following that, we define the mmlib_xlink class to set the "x" dismissal icon to a boldfaced, red font and to display a cursor when a user hovers her mouse over it.

Saving State with User Preferences

In many instances, you may need to persistently store small amounts of personalization information for a user. One of the features available within the OpenSocial gadgets JavaScript libraries provides a facility to help you do just that.

To integrate this feature, you need to take a few steps:

1. Within the ModulePrefs node of the gadget spec file, add a Require element including setprefs to enable the flash JavaScript library.
   - Include: <Require feature="setprefs"/>
2. Add a UserPref node with the value matching the user preference element you wish to persistently store.
3. When you wish to set a new user preference, you will need to call the set() method of the gadgets.Prefs object.
   - Method call: set(...);

There are several methods available that provide user preference getting and setting abilities, listed in Table 4-3.

Table 4-3. User preference methods

Method	Description
set	Allows you to set the persistent state of a user preference variable. Parameters include:
	Variable name *(string)* The name of the UserPref variable to set for the current user
	Value *(mixed)* The value of the UserPref variable
getString	Obtains a UserPref string. Parameters include:
	Variable name *(string)* The name of the UserPref variable to get for the current user

Method	Description
getInt	Obtains a UserPref integer. Parameters are the same as the getString method.
getBool	Obtains a UserPref Boolean. Parameters are the same as the getString method.

```
<Module>
    <ModulePrefs>
        <Require feature="setprefs" />
    </ModulePrefs>
    <UserPref name="count" default_value="0" datatype="hidden" />
    <Content view="canvas">
        <![CDATA[
        <div id="myNum">0</div>
        <button onclick="increment();">Add 1</button>
        <button onclick="decrement();">Subtract 1</button>

        <script type="text/javascript">
        var outputContainer = document.getElementById('myNum');
        //set prefs variable
        var prefs = new gadgets.Prefs();

        function increment(){
            //capture current UserPref value
            var count = prefs.getInt("count");

            //set new user pref and increment counter
            prefs.set("count", count + 1);
            outputContainer.innerHTML = count + 1;
        }

        function decrement(){
            //capture current UserPref value
            var count = prefs.getInt("count");

            //set new user pref and decrement counter
            prefs.set("count", count - 1);
            outputContainer.innerHTML = count - 1;
        }
        </script>
        ]]>
    </Content>
</Module>
```

 The full code for this sample is available at *https://github.com/jcleblanc/programming-social-applications/blob/master/chapter_4/saving_state_with_userprefs.xml*.

The preceding example demonstrates the process by which you get and set user preference variables. We create buttons to call our increment and decrement functions and, once hit, each function captures the current user preference count variable and either increments or decrements it.

Setting Your Gadget Title Programmatically

In certain circumstances, you may need to programmatically reset the title of your gadget—for example, if you are attempting to personalize all elements of the application to the current user's profile. In this case, you may want to capture profile information about the user, such as his name, and reset the gadget title to something like "Erik's Task List."

To integrate this feature, take these steps:

1. Within the `ModulePrefs` node of the gadget spec file, add a `Require` element to enable the `settitle` JavaScript library.

   - Include: `<Require feature="settitle"/>`

2. When you wish to reset the gadget title, call the `setTitle()` method of the `gadgets.window` object.

   - Method call: `gadgets.window.setTitle();`

```
<Module>
   <ModulePrefs>
      <Require feature="settitle" />
   </ModulePrefs>
   <Content view="canvas"><![CDATA[
      <form name="titleForm">
         Input new gadget title<br />
         <input type="text" name="newTitle"><br />
         <button onclick="setTitle();">Set New Title</button>
      </form>

      <script type="text/javascript">
      function setTitle(){
         //capture user title input
         var newTitle = form.newTitle.value;

         //set the gadget title
         gadgets.window.setTitle(newTitle);
      }
      </script>
   ]]></Content>
</Module>
```

 The full code for this sample is available at *https://github.com/jcleblanc/ programming-social-applications/blob/master/chapter_4/setting_gadget _title.xml.*

In the preceding example, we include the `Require` statement to initialize the `settitle` library. Within the `Content` section, we set up a simple form with an input box and button. The input box allows the user to enter a new title; when he clicks the "Set New Title" button, the `setTitle` function executes. `setTitle` captures the input from the form and then calls the `gadgets.window.setTitle()` method, passing through the title as the parameter to set the gadget title.

Integrating a Tabbed Gadget User Interface

The OpenSocial JavaScript libraries define several easy methods for creating a tabbed environment within your gadgets.

To integrate the tabbed UI feature set, you need to take a few steps:

1. Within the `ModulePrefs` node of the gadget spec file, add a `Require` element to enable the `tabs` JavaScript library.
   - Include: `<Require feature="tabs"/>`
2. Within the gadget JavaScript layer, insert a `TabSet` constructor method call for the tabbed UI features.
   - Method call: `var tabs = new gadgets.TabSet(__MODULE_ID__, "Default Tab ID");`
3. To create a new tab within the `TabSet`, call the `addTab()` method of the `tabs` Java-Script library.
   - Method call: `tabs.addTab(tabName, optParams);`

The `addTab()` method accepts the following parameters:

`tabName` *(string)*
: The name identifier for the tab to be created.

`optParams` *(object)*
: A series of optional parameters that may be used to customize the tab being created. This object may be replaced with a string to signify the `id` for the tab. The `add Tab()` optional parameters include:

`callback` *(function reference)*
: A reference to a JavaScript function to be called when a tab is selected. The tab `id` is passed in as a parameter to the callback function when executed.

`contentContainer` *(DOM node reference)*
: A reference to an HTML entity node out of which the tab content is created. This parameter can be the result of obtaining an element using `document .getElementById("ID")`. If the DOM node does not exist, it will be created.

`index` *(number)*
: The numeric index at which the new tab should be inserted. If this value is not included, the new tab will be inserted at the end of the tab list.

`tooltip` *(string)*
: A tool tip that is displayed to a user when she hovers her mouse over a tab.

The addTab() method contains enough abstraction to allow developers to define the tab and its content in many different ways within their gadgets.

The Basic Gadget

Here is the gadget we will use as a foundation for the tab examples that follow:

```
<Module title="Tabs Example">
  <ModulePrefs>
    <Require feature="tabs" />
  </ModulePrefs>
  <Content view="canvas">
    <![CDATA[
    ... Content ...
    ]]>
  </Content>
</Module>
```

This gadget includes a Require element that will integrate the OpenSocial tabs JavaScript library and a Content section for a canvas view.

Creating a Tab from Markup

One method for defining a tab's content is to create a tab out of an existing HTML DOM node, such as a div. This is an excellent tab method to use if you are trying to promote Model-View-Controller (MVC) design patterns, which separate markup from programming logic.

Applying what we have learned thus far about the tab creation methods in a gadget XML spec, we can build out a tab using a base HTML node as our foundation:

```
<Content view="canvas">
  <![CDATA[
    <div id="tab1" style="display:none;">This is the content of Tab 1</div>
    <div id="tab2" style="display:none;">
      <b>Heading for Tab 2</b><br />
      See more details on <a href="http://www.mysite.com">my site</a>.
    </div>

    <script type="text/javascript">
    //create a new tabset object with the default tab set
    var tabs = new gadgets.TabSet(__MODULE_ID__, "Second Tab");

    //create two tabs out of our markup
    tabs.addTab("First Tab ", "tab1");
    tabs.addTab("Second Tab", "tab2");
    </script>
  ]]>
</Content>
```

The full code for this sample is available at *https://github.com/jcleblanc/ programming-social-applications/blob/master/chapter_4/creating_tabs _from_markup.xml.*

In this example, we create two tabs, one with just plain text and another with additional HTML markup within the div node. To prevent a jarring UI switch, we set the display for both tabs to none to hide them until they're built.

Within the script block, we create a new TabSet object with the module ID as the first parameter and the name of the default tab as the second parameter. This optional second parameter specifies which tab loads first by default. Finally, we call the add Tab(...) method for both new tabs, passing in the tab name as the first parameter and the tab ID as the second parameter. This tab ID is the same ID we used in our div nodes, which ensures that they're treated as the content of the tab.

This example gives us two tabs using our HTML markup as the content.

Creating a Tab from JavaScript

Another method for creating tab content is to generate it from the JavaScript layer rather than working with HTML markup like we did in the previous example. This approach can be beneficial when your content is generated based on data obtained through an AJAX request to some server-side logic, or when JavaScript logic is required.

Using our base tab gadget, we'll edit the Content section to build tabs using JavaScript logic:

```
<Content view="canvas">
   <![CDATA[
     <div id="tabObject"></div>

     <script type="text/javascript">
     //callback to be executed when tab is selected
     function runCallback(tabID){
        var selectedTab = document.getElementById(tabID);
        selectedTab.style.color = "#da1d1d";
     }

     //create a new tabset object
     var tabs = new gadgets.TabSet();

     //create new tabs
     var tab = tabs.addTab("My Tab ", {
        callback: runCallback,
        contentContainer: document.getElementById("tabObject"),
        tooltip: "Select this tab for more details"
     });
     tabs.addTab("Content Tab");

     //alter the content of the tab
```

```
    var tabContent = "<b>My New Tab</b>";
    document.getElementById(tab).innerHTML = tab1Content;
    </script>
  ]]>
</Content>
```

 The full code for this sample is available at *https://github.com/jcleblanc/programming-social-applications/blob/master/chapter_4/creating_tabs_from_javascript.xml*.

In this example, we start by creating a `div` node, which will house one of our tabs. In the `script` block, we initialize a new `TabSet` object. Following this, we create two tabs.

With the first tab, we capture the return value of the `addTab()` method. This return value is the ID for the newly created tab, and may be used to change the tab content. Within the first `addTab()` method, we specify an object for the second parameter, meaning that we want to further customize the tab. In the object, we set a callback function (to `runCallback()`), which will be executed when the tab is selected; a content container (our initial `div` node), which is where the tab will be created; and a tool tip to be displayed when a user hovers his mouse over the tab.

The second tab is much simpler. We just call the `addTab()` method with the name of the tab. Since we don't specify an HTML DOM node to house the tab, the node will be automatically created on our behalf.

Now that we have created our tabs, we can begin editing the content. At the bottom of the `script` block, we create a new string of content for the first tab. Since we already have the ID of the first tab from the return value of `addTab()`, we set the `innerHTML` of that node to our new content.

In addition to setting the content at load time, we have also attached a callback to the first tab (`runCallback()`), which is executed when the tab is selected and passes in the selected tab ID as a parameter to the callback. When that tab is selected and the callback executes, we capture the tab node selected and set the tab's text color to red.

Using any combination of this JavaScript-based functionality, you can create highly scalable and dynamic tab sets.

Getting and Setting Information About the TabSet

In the previous examples, we explored a rich layer of customization for building tabs. In addition to this functionality, OpenSocial defines many helper methods for obtaining and setting information about the current `TabSet`. You can think of a `TabSet` as a container for one or more tabs, whereas a tab is just a single piece of the whole set. These helper methods enable you to vastly extend your tab functionality.

The examples that follow assume that you have already created this TabSet object:

```
var tabs = new gadgets.TabSet();
```

Aligning tabs

Should you need to align the tabs to a different horizontal position on the TabSet, you can use the alignTabs(...) method. The first parameter is the string position (left, right, or center), and the second optional parameter is the numeric offset from that position (in pixels):

```
tabs.alignTabs("right", 50);
```

Showing and hiding tabs

The displayTabs() method allows you to show or hide the TabSet tabs. The only parameter is a Boolean that specifies whether you want the tabs displayed (true) or not (false):

```
tabs.displayTabs(false);
```

Obtaining the parent container

To obtain the parent container of the TabSet, use the getHeaderContainer() method. This method returns the HTML element containing the TabSet:

```
var headerContainer = tabs.getHeaderContainer();
```

Obtaining the currently selected tab

To get the currently selected tab, you can use the getSelectedTab() method. This method returns an OpenSocial tab object, from which you can learn further information about the tab, as described in the upcoming section "Getting and setting information about a tab" on page 116:

```
var tab = tabs.getSelectedTab();
```

Obtaining all tabs

The getTabs() method returns all TabSet tabs as an array of OpenSocial tab objects:

```
var allTabs = tabs.getTabs();
```

Removing a tab

To programmatically remove a tab from a TabSet, use the removeTab() method. This method accepts one parameter, the numeric tab index of the tab to be removed:

```
tabs.removeTab(2);
```

Setting the selected tab

You can use the `setSelectedTab()` method to programmatically change the currently selected tab. This method accepts one parameter, the numeric tab index of the tab to be selected. When the tab is selected, the callback for it (if defined) will be fired unless the tab was already selected:

```
tabs.setSelectedTab(1);
```

Swapping tab positions

Should you want to swap the positions of two tabs, you can use the `swapTabs()` method. This method takes two parameters, the numeric tab indexes of the two tabs to be swapped. During the swap, the selected tab will not change, and no callback functions will be executed:

```
tabs.swapTabs(2, 3);
```

Getting and setting information about a tab

When you have an OpenSocial tab object available, you can run a series of methods against the object to provide additional levels of customization. You can obtain a tab object through the `TabSet` methods `getSelectedTab()` or `getTabs()`.

The following examples assume that we have already obtained an OpenSocial tab object:

```
var tabs = new gadgets.TabSet();
... Build Tabs ...
var tab = tabs.getSelectedTab();
```

Getting the callback of a tab

Using the `getCallback()` method, you can obtain a reference to the callback function that's associated with selecting a tab. You can use this method to execute a callback function programmatically without actually selecting the tab:

```
var callback = tab.getCallback();
```

Obtaining the content container

To obtain the HTML element that contains the tab content, use the `getContentContainer()` method:

```
var tabContainer = tab.getContentContainer();
```

Obtaining the tab position

For some of `TabSet`'s tab manipulation methods, you must pass the numeric tab index for the tab you want to remove or swap. Using the `getIndex()` method returns the index number of the tab:

```
var tabIndex = tab.getIndex();
```

Obtaining the tab name

To obtain a tab name, you can use the `getName()` method. This method returns a string containing the tab name:

```
var tabname = tab.getName();
```

Obtaining the tab label

Using the `getNameContainer()` method returns the HTML element that contains the tab label:

```
var labelContainer = tab.getNameContainer();
```

Extending Shindig with Your Own JavaScript Libraries

 The full code for this sample is available at *https://github.com/jcleblanc/ programming-social-applications/tree/master/chapter_4/countdown_fea ture*.

In Chapter 3, we discussed the process of installing Shindig to run your own OpenSocial container to host applications. Thus far, this chapter has outlined the "out of the box" JavaScript components that are available to you in a Shindig container, but what if you want to create your own JavaScript libraries and features to extend those native offerings?

As with the default feature libraries, adding new JavaScript libraries and features to Shindig in order to make them available to your gadget is a simple, multistep process. Let's look at a practical example to showcase how to do this. We'll add a new JavaScript library feature to create a countdown clock that's displayed in a gadget.

First, from the root of your Shindig installation directory, go to the JavaScript *features* directory:

```
cd features/src/main/javascript/features
```

This is where the JavaScript features we've explored thus far are housed, and where we'll create a new one. Create a new directory called "countdown" and then move into it:

```
mkdir countdown
cd countdown
```

Now we need to create the files that will define our JavaScript library feature. Create a new file called *countdown_base.js*. This file will house the JavaScript that will run our countdown clock. Within the JavaScript file, add the following code:

```
gadgets['countdown'] = (function(){
    var time_left = 10;                        //number of seconds for countdown
```

```javascript
var output_element_id = 'countdown';          //node to output time to
var keep_counting = 1;                        //whether to keep counting
var no_time_left_message = "Time's Up!!!";    //message to display when time's up

//decrement time left and check whether time has expired
function countdown() {
    if(time_left < 2) {
        keep_counting = 0;
    }

    time_left = time_left - 1;
}

//add leading 0's on single digit numbers
function add_leading_zero(n) {
    if(n.toString().length < 2) {
        return '0' + n;
    } else {
        return n;
    }
}

//format countdown output string
function format_output() {
    var hours, minutes, seconds;
    seconds = Math.floor(time_left % 60);
    minutes = Math.floor(time_left / 60) % 60;
    hours = Math.floor(time_left / 3600);

    seconds = add_leading_zero( seconds );
    minutes = add_leading_zero( minutes );
    hours = add_leading_zero( hours );

    return hours + ':' + minutes + ':' + seconds;
}

//display time left
function show_time_left() {
    document.getElementById(output_element_id).innerHTML = format_output();
}

//display time expired message
function no_time_left() {
    document.getElementById(output_element_id).innerHTML = no_time_left_message;
}

return {
    //countdown function
    count: function () {
        countdown();
        show_time_left();
    },

    //control timer
    timer: function () {
```

```
            this.count();

            if(keep_counting) {
                setTimeout("gadgets.countdown.timer();", 1000);
            } else {
                no_time_left();
            }
        },

        //counter initialization
        init: function (t, element_id) {
            time_left = t;
            output_element_id = element_id;
            this.timer();
        }
    };
})();
```

The first thing that we need to do to define our core JavaScript is to assign the functionality to a custom gadgets object, `gadgets['countdown']`. We then include any JavaScript functionality that is necessary to run the feature but is not accessible by calling directly into the JavaScript feature. Next, we issue a series of functions in the return object. These are the functions that we will make requests to in order to initialize the JavaScript feature; for example, we'll make a request to the `init(...)` function to create the countdown feature.

Since we assigned the return functionality to a `gadgets` object, returning these functions allows us to initialize the countdown by calling `gadgets.countdown.init(...)`.

Now we need to create a new file, *taming.js*, which will allow us to make certain methods available to a gadget if Caja is being employed:

```
var tamings___ = tamings___ || [];
tamings___.push(function(imports){
    ___.grantRead(gadgets.countdown, 'init');
    ___.grantRead(gadgets.countdown, 'timer');
    ___.grantRead(gadgets.countdown, 'count');
});
```

We specify that we want to make our three return functions available when Caja is being employed.

Our last file, *feature.xml*, names the feature and specifies the files that provide the code (namely, our JavaScript) needed to run that feature:

```
<feature>
    <name>countdown</name>
    <dependency>globals</dependency>
    <gadget>
        <script src="countdown_base.js"/>
        <script src="taming.js"/>
    </gadget>
    <container>
        <script src="countdown_base.js"/>
```

```
        <script src="taming.js"/>
    </container>
</feature>
```

We name the feature "countdown" and state that *countdown_base.js* and *taming.js* should be used for the container and gadget.

Now we just need to add our new feature to the list of features to be loaded by the container. Go to the *features* directory and open the *features.txt* file:

```
cd features/src/main/javascript/features
vim features.txt
```

Add the following line to the file:

```
features/countdown/feature.xml
```

If you don't want to manually edit the file, you can run the following command from the *features* directory:

```
ls -R1a **/*.xml > features.txt
```

At this point, we are ready to start using our new feature in our gadget. To integrate our countdown feature into one of our existing gadgets, we simply need to add the `Require` node with the appropriate feature name:

```
<Require feature="countdown"></Require>
```

When we expand this out into a full-fledged sample gadget, we see how the feature is used:

```
<?xml version="1.0" encoding="UTF-8"?>
<Module>
    <ModulePrefs title="Countdown Application">
        <Require feature="countdown"/>
    </ModulePrefs>
    <Content type="html">
        <![CDATA[
        <div id="countdown">...</div>

        <script type="text/javascript">
        //calculate time left from current to future time
        var currentTime = new Date();
        var futureTime = new Date("September 26, 2011 17:55:00");
        var timeLeft = (futureTime - currentTime) / 1000;

        //initialize counter
        gadgets.countdown.init(timeLeft, 'countdown');
        </script>
        ]]>
    </Content>
</Module>
```

In the `ModulePrefs` node, we have included our `Require` statement. The countdown feature functionality is loaded within the `Content` node. We include the `div` node where we want to render the counter. Next, in the `script` block, we calculate the time between

---

the current time and some date in the future. We can then initialize the feature by calling the gadgets.countdown.init(...) method, passing in the time remaining and a string representing the ID of the node in which the countdown should be rendered.

Using this method, you can create and use custom JavaScript library features.

Putting It All Together

 The full code for this sample is available at *https://github.com/jcleblanc/ programming-social-applications/blob/master/chapter_4/chapter_final .xml.*

At this point, you should now have Shindig set up to host OpenSocial gadgets and understand the XML markup that is used as the foundation for defining those gadgets. You may have also installed Partuza to see the architecture of a full end-to-end social networking container. Let's combine all of these lessons to create a real gadget using our Shindig installation and OpenSocial gadget knowledge.

We will integrate the following OpenSocial concepts and techniques in our gadget:

- Building a gadget XML spec, including using views
- Setting and getting user state information with user preferences
- Building tabs using the OpenSocial tabs library
- Displaying messages with the OpenSocial minimessage library

Building the Gadget XML File

The first element of the sample to set up is the core gadget architecture that will be used:

```
<Module>
    <ModulePrefs title="Chapter 4 Example"
                 description="Displays some of the key concepts
                              learned in chapter 4"
                 author="Jonathan LeBlanc"
                 author_link="http://www.jcleblanc.com">
        <Require feature="opensocial-0.9"/>
        <Require feature="tabs" />
        <Require feature="minimessage"/>
        <Require feature="setprefs"/>
        <Locale lang="en" country="us" />
    </ModulePrefs>
    <UserPref name="contactMethod"
              default_value="email"
              datatype="hidden" />
    <UserPref name="contactEmail"
              default_value="None Entered"
              datatype="hidden" />
```

```
<UserPref name="contactTwitter"
          default_value="None Entered"
          datatype="hidden" />
<Content type="html" view="canvas, home, profile">
  <![CDATA[

  ]]>
</Content>
</Module>
```

Within the `ModulePrefs` node, we set our metadata about the gadget and then define the JavaScript libraries required to run the gadget. These match the features we are using, which include OpenSocial 0.9, tabs, `minimessage`, and `setprefs`. Next, we indicate support for US-based English in our `Locale` element.

Since we will be using stored user preferences, we set the `UserPref` elements next, specifying the three strings we would like to temporarily store (contact method, email, and Twitter). All three strings have default values set (in case the user doesn't input his contact information) and are hidden.

Last, we create a `Content` section to host the HTML, CSS, and JavaScript of the gadget inline to the XML file. This single `Content` element will display similar content between three views (`canvas`, `home`, and `profile`).

Now that we have our architecture established, we have to fill the `Content` section with the CSS and HTML markup needed for the gadget:

```
<style type="text/css">
.tablib_table{ margin-top:10px; }
#messageWindow{ padding:5px;
                margin:5px; }
#tabSetting, #tabInfo{ padding:5px; }
#displayPrefs{ background-color:#eaeaea;
               margin:10px 5px;
               padding:5px;
               display:none; }
</style>

<div id="tabSetting">
   <div id="messageWindow">
      Please click on the "More Information" tab for helpful links
   </div>
   <form name="contactInfo">
      <p>
         <input type="radio" name="contactMethod" value="twitter" />
         Twitter<br />

         <input type="radio" name="contactMethod" value="email" />
         E-Mail
      </p>

      <p>
         <label for="contactEmail">Email Address: </label>
         <input type="text" id="contactEmail" />
```

```
        </p>

        <p>
            <label for="contactTwitter">Twitter Address: </label>
            <input type="text" id="contactTwitter" />
        </p>

        <button onclick="savePrefs();return false;">Save Preferences</button>
        <button onclick="showPrefs();return false;">Show Preferences</button>

        <div id="displayPrefs">
            <b>User Preferences:</b><br />
            Contact Method: <span id="listMethod"></span><br />
            E-Mail Address: <span id="listEmail"></span><br />
            Twitter Address: <span id="listTwitter"></span>
        </div>
    </form>
</div>
<div id="tabInfo">
    More information about features in this chapter:
    <ul>
        <li>OpenSocial: http://www.opensocial.org/</li>
        <li>OpenSocial Wiki: http://wiki.opensocial.org/</li>
        <li>Shindig: http://shindig.apache.org/</li>
        <li>Partuza: http://code.google.com/p/partuza/</li>
    </ul>
</div>
```

We start the gadget markup by adding a few styles for our containers. These are just standard markup styles, but there's one point to make here about the tablib_table class. When an OpenSocial message, tab, or any other JavaScript library–generated component is rendered, there are classes assigned to the markup, which means that new classes and styles can be applied to those components. In the case of tablib_table, we are adding a top margin to the tab set.

The HTML markup that follows contains the content of the two tabs that we will display in the application. The first one, the settings tab, contains a message window that will display information about the second tab. The second tab is a form element containing buttons that will allow a user to pick her preferred contact method, as well as two input boxes that will allow her to input her email address and Twitter handle. At the bottom are two buttons to control how user preferences are set and displayed. These two buttons will execute their respective JavaScript functions to execute the required set or get method. Below the buttons is a box, hidden by default, that will display the user's preferences. The second tab will simply display a series of links to additional resources.

Now that we have the XML architecture, styles, and markup ready, we can put everything to work by applying the appropriate OpenSocial JavaScript library methods:

```
<script type="text/javascript">
var prefs = new gadgets.Prefs();
```

```
//get user preferences and save them
function savePrefs(){
   var method = "email";

   //loop through all options to see which contact methods was checked
   for (var i=0; i < document.contactInfo.contactMethod.length; i++){
      if (document.contactInfo.contactMethod[i].checked){
         method = document.contactInfo.contactMethod[i].value;
      }
   }
   var email = document.contactInfo.contactEmail.value;
   var twitter = document.contactInfo.contactTwitter.value;

   //set preferences
   prefs.set("contactMethod", method);
   prefs.set("contactEmail", email);
   prefs.set("contactTwitter", twitter);

   if (document.getElementById("displayPrefs").style.display == "block"){
      showPrefs();
   }
}

//display preferences from stored values
function showPrefs(){
   document.getElementById("displayPrefs").style.display = "block";
   document.getElementById("listMethod").innerHTML =
      prefs.getString("contactMethod");
   document.getElementById("listEmail").innerHTML =
      prefs.getString("contactEmail");
   document.getElementById("listTwitter").innerHTML =
      prefs.getString("contactTwitter");
}

//create a new tabset object with the settings tab set
var tabs = new gadgets.TabSet("tabSet1", "Setting Configuration");
tabs.alignTabs("left", 50);

//create two tabs
tabs.addTab("More Information", {
   contentContainer: document.getElementById("tabInfo"),
   tooltip: "Select this tab for more details"
});
tabs.addTab("Setting Configuration", "tabSetting");

//display message window about more information
var message = new gadgets.MiniMessage("message1");
message.createTimerMessage(document.getElementById("messageWindow"), 2);
</script>
```

The first two functions within our JavaScript block set and get user preferences, and are triggered from the markup buttons. The savePrefs() function will capture the user preferences entered in the settings form and then, using the setPrefs JavaScript library functions, will temporarily store those session values via the prefs.set() method. If the preference display box is currently visible, the `showPrefs()` method will be executed to update the values.

The `showPrefs()` function sets the preference display box to a visible status and then calls the `prefs.getString()` method to capture the previously stored user preferences. These preferences will be input into their matching value objects in the preference display box. If user preferences were not previously stored in the system, the default values set in the `UserPref` elements of the XML spec will be displayed instead.

The first automatic code block that will be executed creates the `TabSet` to hold the two tabs we will create with our markup, and specifies the settings tab as the default tab to open. Once we've created the object, we align the tabs horizontally on the left and offset them from the left by 50 pixels. We then begin generating our tabs.

The first block will generate the "More Information" tab with a configuration object. The object sets the HTML block (`contentContainer`) that will be used to generate the content of the tab, and then adds a tool tip to the tab so that when a user hovers her mouse over it, a short alternative-text note will appear. The second tab just sets the title of the same tab, and the second parameter matches the `div` node that contains the tab content.

Now that our tabs are created, we display a brief timer-status message to the user to inform her of the second tab's content. Using the OpenSocial `minimessage` JavaScript library, we create a new message window object. Finally, we call `createTimerMessage()` to generate a timed message, which we set to expire after two seconds, and use the message object we created in the settings tab as the message content.

Displaying the Gadget Using Shindig

Our gadget XML file is now ready to be displayed within an OpenSocial container. Our next task is to place it in a location where Shindig can access it. You can upload the XML file to a personal web server, use a social coding site like github (linking to the raw code URL, such as *http://github.com/jcleblanc/programming-social-applications/raw/master/opensocial-gadgets/ch3_tabbed_preferences.xml*), or put the XML file within your localhost web server to be served from there (e.g., *http://localhost/ch3_tabbed_preferences.xml*). In this example, we'll place the XML file within our localhost directory and serve it from there.

Open a web browser. The URL syntax for our local Shindig container is *http://shindig/gadgets/ifr?url=XML_URL*. We can run that URL with our localhost file location to load the gadget, which gives us a URL like *http://shindig/gadgets/ifr?url=http://localhost/ch3_tabbed_preferences.xml* (assuming we named the file *ch3_tabbed_preferences.xml*). Navigate to that URL.

You should be presented with a gadget with two tabs, as displayed in Figure 4-1, with the "Setting Configuration" tab opening by default. Once that initial tab loads, the timed yellow message will be displayed. The second tab should display a series of links to more information.

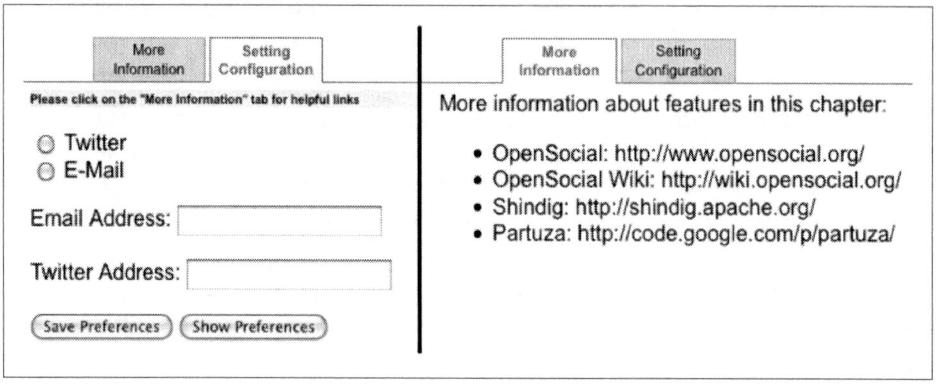

Figure 4-1. Chapter 4 gadget rendered

This example sums up many of the core lessons we've learned in this book thus far. We've created a gadget that successfully loads a user interface and interacts with a simple data store and the OpenSocial JavaScript libraries.

CHAPTER 5

Porting Applications, Profiles, and Friendships

As we dive further into the social and profile features of the OpenSocial specification, this chapter will look into using a container user's social information to personalize applications. We'll also explore how the social details between containers differ, how to port them from one social container to the next, and how to balance client- and server-side components in this context. After breaking down the social profile into its individual parts, I'll provide code to show you how to use the JavaScript APIs.

What You'll Learn

This chapter will focus on the core concepts behind capturing and using a user's social profile information, making external data requests from a container, and porting applications from one container to another. Our specific focus areas will be:

- Porting a Facebook application to an OpenSocial container, and porting applications between different OpenSocial containers
- Accessing and using user profile information
- Increasing an application's base with user friendships

At the end of the chapter, we will roll the lessons we've learned into a project to build a full social application that promotes user growth.

Evaluating OpenSocial Container Support

Since OpenSocial is an open source specification for social containers, it has been implemented across many sites with differing levels of integration. This text generally refers to OpenSocial 1.0 or 0.9, so we will focus on containers that support that Java-Script API version. OpenSocial 0.9 contains the same engineering specifications as 1.0, but 1.0 contains new definitions on how to split up the specification to be more applicable to each container environment.

There are a number of containers available that currently implement these JavaScript API specification versions. They are listed in Table 5-1.

Table 5-1. OpenSocial application development containers

Container	OpenSocial version	Developer site
Creyle	0.9	http://developer.creyle.jp/
Cyworld	0.9	http://devsquare.nate.com
Google Friend Connect	0.9	http://code.google.com/apis/friendconnect
GROU.PS	0.9	http://grou.ps/groupsdev
iGoogle	0.9	http://code.google.com/apis/igoogle/
iWiW	0.9	http://dev.iwiw.hu/
MySpace	1.0	http://developer.myspace.com/
XING	0.9	https://www.xing.com/net/opensocialpartner
Yahoo!	0.9	http://developer.yahoo.com/yap
VZ-Netzwerke	0.9	http://www.studivz.net/Developer

These containers have different localization support, depending on their country of origin and user reach.

Many other containers currently implement older versions of the OpenSocial specification, including those listed in Table 5-2.

Table 5-2. Containers implementing older versions of the OpenSocial specification

Container	OpenSocial version	Developer site
Avatars United	0.8.1	http://developer.avatarsunited.com/
Friendster	0.7	http://www.friendster.com/developer
goo Home	0.8.1	http://developer.home.goo.ne.jp/
hi5	0.8	http://developer.hi5.com/
Hyves	0.7	http://trac.hyves-api.nl/
itimes	0.8	http://www.itimes.com/os_sandbox.php
LinkedIn	0.8	http://developer.linkedin.com/index.jspa
Lonely Planet	0.8	http://lplabs.com/groups/
Netlog	0.8	http://en.netlog.com/go/developer
Ning	0.8.1	http://developer.ning.com/
orkut	0.8.1	http://sandbox.orkut.com/
Socialtext	0.8	http://www.socialtext.net/open/index.cgi?socialtext_widgets

Container	OpenSocial version	Developer site
Sonico	0.8	http://sandbox.sonico.com/app_dev_pres.php
Webjam	0.8.1	http://www.webjam.com/developers/opensocial
Webon	0.8	http://team.webonsites.com/

Implementations of the specification are also expanding into enterprise-level software, which provides an internalized social network for employees of a company. Examples are listed in Table 5-3.

Table 5-3. OpenSocial containers in the enterprise space

Container	OpenSocial product integration
Alfresco	Alfresco Share
Atlassian, Inc.	JIRA (Bug Tracker) and Confluence (Enterprise Wiki)
Cisco	Cisco Pulse
eXo Platform	eXo Portal Product
IBM	IBM Rational, Lotuslive
Jive	Jive Apps Framework
SAP	12sprints, SAP Social Network Analyzer (SNA)
SocialText	Dashboard module

Core Components of the OpenSocial Specification

In the early days of OpenSocial, its sole intention was to offer developers portability between containers and the ability to build gadgets to run on many different containers simultaneously. This works well if all of the containers, sites, and companies implementing OpenSocial have the same goals.

As OpenSocial implementers became more diverse, exploring new realms such as moving the social experience into enterprise-level software, this narrow definition no longer sufficed. Because the ways in which people used the OpenSocial specification were changing, the specification itself needed to change to meet the community's needs.

As of OpenSocial 1.0, the specification offers five models that define differing levels of integration and provide, in most cases, a subset of features from the global specification:

Core API server
> A subset implementation for containers that want to provide a method for exposing their data through standard web services

Core gadget container
> Enables a container to render gadgets, but does not provide functionality for accessing social details

Social API server
> A subset implementation for containers that want to provide a method for exposing their social data through standard web services

Social gadget container
> A subset implementation that allows a container to render gadgets and grants those gadgets access to social information from the container

OpenSocial container
> A fully implemented social container that includes the complete feature set of the social API server and the social gadget container

Each specification provides a certain subset of the OpenSocial specification—whether that is enabling social features, data retrieval, or RESTful HTTP access to social URI endpoints.

Core API Server Specification

You can use the core API server specification to enable a RESTful request architecture within a container to get and set core data. This feature set does not provide the social data references included in the social API server or social gadget container implementations.

This portion of the specification includes REST and RPC standards for making requests and providing a uniform response structure back from the request.

This implementation can be valuable for publishers who want to provide a standardized method for developers to collect and syndicate stories or articles to their sites, but whose sites do not include a social container with user logins, profiles, and communication methods between individuals.

Full specification requirements for the core API server implementation are available at *http://opensocial-resources.googlecode.com/svn/spec/1.0/Core-API-Server.xml*.

Core Gadget Container Specification

The core gadget container specification gives a container the means to host OpenSocial gadget applications. This feature set includes all the functionality associated with how a gadget renders and collects data, but does not include the social functionality and integration built into the social gadget container specification.

There are a number of features and functions included in the core gadget container, such as:

- The core gadget XML file definitions for creating an application, as well as features for accessing proxied content, content rewriting, and data pipelining
- Making and handling OAuth and signed requests

- The OpenSocial JavaScript API implementations not relating to social interaction, including the gadgets specification and subsets of the opensocial and osapi specifications
- Localization support and a series of recommended features of the JavaScript API gadget specification

This option is valuable for implementers who want to allow third-party developers to build applications and host content on their sites in a standard way, but without access to social features such as profile information, activity streams, or social engagement.

Traditionally, applications of this type are closed Flash games without social hooks, or business applications that provide a window into some user data from a company's core site, such as a SlideShare application that displays your recent presentations without providing your full profile interaction.

Full specification requirements for the core gadget container implementation are available at *http://opensocial-resources.googlecode.com/svn/spec/1.0/Core-Gadget.xml*.

Social API Server Specification

The social API server specification is used for containers that wish to provide a developer the means to leverage their social data, but do not wish to host applications themselves.

This implementation means that containers provide a RESTful method for developers to get, update, insert, and delete their social data. This social data may include:

- OpenSocial `Person` information (the user profile), including a user's friendships and relationships
- Activity information and actions taken by the user
- Direct messages sent or to be sent by a user
- Group information associated with the user
- Albums and media items

This option is best suited for containers that have a social experience built in but have no desire to integrate applications. These containers may include sites that allow geolocation for their users and commenting about status updates—data that developers can then link to programmatically. Even though the container does not host applications itself, this implementation lends itself well to building applications on mobile devices or other sites that leverage the container's data sources.

Full specification requirements for the social API server implementation are available at *http://opensocial-resources.googlecode.com/svn/spec/1.0/Social-API-Server.xml*.

Social Gadget Container Specification

The social gadget container specification includes a complete standardization of the feature set that allows a container to host OpenSocial applications that leverage its social data, but does not include the API server specifications of a social implementation.

This portion of the specification provides the functionality of the core gadget container specification, but does not exclude the social features. The features and functions in this specification include:

- The core gadget XML file definitions for creating an application, and features for accessing proxied content, content rewriting, templating, and data pipelining
- Making and handling OAuth and signed requests
- The OpenSocial JavaScript API implementations, including the full gadgets, the opensocial and osapi specifications for providing data-request and -manipulation tools, and functions to extract and modify social information
- Localization support and a series of recommended features of the JavaScript API gadget specification

This implementation is best for OpenSocial containers that want to allow developers to build applications within them but do not want to allow those developers to pull their social information onto third-party sites.

Full specification requirements for the core API server implementation are available at *http://opensocial-resources.googlecode.com/svn/spec/1.0/Social-Gadget.xml*.

OpenSocial Container Specification

To meet the requirements of the OpenSocial container specification, a container must implement the specifications for a social API server as well as a social gadget container (both of which have been described in detail in the preceding sections).

The main capabilities of a full OpenSocial container implementation are:

- Allowing developers to build applications within the container that can leverage its social data
- Providing a means by which users can pull data (social or otherwise) from the container and onto third-party sites or applications

Cross-Container Development and Porting

Although the OpenSocial specification was originally meant to allow developers to port applications fairly easily from one OpenSocial container to the next, it has evolved to provide containers with the flexibility to implement only the particular social or implementation features they need. What this means for developers is that there are generally a few implementation differences when working between distinct OpenSocial containers.

In the sections that follow, we'll discuss some development practices you can use in your applications to expedite cross-container porting.

Use a Blended Client-Server Environment

Other than employing iframes to protect application content from malicious code attacks, several containers add layers of protection by securing client-side code and markup. One such project, Caja (see Chapter 8), aims to mitigate concerns over the security of iframes. Securers like Caja work by rewriting the client-side code base to a secure version, causing a larger code base to be used. These securers increase load time beyond the natural overhead imposed by the loading of the container itself.

On the other hand, loading an initial social data set and visual layer through a server-side implementation, executing requests to REST social endpoints, will decrease load time on application startup.

Once the application has loaded, using AJAX functionality through either the Open-Social toolset or standard AJAX requests will allow it to communicate seamlessly with the server as the user interacts with it.

Decouple Social Features from Mainstream Application Code

One difficult aspect of migration is understanding the differences between the social features and the request methods or endpoints of each container. This problem is compounded when social request logic is deeply ingrained in the core application code base.

Decoupling social logic from the main visualization and controller code is one method for easing the pain of migration. You can start this process by mapping the social endpoints, or social data request code, to variables and creating separate function logic for parsing container-specific social structures. At the end of this process, you will have functionality that resembles a container's API, where functions can be defined for obtaining and parsing connections, activities, or any number of other social features. Using logic like this allows you to include simple function calls in your mainstream code, meaning that if you need to make changes to that functionality, you have to update only those modularized functions.

Avoid Using Container-Specific Tags

It goes without saying that if abstraction eases the pain of migration, then using container-specific tags to implement functionality like commenting widgets or tabs will only worsen it. Although container-specific tags and markup will initially ease feature integration, once entrenched in program development logic, they'll make migration a not-so-trivial task. Not only will the developer have to reimplement the functionality behind the tags using a new container's architecture, but he'll need to have a deeper understanding of their social hooks—such as whether the widget sends an activity update, parses friendship data, etc.

You should avoid any container-specific markup or client-side code if you'll potentially be porting the application to a new container.

Porting Applications from Facebook to OpenSocial

As developers search for new mediums to push their applications to, at some point they'll probably ask themselves, *what are the differences between Facebook and OpenSocial platforms*, and *how do I port applications from one container to the next?* While the Facebook and OpenSocial platforms have mainly incompatible development practices, there are many techniques you can employ to ease the transition between the two. We'll cover these next.

Employ iframes for Non-Social-Application Constructs

Many developers choose a very easy approach when creating applications to be portable from one container to the next: serving up the entire application in a single iframe. With this method, the application being loaded is a page on the developer server. Both Facebook and OpenSocial allow developers to use a standard HTML iframe, which means that when the application is ported from Facebook to OpenSocial, none of the code needs to be modified to serve it up.

The major problem with this approach emerges when you try to leverage the client-side methods and constructs, as well as potential container-specific tags, within the iframe content. By simplifying the cross-container development efforts, you lose the easy-to-use features that containers provide for accessing a user's social details, such as the OpenSocial JavaScript libraries and methods. There are methods you can use to pass along OAuth access tokens to the iframe to sign requests to the container REST URIs, but working with social profile data becomes far more complicated.

You can think of iframes in an application in a similar way to a surgeon's tools. The surgeon has a few options available to her; she can use a butter knife or a scalpel. Both tools will eventually do the job, but one is much messier than the other. The butter-knife approach in our scenario is encasing the entire application in an iframe. Using the scalpel approach, we can selectively introduce iframes where appropriate.

This raises the question: when *is* the appropriate time to use an iframe? The simple answer is that you should use iframes to wrap sections that do not require the container user's social data—for example, when generating nonsupported HTML or JavaScript constructs in Facebook.

Abstract Facebook Function Logic

If your development practice is to use server-side languages to make RESTful requests to Facebook servers for social data, then configuring social endpoint mappings will make swapping containers a much easier process. You should map all container-specific social endpoints within configuration files, as well as the paths to required social data within the returned social constructs. If the container changes, you'll need to update these mappings to match the paths of the new container.

Separate Visual Markup from Programming Logic

In a normal application, employing programming design pattern concepts such as Model-View-Controller (MVC) allows developers to separate programs into logical chunks. In MVC's case, program logic is separated into the base data sources (model), the data visualization (view), and the program event handlers, data request, and flow logic (controller). If you follow design pattern precepts, switching containers with different visual/markup standards simply means having to swap out the view—instead of having to rewrite program logic, event handlers, and data transitioning flows, as would be the case with an embedded visual/programming logic.

Use REST Endpoints, Not FQL

While the Facebook Query Language (FQL) might be easy to work with (since it has an SQL-like syntax and provides easy access to users' social data), if you use FQL in your application, you're in for a major overhaul when porting it from Facebook to an OpenSocial container.

This reiterates the point covered earlier in the "Abstract Facebook Function Logic" section. All social reference feeds should be pulled from a container's REST endpoints, and all container-specific paths should be mapped into a series of configuration variables so that they can be easily updated for a new container when the application is ported.

Employ a Server-Side Heavy Code Implementation

If your Facebook application does not employ an iframe approach to client-side development, then you've most likely developed (or will be developing) it using the Facebook HTML and JavaScript subsets, FBML and FBJS. This approach provides a secure subset of client-side code functionality for developers to build their applications. But what it means for porting application between Facebook and OpenSocial containers is that you'll have to rewrite the entire client-side markup and scripts to standard HTML and JavaScript.

When developing applications to be portable between containers, you should never introduce proprietary implementations when open, standard methods are available.

Facebook is migrating away from this FBML/FBJS approach and has a plan in place to move toward using iframes exclusively for Facebook application development. However, older applications implementing FBML/FBJS will continue to be supported.

Personalizing Applications with Profile Data

As social networking sites become more deeply ingrained in our daily lives, it is increasingly obvious that many people don't have any qualms about publishing all kinds of information—personal details, photos, their physical location, and more—to their profiles. While this is a mounting concern from a privacy and "good sense" perspective, for an application developer it's a wealth of knowledge that you can use to personalize applications. This personalization can include anything from demographically targeted ads to gender-specific marketing. With all of this information readily available, the benefit here is quite clear.

Let's look at this from another angle. One thing that many users no longer tolerate is having to build multiple profiles for every application or social network they use. If someone is using an application on a popular social network like Facebook or MySpace, why should he have to input the exact same information in that application that he has already painstakingly entered into his profile? The simple fact is he doesn't have to— and that's why it's vital to capture and use his profile information to precustomize his experience in your application.

The Person Object

Within the confines of an OpenSocial container, a human being is represented by a Person object. The Person object is used to collect a user's history, personality, and information in a single place. Depending on the container implementing the Person object, there may be a wide variation in what information makes up the Person object for a particular user. OpenSocial defines an array of data points for the user, as well as a series of helper methods for easily accessing that data, all of which are available from the global Person object.

Person Data Extraction Methods

The helper methods defined for extracting Person data are:

- `opensocial.Person.getAppData`
- `opensocial.Person.getDisplayName`
- `opensocial.Person.getField`
- `opensocial.Person.getId`
- `opensocial.Person.isOwner`
- `opensocial.Person.isViewer`

The OpenSocial specification includes a number of alternate, streamlined methods for capturing a lot of the same social data you would through the aforementioned methods. These are embedded within the lightweight JavaScript API references.

Each method listed in the following sections supports several parameters, which are used to specify the data to be returned by the REST request to the container's social endpoints.

osapi.people.get

`get` is the generic call within the lightweight JavaScript API methods to collect a user's data, and can be used to retrieve most of the social details you will want to leverage.

The `osapi.people.get(...)` method accepts a JSON object to define the type of information you want, and takes the form:

```
osapi.people.get(params)
```

Parameter list. The `params` list may consist of:

auth *(AuthToken)*
> An optional authorization token for requesting data.
>
> Example value: `HttpRequest.Authorization`

userId *(string or array of strings)*
> A string or array of strings that defines the user about whom you want to collect data. You may use short identifiers such as `@me`, `@viewer`, or `@owner`.
>
> Example value: `'@owner'` or `['@me', '@owner']`

groupId *(string)*
> A string defining a group of people about whom you want to collect data. This value is especially useful when you're trying to collect profile information for friends of the viewer or owner. You may use short identifiers such as `@self` or `@friends`.
>
> Example value: `'@friends'`

fields *(array of strings)*
> An array of strings identifying the `Person` fields you want to collect.
>
> Example value: `['name', 'gender']`

count *(integer)*
> The number of results to be returned from the request.
>
> Example value: `10` (return 10 results)

startIndex *(integer)*
> The offset from the beginning at which results should be returned. You can use this parameter to skip starting results if they're unwanted.
>
> Example value: `5` (start at the fifth result)

startPage *(integer)*

An integer value that defines the first page you want results returned for. This option is useful when you're trying to improve loading performance by reducing the processing time for `Person` data requests.

Example value: `2` (start at the second page of results)

Example request. Using the preceding parameters as a guide, we can put together a simple request to capture the application owner's name and gender. We use the `userId` key with a value of `@owner` and then input name and gender under the `fields` key.

Finally, we bundle the request with the `execute` method to initiate the REST request to the container's social endpoints.

```
//opensocial person data request
osapi.people.get({userId: '@owner', fields: ['name', 'gender']}).execute(
    function(result){
        var name = (result.name) ?
                    result.name.givenName + " " + result.name.familyName : "";
        var gender = (result.gender) ? result.gender : "Unknown";
    }
);
```

The `execute` method accepts a function reference to call once the REST request completes. The function will be called with the result set, after which we can parse the results to capture the data values we requested.

osapi.people.getViewer

The `getViewer` request is a convenience method to allow a developer to capture `Person` information for the person currently viewing the application. This method is the same as using the `osapi.people.get(...)` method with the following parameters set:

```
osapi.people.get({userId: '@viewer'})
```

Parameter list. The parameters available in the `getViewer` method are:

auth *(AuthToken)*

An optional authorization token for requesting data

Example value: `HttpRequest.Authorization`

fields *(array of strings)*

An array of strings identifying the `Person` fields you want to collect

Example value: `['name', 'gender']`

Example request. As with the previous get method, we can use the `getViewer` method to capture social details. Since the request is targeted to the current application user, we don't need to specify the `userId` parameter and only need the `fields` list:

```
//capture viewer data
osapi.people.getViewer({fields: ['name']}).execute(function(result){
    var name = (result.name) ? result.name.givenName + " " + result.name.familyName : "";
});
```

---

osapi.people.getViewerFriends

The getViewerFriends request is a convenience method to allow a developer to capture Person information for the friends or connections of the person currently viewing the application. This method is the same as using the osapi.people.get method with the following parameters set:

```
osapi.people.get({userId: '@viewer', groupId: '@friends'})
```

Parameter list. The parameters available in the getViewerFriends method are:

auth *(AuthToken)*
> An optional authorization token for requesting data.
>
> Example value: HttpRequest.Authorization

fields *(array of strings)*
> An array of strings identifying the Person fields you want to collect.
>
> Example value: ['name', 'gender']

count *(integer)*
> The number of results to be returned from the request.
>
> Example value: 10 (return 10 results)

startIndex *(integer)*
> The offset from the beginning at which results should be returned. You can use this to skip starting results if they're unwanted.
>
> Example value: 5 (start at the fifth result)

startPage *(integer)*
> An integer value that defines the first page you want results returned for. This option is useful when you're attempting to improve loading performance by reducing the processing time for Person data requests.
>
> Example value: 2 (start at the second page of results)

Example request. In this next example, we make a request to collect the friends of the current application viewer. Using the count parameter, we limit the number of friends returned to 10. These friends are returned as Person objects:

```
//get viewer friends
osapi.people.getViewerFriends({count: 10}).execute(function(result){
   var friends = result.list;
   var html = '';
   for (var i = 0; i < friends.length; i++){
      html += friends[i].name.givenName + ' : ' + friends[i].profileUrl + '<br />';
   }
});
```

Once the request returns, we store the friends array (result.list) in a variable. We then loop through the friends array, storing each friend's name and profile URL.

osapi.people.getOwner

The getOwner request is a convenience method to allow a developer to capture PERSON information for the application owner, not the current viewer. This method is the same as using the osapi.people.get(...) method with the following parameters set:

```
osapi.people.get({userId: '@owner'})
```

Parameter list. The parameters available in the getOwner method are:

auth *(AuthToken)*
> An optional authorization token for requesting data
>
> Example value: HttpRequest.Authorization

fields *(array of strings)*
> An array of strings identifying the Person fields you want to collect
>
> Example value: ['name', 'gender']

Example request. Much like we did for the getViewer call, we will capture the name for the person (in this case, the application owner) but will extend it with the nickname. In many social networks, the nickname is the text identifier by which the person has chosen to be addressed. This nickname identifier is generally more publicly exposed than the full name:

```
//capture owner data
osapi.people.getOwner({fields: ['name', 'nickName']}).execute(function(result){
  var name = (result.name) ? result.name.givenName + " "
          + result.name.familyName : "";
  name += (result.nickName) ? " : " + result.nickName : " : no nickname";
});
```

Once the request returns, we can capture the owner's full name and nickname.

osapi.people.getOwnerFriends

The getOwnerFriends request is a convenience method to allow a developer to capture Person information for the friends of the application's owner, not the current viewer's friends. This method is the same as using the osapi.people.get(...) method with the following parameters set:

```
osapi.people.get({userId: '@owner', groupId: '@friends'})
```

Parameter list. The parameters available in the getOwnerFriends method are:

auth *(AuthToken)*
> An optional authorization token for requesting data.
>
> Example value: HttpRequest.Authorization

fields *(array of strings)*
> An array of strings identifying the Person fields you want to collect.
>
> Example value: ['name', 'gender']

count *(integer)*

> The number of results to be returned from the request.

> Example value: 10 (return 10 results)

startIndex *(integer)*

> The offset from the beginning at which results should be returned. You can use this to skip starting results if they're unwanted.

> Example value: 5 (start at the fifth result)

startPage *(integer)*

> An integer value that defines the first page you want results returned for. This option is useful when you're attempting to improve loading performance by reducing the processing time for Person data requests.

> Example value: 2 (start at the second page of results)

Example request. In this next example, we will collect the friends of the application's owner. We will do so much like we did for the getViewerFriends call, but this time we will be capturing only the thumbnailUrl and only the second page of friend results, given a count of 10 friends. This means that we will be capturing friends 11–20:

```
//get owner friends
osapi.people.getOwnerFriends({'count': 10,
                              'startPage': 2,
                              'fields': ['thumbnailUrl']}).execute(function(result){
    var friends = result.list;
    var html = '';
    for (var i = 0; i < friends.length; i++){
        html += '<img src="' + friends[i].thumbnailUrl + '" alt="thumbnail image" />';
    }
});
```

Once the results have been returned, we loop through the array and store images for thumbnails of all the friends returned.

Fields Available Within the Person Object

A Person object contains a series of fields that are used to define a user's preferences, personal information, location-based details, or interests and hobbies within a social networking container. While most containers do not support the full list of potential object definitions, having numerous key data markers is core to an effective social container.

opensocial.Person.Field.ABOUT_ME

Container support:
Optional

Return type:
String

Interchangeable with short identifier:
aboutMe

Description:
Contains a personalized statement about the user, such as a quote, byline, or series of tags.

Example of return:
`'I am a manager working with Company A'`

opensocial.Person.Field.ACTIVITIES

Container support:
Optional

Return type:
Array of strings

Interchangeable with short identifier:
activities

Description:
Contains a list of the user's favorite activities.

Example of return:
`['hiking', 'fishing', 'air guitar', 'diving']`

opensocial.Person.Field.ADDRESSES

Container support:
Optional

Return type:
Array of OpenSocial `Address` objects

Interchangeable with short identifier:
addresses

Description:
These are physical locations associated with the user such as her work, home, or school addresses. The addresses are returned as an array of OpenSocial `Address` objects.

Example of return:
See "Addresses (opensocial.Address)" on page 162 in the upcoming section "Extending the Person Object".

opensocial.Person.Field.AGE

Container support:
Optional

Return type:
Number

Interchangeable with short identifier:
age

Description:
The user's age as a numeric identifier in years.

Example of return:
25

opensocial.Person.Field.BODY_TYPE

Container support:
Optional

Return type:
OpenSocial BodyType object

Interchangeable with short identifier:
bodyType

Description:
Characteristics about the body type of the user, such as muscular, normal, etc., specified as an OpenSocial BodyType object.

Example of return:
See "Body type (opensocial.BodyType)" on page 163 in the upcoming section "Extending the Person Object".

opensocial.Person.Field.BOOKS

Container support:
Optional

Return type:
Array of strings

Interchangeable with short identifier:
books

Description:
The user's favorite books.

Example of return:

```
['Pride and Prejudice and Zombies', 'Sense and Sensibility and Sea Monsters']
```

opensocial.Person.Field.CARS

Container support:
Optional

Return type:
Array of strings

Interchangeable with short identifier:
cars

Description:
The user's favorite cars.

Example of return:

```
['56 mustang', '2010 Dodge Charger', 'Subaru WRX STI']
```

opensocial.Person.Field.CHILDREN

Container support:
Optional

Return type:
String

Interchangeable with short identifier:
children

Description:
Information about the user's children (if applicable), such as names, ages, etc.

Example of return:

```
'Hansel and Gretel'
```

opensocial.Person.Field.CURRENT_LOCATION

Container support:
Optional

Return type:
OpenSocial Address object

Interchangeable with short identifier:
currentLocation

Description:

This is a static address object identifying the current location of the user, as he has specified. This may include any address (or part of an address) including home, work, school, etc., and is specified as an OpenSocial `Address` object.

Example of return:

See "Addresses (opensocial.Address)" on page 162 in the upcoming section "Extending the Person Object".

---

opensocial.Person.Field.DATE_OF_BIRTH

Container support:

Optional

Return type:

Standard `Date` object

Interchangeable with short identifier:

`dateOfBirth`

Description:

The user's date of birth, specified as a standard `date` object.

---

opensocial.Person.Field.DRINKER

Container support:

Optional

Return type:

OpenSocial `Enum` object

Interchangeable with short identifier:

`drinker`

Description:

The user's drinking status, such as whether she drinks or not, and if so, how often. This data is returned as an OpenSocial `Enum` object.

Example of return:

See "Enum (opensocial.Enum)" on page 164 in the upcoming section "Extending the Person Object".

---

opensocial.Person.Field.EMAILS

Container support:

Optional

Return type:
Array of OpenSocial `Email` objects

Interchangeable with short identifier:
emails

Description:
Email addresses that the user has associated with his profile. This data is represented as an array of OpenSocial `Email` objects.

Example of return:
See "Email (opensocial.Email)" on page 163 in the upcoming section "Extending the Person Object".

opensocial.Person.Field.ETHNICITY

Container support:
Optional

Return type:
String

Interchangeable with short identifier:
ethnicity

Description:
The user's ethnicity.

Example of return:
'Caucasian'

opensocial.Person.Field.FASHION

Container support:
Optional

Return type:
String

Interchangeable with short identifier:
fashion

Description:
The user's views on fashion or any number of fashion-related topics.

Example of return:
'Betsey Johnson is the rock star of fashion for women'

opensocial.Person.Field.FOOD

Container support:
Optional

Return type:
Array of strings

Interchangeable with short identifier:
food

Description:
The user's favorite foods, including food types or specific items.

Example of return:
['Cuban', 'Pluots', 'Orbitz']

opensocial.Person.Field.GENDER

Container support:
Optional

Return type:
OpenSocial Enum object

Interchangeable with short identifier:
gender

Description:
The user's gender, specified as an OpenSocial Enum object.

Example of return:
See "Enum (opensocial.Enum)" on page 164 in the upcoming section "Extending the Person Object".

opensocial.Person.Field.HAPPIEST_WHEN

Container support:
Optional

Return type:
String

Interchangeable with short identifier:
happiestWhen

Description:
When or under what circumstances the user is happiest. This may be an action, place, thing, or any number of other criteria.

Example of return:

`'in the city'`

---

opensocial.Person.Field.HAS_APP

Container support:

Optional

Return type:

Boolean

Interchangeable with short identifier:

hasApp

Description:

A true or false value indicating whether the user has used the current application.

Example of return:

True

---

opensocial.Person.Field.HEROES

Container support:

Optional

Return type:

Array of strings

Interchangeable with short identifier:

heroes

Description:

The user's personal or professional heroes.

Example of return:

`['That guy from that movie', 'Judge Fudge']`

---

opensocial.Person.Field.HUMOR

Container support:

Optional

Return type:

String

Interchangeable with short identifier:

humor

Description:
Personal humor, jokes, favorite comedians, or comedy styles that the user likes.

Example of return:
`'Steve Carell is awesome'`

---

opensocial.Person.Field.ID

Container support:
Required

Return type:
String

Interchangeable with short identifier:
`id`

Description:
The permanent, unique identifier that the container uses to identify the user. This is a required field for all containers. If capturing an anonymous profile (as in the case of a user who is not signed in), the container *must* use -1 as the user ID.

Example of return:
`'NJFIDHVPVVISDXZKT7UKED2WHU'`

---

opensocial.Person.Field.INTERESTS

Container support:
Optional

Return type:
Array of strings

Interchangeable with short identifier:
`interests`

Description:
The user's hobbies, interests, or passions.

Example of return:
`['wine', 'art']`

---

opensocial.Person.Field.JOB_INTERESTS

Container support:
Optional

Return type:
String

Interchangeable with short identifier:
jobInterests

Description:
The user's professional skills, career goals, or general job requirements.

Example of return:
'Yahoo! Developer Network'

opensocial.Person.Field.JOBS

Container support:
Optional

Return type:
Array of OpenSocial `Organization` objects

Interchangeable with short identifier:
jobs

Description:
The user's job history, including organizational information, contact data, and address details. Data is returned as an array of OpenSocial `Organization` objects.

Example of return:
See "Organization (opensocial.Organization)" on page 166 in the upcoming section "Extending the Person Object".

opensocial.Person.Field.LANGUAGES_SPOKEN

Container support:
Optional

Return type:
Array of strings

Interchangeable with short identifier:
languagesSpoken

Description:
Languages the user speaks, represented as ISO 639-1 codes (for more details, see *http://en
.wikipedia.org/wiki/List_of_ISO_639-1_codes*).

Example of return:
['en', 'fr']

opensocial.Person.Field.LIVING_ARRANGEMENT

Container support:
Optional

Return type:
String

Interchangeable with short identifier:
livingArrangement

Description:
The user's living arrangement, such as who she lives with or the type of place she lives in.

Example of return:
'roommates'

opensocial.Person.Field.LOOKING_FOR

Container support:
Optional

Return type:
Array of Enum objects

Interchangeable with short identifier:
lookingFor

Description:
Why the user is interested in using the container or why he is interested in meeting people. Many social networks represent this data as a drop-down list that allows the user to specify whether he is interested in friends, professional connections, dating, etc.

Example of return:
See "Enum (opensocial.Enum)" on page 164 under the upcoming section "Extending the Person Object".

opensocial.Person.Field.MOVIES

Container support:
Optional

Return type:
Array of strings

Interchangeable with short identifier:
movies

Description:
The user's favorite movies.

Example of return:

['Dawn of the Dead', 'Children of Men']

---

opensocial.Person.Field.MUSIC

Container support:
Optional

Return type:
Array of strings

Interchangeable with short identifier:
music

Description:
The user's favorite music.

Example of return:

['The Lonely Planet', 'The Beatles']

---

opensocial.Person.Field.NAME

Container support:
Required

Return type:
OpenSocial Name object

Interchangeable with short identifier:
name

Description:
The name of the person returned as an OpenSocial Name object. For anonymous viewers, the container can return a user-friendly name string such as guest or anonymous, which changes based on internationalization or locale requirements.

Example of return:
See "Name (opensocial.Name)" on page 165 under the upcoming section "Extending the Person Object".

---

opensocial.Person.Field.NETWORK_PRESENCE

Container support:
Optional

Return type:
OpenSocial Enum object

Interchangeable with short identifier:
networkPresence

Description:
The user's current networking status.

Example of return:
See "Enum (opensocial.Enum)" on page 164 in the upcoming section "Extending the Person Object".

opensocial.Person.Field.NICKNAME

Container support:
Required

Return type:
String

Interchangeable with short identifier:
nickname

Description:
The nickname by which the user prefers to be identified, such as a shortened version of his full name. For anonymous users, the container designates a user-friendly nickname such as guest or anonymous, which changes based on internationalization or locale requirements.

Example of return:
'Jon'

opensocial.Person.Field.PETS

Container support:
Optional

Return type:
String

Interchangeable with short identifier:
pets

Description:
The person's pets.

Example of return:
'cat'

opensocial.Person.Field.PHONE_NUMBERS

Container support:
Optional

Return type:
Array of OpenSocial Phone objects

Interchangeable with short identifier:
phoneNumbers

Description:
Phone numbers that the user has designated as associated with her profile.

Example of return:
See "Phone (opensocial.Phone)" on page 167 in the upcoming section "Extending the Person Object".

opensocial.Person.Field.POLITICAL_VIEWS

Container support:
Optional

Return type:
String

Interchangeable with short identifier:
politicalViews

Description:
The user's political affiliation or views. Many containers represent this value as a drop-down list of political parties based on locale.

Example of return:
'Moderate'

opensocial.Person.Field.PROFILE_SONG

Container support:
Optional

Return type:
OpenSocial Url object

Interchangeable with short identifier:
profileSong

Description:

The user's chosen profile song. This data is returned as an OpenSocial `Url` object. One practical example is MySpace, which allows a user to choose a song that plays when other users visit her profile.

Example of return:

See "Url (opensocial.Url)" on page 167 in the upcoming section "Extending the Person Object".

opensocial.Person.Field.PROFILE_URL

Container support:

Optional

Return type:

String

Interchangeable with short identifier:

profileUrl

Description:

The URL by which someone can visit the user's profile directly.

Example of return:

`'http://pulse.yahoo.com/_NJFIDHVPVVISDXZKT7UKED2WHU'`

opensocial.Person.Field.PROFILE_VIDEO

Container support:

Optional

Return type:

OpenSocial `Url` object

Interchangeable with short identifier:

profileVideo

Description:

A personalized video associated with the user's profile. This data is served as an OpenSocial `Url` object.

Example of return:

See "Url (opensocial.Url)" on page 167 in the upcoming section "Extending the Person Object".

opensocial.Person.Field.QUOTES

Container support:
Optional

Return type:
Array of strings

Interchangeable with short identifier:
quotes

Description:
Favorite quotes defined by the user.

Example of return:
```
['Everything is relative. After all, sloths think turtles are hyperactive.']
```

opensocial.Person.Field.RELATIONSHIP_STATUS

Container support:
Optional

Return type:
String

Interchangeable with short identifier:
relationshipStatus

Description:
The user's current relationship status.

Example of return:
```
'married'
```

opensocial.Person.Field.RELIGION

Container support:
Optional

Return type:
String

Interchangeable with short identifier:
religion

Description:
The user's religion or religious views.

Example of return:
```
'agnostic'
```

opensocial.Person.Field.ROMANCE

Container support:
Optional

Return type:
String

Interchangeable with short identifier:
romance

Description:
The user's views on romance or general comments on the subject.

Example of return:
'go love go'

opensocial.Person.Field.SCARED_OF

Container support:
Optional

Return type:
String

Interchangeable with short identifier:
scaredOf

Description:
The user's fears and phobias.

Example of return:
'arachnophobia'

opensocial.Person.Field.SCHOOLS

Container support:
Optional

Return type:
Array of OpenSocial Organization objects

Interchangeable with short identifier:
schools

Description:
List of schools that the user has attended, including high schools and colleges, or any other educational experience. This information is returned as an array of OpenSocial Organization objects.

Example of return:
See "Organization (opensocial.Organization)" on page 166 in the upcoming section "Extending the Person Object".

---

opensocial.Person.Field.SEXUAL_ORIENTATION

Container support:
Optional

Return type:
String

Interchangeable with short identifier:
sexualOrientation

Description:
The user's sexual orientation or preferences.

Example of return:
'Straight'

---

opensocial.Person.Field.SMOKER

Container support:
Optional

Return type:
OpenSocial Enum object

Interchangeable with short identifier:
smoker

Description:
The user's smoking preferences, defined as an OpenSocial Enum object.

Example of return:
See "Enum (opensocial.Enum)" on page 164 in the upcoming section "Extending the Person Object".

---

opensocial.Person.Field.SPORTS

Container support:
Optional

Return type:
Array of strings

Interchangeable with short identifier:
sports

Description:

The user's favorite sports.

Example of return:

```
['hockey', 'football', 'baseball']
```

opensocial.Person.Field.STATUS

Container support:

Optional

Return type:

String

Interchangeable with short identifier:

status

Description:

Short status message, headline, or user state. This is much like updates on Twitter or news feed posts on Facebook.

Example of return:

```
'Currently writing a book'
```

opensocial.Person.Field.TAGS

Container support:

Optional

Return type:

Array of strings

Interchangeable with short identifier:

tags

Description:

Arbitrary tags associated with the user, identifying some group or current communication channel she's affiliated with. These are much like hashtags on Twitter.

Example of return:

```
['engineer', 'evangelist']
```

opensocial.Person.Field.THUMBNAIL_URL

Container support:

Required

Return type:

String

Interchangeable with short identifier:
thumbnailUrl

Description:
The URL to the thumbnail image of the user, defined as a fully qualified absolute URL. For anonymous users, or users who are not signed in, the container can present a link to a default image representation of a profile.

Example of return:
'*http://create.img.avatars.yahoo.com/users/1psAsuhxtAAEBCCNmHA11FhkB.128.png*'

opensocial.Person.Field.TIME_ZONE

Container support:
Optional

Return type:
String

Interchangeable with short identifier:
timeZone

Description:
The user's current time zone. The time zone information returned is the difference in minutes between Greenwich Mean Time (GMT) and the user's local time.

Example of return:
'GMT -7'

opensocial.Person.Field.TURN_OFFS

Container support:
Optional

Return type:
Array of strings

Interchangeable with short identifier:
turnOffs

Description:
The user's personal turn-offs.

Example of return:
['people taller than me', 'abstract art']

opensocial.Person.Field.TURN_ONS

Container support:
Optional

Return type:
Array of strings

Interchangeable with short identifier:
turnOns

Description:
The user's personal turn-ons.

Example of return:
```
['people who have a height <= my own', 'non-abstract art']
```

opensocial.Person.Field.TV_SHOWS

Container support:
Optional

Return type:
Array of strings

Interchangeable with short identifier:
tvShows

Description:
The user's favorite TV shows.

Example of return:
```
['Eureka', 'South Park']
```

opensocial.Person.Field.URLS

Container support:
Optional

Return type:
Array of OpenSocial `Url` objects

Interchangeable with short identifier:
urls

Description:
URLs that the user has associated with her profile—generally personal websites, blogs, or profiles on other sites.

Example of return:

See "Url (opensocial.Url)" on page 167 in the section "Extending the Person Object".

Extending the Person Object

While exploring the `Person` object, you might have noted a need for additional layers of data to help you drill down to exactly the information you want to use. Fortunately, OpenSocial defines extensions to several `Person` fields to allow developers to obtain more specific details. These extensions are broken down into the following subsections.

Addresses (opensocial.Address)

The OpenSocial `Address` object is a standardized way to display an address in an Open-Social application. Address information may contain street information, data about the type of place, and geographically relevant plotting data. For example:

```
"address": {
    "country": "United States",
    "latitude": 37.371609,
    "longitude": -122.038254,
    "locality": "Sunnyvale",
    "region": "California",
    "streetAddress": "701 First Avenue",
    "type": "work"
}
```

Depending on the container's needs or implementation specifications, an OpenSocial `Address` object may contain a number of different fields. These are listed in Table 5-4.

Table 5-4. Address object fields

Key	Description
opensocial.Address.Field.COUNTRY (string)	The country of the address. May be used interchangeably with `country`.
opensocial.Address.Field.EXTENDED_ADDRESS (string)	The extended address specified as a string. May be used interchangeably with `extendedAddress`.
opensocial.Address.Field.LATITUDE (number)	The latitude of the address. May be used interchangeably with `latitude`.
opensocial.Address.Field.LOCALITY (string)	The address locality. May be used interchangeably with `locality`.
opensocial.Address.Field.LONGITUDE (number)	The latitude of the address. May be used interchangeably with `longitude`.
opensocial.Address.Field.PO_BOX (string)	The P.O. box of the address, if available. May be used interchangeably with `poBox`.
opensocial.Address.Field.POSTAL_CODE (string)	The postal/zip code. May be used interchangeably with `postalCode`.

Key	Description
`opensocial.Address.Field.REGION` (string)	The address region. May be used interchangeably with `region`.
`opensocial.Address.Field.STREET_ADDRESS` (string)	The full street address. May be used interchangeably with `streetAddress`.
`opensocial.Address.Field.TYPE` (string)	The type of address or address label (e.g., work, home). May be used interchangeably with `type`.
`opensocial.Address.Field.UNSTRUC TURED_ADDRESS` (string)	The unstructured address that the user entered as a string. May be used interchangeably with `unstruc turedAddress`.

Body type (opensocial.BodyType)

The OpenSocial `BodyType` object is used to define physical information about a person within the confines of the container. For example:

```
"bodyType": {
    "build": "average",
    "eyeColor": "blue",
    "hairColor": "brown",
    "height": 1.905,
    "weight": 83.91
}
```

A container may return a number of fields, listed in Table 5-5, for a `bodyType` query.

Table 5-5. BodyType object fields

Key	Description
`opensocial.BodyType.Field.BUILD` (string)	The user's physical build (e.g., muscular, thin, average). May be used interchangeably with `build`.
`opensocial.BodyType.Field.EYE_COLOR` (string)	The user's eye color. May be used interchangeably with `eyeColor`.
`opensocial.BodyType.Field.HAIR_COLOR` (string)	The user's hair color. May be used interchangeably with `hairColor`.
`opensocial.BodyType.Field.HEIGHT` (number)	The user's height in meters. May be used interchangeably with `height`.
`opensocial.BodyType.Field.WEIGHT` (number)	The user's weight in kilograms. May be used interchangeably with `weight`.

Email (opensocial.Email)

A container may provide email address information about a user through an OpenSocial `Email` object. (However, many containers have restrictions on this data due to privacy and security concerns.) For example:

```
"email": {
    "address": "user@mysite.com",
```

```
        "type": "work"
    }
```

The object itself is small, having only two available fields (Table 5-6).

Table 5-6. Email object fields

Key	Description
opensocial.Email.Field.ADDRESS (string)	The email address, specified as a string. May be used interchangeably with address.
opensocial.Email.Field.TYPE (string)	The email type (e.g., work, home, personal). May be used interchangeably with type.

Enum (opensocial.Enum)

The Enum objects provide a way for containers to use constants for fields that usually have a common set of values. For example:

```
opensocial.Enum.Gender = "MALE"
```

There are a number of potential fields that are defined for use as Enum types (Table 5-7).

Table 5-7. Enum object fields

Key	Description
opensocial.Enum.Drinker (string)	Whether the user drinks and the frequency at which he drinks. The possible values for this field are: • opensocial.Enum.Drinker.HEAVILY • opensocial.Enum.Drinker.NO • opensocial.Enum.Drinker.OCCASIONALLY • opensocial.Enum.Drinker.QUIT • opensocial.Enum.Drinker.QUITTING • opensocial.Enum.Drinker.REGULARLY • opensocial.Enum.Drinker.SOCIALLY • opensocial.Enum.Drinker.YES
opensocial.Enum.Gender (string)	The user's gender. The possible values for this field are: • opensocial.Enum.Gender.FEMALE • opensocial.Enum.Gender.MALE
opensocial.Enum.LookingFor (string)	What the user is looking for from the site. The possible values for this field are: • opensocial.Enum.LookingFor.ACTIVITY_PARTNERS • opensocial.Enum.LookingFor.DATING • opensocial.Enum.LookingFor.FRIENDS • opensocial.Enum.LookingFor.NETWORKING

Key	Description
	• `opensocial.Enum.LookingFor.RANDOM`
	• `opensocial.Enum.LookingFor.RELATIONSHIP`
`opensocial.Enum.Presence` (string)	The user's current state of engagement. The possible values for this field are:
	• `opensocial.Enum.Presence.AWAY`
	• `opensocial.Enum.Presence.CHAT`
	• `opensocial.Enum.Presence.DND`
	• `opensocial.Enum.Presence.OFFLINE`
	• `opensocial.Enum.Presence.ONLINE`
	• `opensocial.Enum.Presence.XA` (eXtended Away)
`opensocial.Enum.Smoker` (string)	Whether the user smokes and the frequency at which he smokes. The possible values for this field are:
	• `opensocial.Enum.Smoker.HEAVILY`
	• `opensocial.Enum.Smoker.NO`
	• `opensocial.Enum.Smoker.OCCASIONALLY`
	• `opensocial.Enum.Smoker.QUIT`
	• `opensocial.Enum.Smoker.QUITTING`
	• `opensocial.Enum.Smoker.REGULARLY`
	• `opensocial.Enum.Smoker.SOCIALLY`
	• `opensocial.Enum.Smoker.YES`

Name (opensocial.Name)

OpenSocial defines a standardized method for relaying the user's name through the OpenSocial `Name` object. This object provides individual pieces, or full strings, of the name and other related fields. For example:

```
"name": {
    "familyName": "LeBlanc",
    "givenName": "Jonathan",
    "unstructured": "Jonathan LeBlanc"
}
```

In addition to basic first and last name data, the OpenSocial `Name` object may contain a number of other fields (Table 5-8), depending on container implementation.

Table 5-8. Name object fields

Key	Description
`opensocial.Name.Field.ADDI` `TIONAL_NAME` (string)	An additional name for the user (e.g., maiden name). May be used interchangeably with `additionalName`.
`opensocial.Name.Field.FAMILY_NAME` (string)	The user's last name (surname). May be used interchangeably with `familyName`.

Key	Description
opensocial.Name.Field.GIVEN_NAME (string)	The user's first name. May be used interchangeably with givenName.
opensocial.Name.Field.HONORIFIC_PREFIX (string)	An honorific prefix for the user (e.g., Mr., Dr.). May be used interchangeably with honorificPrefix.
opensocial.Name.Field.HONORIFIC_SUFFIX (string)	An honorific suffix for the user (e.g., Jr.). May be used interchangeably with honorificSuffix.
opensocial.Name.Field.UNSTRUCTURED (string)	The user's unstructured name as a string. May be used interchangeably with unstructured.

Organization (opensocial.Organization)

The OpenSocial Organization object provides an extensive look into a user's history of work, education, or organizational involvement. This object is used to define a period of time in which the person was involved with some company, school, or organization. For example:

```
"organization": {
    "name": "ACME Bread Makers",
    "title": "Senior Director",
    "description": "Managed a group of 15 bakers",
    "startDate": "2008-07-01",
    "endDate": null
    "address": {
        "country": "United States",
        "latitude": 37.416422,
        "longitude": -122.097408,
        "locality": "Mountain View",
        "region": "California",
        "streetAddress": "846 Independence Ave",
        "type": "work"
    }
}
```

As you can see from the preceding sample, in addition to the Organization object fields, the OpenSocial Address object is included in the return value. This presents a clear view into the organization, including details like its business address. Other than the Address object, several fields are supported in the Organization object. These are listed in Table 5-9.

Table 5-9. Organization object fields

Key	Description
opensocial.Organization.Field.ADDRESS (OpenSocial.Address)	The organization's oaddress, specified as an OpenSocial.Address object. May be used interchangeably with address.
opensocial.Organization.Field.DESCRIPTION (string)	A description of the work the user did at the organization (e.g., projects/course work). May be used interchangeably with description.

Key	Description
opensocial.Organiza tion.Field.END_DATE (date)	The date the user stopped working at the organization. A Null value means that he is still currently with the organization. May be used interchangeably with endDate.
opensocial.Organiza tion.Field.FIELD (string)	The organization's field of work. May be used interchangeably with field.
opensocial.Organiza tion.Field.NAME (string)	The organization's name. May be used interchangeably with name.
opensocial.Organiza tion.Field.SALARY (string)	The user's salary while he was at the organization. May be used interchangeably with salary.
opensocial.Organiza tion.Field.START_DATE (date)	The date the user started working at the organization. May be used interchangeably with startDate.
opensocial.Organiza tion.Field.SUB_FIELD (string)	The organization's subfield (if applicable). May be used interchangeably with subField.
opensocial.Organiza tion.Field.TITLE (string)	The title the user held at the organization. May be used interchangeably with title.
opensocial.Organiza tion.Field.WEBPAGE (string)	The organization's web page. May be used interchangeably with webpage.

Phone (opensocial.Phone)

The OpenSocial Phone object outlines information about the user's phone number. For example:

```
"phone": {
    "number": "867-5309",
    "type": "home"
}
```

As with the OpenSocial Email object, the Phone object contains only two fields for defining the phone number and type, as you can see in Table 5-10.

Table 5-10. URL object fields

Key	Description
opensocial.Phone.Field.NUMBER (string)	The user's phone number. May be used interchangeably with number.
opensocial.Phone.Field.TYPE (string)	The type of phone number (e.g., work, home, cell). May be used interchangeably with type.

Url (opensocial.Url)

The OpenSocial Url object provides information for denoting URL structures. For example:

```
"url": {
    "address": "http://www.jcleblanc.com",
```

```
        "linkText": "Personal Website",
        "type": "website"
    }
```

The Url object contains three fields for defining a URL structure, as shown in Table 5-11.

Table 5-11. URL object fields

Key	Description
opensocial.Url.Field.ADDRESS (string)	The address of the link. May be used interchangeably with address.
opensocial.Url.Field.LINK_TEXT (string)	The text or title associated with the link. May be used interchangeably with linkText.
opensocial.Url.Field.TYPE (string)	The type of link, such as blog, work, or website. May be used interchangeably with type.

Capturing the User Profile

Due to the vast array of methods, social access functions, and container social hooks available, a developer has numerous options for accessing a user's profile data. Two of the most popular consist of standardized AJAX request methods; both provide the same results, but they have radically different ways of getting there.

Old method

The traditional AJAX social request method—used as the primary request functionality up until OpenSocial 0.9—is newDataRequest. Even though it is more laborious, this method is widely used because it is backward compatible.

While method names and parameters for different data fetches change, you still have to call standard methods to set up a data request. When making a get request, we first set up our data request object using the newDataRequest method, as follows:

```
var req = opensocial.newDataRequest();
```

Now that the data request container object is available, we can create the key value parameter list to define the profile data that we capture. Our key indicates that we want to capture PROFILE_DETAILS, and the value array contains the list of OpenSocial Person fields that we want to capture. In this example, we are capturing the user's name and thumbnail URL:

```
var params = {};
params[opensocial.DataRequest.PeopleRequestFields.PROFILE_DETAILS] = [
    opensocial.Person.Field.NAME,
    opensocial.Person.Field.THUMBNAIL_URL
];
```

We then add a newFetchPersonRequest call to our initial data request to indicate that we want to capture Person data from a profile. We will pass in two parameters to this

---

function: VIEWER and params. VIEWER defines the person about whom we would like to capture data. This will normally be either VIEWER (the person using the application) or OWNER (the person who created the application). The params list is the object we created earlier in the script that lists the fields we would like to capture. The second parameter of the add function is the label for the request:

```
req.add(req.newFetchPersonRequest('VIEWER', params),
    'viewer_profile');
```

We then send that request to our response handler (personCallback). This method will issue an AJAX request to capture the data required:

```
req.send(personCallback);
```

Much like with a standard AJAX request, the callback function will take in a parameter (data) that is the object sent back from the container servers. You could parse this object to find the data that you are looking for, but that would require unnecessary effort; there are helper methods set up within OpenSocial to parse the returned data structure, after all, and we should take advantage of them:

```
//response handler
function personCallback(data){
    var viewer = data.get('viewer_profile').getData();
    var name = viewer.getDisplayName();
    var thumb = viewer.getField(opensocial.Person.Field.THUMBNAIL_URL);
}
```

First, we can retrieve the data structure that we are looking for by using the data.get(...) method with the syntax of data.get('*label*').getData(), where *label* is the text that we assigned to the data request in the previous sample. This will return the response data object to us. There are a few commonly used data sets that have their own methods—such as getDisplayName() to return the name of the user (which we have used in the preceding sample) or getId() to capture the user ID—but for the most part, we'll use the getField() method to capture specific Person details. From our callback, we pull out these details by calling getField on our response data object, followed by specifying the field that we want to capture as the parameter. With all of that, you can now capture any user profile details.

New method

With the introduction of the lightweight JavaScript APIs in OpenSocial 0.9 came new and easier methods to streamline the development process and reduce code bloat.

We can accomplish our data retrieval task quickly and easily using OpenSocial's get Viewer or getOwner methods:

```
//opensocial person data request
osapi.people.getViewer({fields: ['name']}).execute(function(data){
    alert('Hello ' + data.name);
});
```

To request details about a person, you need to take a few steps (all chained nicely together, though). Breaking down the request into its individual parts, we have three distinct sections:

- `osapi.people.getViewer(...)` is the method specifying that we want to capture the viewer's profile information. The parameter that we pass into this method is a JSON structure, which defines the fields that we want to return from the profile. In this case, we want to capture the viewer's name.
- `execute(...)` will initialize the viewer data request.
- The callback, listed as the parameter in the `execute` function, will be hit when the viewer data request completes, and will contain the `Person` object returned (result parameter). From this result, we can use standard dot notation to get at the data we requested.

Comparing the old and new methods, we can see that the lightweight JavaScript APIs produce a smaller code footprint with additional layers of method chaining.

Using Friendships to Increase Your Audience

The friendships or connections that a user creates compose a great portion of her social graph, which you can leverage to increase your application's user base and ramp up application activity. Friendships are a reciprocated link between two users. For a developer, friendships provide a way to take advantage of full profile details from a much larger audience of users. In short, when a user creates this type of link with another user, she is telling the container that she knows and trusts the other person with her profile and personal information. This trust relationship permeates the social graph, and developers can build off this trust to get more profile information for people relevant to the original user. These concepts work equally well in a follower model such as Twitter; you're looking for a means of using a physical connection (like a friendship or work contact) to your advantage.

Many of us who belong to any of the popular social networks have either generated or received annoying messages from one of the virally popular games, requesting that you help the user out in some fashion by installing the application. Looking closer at such games, we can see that one major reason they have "gone viral" is because of the huge relevant social graph that they build.

The important word here is *relevant*—something that many social networks struggle with at times. Most social platform users add many people to their social graph other than close friends and family—coworkers, the postman, the cousin of the neighbor you say hi to while getting the paper in the morning—and these connections aren't really what we'd call relevant to the user. These nonrelevant friendships dissolve the social graph into a confusing mass of 1 to 1 people links, which are much more difficult to use to drive user interest.

This means that, for the social container itself, a link between nonrelevant users has far less value than one where the users know each other and interact on a regular basis. This same concept applies to your application: when you are building links between the people who use your application, you must give them a way to interact with, and drive activity from, each other on a regular basis for them to be of any use to you.

Making a Request to Capture User Friendships

Much like our previous `Person` request, we can make a simple `get` request to capture owner friends:

```
//get owner friends
osapi.people.get({userId: '@owner', groupId: '@friends', count: 10})
        .execute(function(result){
    if (!result.error){
        var friends = result.list;
        var html = '';
        for (var i = 0; i < friends.length; i++){
            html += friends[i].name.formatted + '';
        }
    }
});
```

Again, this request can be split up into three individual sections:

- `osapi.people.get(...)` is a standard `get` method that can be used to capture any user data. In this case, we indicate within the JSON passed into this function that we would like to capture information from the owner of the application where the `groupId` is `friends`. These are simple strings stating that we would like to capture the owner's friends.

- `execute(...)` will initialize the owner friend data request.

- The callback, listed as the parameter in the `execute` function, will be hit when the owner friend data request completes, and contains all friend `Person` objects for the owner (`friends` parameter). From this result, we can get the number of friends returned using `.totalResults` or loop through the list of `Person` objects for each friend.

Putting It All Together

 The full code for this sample is available at *https://github.com/jcleblanc/ programming-social-applications/blob/master/chapter_5/chapter_final .xml.*

Now that we understand the importance of the `Person` object in an OpenSocial container and the quantity of information that we can obtain from a user's friendships, we can look more closely into these features and fit them neatly together into an Open-Social gadget.

To showcase these features, we will create a gadget with the following requirements:

- Display profile information for the current viewer, including name, photo, gender, profile URL, and any relevant links associated with the user.
- Display a list of the current viewer's friends.
- When the profile image for a viewer's friend is clicked, that friend's profile will be displayed in place of the original viewer's information.

Let's look at the pieces that will need to be in place to build this gadget.

The Gadget Specification

Our first task, much like with any other gadget, is to implement the XML gadget wrapper for the application markup and content:

```
<?xml version="1.0" encoding="utf-8"?>
<Module>
    <ModulePrefs title="Chapter 5 rollup example"
                 title_url="http://www.jcleblanc.com"
                 description="Displays the profile information for the
                              current user and user friends"
                 author="Jonathan LeBlanc">
        <Require feature="opensocial-0.9"/>
        <Require feature="osapi" />
    </ModulePrefs>
```

We add in the gadget metadata for author, description, title, and the associated title URL. In this gadget, we will be using the OpenSocial lightweight JavaScript library osapi and will not need any other libraries along with this feature. To include osapi, we add in two Require nodes—one for OpenSocial 0.9, which is the lowest OpenSocial version needed for osapi, and one for the osapi library itself.

The Content Markup

The gadget's Content section will contain all the gadget markup inline. We will define the style block to add visual appeal to the application and include the DOM containers we'll drop all of our content in:

```
<Content type="html"><![CDATA[
    <style type="text/css">
    div#gadget{ font:11px arial,helvetica,sans-serif; }
    div#gadget div.header{ background-color:#858585;
                           color:#fff;
                           font-weight:bold;
                           font-size:12px;
                           padding:5px;
                           margin:5px; }
    div#gadget div#railRight{ width:360px;
```

```
                          float:right;
                          border:1px solid #858585;
                          margin:0 0 15px 15px;
                          padding:10px;
                          background-color:#eaeaea; }
    div#gadget div#railRight span{ margin:5px; }
    div#gadget div#railRight div#friendLinks img{ border:0;
                                            margin:5px;
                                            width:50px;
                                            height:50px;
                                            cursor:pointer; }
    div#gadget div#updates{ margin-left:5px;
                        margin-right:390px; }
    div#gadget div#updates div.header{ font-size:15px;
                                  margin:0; }
    div#gadget div#updates div#profileContent img{ margin:10px; }
    div#gadget div#updates div#profileContent div{ font-size:14px;
                                            margin:5px 10px; }
    div#gadget div#updates div#profileContent span{ font-weight:bold; }
    </style>

    <div id="gadget">
      <div id="railRight">
        <div class="header">Other Profiles</div>
        <span>Click on an image below to load the profiles of
            your connections</span>
        <div id="friendLinks"></div>
      </div>
      <div id="updates">
        <div class="header">Current Profile</div>
        <div id="profileContent"></div>
      </div>
    </div>
```

Between the style block and our DOM objects, we are building out an application that
consists of two columns to display our required data fields. We will use an interface
that looks like Figure 5-1 to build this application.

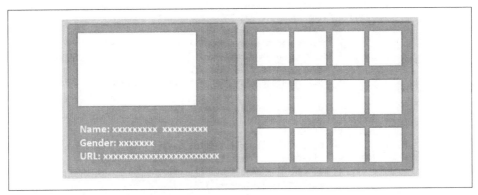

Figure 5-1. Architecture of the Chapter 5 social gadget

Our left column will consist of a display pane for the currently selected user—either the current viewer or any of his chosen friends. A larger version of his profile image will appear at the top, followed by the user's core profile information.

Our right column will contain a view of the application viewer's friends, represented by their profile images. When a profile image is clicked, the left column's display pane will update with the most recently selected profile.

This will be the core of our application visualization.

The JavaScript

The JavaScript layer will act as our controller for the application, providing the data-fetching methods to access profiles and friendships:

```
<script type="text/javascript">
var socialController = {
  //fetch profile photos for friends
  fetchConnections: function(insertID){
    osapi.people.get({userId: "@viewer",
                      groupId: "@friends",
                      count: 36}).execute(function(result){
      var friends = result.list;
      var html = '';
      for (var i = 0; i < friends.length; i++){
        html += "<img src='" + friends[i].thumbnailUrl + "'onclick=
                'socialController.loadProfile(\"" + friends[i].id + "\");' />";
      }
      document.getElementById(insertID).innerHTML = html;
    });
  },

  //load profile for a given user
  loadProfile: function(uid){
    osapi.people.get({userId: uid}).execute(function(result){
      if (!result.error){
        //build basic profile information
        var name = result.name.givenName + " " + result.name.familyName;
        var html = "<img src='" + result.thumbnailUrl
                  + "' alt='profile image' />"
                  + "<div><span>Name:</span> " + name + "</div>"
                  + "<div><span>Gender:</span> " + result.gender + "</div>"
                  + "<div><span>Profile URL:</span> <a href='"
                  + result.profileUrl + "'>" + result.profileUrl
                  + "</a></div><br />"
                  + "<div class='header'>Profile URLs</div>";

        //load all urls for the user
        for (var i = 0; i < result.urls.length; i++){
          html += "<div><span>" + result.urls[i].type + ": </span>"
                + "<a href='" + result.urls[i].value + "'>"
                + result.urls[i].value + "</a></div>";
        }
```

```
                //add new markup to the application
                document.getElementById("profileContent").innerHTML = html;
            }
        });
    }
};

//load friend list
socialController.fetchConnections("friendLinks");

//load viewer profile information
socialController.loadProfile("@viewer");
</script>
]]></Content>
</Module>
```

Our first function, `fetchConnections(...)`, is tasked with fetching the current user's friends and building out the content of the application's right column. We issue a call to the `osapi.people.get(...)` method, passing in a configuration object stating that we want to collect data from the viewer; then *qualify* that by specifying that we want to access the viewer's friends group; and finally *quantify* that by stating that we want to pass back 36 results (or friends). Once that request returns, we build out the profile images for each friend with an `onclick` event to call the `socialController.loadPro file(...)` function. That markup is then injected into the DOM node we have set up for the right column.

Our next function, `loadProfile()`, accepts a user identifier as its single parameter. We issue another request to `osapi.people.get()`, but this time just pass in the `userId` as our configuration object, stating that we want to get the profile of that particular user. When that request completes, we build the markup for the user's name, gender, and profile URL, extracted from the result set returned from our people request. We then loop through each OpenSocial URL object in the profile, adding each one to our return object. Once all of the markup has been generated, we inject it into the left column of our application.

Our last piece of script, below our functions, contains the request methods that we need to call to get our initial markup payload for the application. We call our `fetchConnections(...)` function to grab the viewer's friends; next, we call the `loadPro file(...)` function, passing in the ID of the profile to fetch as the `@viewer` object, which will grab the current user's profile.

Running the Gadget

Once you've loaded the gadget in the container of your choice (or through a local Partuza install), you'll be able to see the full application, providing all of the functionality that we outlined in our requirements, in your browser. It should look like what you see in Figure 5-2.

Figure 5-2. The Chapter 5 social gadget

CHAPTER 6

OpenSocial Activities, Sharing, and Data Requests

One of the biggest challenges with building social applications is figuring out how to promote your applications and leverage external data sources to build in a rich feature set that will keep users' attention and drive a loyal customer base.

Many developers integrate application sharing and activity hooks only as an afterthought; the overall architecture for increasing application use is of little importance to them. The simple fact is that the standard methods that containers set up to promote applications, such as galleries, are not effective drivers of user installs. In many instances, these galleries are oversaturated with thousands of applications and are built to surface the most popular applications at the top. For a new developer, this means not only having to compete with the gallery's numerous applications, but also having to start at the bottom of the pile. This concept is similar to a person's credit history—having no credit is the same as having bad credit.

This is where promoting your application with activities through a regimented sharing process comes into play. Doing so allows you to surface links to your application directly in the user's day-to-day activity stream. In addition, properly augmenting your application with fresh content via data requests will help to draw and keep users' attention, increasing not only your number of installs, but also your daily active users.

What You'll Learn

In Chapter 5, we covered how to customize applications with user profile information and promote application growth through user friendships. This chapter will expand upon those concepts, exploring OpenSocial activities and how to create highly customized applications by building extensive data sources through third-party data requests. Our focus areas in this chapter are:

- Personalizing an application state to a user through social activities
- Increasing application installs by producing activities
- Understanding passive sharing versus direct sharing
- Making data requests to provide rich data sources and increase the number of daily active users
- Making signed data requests to provide security by validating user credentials and data sources

Once you grasp these concepts, you will be well positioned to build highly customizable social applications that promote user growth.

Promoting Your Applications with OpenSocial Activities

A powerful tool for social application developers is the ability to send updates to a user's *activity stream* (or *update stream*). The activity stream, shown in Figure 6-1, is the central news area for the application user and her connections, and is a main communication channel for container users. Using this medium to promote your application with a call to action ensures that you reach the maximum number of users, and can prompt a much higher number of application installs than simply relying on an application gallery.

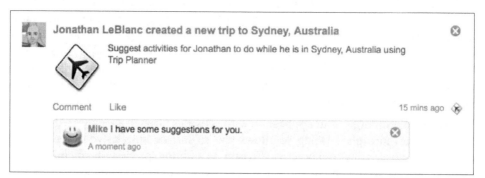

Figure 6-1. An OpenSocial activity stream with images and comments

On most social networking containers, an activity includes these key pieces of data:

- A title describing the action taken by the user.
- A link to the originating source of the update, such as the application itself.
- A description providing more information about the update, or a call to action for other users to add the application.
- An optional media include, such as a video or image, to provide additional visuals to draw in users.
- Comments or *likes* from the user's friends.

Understanding an activity's components will allow a developer to utilize the activity stream to its maximum potential. OpenSocial provides two utilities for interacting with activity updates—one that allows developers to use existing activities to personalize an application experience, and the other for developers who want to produce new activities to drive traffic back to the application itself.

Personalizing an Application Experience by Consuming Activity Updates

Whereas the user's profile comprises the data that she chooses to share and reflects how she sees herself, the user's activity stream shows the reality of what that user does and likes. The activity stream contains information such as application installs, application updates, status and profile information, as well as a gold mine of additional data, all of which can give you insight into the user's online habits, likes, and dislikes. When used in conjunction with the user's profile information, the activity stream gives a developer a great opportunity to target content and advertising directly to that user.

The defining truth in any social network is the user's activity stream. When the user sends messages, the person she's contacting, what she's doing, and what applications she's using all become accessible to a developer via the activity stream.

OpenSocial defines a standard method for capturing these user details:

```
//capture viewer activities
osapi.activities.get({userId: '@viewer ', count: 20}).execute(function(result){
  if (!result.error){
    var activities = result.list;
    var html = ' ';

    //build title and url for each discovered activity
    for (var i = 0; i < activities.length; i++){
      html += 'Activity Title: ' + activities[i].title +
          'Activity URL: ' + activities[i].url;
    }
  }
});
```

 The full code for this sample is available at *https://github.com/jcleblanc/ programming-social-applications/blob/master/chapter_6/activities_cap ture.js*.

In this request, we are making a call to osapi.activities.get(...), indicating that we want to return someone's activity stream. The JSON object provided as the parameter to this request denotes that we want the activities for a userId that matches that of the current application viewer, and we want to return only 20 activities.

Once this request completes, we can parse each activity and use it however we'd like.

Driving Application Growth by Producing Activity Updates

Sadly, many social networking containers are usually oversaturated with applications from their galleries, causing them to relegate applications to undesirable locations to prevent many of their core social features from being overrun by application windows. This raises a major problem for application developers: if your applications are being placed on subtabs or other less-than-prime locations in the container, how will they be surfaced to new users?

One of the best methods you can use to encourage user growth in your application is to promote it through the user's activity stream. The activity stream is one of the few gateways to users that developers can still access if a container does not provide prime real estate for application windows. When a developer taps into the activity stream by setting new updates that draw the user's attention, he generally sees a larger influx of users than he would by just relying on gallery installs.

Thankfully, OpenSocial defines a simple JavaScript method for pushing new activities to this stream, allowing a developer to promote his application through targeted messages.

Pushing an activity to the user activity stream

The method used as of OpenSocial 0.9 to push an update to a user's activity stream is `osapi.activities.create(...)`. This method allows a developer to quickly output a message from an application to an activity stream or any available activity consumption channel provided by the container.

The `osapi.activities.create(...)` method accepts one parameter, a JSON object containing the activity request parameters listed in Table 6-1.

Table 6-1. Activity request parameters for osapi.activities.create

Parameter	Description
activity	An OpenSocial `Activity` object that defines the content of the activity to be sent.
auth	An AuthToken object that defines the authorization type (e.g., `HttpRequest.Authorization`).
appId	The application ID string that denotes the application from which the update was sent. A container may use the application ID to display application details and links back to the application automatically within the update.
groupId	The group string to which the update should be sent (e.g., `@self`).
userId	The user to which the update should be attributed (e.g., `@me`, `@viewer`, `@owner`). This may be either a string or an array of strings.

Using the parameters listed in Table 6-1 as a base, we can build a JavaScript block to enable us to push out an update to the user's activity stream:

```
//insert new activity for the current viewer
osapi.activities.create({
  userId: "@viewer",
```

```
   groupId: "@self",
   activity: {
    title: "My application does all sorts of cool things",
    body: "<a href='http://www.mysite.com'>Click here</a> for more information",
    url: "http://www.mysite.com/"
   }
}).execute();
```

 The full code for this sample is available at *https://github.com/jcleblanc/ programming-social-applications/blob/master/chapter_6/activities_cre ate.js.*

To generate the update, we make a request to `osapi.activities.create(...)` with our JSON object as the parameter. In the update, we specify that the activity stream to which the update should be pushed is that of the current application viewer, and the group to push to is `self`; then, we define an `activity` object to specify the content. Within our `activity` object, we include a title, the URL that the title will link to, and the description (body) of the update. The body of an activity accepts a small subset of HTML tags, including `<b>`, `<i>`, `<a>`, and `<span>`. Executing this code will push an update to the user's activity stream.

Setting an update priority

When pushing out an activity for a user, you need to ensure that application activities can be posted on the user's behalf, even if she has not explicitly granted the application permission to do so. This is where the activity priority comes into play.

You can include an optional flag, `priority`, in an activity push to set the activity's priority. This is a Boolean field that contains a value of `0` (low priority) or `1` (high priority). The value depends on whether the user who is about to push an activity has granted your application permission to do so, and on the container implementation. If you define a high priority (`1`) and the user has not granted your application permission to push out activities on her behalf, the application will attempt to load an authentication flow to prompt her to allow the activity. If you set a low priority (`0`) and the user has not granted your application permission, the update is ignored and no authentication flow will be presented to provide her the option to permit the update to her activity stream.

You can set an activity with a `priority` flag simply by placing the value in the JSON object passed to the push request:

```
//insert new activity for the current viewer with a high priority
osapi.activities.create({
    userId: "@viewer",
    activity: {
        title: "Get more information on my blog",
        url: "http://www.nakedtechnologist.com/",
        priority: 1
```

```
    }
}).execute();
```

 The full code for this sample is available at *https://github.com/jcleblanc/ programming-social-applications/blob/master/chapter_6/activities_cre ate_with_priority.js*.

The preceding example requests the user's permission to push out the activity if she has not already granted the application permission to do so. This may come up if a user has not allowed the application access to her social data, or if she is viewing the application in a preview state.

Including visual media in an update

Adding visual media to an activity that will be displayed to other users will promote richer degrees of interaction with its content, capture user attention more so than standard text and links, and ultimately increase the number of people viewing and installing your application.

An activity push request includes an optional field for mediaItems, through which the developer can embed images, audio, or video into the activity's content.

The method available for creating a media item within OpenSocial is opensocial.new MediaItem(...), which accepts a MIME type defining the media and a URL to the media item itself, such as an image:

```
//create a new media item for an image
var imageUrl = "http://www.mysite.com/image.jpg";
var mediaImg = opensocial.newMediaItem("image/jpeg", imageUrl);
var mediaObj = [mediaImg];

//build parameter list for the activity
var params = {};
params[opensocial.Activity.Field.TITLE] = "Posting my image";
params[opensocial.Activity.Field.URL] = "http://www.myserver.com/index.php";
params[opensocial.Activity.Field.BODY] = "Testing <b>1 2 3</b>";
params[opensocial.Activity.Field.MEDIA_ITEMS] = mediaObj;
var activityObj = opensocial.newActivity(params);

//make request to create a new activity
osapi.activities.create({
    userId: "@viewer",
    activity: activityObj
}).execute();
```

 The full code for this sample is available at *https://github.com/jcleblanc/ programming-social-applications/blob/master/chapter_6/activities_cre ate_with_media.js*.

The process of including a media object in the preceding example comprises three steps. The first task is to create a new media item object, making a request to opensocial.new MediaItem(...) to create the structure. The first parameter specified, image/jpeg, is the MIME type denoting what type of data we are creating. The second parameter is the string specifying the URL to our image. As is typical when embedding media into an activity, we then create an array out of that object.

The second step is to create our activity object to house all of our activity's data, including the media object. The activity parameters can be specified as a JSON object or by calling the opensocial.newActivity(...) method to generate the required structure. We create entries for the title, body, and URL as the base text data to populate the activity. We then add the media item via the opensocial.Activity.Field .MEDIA_ITEMS entry, inputting the array containing the media object we created in the previous step. Next, we call the opensocial.newActivity(...) method to generate the activity structure.

In the final step, we make a request to create the activity. We pass in the userId of the user we would like the activity to be posted for—in this case, the current viewer—and then insert our activity based on the object we created earlier.

These steps will post out an activity containing an image. You can follow the same process to insert a video or audio stream—just keep in mind that you'll have to set the URL and a correct MIME type for the data being presented.

Direct Sharing Versus Passive Sharing

There are two main categories for the methods a developer can employ to promote his applications: *direct sharing* and *passive sharing*. These two options dictate under what circumstances an activity will be published on a user's behalf and whether that user is aware of the update being posted.

There are a few schools of thought where sharing is concerned. As we've discussed, many developers promote application notifications to the user's activity stream, thus displaying the notification to all of the user's friends, and believe that more notifications equals more visibility. Let's assume that a user has five or more applications installed, all promoting out as many activities as they can and all being broadcast to that user's friends. But what if the container provides a means by which a user can hide all application notifications in case they become too invasive and overrun his activity streams? The fact is, almost every container supporting applications *does* provide a way for users to hide such notifications, so application developers need to be careful about which, and how many, notifications they send. This is where direct and passive sharing come into play. Each option has some drawbacks and benefits, which we'll examine next.

Direct Sharing

Direct sharing is the concept of setting up applications to share activities based on the user's actions, with that user's knowledge and consent. The user gives consent when she accepts an option to share the application, asks for help in an application, or promotes some goal or accomplishment she has achieved in the application.

The main reason why implementers employ a direct sharing mechanism is because the user is aware of the actions that the application is taking on her behalf, and is therefore less likely to either turn off (hide) application sharing (via the container or application configuration) or to uninstall the application because she feels her trust has been violated. Maintaining this trust relationship is very important when you are trying to build a community around your application. You want users to feel confident that they can use your application without having it do things that they view as malicious or unwarranted.

The biggest disadvantage to direct sharing is the number of activities that will be produced by the application. Unless the application is set up such that it strongly encourages a user to share an activity, many users will not wish to post activities to their streams, which would promote the application to their friends. Social networking container users have quickly become disenchanted with the flood of application activities being posted by their friends. And because most containers provide a mechanism for users to block application activities from their streams, this presents another challenge for the application developer attempting to promote his application.

To mitigate these issues, *selective promotion* of application events takes into account both the user on whose behalf the activity is being posted as well as her friends who will be seeing the update. Oversaturating a user's stream with your activities is a sure-fire way to have her block your application. Push activities *in moderation*.

Direct sharing may be as simple as providing a call to action and an incentive for a user to share to her activity stream:

```
<div id="msgNode"></div>
<div id="shareMsg">
   Tell your friends that you've updated your profile and earn 5 app bucks!<br />
   <button onclick="addActivity();">Share</button>
</div>

<script type="text/javascript">
//make request to create a new activity
function addActivity(){
   osapi.activities.create({
      userId: "@viewer",
      activity: {
         title: "I've updated my profile - click to see the updates",
         url: "http://www.container.com/myapp"
      }
   }).execute(function(){
      //activity has been shared - display success message
```

```
        document.getElementById("msgNode").innerHTML = "Your message has been shared";
        document.getElementById("shareMsg").style.display = "none";

        //logic to add 5 app bucks to user profile
    });
}
</script>
```

 The full code for this sample is available at *https://github.com/jcleblanc/ programming-social-applications/blob/master/chapter_6/sharing_direct .html*.

Breaking down this example, we can see that the user is presented with some text and a button requesting that she share the fact that she has updated her profile. Once the user clicks on the share button, the activity is pushed to her stream and she receives confirmation of the update.

Passive Sharing

In contrast to direct sharing, passive sharing is the process of pushing out activities on a user's behalf without his direct knowledge that the activity is being posted. We see this in action in social applications like Foursquare or Gowalla, which automatically post out locations where the user has checked in. The user is aware that he has granted such applications permission to push activities on his behalf, but he is not involved in the process of actually pushing out each individual activity.

This method of sharing has its benefits and drawbacks. A user has technically allowed your application permission to push out activities on his behalf, so that gives you the freedom to define how you'll actually use that permission. The main benefit here is that, unlike with the direct sharing method, you can guarantee that certain user actions will produce certain activities. This allows you to increase the number of activities posted from your application in the hopes of reaching a much larger audience.

The main drawback to this method is the same as the benefit: numerous activities can be posted out on the user's behalf *without him actually being involved in or aware of the process*. There are a couple of key negatives here:

- A user has a prearranged trust relationship set up with your application, whereby the application may access his social profile and do things on his behalf. Abusing that trust relationship by posting numerous activities can result in the user hiding all your activities, revoking permission to post out activities on his behalf, or un-installing your application altogether.

- There are many applications posting numerous activities to the user's stream. These activities are visible to the user's connections. If one application oversaturates the user's stream with activities, his connections will tend to hide activities from that application or uninstall the application altogether. This means you lose the potential to expand your application's user base.

The most important rule—with either form of sharing—is moderation. Do not take advantage of your user's trust by posting an inordinate number of activities, or the user will be more likely to turn against the application.

A passive sharing event may be introduced as a simple profile update that in turn sends an activity stating that an update has been posted:

```
<!-- INSERT: Form elements to update the profile -->
Update your profile
<button onclick="updateProfile();">Update Profile</button>

<script type="text/javascript">
//function to update the user profile
function updateProfile (){
   //INSERT: request scripts to update user profile

   //make request to update profile
   osapi.activities.create({
      userId: "@viewer",
      activity: {
         title: "I've updated my profile - click to see the updates",
         url: "http://www.container.com/myapp"
      }
   }).execute();
</script>
```

 The full code for this sample is available at *https://github.com/jcleblanc/ programming-social-applications/blob/master/chapter_6/sharing_pas sive.html*.

This example is similar to the one we looked at for direct sharing. The subtle difference here is that the activity share push is tied to the profile update without the user being aware of the action or being notified when it has taken place.

The example has a number of form fields that allow the user to update his profile and click a button to save his changes. Once the user clicks the button, the function called will make a server request to update his profile. Once the request is sent, an update is pushed out on the user's behalf, without giving him any notification or warning.

Balanced Sharing

One way to reap the benefits but avoid the drawbacks of the direct and passive sharing approaches is to attempt to integrate both into a *balanced sharing* mechanism. If employed correctly, this technique guarantees you a certain number of activities posted per user action while maintaining the trust relationship you've established with the user.

The balanced sharing technique is built on a few main concepts. The first is the use of passive sharing and determining the appropriate actions to tie it to. If passive shares are tied to heavily trafficked user actions, you will end up flooding the user's activity stream with an abundance of messages that she knows nothing about. Passive sharing should be used only for major actions, such as the user completing a lengthy task, earning a badge, or making major upgrades to her profile or application content. This will ensure that a certain number of activities are promoted without monopolizing the user's stream.

The direct sharing technique, on the other hand, should be tied to every other instance for which you would like the application to post out messages. This could be invite flows, requests for help or content from friends, sharing content from the application, and more. You can make your calls to action more enticing to users by providing benefits—such as virtual currency or promotional upgrades—for posting the updates.

Using moderation and maintaining the trust relationship you have with your users can help you build out a rich activity-promotion base within your application. In this way, your users do all of the application promotion for you by publishing activities to their friends and connections.

Making AJAX and External Data Requests

During normal program flow, you may need to modify your application or augment the server data sources, such as a database, with new content. To meet this need, OpenSocial makes available an `http` request method through the standard JavaScript library.

Developers can use this method to make RESTful requests (GET, PUT, POST, DE-LETE) between the application and the server to alter their state without impacting the user experience.

The methods you can use to make these requests are all under the `osapi.http` object and include:

- `osapi.http.get(url, params)`
- `osapi.http.put(url, params)`
- `osapi.http.post(url, params)`
- `osapi.http.delete(url, params)`

In addition to the URL to make the `http` request to, there are a number of parameters you can introduce within these request calls. They are listed in Table 6-2.

Table 6-2. http request parameters

Parameter	Description
authz (string)	The authorization method to use when sending data to the server. This value may be none (default), signed, or oauth.
body (string)	For PUT and POST requests. The data to be sent to the server from the request.
format (string)	The format of the data returned. This value may be json (default) or text.
headers (string/array of strings)	Optional headers to send with the data request.
oauth_service_name (string)	The service element in the gadget spec to use for the request. Default is an empty string (" ").
oauth_token_name (string)	The OAuth token to use in the request. Default is an empty string (" ").
oauth_request_token (string)	A token that is preapproved by the provider for accessing the content of the request.
oauth_request_token_secret (string)	The secret associated with the request_token.
oauth_use_token (string)	Should the OAuth token be used in the request? Possible values are always, if_available, or never.
refreshInterval (integer)	Period of time for which the container may cache the return data.
sign_owner (Boolean)	Should the request be signed and pass the owner ID? Default is true.
sign_viewer (Boolean)	Should the request be signed and pass the viewer ID? Default is true.

Many of the requests used for insecure data will include only a small portion of these parameters, including format, body for POST or PUT requests, and refreshInterval to increase performance.

The authz, sign_*, and oauth_* parameters may be introduced to the request if you need to make a secure data request and verify the sender's identity.

Making Standard Data Requests

Unless you're building a site that requires a secure data transfer, you'll access the majority of your data through standard RESTful server requests. You can make these standard requests through osapi.http.*method*, where *method* is get, put, post, or delete.

Since we are using the osapi JavaScript functionality, we will need to add a Require statement to make the request methods available for us to use. Once the methods are available, we can use them to build out a functional example to capture data from an external source and display the content within the application.

The following example will make a GET request to Flickr via the Yahoo! Query Language (YQL) to return photos that match the search term "Montreal." Those results are then parsed, and <img> tags are generated based on the results of each photo and displayed within the application:

```
<?xml version="1.0" encoding="utf-8"?>
<Module>
```

```
<ModulePrefs title="GET Request to Flickr via YQL">
    <Require feature="osapi"/>
</ModulePrefs>
<Content type="html" view="canvas">
    <![CDATA[
    <div id="imgContainer"></div>

    <script type="text/javascript">
    //GET request callback
    function requestCallback(response){
        var photolist = response.content.query.results.photo, html = "";

        //loop through each image and create an <img> tag
        for (var i in photolist){
            if (photolist.hasOwnProperty(i)){
                html += "<img src='http://farm" + photolist[i].farm +
                        ".static.flickr.com/" + photolist[i].server +
                        "/" + photolist[i].id +
                        "_" + photolist[i].secret +
                        ".jpg' alt='" + photolist[i].title +"' /><br />";
                document.getElementById('imgContainer').innerHTML = html;
            }
        }
    }

    //make GET request
    var url = "http://query.yahooapis.com/v1/public/yql?q=select%20*%20from%20
               flickr.photos.search%20where%20text%3D%22Montreal%22&format=json";
    osapi.http.get({
        "href": url,
        "format": "json"
    }).execute(requestCallback);
    </script>
    ]]>
</Content>
</Module>
```

 The full code for this sample is available at *https://github.com/jcleblanc/
programming-social-applications/blob/master/chapter_6/data_request
.xml*.

The first thing that we define here is the gadget specifications needed to run the example—namely, the Require element for the osapi library under ModulePrefs. We then create the Content section to display the application's canvas view.

Our program execution starts at the bottom of the Content section. We define the URL that we will call—in this case, a URL to YQL with the Flickr search string. We then call our osapi.http.get(...) method to initiate the call. We pass the URL as the href parameter and specify that we are expecting JSON to be returned. Last, we execute the request with the execute(...) method, passing in the callback function reference we want to call when the request completes.

Once the request completes, the requestCallback function will be executed, passing in the data response object as the parameter to the function. We drill down to the start of the repeating photo return values, and then loop through each object in that repeating list.

For each photo that we find in the list, we use the data that is returned from the request to generate <img> tags for each Flickr URL. Once the HTML content is generated for all images, we dump the content into the div node we set up at the top of the Content section.

Pushing Content with Data Requests

When making data requests, you may sometimes need to push content to the server to which you are connecting—for example, if you are pushing new user configuration settings to your server in order to update the database record for the user:

```
<label for="user"></label>
<input type="text" name="user" id="user" /><br />
<label for="pass"></label>
<input type="hidden" name="pass" id="pass" />
<button onclick="updateRecord();">Update User</button>
<div id="response"></div>

<script type="text/javascript">
function updateRecord(){
   //set up url and post data
   var url = "http://www.mysite.com/updateUser.php";
   var postData = "user=" +
      encodeURIComponent(document.getElementById("user").value) + "&pass=" +
      encodeURIComponent(document.getElementById("pass").value);

   //POST data object to URL
   osapi.http.post({
      "href": url,
      "body": postData,
      "format": "text"
   }).execute(function(response){
      document.getElementById("response").innerHTML = "Data Posted";
   });
}
</script>
```

 The full code for this sample is available at *https://github.com/jcleblanc/ programming-social-applications/blob/master/chapter_6/data_request _content.html*.

In our POST request, we set up the markup to allow a user to input her username and password. These values represent the information that we will pass to the server to update the user record. We also set up a div to display a confirmation that the message

---

was sent. When the user clicks the button, the `updateRecord()` function will be executed.

In the `updateRecord()` function, we set the URL that we will be calling and then put together the POST key/value pairs based on the input fields. These are ampersand-separated pairs of data.

Finally, we make an HTTP POST request using the `osapi.http.post(...)` method, passing in the `href`, format, and the POST data that we want to send with the request. The `execute()` method initiates the request, executing the callback when complete. The callback then pushes a simple success message to our message `div`.

Using Signed Requests to Secure a Data Connection

With a normal HTTP request sent via an application using the `osapi.http` methods, the container itself acts as a proxy, forwarding any parameters passed through a request directly to the server to which the request is being made without modifying them (Figure 6-2).

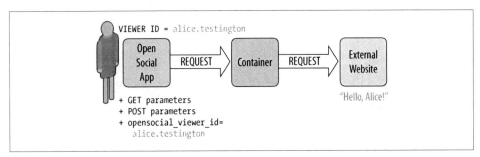

Figure 6-2. A user making a request to an external website through the container without OAuth authorization

When you're collecting data from an external source where security is not an issue or where user validation is not a concern, this insecure method of data transference may suffice.

But let's take a look at a different use case for making a request. Instead of just collecting some random insecure data, let's say we are now making a POST request to a server to update the configuration information for a user. All of the parameters passed to the server are set within the application itself, including the user identifier. Since this request is completely exposed, a user simply running Firebug or modifying the request can spoof his identifier to alter or get information on a different user. Figure 6-3 shows the request to the server, which still appears completely valid despite the fact that a malicious user has now been granted access to information about another user.

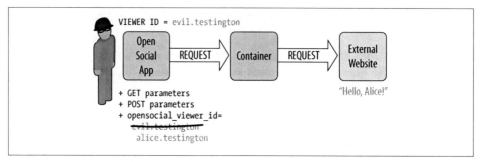

Figure 6-3. A malicious user making a request to an external website, successfully posing as a valid user without OAuth authorization

This is the exact use case that signed requests within the OpenSocial `osapi.http` request methods aim to address. Signed requests will still allow developers to pass parameters and requests from the application to a server, but the container now takes a more active role. When a signed request is proxied through the container, as displayed in Figure 6-4, it validates the user sending the request and appends her identifier. In addition to the identifier, the request includes a cryptographic hash that allows the third-party server to validate that the identifier passed is legitimate.

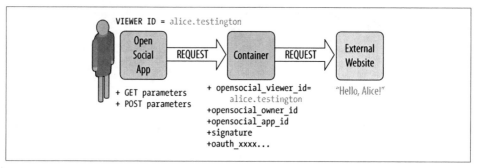

Figure 6-4. A user making a request to an external website through the container with OAuth authorization

With this validation step in place, any malicious user attempting to spoof his identification on a server by passing credentials for another user will have those credentials overwritten with his actual values. Viewer and owner identifiers, in addition to parameters such as the application ID, may also be passed along with the request, provided the user credentials were verified as valid (Figure 6-5).

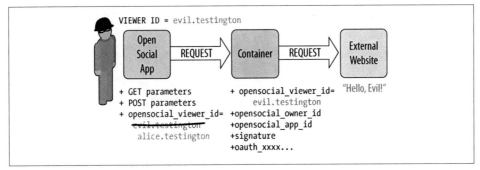

Figure 6-5. A malicious user making a request to an external website, unsuccessfully posing as a valid user with OAuth authorization

When you're making a signed request, the server to which the request is being made always receives the following parameters:

opensocial_owner_id
: The unique identifier for the application's owner

opensocial_app_url
: The qualified URL of the application making the server request

Other than these required parameters, containers can optionally send additional verification data sources, including:

opensocial_viewer_id
: The unique identifier for the current viewer of the application.

opensocial_instance_id
: Should the container support multiple instances of an application, you can include this identifier to specify the application instance sending the request. Between this variable and the opensocial_app_url, you can identify the instance of a particular application in a container.

opensocial_app_id
: A unique identifier for the application. This parameter is generally used to maintain backward compatibility with version 0.7 of the OpenSocial specification.

xoauth_public_key
: The public key used to sign the request. If a container does not use public keys to sign requests, or if it has another means of distributing keys with the request server, this parameter may be omitted.

In addition to these parameters, the server will also be sent a series of OAuth credentials to verify the signed request. These parameters include:

- oauth_consumer_key
- oauth_nonce

- oauth_signature
- oauth_signature_method
- oauth_timestamp
- oauth_token

Simply making a signed request does not guarantee that the request will be tamper-proof. The server to which the request is being made will need to take the additional step of validating the signed request to ensure the legitimacy of the data transferred.

Making a signed request

You can easily make signed requests by using the request syntax we have already learned in conjunction with the authz parameter:

```
//make a signed HTTP GET request
osapi.http.get({
    'href' : 'http://www.mysite.com/editUser.php',
    'format' : 'json',
    'authz' : 'signed'
}).execute(callback);
```

Within the GET request, we define the URL that we wish to make a signed request to, specify the data format and, most importantly, state that the authentication (authz) will be signed. This will initiate a signed HTTP GET request.

Validating a signed request on the server

As noted previously, simply making a signed request to the server is not enough to ensure that the request is actually valid. A person with malicious intent may attempt to spoof a signed request to the server. This is where a developer may use OAuth signature validation to verify that a signed request actually came from the correct source.

There are a few things that we'll need in order to validate the request:

- The OAuth library from *http://code.google.com/p/oauth/*, which is used in the server-side file validation. This example uses the PHP OAuth 1.0 Rev A library at *http://oauth.googlecode.com/svn/code/php/*.

- If the container uses a public key certificate as a validation method, we will need that public key certificate. For a list of the numerous public key certificates for different containers and links to the certifications, go to *https://opensocialresources.appspot.com/certificates/*. Note, however, that this is just a convenience site and is not supported or approved by the containers. To integrate the best security measures, you should check the container's documentation to find the most current public key certificate.

The validation of a signed request comprises two parts. First, within the client-side code, we need to make a signed request to a server-side script. Then, we take the parameters sent to the server-side script and validate them using the OAuth library. We'll detail this two-part process next.

Making the signed JavaScript request. Making a signed request within the JavaScript layer embedded in the gadget XML Content section will pass along OAuth, container, and user credentials that can be used to validate the request.

Setting up such a request is as simple as making a signed `osapi.http.get` request to the server-side script, as we saw in the earlier section "Making a signed request" on page 194:

```
<?xml version="1.0" encoding="utf-8"?>
<Module>
    <ModulePrefs title="Validating a Signed AJAX Request">
        <Require feature="opensocial-0.9"/>
        <Require feature="osapi"/>
    </ModulePrefs>
    <Content type="html" view="canvas">
        <![CDATA[
        <div id="validationResponse"></div>

        <script type="text/javascript">
        function dataCallback(response){
            document.getElementById("validationResponse").innerHTML =
                "Request was verified as: " + response.data.validation;
        }

        osapi.http.get({
            "href" : "http://www.mysite.com/validate.php",
            "format" : "text",
            "authz" : "signed"
        }).execute(dataCallback);
        </script>
        ]]>
    </Content>
</Module>
```

 The full code for this sample is available at *https://github.com/jcleblanc/ programming-social-applications/blob/master/chapter_6/request_signed .xml*.

The gadget itself contains the Require statements for the `osapi.http.get(...)` request and the required Content section to host the scripts. In the Content section, we have a div node to display the validation message from the callback, and the callback from the HTTP request itself. In a production application, you could check the validation message coming back from the server. If the response is valid and contains new markup, you can insert it on the page. If the response is invalid, you should display a message to this effect, stating that the request could not be completed at this time.

The `osapi.http.get(...)` request following the callback will then make the signed GET request to the server-side script.

Validating the signed request on the server (RSA-SHA1 with public key certificate). Once the request has passed through the container proxy layer and hits the server-side script (in this example, *http://www.mysite.com/validate.php*), the parameters should now hold all the container, user, and OAuth credentials needed to validate the request.

Many of the most popular social networking containers use public key certificates to validate a request via RSA-SHA1. In this example, we use one of these certificates to validate the request.

 If the container in question does not use public key certificates to validate the requests, or if you wish to use HMAC-SHA1 rather than RSA-SHA1, you will need to set up a secret key with the container and use that instead of the public key certificate.

```php
<?php
require_once("OAuth.php");

class buildSignatureMethod extends OAuthSignatureMethod_RSA_SHA1 {
    public function fetch_public_cert(&$request) {
        return file_get_contents("http://www.fmodules.com/public080813.crt");
    }
}

//construct request method based on POST and GET parameters
$request = OAuthRequest::from_request(null, null, array_merge($_GET, $_POST));

//create new signature method from created class & public key certificate
$signature_method = new buildSignatureMethod();

//validate signature
@$signature_valid = $signature_method->check_signature($request, null, null, $_GET
["oauth_signature"]);

$response = array();
if ($signature_valid) {
    //validated signed request - send valid message
    $response['validation'] = "valid";
} else {
    //invalid signed request - send invalid message
    $response['validation'] = "invalid";
}

//print response object
print(json_encode($response));
?>
```

The full code for this sample is available at *https://github.com/jcleblanc/ programming-social-applications/blob/master/chapter_6/request_signed _validate_rsa_sha1.php*.

The `require_once(...)` statement at the beginning of the example is the OAuth file that we downloaded earlier from *http://oauth.googlecode.com/svn/code/php/*.

The first thing to note about the validation script is the class `buildSignatureMethod` at the beginning. This class extends the RSA_SHA1 OAuth signature method of the *OAuth.php* file and simply contains a function to fetch and return the contents of a public key certificate file. You should not make a request to capture this file's data each time a signed request needs to be validated. Instead, the contents should be added to a key cache based on the values of several parameters passed to the server-side file, and only updated when these values change. These parameters include:

- `xoauth_signature_publickey`
- `oauth_consumer_key`
- `oauth_signature_method`

Next, we build a new OAuth request object based on the GET and POST parameters sent via the request. These parameters contain the OAuth and container parameters from the container proxy script used during the signed data request. This OAuth request object will be used to validate the signature provided. Using our public key certificate fetching class, we build a new signature based on that public key certificate.

Using the `check_signature(...)` method, we then verify that the signature provided is valid and store the result. Based on that signature's validation, we store either a valid or invalid message and return a JSON object of the response back to the client-side script.

Validating the signed request on the server (HMAC-SHA1). If a public key certificate is not available for the container you are working with, you can take a different approach for validating the signed request on the server. Rather than using RSA-SHA1, we will validate via HMAC-SHA1.

Instead of using a public key certificate as our method for validating the request, we can build a new OAuth request object from the OAuth data that was sent through the signed request:

```php
<?php
require_once("OAuth.php");

$key = "KEY HERE";
$secret = "KEY HERE";

//Build a request object from the current request
$request = OAuthRequest::from_request(null, null, $_REQUEST);
$consumer = new OAuthConsumer($key, $secret, null);
```

```php
//Initialize signature method
$sig_method = new OAuthSignatureMethod_HMAC_SHA1();

//validate passed oauth signature
$signature = $_GET['oauth_signature'];
$valid_sig = $sig_method->check_signature(
    $request,
    $consumer,
    null,
    $signature
);

//check if signature check succeeded
if (!$valid_sig) {
    //SIGNATURE INVALID - Produce appropriate error message
} else{
    //SIGNATURE IS VALID - Continue with normal program execution
}
?>
```

 The full code for this sample is available at *https://github.com/jcleblanc/ programming-social-applications/blob/master/chapter_6/request_signed _validate_hmac_sha1.php*.

Much like with the previous example, we start by including our PHP OAuth library (available at *http://oauth.googlecode.com/svn/code/php/*). This will allow us to create our OAuth request object and consumer object, and validate the signature. In addition to the library, we include our OAuth consumer and secret as variables in order to construct a new OAuth consumer.

Our next task is to build our request and consumer OAuth objects. We first make a request to OAuthRequest::from_request(...) to build the request object. We set the first and second parameters to null, as they are not required. These parameters represent the HTTP method and HTTP URL, respectively. The third parameter is the $_REQUEST object, which will contain all the OAuth request information we need to build the object. We then create a new OAuthConsumer object, passing in the OAuth key and secret. The third parameter in this request method, which we set to null, is the callback URL for the OAuth process.

Our next task is to build a new signing object by creating a new instance of OAuth SignatureMethod_HMAC_SHA1(). We'll then be able to run comparisons between it and the signature that was passed through the signed request in order to ensure that the latter is valid.

We begin the next block by collecting the OAuth signature that was passed through the signed request. Once we've obtained that signature, we use our new signature instance to make a request to the check_signature(...) method. For the parameters list, we pass through the OAuth request object and OAuth consumer object, set the token value to `null` (since it isn't needed), and finally, add the signature passed through the request for comparison.

Now we can use the value passed back from that request to verify whether the signature comparison completed successfully (i.e., whether the signature passed through was valid). If so, we can continue processing the signed request as needed. If not, an error message should be published.

Putting It All Together

 The full code for this sample is available at *https://github.com/jcleblanc/ programming-social-applications/blob/master/chapter_6/chapter_final .xml*.

Now that you have the knowledge you need to leverage a gadget's social features, we'll put it to use in a sample gadget. This gadget will display the activity stream of the viewer's friends, display their profile images, and then provide a method for the viewer to add a new activity to his stream.

First, we need to build the gadget markup. In this example, we'll just need the lightweight `osapi` JavaScript library, so we'll include that feature in the gadget. We then define the view in which the Content node will be loaded:

```
<?xml version="1.0" encoding="UTF-8"?>
<Module>
    <ModulePrefs title="Chapter 4 Example"
                 description="Display social information fetch and push abilities">
        <Require feature="opensocial-0.9"/>
        <Require feature="osapi" />
    </ModulePrefs>
    <Content type="html" view="canvas">
        <![CDATA[
        <!-- view content -->
        ]]>
    </Content>
</Module>
```

We now need to include our styles and markup in the Content node. For this example, we use styles to position the page elements and set their font, colors, and spacing. This markup will build a container with two columns. The left column will display the recent updates of the viewer's friends, and the right column will display profile images for 12 of those friends. Below the photos is a form to allow the user to input a title, description, and URL to push out a new activity to his stream:

```
<style type="text/css">
div#gadget{ font:11px arial,helvetica,sans-serif; }
div#gadget div.header{ background-color:#858585;
```

```css
                    color:#fff; font-weight:bold;
                    font-size:12px;
                    padding:5px;
                    margin:5px; }
div#gadget div#railRight{ width:360px;
                    float:right;
                    border:1px solid #858585;
                    margin:0 0 15px 15px;
                    padding:10px;
                    background-color:#eaeaea; }
div#gadget div#railRight div#friendLinks img{ border:0;
                                    margin:5px;
                                    width:50px;
                                    height:50px; }
div#gadget div#railRight form{ margin:10px 5px; }
div#gadget div#railRight form label{ font-weight:bold; }
div#gadget div#railRight form input{ width:300px; }
div#gadget div#updates{ margin-left:5px;
                    margin-right:390px; }
div#gadget div#updates div.header{ margin:0; }
</style>

<div id="gadget">
    <div id="railRight">
        <div class="header">Other Profiles</div>
        <div id="friendLinks"></div>
        <div class="header">Update Your Friends</div>
        <form name="addActivity" onSubmit="return false;">
            <label for="title">Title:</label><br />
            <input type="text" name="title" id="title" /><br />

            <label for="description">Description:</label><br />
            <input type="text" name="description" id="description" /><br />

            <label for="url">URL:</label><br />
            <input type="text" name="url" id="url" /><br /><br />
            <button onclick="socialController.addActivity();">Add Activity</button>
        </form>
    </div>
    <div id="updates">
        <div class="header">Updates From Your Connections</div>
        <div id="updateContent"></div>
    </div>
</div>
```

The last piece of the gadget is the JavaScript layer. This section contains three functions to handle the getting and setting of the gadget's social data. These functions act as constructors for the social data sources and promote application data to the user's friends:

```javascript
<script type="text/javascript">
var socialController = {
    //fetch profile photos for friends
    fetchProfile: function(insertID){
        //make GET request for 12 viewer friend profiles
```

```
        osapi.people.get({userId: "@viewer",
                          groupId: "@friends",
                          count: 12}).execute(function(result){
            var friends = result.list;
            var html = '';

            //for each friend found, create a profile image linked to their profile
            for (var i = 0; i < friends.length; i++){
                html += "<a href='" + friends[i].profileUrl + "'><img src='"
                         + friends[i].thumbnailUrl + "' /></a>";
            }
            document.getElementById(insertID).innerHTML = html;
        });
    },

    //fetch update stream for friends
    fetchUpdates: function(insertID){
        //make GET request for 30 viewer friend activities
        osapi.activities.get({userId: "@viewer",
                              groupId: "@friends",
                              count: 30}).execute(function(result){
            var activities = result.list; var html = '';

            //for each activity, create a title linked to their source
            for (var i = 0; i < activities.length; i++){
                html += "<p><a href='" + activities[i].url + "'>"
                         + activities[i].title + "</a><br /></p>";
            }
            document.getElementById(insertID).innerHTML = html;
        });
    },

    //insert a new activity for the current viewer
    addActivity: function(){
        osapi.activities.create({userId: "@viewer", groupId: "@self",
            activity: {
                title: document.getElementById("title").value,
                body: document.getElementById("description").value,
                url: document.getElementById("url").value
            }
        }).execute();
    }
};

//initialize data requests
socialController.fetchProfile("friendLinks");
socialController.fetchUpdates("updateContent");
</script>
```

The fetchProfile() function captures profile photos and profile URLs for the viewer's friends. This information is then used to create a series of image tags and insert that HTML into the gadget markup.

The fetchUpdates() function captures updates from the viewer's friends, creates markup for the linked titles, and inserts that markup into the application's left column.

The last function, `addActivity()`, inserts a new activity into the viewer's stream when he enters a title, description, and URL for that activity in the right column.

The last two lines of the JavaScript call the social data fetch functions to populate the application once it loads. When the gadget is loaded, it will render with the social features we've defined in our `div` nodes, appearing like Figure 6-6.

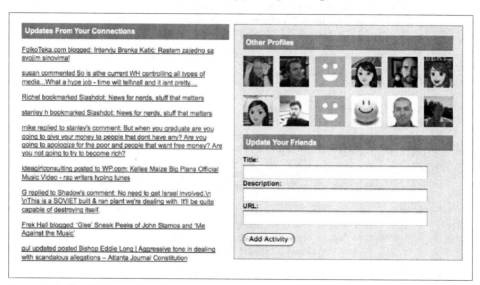

Figure 6-6. The Chapter 6 example gadget, showcasing activity and social profile capabilities

This application contains some of the core social features that you can use to promote application growth and user customization. Using even a subset of these features will help you target user preferences, get the users to promote your application for you, and draw users' social friendships into the application context.

CHAPTER 7

Advanced OpenSocial and OpenSocial Next

Using OpenSocial techniques and tools, developers can create very extensible applications and utilities. This chapter will explore those features in more depth and cover what is coming up for OpenSocial in the future.

What You'll Learn

In this chapter, we will examine some of the more advanced features for building OpenSocial gadgets. In addition to technical implementations, we will dive into some upcoming improvements to the specification and how they'll work with different distributed web frameworks in the future.

The topics that we will explore include:

- Building data sources with data pipelining
- Creating an extensible markup layer with templating
- Extending features with OSML
- Exploring the OpenSocial REST APIs
- The new specification and improvements over current functionality
- How distributed web frameworks will play a major role in the future of OpenSocial

Once we understand the core features discussed in this chapter, we will apply the lessons we have learned to build out the architecture of an advanced OpenSocial gadget.

Data Pipelining

There comes a time in every developer's career when he realizes that embedding a data source directly into the application markup makes for an application that is not only hard to maintain and debug, but is also not scalable in the long run. Separating out a data source—such as a JSON or XML object obtained from a third-party resource—from the page markup, or visual layout, is key to building applications that are modular, easy to maintain, and highly scalable.

The first part of this process involves the data retrieval methods that make the raw information available to your application, which is where we'll begin our discussion of *data pipelining*. Data pipelining allows developers to pull in a data source from some third-party resource and make it available within the gadget code base. The reasoning behind such an implementation is twofold:

- It provides developers with an easy and scalable method for accessing a raw data source, without them having to embed a mechanism to make and handle the request.

- The data source can be used in a multitude of ways to build a rich data source/template interaction.

Before data pipelining became available within the OpenSocial specification, developers had to make the request through standard HTTP requests and handle the data source themselves:

```
<script type="text/javascript">
function requestCallback(response){
    var data = response.content;
    //build data source
}

//define URL to make GET request to
var url = "http://www.mysite.com/dataSource.php";

//make GET request
osapi.http.get({
    "href": url,
    "format": "json"
}).execute(requestCallback);
</script>
```

To fetch the data source, we make the HTTP GET request to a defined URL, specifying the format that needs to be returned. Once the request completes, our callback is hit and we can begin to handle the data results that are returned.

While this is not an extensive amount of code, and the HTTP GET request function can be repurposed for a multitude of application request needs, the simple fact is that the majority of developers will be making data requests to capture some raw information as soon as the application loads. Unless you're feeding your users static content without customizing their experience through a data source, these data requests will be integral to your initial load.

This is where data pipelining comes into play. We can easily shrink down the previous request and make the raw data source available to us using the following method:

```
<script type="text/os-data" xmlns:os="http://ns.opensocial.org/2008/markup">
    <os:HttpRequest key="myData" href="http://www.mysite.com/dataSource.php" />
</script>
```

To define our data source and initiate the HTTP request, we just have to embed a few nodes within the gadget code. We create a script node with two attributes:

type
: Defines the type of request to be embedded in the script node. To specify a data pipelining source, set this value to `text/os-data`.

xmlns:os
: The XML namespace markup definition for the os namespace. This value should be set to *http://ns.opensocial.org/2008/markup*.

We then define an HTTP data request using the `os:HttpRequest` node, which is one of the data request methods that can be used as a data pipe.

We can also make available multiple data requests within the context of a data pipe by embedding the calls together with different keys:

```
<script type="text/os-data" xmlns:os="http://ns.opensocial.org/2008/markup">
    <os:HttpRequest key="myData" href="http://www.mysite.com/dataSource.php" />
    <os:ViewerRequest key="viewerProfile" fields="name, gender, age, status" />
</script>
```

Using such requests, we make the data source available to the gadget. To use the data pipelining library functionality, we need to add a `Require` statement to load in the required library, `opensocial-data`. When we put these concepts together, we get a base-level gadget that integrates an external data source:

```
<?xml version="1.0" encoding="UTF-8"?>
<Module>
    <ModulePrefs title="Loading data via Data Pipelining">
        <Require feature="opensocial-data" />
    </ModulePrefs>
    <Content type="html">
        <![CDATA[
        <script type="text/os-data" xmlns:os="http://ns.opensocial.org/2008/markup">
            <os:HttpRequest key="myData" href="http://www.mysite.com/dataSource.php"/>
        </script>
        ]]>
    </Content>
</Module>
```

 The full code for this sample is available at *https://github.com/jcleblanc/programming-social-applications/blob/master/chapter_7/data_pipelining.xml*.

The preceding gadget sample integrates the `Require feature="opensocial-data"` node to make available the OpenSocial JavaScript library functions for data pipelining. It defines a Content section to display when the gadget loads. In the Content section, we integrate a script node to make an HTTP request to our data source, using the key myData to store the result set.

The real value in using data pipelining emerges when the data object is tied into a template via OpenSocial templating, which we'll discuss in the upcoming section "OpenSocial Templating" on page 218.

Data Request Types

A developer may want to request several types of data to help build his application base. For example, he might want the user's profile information or a series of activities from the user's friends, or he might want to simply make a remote data request for a raw JSON feed. Fortunately, OpenSocial defines a series of data request types that allows developers to easily load social, private, or public data sources for use within their applications.

Container requests with <os:DataRequest>

Within the OpenSocial social API server and core API server specifications (described in Chapter 5), there are several definitions for REST endpoints to collect data from the container. This data may be social in nature, such as a user's profile or activity information (in the case of the social API server), or simply be container-specific data not tied to the user's social information (as in the case of the core API server). The Data Request tag provides a method for developers to collect this information easily, making it available within their program flow.

Much like with any other data pipelining feature, the developer must add the Require feature="opensocial-data" tag in the gadget XML file in order to use the DataRequest tag. Once the feature is available, pulling in the data source is a trivial matter of specifying the REST method that you would like to fetch and the parameters that should be sent to that endpoint:

```
<script type="text/os-data" xmlns:os="http://ns.opensocial.org/2008/markup">
    <os:DataRequest key="userFriends" method="people.get" userId="@viewer"
                    groupId="@friends" startIndex="20" count="10"/>
</script>
```

 The full code for this sample is available at *https://github.com/jcleblanc/ programming-social-applications/blob/master/chapter_7/data_request _container.xml*.

The preceding sample shows one type of request you can make—in this case, to capture the friends of the current application viewer. The container REST endpoints to collect data may all be used in the context of this request. There are several defined attributes that you can specify for the DataRequest tag, as listed in Table 7-1.

Table 7-1. DataRequest attributes

Attribute	Description
key (string)	A name to serve as the root node of the data source.
method (string)	The REST endpoint and operation to be called, such as `people.get` or `activities.get`. The `.update`, `.create`, and `.delete` operations are not supported.
Dynamic attributes	Any other attributes that may be specified for the REST endpoint, such as `startIndex`, `count`, etc. All dynamic attributes will be passed as strings to the endpoint.

Using the dynamic attributes available for each REST endpoint in conjunction with the method itself will allow you to easily bring in the container's core data set (social or otherwise).

External data requests with <os:HttpRequest>

If you are an application developer who wants to leverage some third-party data source to populate dynamic content upon the loading of your application, you'll use the `HttpRequest` tag to accomplish that. Functioning in a way similar to a standard `osapi.http.get` request, `HttpRequest` lets developers access third-party sources, make signed requests, and verify those requests via OAuth credentials:

```
<script type="text/os-data" xmlns:os="http://ns.opensocial.org/2008/markup">
    <os:HttpRequest key="myData" href="http://www.mysite.com/dataSource.php"
                    format="text" />
</script>
```

> The full code for this sample is available at *https://github.com/jcleblanc/ programming-social-applications/blob/master/chapter_7/data_request _external.xml*.

At a base level, a simple `HttpRequest` tag can simply query a data source and make it available to the rest of the gadget code. This tag offers an extensive amount of functionality that builds upon core features to allow developers to add security levels, request-source checks, and caching layers. Table 7-2 lists the attributes you can specify for `HttpRequest`.

Table 7-2. HttpRequest attributes

Attribute	Description
authz (string)	The authorization method to use when sending data. The values may be none (default), `signed`, or `oauth`.
format (string)	The format of the data to be returned. Values may be `json` (default) or `text`.
href (string)	The URL to make the request to.
key (string)	A name to serve as the root node of the data source.

Attribute	Description
method (string)	The HTTP method to use for the request, either get (default) or post. If the params attribute is set, making a post request will send the params with a content type of application/x-www-form-urlencoded. If you're making a get request with params, they will be appended to the URL.
params (string)	Parameters to be sent to the URL endpoint. The parameters should be ampersand delimited and follow the format param1=a&param2=b.
oauth_request_token (string)	A request token that is preapproved by the provider to permit resource access.
oauth_request_token_secret (string)	The secret key associated with the request token.
oauth_service_name (string)	The service element in the gadget spec to be used when making the request. Default value is "".
oauth_token_name (string)	Identifies the OAuth token to be used to make the request. Default value is "".
oauth_use_token (string)	Value to determine whether an OAuth token should be used to make the request. Available values are always, if available, or never.
refreshInterval (integer)	The amount of time that the container can cache the data for.
sign_owner (Boolean)	Whether to sign the request and include the current viewer ID. Defaults to true.
sign_viewer (Boolean)	Whether to sign the request and include the owner ID. Defaults to true.

Using this extensive list of attributes, you can verify the source of a signed request based on OAuth parameters, and have the container cache the data obtained for a certain amount of time, which improves performance if the data source does not change frequently.

People data requests with <os:PeopleRequest>

If you are building a social application, in many instances you will need to get profile information for one person, more than one person, or for entire groups. The People Request tag provides you with this functionality, enabling you to highly customize the data that will be returned by the request:

```
<script type="text/os-data" xmlns:os="http://ns.opensocial.org/2008/markup">
    <os:PeopleRequest key="viewerFriends" userId="@viewer" groupId="@friends"
                    startIndex="10" count="20"/>
</script>
```

 The full code for this sample is available at *https://github.com/jcleblanc/ programming-social-applications/blob/master/chapter_7/data_request _people.xml*.

Developers making requests using the PeopleRequest tag can capture the complete profile information for a set of users, or only a subset. Prior to returning, this profile information may be sorted to display content in the form you need. The attribute tags listed in Table 7-3 give you this sorting capability.

Table 7-3. PeopleRequest attributes

Attribute	Description
count (integer)	The number of people to return.
filterBy (string)	The type of filter to be applied against the retrieved users. This matches the REST specification.
filterOp (string)	The type of filter to be applied against the retrieved users. This matches the REST specification.
filterValue (string)	The type of filter to be applied against the retrieved users. This matches the REST specification.
fields (list of strings)	A comma-delimited list of OpenSocial Person fields to return.
groupId (string)	The group of users that should be returned. The values may be @self (default) to return the users listed in the userId attribute, @friends to get user friend profiles, or any string representing a group.
key (string)	A name to serve as the root node of the data source.
sortBy (string)	The name of the field to be used to sort the returned people. This is used in conjunction with the sortOrder parameter to determine sort order.
sortOrder (string)	The sort order of the results. This may be either ascending (default) or descending.
startIndex (integer)	The numeric start index for the result set.
userId (list of strings)	A comma-delimited list of user IDs to use with the groupId attribute. Besides a user ID, this value can be @me, @viewer, or owner.

A PeopleRequest is valuable when you're building applications to promote user growth through viewer friendships, which may take the form of inviting people to use the application or sharing application content with links back to the application itself.

Viewer and owner data requests with os:ViewerRequest and os:OwnerRequest

For any social application, it is important to personalize your content for the current viewer in order to prefill form configurations, customize the user experience, and/or leverage user preferences to target advertising or upsell products. Owner information can include a profile for the application creator, which means the developer can build a profile view of himself in his application. Both viewer and owner profile information can be easily obtained through a respective pair of tags. Here, we capture a portion of data from a viewer using the ViewerRequest tag:

```
<script type="text/os-data" xmlns:os="http://ns.opensocial.org/2008/markup">
  <os:ViewerRequest key="viewerData" fields="nickname, gender"/>
</script>
```

 The full code for this sample is available at *https://github.com/jcleblanc/ programming-social-applications/blob/master/chapter_7/data_request _viewer.xml*.

Likewise, we can obtain the application owner's profile information using a similar syntax, but with the `OwnerRequest` tag:

```
<script type="text/os-data" xmlns:os="http://ns.opensocial.org/2008/markup">
    <os:OwnerRequest key="ownerData" fields="name, birthday"/>
</script>
```

 The full code for this sample is available at *https://github.com/jcleblanc/programming-social-applications/blob/master/chapter_7/data_request _owner.xml*.

These two tags have a couple of attributes available, listed in Table 7-4, that allow you to collect just the subset of profile information needed for the data source.

Table 7-4. ViewerRequest and OwnerRequest attributes

Attribute	Description
fields (list of strings)	A comma-delimited list of OpenSocial Person fields to return.
key (string)	A name to serve as the root node of the data source.

This pair of tags provides a simple method for capturing data for the current viewer or the application owner, allowing you to personalize the user experience with profile content.

Activity data requests with <os:ActivitiesRequest>

The last type of data request available is the `ActivityRequest` tag, used for collecting activity data for a user or group of users. This tag is simple to implement but provides an extensive amount of functionality:

```
<script type="text/os-data" xmlns:os="http://ns.opensocial.org/2008/markup">
    <os:ActivitiesRequest key="ViewerActivities" userid="@viewer" startIndex="40"
                          count="20"/>
</script>
```

 The full code for this sample is available at *https://github.com/jcleblanc/programming-social-applications/blob/master/chapter_7/data_request _activities.xml*.

Developers can return full activity streams or only portions, depending on the fields available in the OpenSocial `Activity` object, and define paging and return limits on the activities fetched. Table 7-5 lists the supported attributes for the `ActivityRequest` tag.

Table 7-5. *ActivitiesRequest attributes*

Attribute	Description
activityIds (list of strings)	A comma-delimited list of activity IDs to retrieve. If this is set, the userId and groupId attributes will be ignored.
appId (string)	The application ID for which activities should be returned. The default value is the current application.
count (integer)	The number of activities to return.
fields (list of strings)	A comma-delimited list of OpenSocial Activity fields to return. If this is set, the userId and groupId attributes will be ignored.
groupId (string)	The group of users that should be returned. The values may be @self (default) to return the users listed in the userId attribute, @friends to get user friend activities, or any string representing a group.
key (string)	A name to serve as the root node of the data source.
startIndex (integer)	The starting index to start returning data results from.
startPage (integer)	The page to return results for. If 20 results are returned in each request, and there are 40 results, page 1 would be defined as 1–20, and page 2 would be defined as results 21–40.
userId (list of strings)	A comma-delimited list of user IDs to use with the groupId attribute. Besides a user ID, this value can be @me, @viewer, or owner.

Activity stream information gives developers an opportunity to customize the user experience based on the content of user's activities. You can use this information to find when users have installed applications, which people they have followed, or to review the user's friends' activities to get an encapsulated look at the user's social graph.

Making Data Available to Proxied Data Requests

We talked about the differences between using proxied and inline content within a gadget in Chapter 3 in the section "Inline Versus Proxy Content" on page 89. Depending on the architecture and needs of their application development environment, many developers may prefer the proxied content approach for its ease of use.

If the markup for the Content sections of your gadget is defined with a proxied data source, the way you make container data sources available to that file is very similar to the methods we have used in earlier sections:

```
<Content type="url" view="canvas" href="http://www.mysite.com/canvas.php">
  <os:PeopleRequest key="ownerFriends" userId="@owner"
                    groupId="@friends" startIndex="10" count="20"
                    fields="name,nickname,gender,birthday" />
</Content>
```

 The full code for this sample is available at *https://github.com/jcleblanc/ programming-social-applications/blob/master/chapter_7/data_request _proxied.xml.*

We define our `Content` node, with our proxied content being loaded through the file specified in the `href` attribute. Normally, when using proxied content, we would have a self-closing `Content` node, but to add the container data we instead embed the data source that we are looking for—in this case, a subset of the application owner's friends.

Once the proxied content source is fetched, all of the data sources requested will be passed to the file as POSTed JSON objects. If the container cannot also send the `open social_owner` parameter (which contains the unique identifier for the owner) to the third-party server, then references to `@owner` will return a 403 forbidden HTTP error. The same would hold true if we were using the `@viewer` or `@me` values and the container could not send the `opensocial_viewer` parameter.

Working with Pipelined Data on the Client

There are several methods for working with pipelined data within the defined gadget. One method is defining a template to render the content of a data pipe, which we will discuss later in this chapter. Another method is to use the JavaScript APIs defined for working with data pipes.

The data sources for a gadget are stored within the gadget context, which we can obtain using a simple method call:

```
opensocial.data.getContext();
```

Using this as our base data, we can call methods to get data, set data, and build data change listeners around the data sources. We'll go over these actions next.

Getting data objects

 The full code for this sample is available at *https://github.com/jcleblanc/ programming-social-applications/blob/master/chapter_7/pipeline_get _data.xml.*

Now that you understand the gadget context concept, we can use a series of methods to manipulate the data sources. To start, you can easily set up the method for obtaining an object from a data pipe, `getDataSet()`, using the following format:

```
opensocial.data.getContext().getDataSet(key);
```

There is one parameter that is passed in to the `getDataSet()` method:

key *(string)*
    The data pipe key where the new object should be inserted

Let's assume that the gadget we are building will capture a small set of fields from the current application viewer as well as the same set of fields from the viewer's friends. Our first task is to set up the data pipelining request to load the data sources:

```
<script type="text/os-data" xmlns:os="http://ns.opensocial.org/2008/markup">
    <os:ViewerRequest key="viewerData" fields="name, nickname, gender"/>
    <os:PeopleRequest key="viewerFriends" userId="@viewer"
                      groupId="@friends" count="50"
                      fields="name, nickname, gender" />
</script>
```

Once our data sources are available, we can use the OpenSocial data pipe JavaScript fetch function, getDataSet(), using the key defined for the data pipe to work with the information sources that we obtained:

```
var viewerSrc = opensocial.data.getContext().getDataSet('viewerData');
var viewerFriendSrc = opensocial.data.getContext().getDataSet('viewerFriends');
var viewerName = viewerSrc.name;
```

Using our gadget context in conjunction with the getDataSet function, we can pass in the key that we defined for our data sources to store the JSON return object from the requests; then, we can pull out the information we requested from the object.

Adding content to an existing data object

 The full code for this sample is available at *https://github.com/jcleblanc/ programming-social-applications/blob/master/chapter_7/pipeline_add _data.xml.*

Getting content from a set container data source is a great method for adding customizations and features geared toward a specific user or group of users. There may be times, though, when you want to take the initial set of data provided by the container and augment it based on another service's data source. The putDataSet() method helps you do just that. This method allows for a few parameters to be passed in and takes the following form:

```
os.data.getDataContext().putDataSet(key, json)
```

The parameters that can be passed in are:

key *(string)*
   The data pipe key where the new object should be inserted

json *(object)*
   The new JSON object to be inserted into the result set of the data pipe

Let's look at a practical example. Let's say you have a product store that you want to search based on the application user's interests to help you surface products that the user may like. We can start with a data pipe that captures the user's interests:

```
<script type="text/os-data" xmlns:os="http://ns.opensocial.org/2008/markup">
    <os:ViewerRequest key="viewerInterests" fields="interests"/>
</script>
```

This generates an array of strings listing all of the current application user's interests. If we were to then use those interests to query our product database, we could return a number of products based on those interests, giving us a new object structure:

```
var newData = {
    "product1": "http://www.mysite.com/product.php?id=123",
    "product2": "http://www.mysite.com/product.php?id=456",
    "product3": "http://www.mysite.com/product.php?id=789"
};
```

We can then store the new product JSON object that we created with the original viewer interests that were returned from our search:

```
os.data.getDataContext().putDataSet('viewerInterests', newData);
```

We call the `putDataSet` method, passing in the key `viewerInterests`, which is the same key we used for the original data pipe. We then pass through the JSON object as our second parameter.

Listening for changes to the data object

 The full code for this sample is available at *https://github.com/jcleblanc/ programming-social-applications/blob/master/chapter_7/pipeline_listen _data_changes.xml*.

If you have changes being made dynamically to a data pipe, you might need to integrate a check to perform an action within the gadget once the data set has changed.

The `registerListener()` method provides a way for developers to listen to changes to one, several, or all data pipes within the gadget. The method takes the following format:

```
os.data.getDataContext().registerListener(keys, callback(keys))
```

The parameters you can add to the method are:

keys *(string or array of strings)*
> The data pipe key that the listener should be attached to. This value may be either a string (for a single data pipe) or an array of strings (for multiple data pipes). Wildcards (*) may be used here to attach listeners to all data pipes in the current gadget context.

callback *(function reference)*
> The function to be called when the information in a data pipe has changed. The parameter passed through to the function is an array of strings including all keys whose data source has changed.

Looking at a practical example for this functionality, let's say that we have a data pipe that captures all of the user's profile information:

```
<script type="text/os-data" xmlns:os="http://ns.opensocial.org/2008/markup">
  <os:ViewerRequest key="viewerData" />
</script>
```

We then take this information in our gadget and display a form field for a new profile, prefilled with all of the user's social information we have just obtained. The user has the option to edit this information and resubmit it. If she submits changes to her profile, we call the putDataSet() method to add an amendment of the user's profile information. Once this change has been made, we want to be able to show the user that the new data has been added to her profile. This is where we can use a listener to trigger a user notification:

```
opensocial.data.getDataContext().registerListener('viewerData', function(keys){
  //get hidden div with a success message
  var successMsg = document.getElementById('Message');

  //display the success message
  successMsg.style.display = 'block';
});
```

Using these methods, we can create a full notification loop for the user: first, we provide her with an autogenerated profile that she can update and save; once she has saved her edits, we fire an event handler to alert her that the change has been made.

Handling Errors Produced by the Data Pipe

When using data pipelining, you may encounter instances when the container cannot provide the information the gadget requested. Errors can result if invalid data pipe requests are being made, if the container failed to generate the data, if the current permission level granted to the application by the user is insufficient, or for any number of other possible reasons. No matter what the event that triggered the error might be, the error state should be handled within the gadget.

Let's explore a practical example of an error case. Assume that we are trying to set up two data pipes—one to collect an external data source, and another to obtain the activities of the current viewer's friends:

```
<script type="text/os-data" xmlns:os="http://ns.opensocial.org/2008/markup">
  <os:ActivitiesRequest key="viewerActivities" userid="@viewer"
                        count="20" groupId="@friends" />
  <os:HttpRequest key="dataStore" href="http://www.mysite.com/storedData.php"
                  format="json" refreshInterval="500" />
</script>
```

If the application does not have permission to access the activities of the viewer's friends and our external server for the stored data is down, an error will result. There is a standard error response that should be sent within all containers to display an error message. In the case of our preceding example, a JSON object will contain both error responses (one for the standard error message and one for the down server):

```
{ viewerActivities: {
    error: {message: 'Server error', code: 500}
},
dataStore: {
    error: {message: 'Server error', code: 500}
}}
```

The error messages will differ depending on how we have set up the data sources for our gadget's Content sections, either as proxied or inline markup:

Proxied content
> The error message will be sent as POST parameters to the URL defined in the href attribute of the Content section.

Inline content
> If a portion of the data return contains an error, those errors will not be modified. If the entire request fails, the error will be cloned in each item, modifying the request object.

Dynamic Parameters

Dynamic parameters refer to the ability to build a data request's parameters based on the response structure of another request or on standard gadget view parameters or user preferences.

There are several cases where using dynamic parameters would be incredibly useful when you're making requests for data from the container or from an external source:

- If you are using variables passed from the container or into the view to control the type of information to be obtained
- If there were custom user preferences set during the program flow that need to be used to capture particular information from the source
- If the information used in the attributes of one data pipe request (e.g., os:DataRequest()) should be based upon the result set of another, earlier data pipe request (e.g., os:PeopleRequest())

Dynamic parameters may be applied to a number of attributes within the data pipe tags. Creating a data pipe from a DataRequest call allows the developer to include dynamic parameters in any attribute of the tag, with the exceptions of key and method. Other than a DataRequest call, dynamic parameters may be included in a number of alternate attributes for other calls, as shown in Table 7-6.

Table 7-6. Dynamic parameter attributes

Attribute	Request types implementing
activityIds	os:ActivitiesRequest
count	os:PeopleRequest, os:ActivitiesRequest
fields	os:PeopleRequest, os:ViewerRequest, os:OwnerRequest, os:ActivitiesRequest

Attribute	Request types implementing
filterBy	os:PeopleRequest
filterOp	os:PeopleRequest
filterValue	os:PeopleRequest
groupId	os:PeopleRequest, os:ActivitiesRequest
params	os:HttpRequest
sortBy	os:PeopleRequest
sortOrder	os:PeopleRequest
startIndex	os:PeopleRequest, os:ActivitiesRequest
userId	os:PeopleRequest, os:ActivitiesRequest

These attribute parameters can add an entirely new dimension of customization to a gadget—whether you are passing in social data as parameters to a data request in order to process customized solutions for particular users, or building paging attributes to obtain chunks of a larger data set.

When you're using dynamic parameters as the attribute values within a tag, you can combine them with other dynamic parameters, static text, or both. All mixed string values within an attribute will be concatenated when the attribute is evaluated.

Let's explore a few ways that you can use these types of dynamic data sets to affect the end result set for a gadget.

Using values from UserPrefs and ViewParams as attributes

Per the data pipelining specifications, UserPrefs and ViewParams are reserved keywords, meaning they're sets of data that are supplied to a gadget:

- ViewParams refers to any parameters that are passed in to the gadget rendering process. This object refers to the same data set that you would obtain by making a gadget data request to the gadgets.views.getParams() method.

- UserPrefs refers to the user preferences that are defined within a gadget and may include any number of stored data sets. Making a request to get a user preference by calling ${UserPrefs.PREF} will obtain the same data source as if you made a gadget data request to gadgets.Prefs.getString("PREF").

With these data sets so openly available to us, we can use ViewParams or UserPrefs to control data paging requests, counts, or any other control mechanisms we require:

```
<os:PeopleRequest key="viewerFriends"
                  userId="@viewer"
                  groupId="@friends"
                  startIndex="${ViewParams.nav.first}"
                  count="30"/>
```

In the preceding example, we control data paging based on the `ViewParams` that are passed in to the gadget. This allows us to capture subsets of the viewer's friends instead of making a larger data request for the results.

Using values from a data pipe as attributes

Besides injecting dynamic attribute values into your gadget based on data that is passed in to it, you may pass parameters through to data requests based on the result set of another request.

Let's assume that our previous request for viewer friends returned a data set containing the IDs of the individuals. We can use the results of that data pipe to alter the results of our new data pipe:

```
<os:HttpRequest href="http://www.mysite.com/process?ids=${viewerFriends.ids}"/>
```

Here, we make an external data request to our processing script at *http://www.mysite .com/process*, passing in a query parameter, `ids`. The value of `ids` is the result set returned by our previous request with the key of `viewerFriends`.

OpenSocial Templating

As you've seen in many of the OpenSocial gadgets in the earlier chapters, two of the most widely used and accepted approaches to developing the visualization layer within a gadget are to insert new content directly into the `innerHTML` of a DOM node, or to dynamically create new nodes and inject them into the DOM structure through the JavaScript layer. One major issue with these approaches is that you mix your markup and script layers, which makes the code base difficult to maintain, very hard to reuse, and unwieldy.

As we talked about in the section "Porting Applications from Facebook to OpenSocial" on page 134 in Chapter 5, one key to making a portable application is to separate visual markup from programming logic. In the traditional approaches to gadget development I just mentioned, markup and programming logic is *not* split. This means that application portability is a major concern, and you risk limiting the reach of your application within different containers.

OpenSocial templating provides a way for developers to create a UI that is driven by a data source, such as through data pipelining. This approach separates out programming logic from the markup layer, extending all of the benefits of portability that come with that separation. In addition, this approach gives you a code base that is easily maintainable, reusable, and that reduces code bloat with redundant functions and code blocks.

OpenSocial templates offer several features for defining a markup layer on top of a data object, further reducing the markup required to define the sections and functionality we need. These features include embeddable expressions, special variables, conditional content, special tag definitions, and a host of other tools.

Templates are not a replacement for JavaScript and do not provide the full range of functionality that you get from a JavaScript layer. For advanced functionality or user interaction, the gadget should still provide the JavaScript controller layer to handle the required features.

To integrate OpenSocial templating within your gadget, you must first include the `Require` node for the feature within the `ModulePrefs` of the gadget:

```
<ModulePrefs>
    <Require feature="opensocial-templates" />
</ModulePrefs>
```

Now you can use the template structure within the gadget `Content` sections. Creating a template in the content that leverages a data structure or pipe takes only a small amount of effort.

To specify an OpenSocial template within your markup, wrap the markup in a `script` block with a type of `text/os-template`. This indicates that the enclosed markup should be treated as a template block. Inside the block, we can place any markup we wish, adding data sources by using the format ${*source*}:

```
<script type="text/os-template">
  <img src="${Viewer.urls.address}" />
</script>
```

The data source reference used here, `Viewer.urls.address`, has a structure representative of the root JSON data that was returned for that source:

```
${Viewer.urls.address}
```

and renders down to the following JSON attribute:

```
Viewer["urls"]["address"]
```

Data pipelining requests or custom data objects are typically used within these blocks to make rich data sources available to the template.

The OpenSocial specification reserves several attributes for future use, including:

- `autoRender`
- `id`
- `name`

A Different Approach to Markup and Data

As we've just discussed, OpenSocial templating is a different approach for handling the visualization of data sources. Let's take a practical look at what this means. Let's assume that we have set up a data request that captures user profile information, and that source returns a JSON structure with the viewer's profile details:

```
var userData = {
    name: "John Smith",
    gender: "Male",
    thumbnailUrl: "http://www.johnsmith.com/img/profile.jpg",
    profileUrl: "http://www.container.com/johnsmith"
}
```

Now that we have a data source, we want to use it to build out a user badge. We have a few options for how we can do this, which we'll cover next.

Dynamically creating the DOM nodes

One approach that is used frequently within the context of gadget construction is to create any required DOM nodes dynamically within the JavaScript layer. This means that all styles, content, and node sources are built using the node property setters:

```html
<div id="profile"></div>
<script type="text/javascript">
var profileNode = document.getElementById("profile");

//build profile image
var imgThumb = document.createElement("img");
imgThumb.src = userData.thumbnailUrl;
imgThumb.setAttribute("style", "float:left; margin-right:10px;");
profileNode.appendChild(imgThumb);

//build profile content text node
var spanProfile = document.createElement("span");
spanProfile.innerHTML = "Name: " + userData.name + "<br />Gender: "
                        + userData.gender + "<br />Profile: ";
profileNode.appendChild(spanProfile);

//build profile link
var linkProfile = document.createElement("a");
linkProfile.href = userData.profileUrl;
linkProfile.innerText = "Click Here";
profileNode.appendChild(linkProfile);
</script>
```

 The full code for this sample is available at *https://github.com/jcleblanc/ programming-social-applications/blob/master/chapter_7/node_creation _dynamic.html*.

You probably noticed one issue immediately with this code: its bulk. For each newly created DOM node, we need individual calls to set all of its properties, such as `href`, styles, and any others we require.

On top of that, building out nodes dynamically this way does not lend itself to code reuse. Each line of code is set up to build out a specific element or property, so it becomes difficult to reuse whole sections of the code for other purposes.

Finally, this approach embeds the markup so tightly into the JavaScript functionality that it makes it hard to maintain the code and parse the relevant differences between each section. Just having a few nodes does not make for an extremely complicated code base, but let's say that we use this type of functionality extensively to build out several sections of our gadget. This leads to a bloated, complex code base that is very difficult to maintain and debug.

Building an InnerHTML string

Our next approach, and arguably one of the most popular ones, is to inject new DOM node markup into the gadget through a DOM node's innerHTML method. This method involves specifying a string that contains the markup that should be injected into the gadget, and then setting the innerHTML of another node currently on the page to the markup specified in that string:

```
<div id="profile"></div>
<script type="text/javascript">
//create html string
var profileHtml = "<img src='" + userData.thumbnailUrl + "' style='float:left; "
                + "margin-right:10px;' />Name: " + userData.name + "<br />Gender: "
                + "userData.gender<br />Profile: <a href='" + userData.profileUrl"
                + "'>Click Here</a>";

//insert html into profile node
document.getElementById("profile").innerHTML = profileHtml;
</script>
```

 The full code for this sample is available at *https://github.com/jcleblanc/programming-social-applications/blob/master/chapter_7/node_creation_innerhtml.html*.

While this approach is very simple to implement, we're once again embedding our markup layer directly into the JavaScript portion of the code. We can attempt to indent the markup structure to make it easier to maintain, but once we start applying content load conditionals—wrapping the content into individual blocks—the scripts become bloated and difficult to parse and debug.

The OpenSocial templating approach

The OpenSocial templating approach seeks to remove the necessity of embedding markup within JavaScript by providing some simple methods for creating markup with template syntax instead:

```
<script type="text/os-template">
  <img src="${userData.thumbnailUrl}" style="float:left; margin-left:10px;" />
  Name: ${userData.name}<br />
  Gender: ${userData.gender}<br />
```

```
        Profile: <a href="${userData.profileUrl}">Click Here</a>
    </script>
```

 The full code for this sample is available at *https://github.com/jcleblanc/ programming-social-applications/blob/master/chapter_7/node_creation _os_templating.xml.*

Here we have a specialized script block that tells the OpenSocial container that this markup should be treated as a template. The markup is not mixed with any JavaScript constructs, so it's easier to maintain because it is visually one complete structure. This templating approach provides us with a much cleaner way to work with our data, markup, and script layers by separating them out into their logical pieces.

Rendering Templates

OpenSocial templates can be rendered in two ways:

- Automatic rendering of the template on gadget load
- Rendering the template via the JavaScript API

The first method listed, automatic rendering of the template, is the more widely accepted. Containers may disable the use of the JavaScript API for rendering templates on one, more, or all of their available views if they so choose. If this is the case, then only the automatic rendering method will be available. Despite this possibility, we'll look at the implementation requirements for both types of template rendering. We'll explore the concepts behind automatic rendering of templates next, and we'll discuss using the template JavaScript API to work with and control templates via JavaScript methods later in the chapter, in the section "JavaScript API" on page 244.

Automatic rendering

Template markup placed within a `script` block with the type set to `text/os-template` is automatically rendered when the gadget loads. Should you want to prevent template blocks from automatically rendering, you can set a `Param` node within the `Require` element for the `opensocial-templates` feature to be disabled, as follows:

```
<Require feature="opensocial-templates">
    <Param name="disableAutoProcessing">true</Param>
</Require>
```

By default, the template markup will be inserted into the gadget in the location where the `script` block is placed within the gadget.

Should we want to embed a template within our existing HTML markup to display a welcome message to the current viewer, we can set up a template to pull the name from a data pipe with the key of `Viewer`:

```
<div>
   <script type="text/os-template">
      Hello ${Viewer.name}!
   </script>
</div>
```

Once the gadget loads, the template will render down to the request data and markup:

```
<div>
   Hello Mary!
</div>
```

You can obtain data sources for templates from several different places in the gadget. For instance, you can create a data pipe that will make itself available to the root data context for the gadget, or you can use the JavaScript API `opensocial.data.DataContext.putDataSet()` method within the data pipelining section of the specification.

Ensuring that data is available for a template prior to loading. When working with templates, you may have times when you want to initialize a template only if certain data sets are available for it to process. Templates have an attribute available to them for exactly this use case: `require`.

The `require` attribute accepts a string of comma-separated keys that refer to their associated data sets, generated through sources like data pipes. If any of the required data sets are not available, the template rendering process will be deferred until a time when they are all available:

```
<script type="text/os-template" require="Viewer, Ratings">
   Welcome ${Viewer.name}<br />
   You most recently rated ${Ratings.last.title} with a rating
   of ${Ratings.last.rating}
</script>
```

In the preceding example, we require the data objects with keys set to `Viewer` and `Ratings` to be available before the template is rendered.

Rerendering templates with updated data sources. As we have already covered in our discussion of data pipelining, data pipes may be updated with the `opensocial.data.DataContext.putDataSet(...)` JavaScript method. This means that our core data can change at a whim, but we have not yet explored a method for updating the templates that implement that data.

Templates can be set to automatically update when a data source they are implementing changes. This provides wonderful functionality, because it means that we don't have to manually update the HTML nodes when we need to update a piece of the data.

To activate the auto-update functionality, we add a new attribute, `autoUpdate`, to our template script block and set its value to `true`. Now, when the data pipes implemented in the template are updated via the `opensocial.data.DataContext.putDataSet(...)` method, our template will automatically rerender its content based on the new data set:

```
<script type="text/os-template" require="Viewer" autoUpdate="true">
   Hello ${Viewer.name}!
```

```
    </script>

    <p>Welcome to our site</p>

    <script type="text/javascript">
        //update the viewer object
        function updateViewer(viewerObj) {
            opensocial.data.DataContext.putDataSet("Viewer", viewerObj);
        }
    </script>
```

In the preceding example, a greeting will be displayed to the current viewer. When the `Viewer` data pipe is updated via the `updateViewer` function, the template will be rendered and its markup updated. Any markup outside the template's bounds—in this case, `<p>Welcome to our site</p>`—will not be updated.

Rendering data using custom tags. Template structures provide a number of features and functionality to reduce code bloat, promote usability, and enable code reuse. At the same time, embedding all content within a single template block is not always the most ideal setup for debugging code structure.

Within a template, developers can add XML references to include custom tags. These custom tags give the developer a way to define blocks of markup and functionality— such as button sets, template structures, message functions, and many other features—that can be reused easily within other sections of the template. This provides a clean working interface for the code, allowing for quicker development with a focus on modularity.

You can implement a custom tag quickly using a few features. The custom tag's look and feel is similar to the standard development of other OpenSocial templates:

```
<script type="text/os-template"
        tag="app:login"
        xmlns:app="http://www.mysite.com/app">
    <form action="login.php" method="post">
        <p>
            <label for="username">Username:</label>
            <input type="text" name="username" />
        </p>
        <p>
            <label for="password">Password</label>
            <input type="hidden" name="password" /><br />
        </p>
        <p>
            <input type="submit" value="Login" />
            <input type="reset" value="Reset" />
        </p>
    </form>
</script>
```

The main difference in this implementation is the `tag` attribute attached to the `script` node, which indicates that the block of markup following it will be created and used as a custom tag. In the preceding example, we create a `login` tag to allow us to display a username/password login at any point in our application.

Custom tags must be implemented within a namespace. In addition to the preceding method, which contains a custom URL for the `app` namespace, you can create these namespaces using the following syntax:

```
os.createNamespace("app", "http://www.mysite.com/app");
```

Creating custom tags in the default HTML namespace is not allowed, so you must employ one of the two implementations I've described.

When you wish to incorporate the custom tag in your template markup, you can simply include the XML node of the same name as the custom tag namespace:

```
<script type="text/os-template">
  <app:login/>
</script>
```

Passing parameters through custom tags. In addition to containing blocks of HTML, custom tags also support parameter structures within their definition. This helps in allowing code to be reused at different places within a gadget. These parameters are passed back through to the template being used and can be set up as XML attributes or elements to leverage the stored data sets:

```
<script type="text/os-template">
  <app:preferences name="Lucas Bell">
    <template theme="dark" />
    <template language="EN" />
  </app:preferences>
</script>
```

We can set access to this stored data within our visual template:

```
<script type="text/os-template"
        xmlns:app="http://www.mysite.com/app"
        tag="app:preferences">
  <div id="themeWrap" class="${My.template.theme}">
    Theme preferences for: ${My.name}<br />
    Language Requested: ${My.template.language}
  </div>
</script>
```

Much like creating custom tags to reuse markup throughout your application sections, here you create custom tags to reuse stored data sets throughout the template building process. This is also an excellent way to separate data and visualization layers, promoting debugging ease and code readability.

Expressions

In the context of OpenSocial templates, *expression* refers to an evaluation of some data source that is embedded directly into a markup structure.

Expressions can be rendered in a template using a simple syntax:

```
${Expression}
```

Expressions may be embedded inside text nodes and attributes, but will not be honored by an implementing container if they are inside custom tags and attribute names—a subject we will explore later in this chapter.

In addition to basic data rendering, most standard arithmetic expressions and data comparison features can be applied to expressions:

```
Next Index: ${Index + 1}
```

The functionality of these expressions is based on a modified version of the JSP expression language. Even though there are definitions for these arithmetic and comparison features, some operators use an XML escaped alternative for comparisons, such as when implementing OpenSocial template os:If statements. These escaped versions are listed in Table 7-7.

Table 7-7. Escaped versions of comparison operators

Conditional	Escaped string	Description
<	lt	Less than
>	gt	Greater than
<=	lte	Less than or equal to
>=	gte	Greater than or equal to
&&	and	And
==	eq	Equals
!=	neq	Not equals
||	or	Or
!	not	Not

By default, expressions are evaluated as escaped strings before they are inserted into the HTML document. Expressions are the basis for the majority of what we do with OpenSocial templates, so it's crucial that you have a basic understanding of them.

Special Variables

OpenSocial has a set of reserved special variables for working with template data objects and processing the template. These variables—Context, Cur, My, and Top—each have different groups of data that they can access and a different order of precedence during loading. With the exception of ${Context}, special variables are not required when you're referencing data. Since the variables are not required, expressions will be evaluated against the *available* special variables using the following precedence load order:

1. ${Cur}

2. ${My}

3. ${Top}

Context

The ${Context} variable contains additional information—relating to currently processed data objects and identifiers for the template—that is used during the processing of the current template. This information provides context for the data that is being processed or rendered.

${Context} contains three variables:

Count
> The total number of results available in the current data object being processed within a repeater structure. This alters the flow of a repeater element based on the total number of results.
>
> Use: ${Context.Count}

Index
> The current numeric index being processed within a repeater structure. Much like the Count variable, Index allows you to alter the flow of the loop based on the current object index processed.
>
> Use: ${Context.Index}

UniqueId
> Provides a unique identifier for the current template. This value can be used to generate custom IDs for DOM nodes in the template markup.
>
> Use: ${Context.UniqueId}

Cur

The ${Cur} variable refers to the current data object being processed in the OpenSocial templating process. One of its main uses is to refer to the current item being iterated over during a loop through a data structure with repeating sources.

```
<div repeat="${userData.profile}">
  <img src="${Cur.image.thumbnailUrl}" alt="Profile Photo" />
  Name: ${Cur.name}<br />
</div>
```

When you're working with multiple data objects or large amounts of data, ${Cur} is a handy variable to use to maintain context with the currently processed object. You can also use this approach to promote code reuse if you'll be processing multiple objects with a similar structure.

Explicitly setting the source of cur. Should you wish to set the scope of the data to which ${Cur} maps, you can set that value explicitly using the cur attribute.

For instance, if we have the application owner's friends stored in a data object, `owner`
`Friends`, we can set `${Cur}` to reference a particular friend, and then we can use that to
iterate through the URLs associated with the user.

```
<div cur="${ownerFriends[2]}">
    User Website Associations for ${Cur.name}:
    <ul>
        <li repeat="${Cur.urls}">
            <b>${Cur.linkText}:</b> ${Cur.address}
        </li>
    </ul>
</div>
```

This code will display the URLs for the owner's third friend.

My

`${My}` allows developers to access data objects that are passed in to the template by
using a custom tag on the OpenSocial template `script` block.

```
<script type="text/os-template"
        xmlns:app="http://www.mysite.com"
        tag="app:userProfile">
```

The `${My}` variable will be available only within `script` blocks that are invoked using
these custom tags. When you use a data object via `${My}`, the template will first check
for the object reference within the data that is passed through via the tag. If it can't find
the object, the template will then look for an element with the same key name.

```
<script type="text/os-template" xmlns:app="http://www.mysite.com"
        tag="app:userQuestionnaire">
    User: ${My.user.name}<br />
    Question 1: ${My.questions.q1.title}<br />
    Answer: ${My.questions.q1.response}
</script>
```

This variable provides an additional way to access groups of data structures within a
template. If any of these data references were not available within the custom tag, the
template would search for the data in the main objects.

Top

`${Top}` is a variable that provides references to all of the data available within the current
template, accessible by the data source key. This reference variable makes it easy to
mash up data sources, compare objects, and perform a number of other functions.

```
<div If="${Top.Viewer.name == 'John Smith'}">
    Hello ${Top.Viewer.name}! This is a personal message for you.
</div>
```

Conditionals

Using *conditional statements*, a developer can create portions of the template markup that will be displayed only if certain criteria are met. These statements are valuable for creating content targeted to a specific user base and can be used to build out a scalable, engaging template system within the application.

Conditional statements are evaluated as Boolean values, meaning that null or empty strings will be evaluated as false and content within the node will not be rendered. In addition, conditionals may be applied to any variable or node within an OpenSocial template, with the exception of the os:If and os:Repeat variables.

There are two methods for defining a conditional statement within an OpenSocial template. In this example, let's assume that we are starting with a data pipe that contains some user-based rating information about a series of movies.

```
movies: [
    {
        title: "The Social Network",
        release: "October 1, 2010",
        rating: 5
    },
    {
        title: "Dinner For Schmucks",
        release: "July 30, 2010",
        rating: 2.5
    },
    {
        title: "Alone in the Dark",
        release: "January 28, 2010",
        rating: 1
    }
];
```

Using this as our base, next we'll explore how to create conditional statements to generate markup for the movies, with optional content sections for good or bad movies.

Method 1: Escaped values

The first method is to build a conditional structure where the data values within the block are output as escaped strings. This means that if the data value is:

```
<b><i>Text</i></b>
```

then the output of the data tag will also be:

```
<b><i>Text</i></b>
```

instead of:

> ***Text***

In other words, rather than having the text rendered with the bold and italics applied to it, we want to just display the string representation of the markup.

Using this method, we can easily add a conditional to any DOM node in our template markup. For instance, let's assume we have a loop structure set up to iterate through each movie object. Within each loop, the movie information for the current object is displayed; but if the movie receives either a high or low rating, a message appears, recommending that users see the movie or steering them away from it, respectively. The content of each loop in the template would look something like the following:

```
<div if="${Cur.rating == 1}">
    ${Cur.title} received a rating of 1 out of 5 stars and is most
    likely a poor movie to see.
</div>
<div if="${Cur.rating == 5}">
    ${Cur.title} received a rating of 5 out of 5 stars and would
    be a great movie to see.
</div>
<div>
    <b>Movie Title:</b> ${Cur.title}<br />
    <b>Release Date: </b> ${Cur.release}<br />
    <b>Rating: </b> ${Cur.rating}/5 stars
</div>
```

The preceding example has two div sections with if attributes applied to them. These attributes allow us to specify the conditions under which the div and its content will be loaded. In this case, we are checking to see if the rating of the current movie object is a 5 (good movie) or a 1 (bad movie) and providing the corresponding feedback to the user in each case.

Method 2: Nonescaped values

The second method is to encase the markup inside a conditional statement block using os:If. This will output any data values rendered within the block as nonescaped strings, so the markup values within the content will be maintained.

We can easily adjust our example from the first method to fit the new block style of the os:If variable:

```
<os:If condition="${Cur.rating == 1}">
    <div>
        ${Cur.title} received a rating of 1 out of 5 stars and is most
        likely a poor movie to see.
    </div>
</os:If>
<os:If condition="${Cur.rating == 5}">
    <div>
        ${Cur.title} received a rating of 5 out of 5 stars and would
        be a great movie to see.
    </div>
</os:If>
<div>
    <b>Movie Title:</b> ${Cur.title}<br />
    <b>Release Date: </b> ${Cur.release}<br />
    <b>Rating: </b> ${Cur.rating}/5 stars
</div>
```

The main difference from the first method is that the `os:If` variables are elements on their own, as opposed to being embedded in a DOM node in the template. In addition, the use of `if` or `repeat` attributes within the `os:If` variable is not supported.

Rendering content on the existence of a value

As we've seen in the previous examples, using conditionals can be an excellent way to display content if some sort of criteria returns true, but what if you simply want to check for the existence of an object? To accomplish this, we can specify the variable reference as the condition to be checked:

```
<os:If condition="${Cur.title}">
    <b>Movie Title:</b> ${Cur.title}<br />
    <b>Release Date: </b> ${Cur.release}<br />
    <b>Rating: </b> ${Cur.rating}/5 stars
</os:If>
```

In this instance, the movie information will be displayed only if the title for the currently iterated object is available. If `null` or a blank string is returned, the condition will evaluate to `false`.

Looping Content

When you're working with large quantities of user social data, one question naturally arises in the context of OpenSocial templating: how do you handle repeating content, such as a list of friends or any measure of activity data? We certainly won't be creating a markup definition for each repeating node in the template, will we? The short answer is no.

Content looping in OpenSocial allows a developer to define a block of markup to be used to render a series of repeating elements, without having to resort to handling each repeating node as a separate instance of markup. There are a few ways to define a loop structure within an OpenSocial template specification, which we'll go over next.

Method 1: Escaped values

The first method is to build a loop structure that outputs the value of a piece of data as an escaped string, much like we saw with conditional statements. Let's say that we have a customized subset of activity data that is returned to us through a data pipe request:

```
activities: [
    {
        title: "Jonathan just added a new comment on Twitter",
        body: "See what Jonathan is saying by adding him to Twitter",
        url: "http://www.twitter.com/jcleblanc"
    },
    {
        title: "Michael updated his profile",
        body: "See more about what Michael is doing",
```

```
        url: "http://www.container.com/profiles/michael"
    },
    {
        title: "Diane just posted a comment on your wall",
        body: "Reply to Diane's message",
        url: "http://www.container.com/messages"
    }
];
```

This content structure has several repeating nodes within the object that we can use to build out a complimentary repeating block within an OpenSocial template:

```
<script type="text/os-template">
    <ul>
        <li repeat="${activities}">
            <a href="${Cur.url}">
                ${Cur.title}
            </a><br />
            ${Cur.body}
        </li>
    </ul>
</script>
```

We wrap our template content in our `script` block with the specialized type definition to start out the template declaration. The markup within the `script` block first defines an unordered list to display the activities. Instead of defining a list item for each element, we simply define a single `<li>` that contains the repeat declaration:

```
<li repeat="${activities}">
```

Here we've stated that this element and its content should be repeated based on the objects contained within `activities`, which we defined earlier. Within the repeated element, we can easily refer to the current object being exposed in the loop by using a provided reference variable:

```
${Cur.title}
```

`${Cur}` allows us to refer to the current object in the loop in question. In this way, we can create an entire markup construct with a smaller code base than we would by defining straight markup. Given the preceding loop, the application would render the complete markup structure for all repeated objects that we iterated over:

```
<ul>
    <li>
        <a href="http://www.twitter.com/jcleblanc">
            Jonathan just added a new comment on Twitter
        </a><br />
        See what Jonathan is saying by adding him to Twitter
    </li>
    <li>
        <a href="http://www.container.com/profiles/michael">
            Michael updated his profile
        </a><br />
        See more about what Michael is doing
    </li>
```

```
<li>
    <a href="http://www.container.com/messages">
        Diane just posted a comment on your wall
    </a><br />
    Reply to Diane's message
</li>
</ul>
```

Method 2: Nonescaped values

The alternate method for looping within an OpenSocial template is to use the `os:Repeat` tag. This will instruct the template to render any code within the data objects being displayed as actual markup—not just the string representations of the markup.

The looping structure is essentially the same as the previous example, but instead of applying a `repeat` attribute to the block of markup to be repeated, we wrap the entire block in the `os:Repeat` tag. If we modify our previous example, the repeat tag would look like:

```
<script type="text/os-template">
    <ul>
        <os:Repeat expression="${activities}">
            <li>
                <a href="${Cur.url}">
                    ${Cur.title}
                </a><br />
                ${Cur.body}
            </li>
        </os:Repeat>
    </ul>
</script>
```

This produces the same results as the previous example. In addition to the standard repeat syntax, you can use the `var` attribute to assign a different variable name to the repeater:

```
<os:Repeat expression="${activities}" var="myActivities">
    <li>
        <a href="${myActivities.url}">
            ${myActivities.title}
        </a><br />
        ${myActivities.body}
    </li>
</os:Repeat>
```

Working with nested repeaters

When working with repeaters, you may need to nest multiple loop structures together to get the desired visual results. But nesting repeaters has its own challenges when it comes to accessing the current result object in the loop using `${Cur}`.

Variable naming is an excellent method for obtaining the desired object data if you're using nested repeaters. It allows you to access the current object of the current or parent loop (if the parent is subsequently named). When you specify a var attribute, the object being iterated over will be stored in the variable name (e.g., ${MyActivities}) as well as within ${Cur}.

For instance, let's assume that we have the same activity data within the activities object for each one of the user's friends, stored in the variable friends. Our friend data object contains the name of the friend and an association to the activity data. We may want to display an unordered list of activities for each friend, using multiple repeaters:

```
<div repeat="${friends}" var="myFriends">
   <b>Activities for ${myFriends.name}</b>
   <div repeat="${activities}" var="myActivities">
      <a href="${myActivities.url}">
         ${myActivities.title}
      </a><br />
      ${myActivities.body}
   </div>
</div>
```

Using var names, not only can we ensure that we are accessing the exact data that we want, but we also keep our template code readable so that when we're working with it later, we can follow the object references more easily than if we'd used ${Cur} throughout.

Specifying an index variable for the repeater

Using the ${Context} special variable is handy for capturing the index of the current object being iterated over, but what if you are working with nested repeaters and want to access the indices for both loops within the inner loops? Support for this type of functionality is valuable if you are working with a grid interface for your application, separating loops into x and y planes.

This type of problem is exactly what custom indices attempt to solve. Using the index attribute on a repeater will allow you to access that variable at any point within the loop structure:

```
<div repeat="${xplane}" index="x">
   <div repeat="${yplane}" index="y">
      <span id="${x}_${y}">
         Current grid index is ${x} : ${y}
      </span>
   </div>
</div>
```

We apply CSS styles to build a visual grid of our divs. Using the index values, we can then keep track of which grid section we are currently in. These indices can be applied to the id attributes of the divs, for instance, to give us tracking capabilities.

Looping with context

During the course of a loop, you may need to use or collect the current index of, or the total number of results available within, the looped object. This is the purpose of the special variable ${Context}. As we discussed earlier, ${Context} contains three reference objects you can use within the context of a loop:

UniqueId
> A unique identifier for the current template being processed

Index
> The index number of the current object being iterated over

Count
> The total number of objects to be iterated over

Using this special variable, you can add another dimension to the markup to be generated from the loop:

```
<ul>
    <li repeat="${activities}">
        Activity ${Context.Index + 1} of ${Context.Count}<br />
        <a href="${Cur.url}">
            ${Cur.title}
        </a><br />
        <div id="${Context.UniqueId}-${Context.Index}">${Cur.body}</div>
    </li>
</ul>
```

In the preceding template, we apply the ${Context} variable to the existing template markup that we built earlier. When this result renders, the user will be presented with markup containing the current index number (e.g., Activity 1 of 10) above every activity that is generated:

```
<ul>
    <li>
        Activity 1 of 3
        <a href="http://www.twitter.com/jcleblanc">
            Jonathan just added a new comment on Twitter
        </a>
        <div id="tpl1234-1">
            See what Jonathan is saying by adding him to Twitter
        </div>
    </li>
    <li>
        ...
```

Looping with conditionals

One of the best methods for customizing a loop structure is to apply conditional statements to the loop itself, specifying that you want the loop to run only if a specific condition has been met. Repeaters will be evaluated before conditionals, meaning that when a conditional is used within a repeater, the conditional will be applied to each result within the repeating data set, much like running a standard loop with an `if` statement embedded:

```
for (var i = 0; i < result.length; i++){
    if (result[i] === "value"){
        //render markup
    }
}
```

Our first method, using the `repeat` attribute on the block to be repeated, applies the conditional statement directly within the same node:

```
<li repeat="${activities}" if="${Cur.url == 'http://www.container.com/messages'">
    <a href="${Cur.url}">
        ${Cur.title}
    </a><br />
    ${Cur.body}
</li>
```

This would render the markup only for any object whose URL is *http://www.container .com/messages*.

If we want to use this same type of conditional loop on an `os:Repeat` tag, we have to implement it in a slightly different manner. `os:Repeat` does not support `repeat` or `if` attributes, so we will need to embed them within the repeater block:

```
<os:Repeat expression="${activities}">
    <os:If condition="${Cur.url == 'http://www.container.com/messages'">
        <li>
            <a href="${Cur.url}">
                ${Cur.title}
            </a><br />
            ${Cur.body}
        </li>
    </os:If>
</os:Repeat>
```

These two statements are equivalent in the order of their execution. Using this mix of repeaters and conditionals, developers can build scalable template designs suited to their application needs.

Marrying Data Pipelining and Templating

 The full code for this sample is available at *https://github.com/jcleblanc/ programming-social-applications/blob/master/chapter_7/pipeline_with _templating.xml*.

We've explored the vast potential and power in both data pipelining and templates, which integrate rich data sets and visualization templates, respectively, into a gadget.

Alone, each feature is a wonderful addition to any gadget, but their power really lies in being married into one cohesive unit.

Let's take a look at an example of how we can merge these two technologies together to build out a data set based on the result set of an external data source. In this example, we want to scrape the main page of *http://www.reddit.com* to capture its top headlines. Using this data source, we want to display all links within our gadget.

Our first task is to build out the `ModulePrefs` section of our OpenSocial gadget, integrating all data pipelining and templating requirements:

```
<?xml version="1.0" encoding="utf-8"?>
<Module>
    <ModulePrefs title="Reddit Headline Fetch"
                 title_url="http://www.jcleblanc.com"
                 description="Obtains reddit.com headlines via YQL using data
                             pipelining and visualizes using OS templates"
                 author="Jonathan LeBlanc">
        <Require feature="opensocial-0.9"/>
        <Require feature="opensocial-data" />
        <Require feature="opensocial-templates" />
    </ModulePrefs>
```

Within the `ModulePrefs` node, we need to set up the `Require` elements for the features that we will need in our gadget. For this use case, we need to implement at least Open-Social version 0.9 (`opensocial-0.9`) as well as the OpenSocial data (`opensocial-data`) and OpenSocial templates (`opensocial-templates`) features.

The next section, where we actually use these features, is our `Content` section. This is where we make an external data request to scrape *http://www.reddit.com* and loop through all headlines to display them in the gadget:

```
<Content type="html">
    <![CDATA[
    <script type="text/os-data"
            xmlns:os="http://ns.opensocial.org/2008/markup">
        <os:HttpRequest key="reddit" href="http://query.yahooapis.com/v1/public/
            yql?q=select%20*%20from%20html%20where%20url%3D%22http%3A%2F%2F
            www.reddit.com%22%20and%0A%20%20%20%20%20xpath%3D'%2F%2Fa%5B
            %40class%3D%22title%22%5D'&format=json"/>
    </script>
    <script type="text/os-template" require="reddit">
        <ul>
            <li repeat="${reddit.content.query.results.a}">
                <a href="${Cur.href}">${Cur.content}</a>
            </li>
        </ul>
    </script>
    ]]>
</Content>
</Module>
```

The first `script` block in our `Content` section is the data pipelining feature. Within the data pipe, we make an `os:HttpRequest` to get an external data source and set the key for the return data to reddit. The href source of our data is an HTML page-scrape query using the Yahoo! Query Language (YQL). This query obtains the HTML from *http://www.reddit.com*, drills down to the headlines using an XPath string, and returns all headline results as a JSON object.

Once the data returns, the reddit variable should comprise an array of anchor objects. This data source will look something like the following:

```
"a": [
    {
        "class": "title",
        "href": "http://www.youtube.com/watch?v=Lk3ibIGKTYA",
        "rel": "nofollow",
        "content": "\"Your\ncar has a broken headlight and, oh no, pack of wolves
                coming down\nthe road\""
    },
    {
        "class": "title",
        "href": "http://imgur.com/6DfnY.png",
        "content": "I'm not sure which system\nthis is referring to [PIC]"
    },
    ...
```

We then define a second script block for our template, requiring our reddit variable in order to render the template. Our markup sets up an unordered list and then repeats the <li> tags for each anchor tag returned in our result set. Each <li> will then contain an anchor tag pointing to the headline URL and display the text of the headline for the link.

With just a minimal amount of effort, we have laid the foundation for a gadget that is based on a dynamic list of data, providing users with new results each time they visit the gadget. In doing so, we are building our gadget to update its content without us ever having to lift a finger after the initial construction is complete.

Other Special Tags

In addition to the special tags we have already seen, os:Repeat and os:If, OpenSocial templates define a couple of reserved tags to enable developers to display data objects that are richer than simple strings. These special tags are os:Html and os:Render.

os:Html

When rendering data within escaped expressions or loops (i.e., not os:Repeat or os:If blocks), developers run into the issue that because all data is displayed as strings, they're prevented from using a lot of rich data sets. When you're using third-party data sources that are not necessarily trusted, this practice is a good option for sanitizing content. When a part of the source data *is* trusted, however, we need a means of rendering that data with the markup intact. This is where the os:Html tag comes in handy.

`os:Html` provides a means for a developer to render a block of data without having it automatically escaped and displayed as a string. The markup is rendered intact and applied to the template.

You use `os:Html` through the `code` attribute of the tag. Any data values within the `code` attribute are evaluated as a string and then rendered as HTML. For instance, if you have an object containing the viewer's friends, and in that object you also have a name and a badge that contains HTML, you can easily render the badge HTML using the `os:Html` tag as follows:

```
<div repeat="${Top.ViewerFriends}">
    Name: ${Cur.name}<br />
    Badge:<br />
    <os:Html code="${Cur.badge}" />
</div>
```

Once rendered, `name` will be displayed as an escaped string and `badge` will be displayed as markup.

os:Render

When working with custom tags containing reusable blocks of content, you may need to render that content within the template markup. You can do this using the `os:Render` tag.

`os:Render` allows you to define a location from which to pull the custom block of content using the `content` attribute of the tag. The value of the `content` attribute in this case should be an immediate child of an `os-template` block.

For example, let's say we are building an application that has multiple page structures but maintains a universal header and footer. We can use the `os:Render` tag to specify the sections where we want to integrate this content:

```
<script type="text/os-template"
        tag="app:pageTemplate"
        xmlns:os="http://opensocial.org/templates"
        xmlns:pageTemplate ="http://www.mysite.com/app">
    <div class="header"><os:Render content="header"/></div>
    This is the content of my current page, using a universal
    header and footer
    <div class="footer"><os:Render content="footer"/></div>
</script>
```

Within an `os-template` `script` block, we define the XML namespaces that will be used, and then insert the `tag` attribute to refer to the custom tag that we will use to define the header and footer. We then implement the content of our template. At the beginning and end of the content block, we have two `div` nodes. These nodes contain our `os:Render` tags, which specify the node that will need to be inserted into that section.

In an alternate `script` block, we can define the custom tag nodes that will be used for the content of the header and footer sections:

```
<script type="text/os-template"
        xmlns:app="http://www.mysite.com/app"
    <app:pageTemplate>
      <app:header>
        <div id="navItems">
            <a href="/home">Home</a> |
            <a href="/profile">Profile</a> |
            <a href="/tasks">Tasks</a>
        </div>
      </app:header>
      <app:footer>
        <div id="copyright">
            Copyright &copy; 2011
        </div>
      </app:footer>
    </app:pageTemplate>
</script>
```

Our `script` block defines the XML namespace that we will use for the custom tags, and then defines the custom tag that should be used for these values, `app:pageTemplate`. Within `app:pageTemplate`, we specify our header and footer nodes with their associated content, which is what will be inserted via the `os:Render` tags. If there were multiple child nodes with the same name (e.g., two header nodes), the results of both nodes would be merged and returned as one block.

When rendered, the template will generate the following markup:

```
<div class="header">
    <div id="navItems">
        <a href="/home">Home</a> |
        <a href="/profile">Profile</a> |
        <a href="/tasks">Tasks</a>
    </div>
</div>
    This is the content of my current page, using a universal
    header and footer
<div class="footer">
    <div id="copyright">
        Copyright &copy; 2011
    </div>
</div>
```

Using `os:Render` and custom tags can help increase code reuse, general usability, and ease of debugging. When you're building out a large-scale application, tags like these can vastly reduce the amount of time spent on development and on repairing bugs.

Template Libraries

Creating inline markup within an OpenSocial template can be an excellent option for small-scale applications, where developing simple tags may help provide some measure of reusability in the code base. Even though this is a fine approach, as the application logic increases in complexity and you create more and more custom tags, you may need to separate out a gadget's reusable logic even further. *Template libraries* can help you do this.

Template libraries are standalone XML files that provide a gadget with functionality such as:

- Global JavaScript functions
- Global styles
- Simple custom tags with simple markup
- Complex custom tags with markup, local CSS, and local JavaScript

Template libraries provide a central location for global JavaScript, CSS, and tags that may be reused throughout the program flow. Using them can help to reduce code bloat, make the gadget easier to work with, and make debugging easier.

Creating a template library

A template library is a standalone XML file containing a number of sections that you can use to define fully enclosed custom tags or global functionality for the gadget. The XML template file follows a standardized template syntax with a number of potential sections and functions:

```
<Templates xmlns:temp="http://www.mysite.com/temp">
  <Namespace prefix="temp" url="http://www.mysite.com/temp"/>

  <Style>
    <!-- global library styles -->
    .inlineText { font:11px arial,helvetica,sans-serif;
                  color:#c0c0c0; }
  </Style>

  <JavaScript>
    <!-- global library functions -->
    function makeRequest(url){
      //make cross-domain request
    };
  </JavaScript>

  <!-- simple declarative tag temp:customTag -->
  <Template tag="temp:footerTag">
    <!-- markup for temp:footerTag -->
    <div class="footer">Copyright &copy; 2011</div>
  </Template>

  <!-- complex tag temp:headerTag with local CSS and JavaScript -->
  <TemplateDef tag="temp:headerTag">
    <Template>
      <!-- markup for temp:headerTag -->
      <div class="header">
        <a href="/home">Home</a>
      </div>
    </Template>
```

```
    <Style>
       <!-- local CSS styles for temp:headerTag -->
       .error{ color:#d41a1a;
               font-weight:bold; }
    </Style>
    <JavaScript>
       <!-- local JavaScript functions for temp:headerTag -->
       function processTemplateData(){
          //javascript to process template data
       };
    </JavaScript>
  </TemplateDef>
</Templates>
```

The root node of the template, `Templates`, defines all of the namespaces that will be used in the template file, including those for all custom tags. Your namespaces should take the form of `xmlns:`*`prefix=`*`"`*`namespace url`*`"`. For instance, should we need to integrate any OpenSocial tags under the `os` namespace, we would include `xmlns:os="http://www.opensocial.org/"` here.

We then have to add in a `Namespace` node to declare the custom namespace for the OpenSocial Templates API. Only one namespace should be defined for each library file. The `Namespace` node includes two attributes: the prefix of the namespace and its associated URL.

Our next two node sections are `Style` and `JavaScript`. These sections define global CSS styles and JavaScript functions that will be made available anywhere the template is used.

The `Template` node defines a simple custom tag that may be used within a template. This node will contain simple, reusable markup.

The `TemplateDef` node is a more complex version of the `Template` node. A `Template Def` node may contain its own `Template` node to define the markup to be used by the tag, local styles to be made available to the custom tag through the `Style` node, and local JavaScript to be made available to the custom tag through the `JavaScript` node.

Let's look at a practical example that puts these features to good use. Say we want to define a template structure for our application within the template file definition. This would provide us with all of the custom tags, functions, and styles that we need to maintain a reusable header and footer in our application:

```
<Templates xmlns:temp="http://www.mysite.com/template">
  <Namespace prefix="template" url="http://www.mysite.com/template"/>

  <Style>
     .nodeSpacer{ margin:10px 0;
                  padding:5px; }
     .textSmall{ font-size:9px; }
  </Style>

  <JavaScript>
     //swap the visibility of one page
```

```
            function switchNode(activate, deactivate){
                //get page nodes to swap
                var showNode = document.getElementById(activate);
                var hideNode = document.getElementById(deactivate);

                //switch the display properties of the two pages
                hideNode.style.display = "none";
                showNode.style.display = "block";
            };
        </JavaScript>

        <Template tag="template:footer">
            <div id="footer" class="nodeSpacer textSmall">
                Copyright &copy; 2011
            </div>
        </Template>

        <TemplateDef tag="template:header">
            <Template>
                <div id="header" class="nodeSpacer">
                    <a onclick="requestNavigate('home')">Home</a> |
                    <a onclick="requestNavigate('profile')">Profile</a> |
                    <a onclick="requestNavigate('canvas')">Canvas</a>
                </div>
            </Template>
            <Style>
                #header{ border-top:1px solid #000; }
                a{ cursor:pointer;
                    color:#d41a1a; }
            </Style>
            <JavaScript>
                //navigate to a new container view
                function requestNavigate(view){
                    gadgets.views.requestNavigateTo(view);
                };
            </JavaScript>
        </TemplateDef>
    </Templates>
```

 The full code for this sample is available at *https://github.com/jcleblanc/ programming-social-applications/blob/master/chapter_7/template_li brary.xml.*

In the first two nodes, we define the XML namespace prefix that we will use throughout the template file as `template` and set the namespace URL.

We start out our global definitions by adding in our global CSS styles. The styles include spacers for our header and footer tags and a small text style for our footer.

Within our global `JavaScript` block, we create one function to be made available to any template block that implements this XML template file. It is not being used in this template file but contains functionality to swap the visibility between two nodes.

Next, we define the custom tags to use throughout the application. Our first tag is a Template node containing simple markup. We just create a div node, attach the global style classes, and insert a copyright message.

Our last node is a TemplateDef element that acts as our header. This is a more complex node that requires its own CSS and JavaScript. We include a Template node to hold our gadget header markup; this is simply a series of links that call a local JavaScript function to swap the gadget's current view. We also include the same nodeSpacer global style as we did for the footer node. We then define a Style node that contains the local styles to be applied to all anchor tags within this custom header tag. Our last node, Java Script, contains the function that the anchor tags call to switch the gadget's current view. These styles and scripts are available only to the custom tag in which they are placed, as they are not needed globally.

Properly implemented template files are a powerful tool and give developers a highly scalable foundation upon which to build their applications.

Loading template libraries

Should you require a template library in your gadget, you can add references to the files in the gadget XML file when the Require statement for the opensocial-templates feature is set to use templating.

For example, to define our required template files, we can add one or multiple Param nodes in the Require feature="opensocial-templates" node with a name of require Library. The content of the node is the URL to a publicly available template XML file. If you use a relative URL, an absolute URL will be generated based on the URL of the gadget XML file:

```
<Require feature="opensocial-templates">
  <Param name="requireLibrary">http://www.mysite.com/template1.xml</Param>
  <Param name="requireLibrary">http://www.mysite.com/template2.xml </Param>
</Require>
```

JavaScript API

Throughout this chapter, we have explored how to work with templates that auto-matically render during gadget processing. Autorendering is an excellent method for building an extensible structure for your gadget when it first loads, but it does not cover the extent of functionality that you may require when working with templates.

The templating JavaScript API seeks to address this shortcoming, allowing developers to programmatically render a template into the HTML document of a gadget through the JavaScript layer, as needed. This functionality allows the developer to enjoy the rich functionality and feature set of OpenSocial templates while still maintaining a great amount of freedom in her development practices.

Before we dive into the individual methods of the JavaScript API, note that each example assumes you have the following template defined:

```
<script type="text/os-template"
        tag="gadget:restaurants"
        xmlns:gadget="http://www.mysite.com/gadget">
    <h1>Local Restaurants</h1>
    <ul>
        <li repeat="${restaurants}">
            <b>Name</b>: ${Cur.place}<br />
            <b>Address</b>: ${Cur.address}<br />
            <b>Website</b>: <a href="${Cur.href}">
                ${Cur.href}
            </a>
        </li>
    </ul>
</script>
```

As well as the following data source for the template:

```
var restaurants = [
    { place: "Lovely Sweets &amp; Snacks",
      address: "9 32 E El Camino Real, Sunnyvale CA",
      href: "http://local.yahoo.com/info-21337048-lovely-
            sweets-snacks-sunnyvale" },
    { place: "Vitos Famous Pizza",
      address: "1155 Reed Ave, Sunnyvale CA"
      href: "http://local.yahoo.com/info-21332026-vitos-
            famous-pizza-sunnyvale" },
    ]
);
```

Obtaining and processing the template

The opensocial.template namespace object exposes a number of methods for obtaining and processing templates defined in the gadget.

Obtaining the template. To work in a defined template or to apply a data source to the template, you must first obtain the template object. You do so by making a request to the following method:

```
opensocial.template.getTemplate(tag)
```

The getTemplate(...) method accepts one attribute to be passed, tag, which is a string containing the template tag name with qualifying XML namespace:

```
//obtain the defined gadget:restaurants template
var template = opensocial.template.getTemplate("gadget:restaurants");
```

This method will return the template object registered with tag, or null if the template does not exist.

Processing the template. The opensocial.template.process() method is used to initially process or reprocess currently used templates in a gadget. This method will initiate processing for templates that are ready:

```
opensocial.template.process()
```

There is no return value for this method.

Disabling templating autoprocessing. Should you wish to control when template processing occurs (instead of allowing the gadget rendering to control it for you), you can disable template autoprocessing within the gadget. This is the same as setting the `disable AutoProcessing` attribute within a template:

```
opensocial.template.disableAutoProcessing()
```

Once autoprocessing is disabled, you will need to manually initiate template processing by calling the `opensocial.template.process()` method:

```
//call process() method to begin template processing
function processTemplates(){
    opensocial.template.process();
}

//disable auto-processing of templates
opensocial.template.disableAutoProcessing();

//when required, call processTemplates() function to process templates
processTemplates();
```

This method will throw an exception if the processing has already occurred.

There is no return value for this method.

Rendering the template

Once you've obtained a template through the `opensocial.template.getTemplate(...)` method, you can control where in the gadget's DOM structure the processed template's markup will render. Two methods are available to specify this, as described next.

Rendering the template to a variable. The `opensocial.template.Template.render(...)` method renders an associated template with the data source provided within the gadget markup at the location where the method was called:

```
opensocial.template.Template.render(data)
```

If you do not include the data source, `opensocial.data.DataContext` is used by default:

```
//obtain the defined gadget:restaurants template
var template = opensocial.template.getTemplate("gadget:restaurants");

//render the template with our JSON object
var domNode = template.render(restaurants);
```

The return value of the `render(...)` method contains the DOM element into which the template markup was inserted.

Rendering the template to a DOM node. Much like with the `render()` method, `opensocial.template.Template.renderInto(...)` is responsible for rendering template data into a gadget's HTML. The difference between the two functions is that `renderInto(...)`

allows the developer to set a location where the template markup will be inserted, via a DOM node reference:

```
opensocial.template.Template.renderInto(element, data)
```

Using this method, you gain a great deal of control over where the markup generated from a template will go:

```
//obtain the defined gadget:restaurants template
var template = opensocial.template.getTemplate("gadget:restaurants");

//capture the DOM node that will house the template markup
var insertNode = document.getElementById("restaurantNode");

//render the template with our JSON object
var domNode = template.renderInto(insertNode, restaurants);
```

The return value of the renderInto(...) method contains the DOM element into which the template markup was inserted.

A practical example

Now that we understand how templates work with the JavaScript API, let's explore how we can implement the API's features in our own projects to control the template rendering functionality programmatically as needed, instead of autorendering on gadget load.

In our example, we have a series of world headlines that are to be built on the fly. We want to have a standard template UI to visualize the headline data. We'll apply that template to the visual markup and then insert it within the gadget when ready.

Our first task in this process is to define the OpenSocial template custom tag that will be used to visualize the headlines data set:

```
<script type="text/os-template"
        tag="app:headlines"
        xmlns:app="http://www.mysite.com/app">
    <h1>Current News Headlines</h1>
    <ul>
       <li repeat="${headlines}">
          <b>Headline Rank</b>: ${Context.Index + 1}<br />
          <a href="${Cur.href}">
             ${Cur.title}
          </a>
       </li>
    </ul>
</script>
```

As with our other custom tag template examples, we first start with the os-template script block. Within the script element, we define the tag, app:headlines, that we'll use to denote this template block. We then define the XML namespace that we will use throughout the template process: app.

Within the markup, we include a header, followed by an unordered list to house all of the headlines. The <li> element is set to repeat for each headline. Within the <li>, we display the headline rank based on the order processed in the array, and we show a linked headline title.

Now that our template is in place, we need to set up the JavaScript functionality that will take our raw data source, apply the template, and insert the template back into the gadget markup:

```
<script type="text/javascript">
    //captures the headline template, applies data and inserts into DOM node
    function displayHeadlines(headlineObj, insertNode) {
        var template = opensocial.template.getTemplate("app:headlines");
        var JSONObj = {
            headlines: headlineObj
        }
        var insertObj = document.getElementById(insertNode);
        template.renderInto(insertObj, JSONObj);
    }
```

The JavaScript functionality consists of a single function, displayHeadlines(...). This function requires two attributes to be passed:

headlineObj
> The JSON object containing an array of headline objects

insertNode
> A string representing the ID of the DOM node in which our newly built headline markup will be inserted

Our first task in the JavaScript layer is to capture the raw template that we defined earlier into a variable using the opensocial.template.getTemplate(...) method. The attribute that we pass to this method is the tag name for the template.

We then wrap the JSON in another object, associating the raw headlines data source with its data set name, headlines.

Once that data and the template information are stored in variables, we then capture the DOM node into which we'll insert the content by using the ID passed in to the function; then, we render the template into that node using the renderInto(...) method.

Once the template rendering function is in place, we can begin building both the gadget markup that will house the template and the raw headlines data source:

```
<div id="currentHeadlines"></div>

//build headline JSON object
var headlineObj = [
    { title: "31 of 33 Chile miners released from hospital",
      href: "http://www.cnn.com/2010/WORLD/americas/10/15/
             chile.miners.rescue/index.html" },
    { title: "Yemen posts reward for al Qaeda suspects",
```

```
        href: "http://www.cnn.com /2010/WORLD/meast/10/15/
                yemen.al.qaeda.reward/index.html" },
      { title: "Rights group questions fairness of Cuban spy trial in U.S.",
        href: "http://www.cnn.com /2010/CRIME/10/15/
                cuba.imprisoned.agents/index.html" },
    ]
  );

    //call function to render headlines into template
    displayHeadlines(headlineObj, "currentHeadlines");
</script>
```

We start our markup layer by defining a DOM node that will house the final template. Following that, we define the JSON object that will list off the headlines to be displayed. Our headline objects consist of a title and a link for each result.

Last, we call the rendering function, `displayHeadlines(...)`, passing in the headlines JSON object and the ID of the `div` in which to insert the headline content.

A Few More Tags: The OpenSocial Markup Language

The *OpenSocial Markup Language*, or *OSML*, is a direct subset of OpenSocial templating. We have already seen many expression tags and custom tag definitions used within the gadget template context, but now we'll take that a little bit further and explore some of the other functional tags that are available using this functional template subset.

OSML includes several standard tags that may aid you in your development, including:

os:Name
:   Used to display the name of a particular person

os:PeopleSelector
:   Used to display a person selector box

os:Badge
:   Used to display a standard badge for a user

os:Get
:   Used for loading external HTML content to insert into the gadget

To be able to render and use these tags, the gadget must include a `Require` statement to pull in the necessary JavaScript functionality:

```
<Require feature="osml" />
```

As I already mentioned, OSML is a direct subset of OpenSocial templating. Thus, if we have already included the templating `Require` element, we will not have to include the OSML feature element just described:

```
<Require feature="opensocial-templates" />
```

There are two separate `Require` statements available for including OSML tags because of the restrictions some containers impose on which views a gadget can implement templating on (due to potential performance issues).

The main value in any container-defined tags like these is that they provide secure access to a user's personal information without requiring the user's permission to do so. Since the container will be rendering the content of these tags and the gadget will not be collecting the social data itself, this can give you a quick and easy way to access social details about a user without actually having to handle her personal information.

Let's explore the functionality of these tags a little bit further.

Displaying a Person's Name: os:Name

The `os:Name` tag allows the container to render the user's name. This name may be linked to his profile or additional container capabilities such as hover state. You add this tag using the following format:

```
<os:Name person="${Viewer}" />
```

The `person` attribute may be a `Person` object or a `DataContext` key referring to the user whose name should be displayed (e.g., `${Viewer}`, `${Owner}`).

Creating a Person Selector: os:PeopleSelector

With the `os:PeopleSelector` tag, a developer can add a container-styled drop-down list that allows users to select from a group of people. The tag will also set a form field with the associated value from the drop-down. This tag should be added using syntax similar to the following:

```
<os:PeopleSelector group="${ViewerFriends}" multiple="false" max="10"
    inputName="viewerFriends"/>
```

The `os:PeopleSelector` tag has several attributes that may be assigned to it, as listed in Table 7-8.

Table 7-8. os:PeopleSelector attributes

Attribute	Description
group (string or object)	The group that should be displayed in the drop-down. This may either be an array of OpenSocial Person objects, or a DataContext key that refers to an array of Person objects. This field is required.
inputName (string)	The name of the input box that will be used to store the selected IDs.
max (number)	The maximum number of people that may be selected.
multiple (Boolean)	Whether multiple people may be selected.
onselect (string)	The JavaScript function to invoke when a new person is selected.
var (string)	The top-level DataContext key that is set with the selected IDs.

You add the os:PeopleSelector tag to a gadget using markup similar to the following:

```
<form action="inviteFriends" method="POST">
    <os:PeopleSelector group="${ViewerFriends}"
                       multiple="true"
                       inputName="viewerFriends"/>
</form>
```

Display a Person's Badge: os:Badge

Using the os:Badge tag, a developer can display a standard badge for a user, styled by the container. The badge will usually contain information such as full name, profile link, and badge image. This tag should have syntax similar to the following:

```
<os:Badge person="${Owner}"/>
```

The person attribute may be a Person object or a DataContext key referring to the user whose name should be displayed (e.g., ${Viewer}, ${Owner}).

Loading External HTML: os:Get

The os:Get tag inserts HTML content from an external source into the gadget's DOM. Loaded content will be sanitized prior to insertion and must be completely inline. External CSS and JavaScript includes will be ignored during insertion. Add this tag using syntax similar to the following:

```
<os:Get href="http://www.mysite.com/getUserData?uid=${viewer.uid}"/>
```

The href attribute should be a URL providing the HTML to be inserted.

Localization Support with Message Bundles

In earlier chapters, we looked at the XML elements that make up the core of an Open-Social gadget. This is where the concept of localization in gadgets was first introduced. Expanding upon this topic, we'll reiterate the importance of localization in targeting a worldwide audience, and discuss how to build localization support for multiple languages into your gadgets.

As anyone who has developed frontend systems to be implemented across multiple countries undoubtedly knows, porting a system between languages when it was not developed to handle multiple languages can require major style, formatting, and content revisions. This is especially true when you're working with English character sets and moving to 8-bit.

If you don't intend for your application to ever grow beyond your country of origin, localization support is probably not high on your list of important tasks. Really think about this for a moment—if your application, which currently uses US English, suddenly finds a huge audience in China, will you turn away the additional traffic and monetization potential, or will you work overtime to support that audience's needs?

When taken into consideration *before* construction of a new application begins, localization doesn't have to be a challenging, time-consuming effort. This is where *message bundle* definitions come into play. By providing a means through which developers can define support for sentence structures in multiple languages, message bundles help to remove the barrier of entry for your application users who speak different languages.

In addition, with the extensive number of existing tools in the marketplace that offer highly refined language conversion capabilities, supporting multiple languages is now easier than ever.

Let's start exploring message bundles by looking at their core syntax. Message bundles are simply an XML file with a few nodes defined:

```
<messagebundle>
    <msg name="message">Localized Text</msg>
</messagebundle>
```

The root node of a bundle is `messagebundle`, which consists of a series of `msg` nodes. These `msg` nodes contain an attribute, `name`, that acts as the message identifier when used in the gadget. The node content is the text in the language that the bundle was developed for.

Let's look at a practical example of this type of implementation. Assume for a moment that we want to build a gadget that will define messages in two languages, English and French. We would define two XML files for these bundles and store them on our server:

- English message bundle: *http://www.mysite.com/mbundle_en.xml*

  ```
  <?xml version="1.0" encoding="UTF-8" ?>
  <messagebundle>
      <msg name="greeting">Hello ${viewer.name}</msg>
      <msg name="thankyou">Thank you for using our service</msg>
  </messagebundle>
  ```

- French message bundle: *http://www.mysite.com/mbundle_fr.xml*

  ```
  <?xml version="1.0" encoding="UTF-8" ?>
  <messagebundle>
      <msg name="greeting">Bonjour ${viewer.name}</msg>
      <msg name="thankyou">Merci d'utiliser notre service</msg>
  </messagebundle>
  ```

Now we need to tell the gadget that we want to use these message bundles to define content to support the two languages. We can do this by embedding a `Locale` node within our gadget `ModulePrefs` element:

```
<ModulePrefs>
    <Locale messages="http://www.mysite.com/mbundle_en.xml" />
    <Locale lang="fr" messages="http://www.mysite.com/mbundle_fr.xml" />
</ModulePrefs>
```

These `Locale` nodes can include a few attributes, including `lang`, `country`, and `mes sages` (see Chapter 3 for more information on the `Local` node). The `messages` attribute contains the URL to the XML message bundle file.

Alternately, we can embed the message bundles directly into the gadget `ModulePrefs` element instead of linking to an external file:

```
<ModulePrefs>
  <Locale>
    <messagebundle>
      <msg name="greeting">Hello ${viewer.name}</msg>
      <msg name="thankyou">Thank you for using our service</msg>
    </messagebundle>
  </Locale>
  <Locale lang="fr" country="fr">
    <messagebundle>
      <msg name="greeting">Bonjour ${viewer.name}</msg>
      <msg name="thankyou">Merci d'utiliser notre service</msg>
    </messagebundle>
  </Locale>
</ModulePrefs>
```

This approach can be beneficial for performance reasons, depending on the gadget caching policy of the container that you are working in. If the container hardcaches the gadget, then having everything inline can give you a small performance boost when the gadget loads.

The main issue with running inline message bundles is maintainability. If the gadget integrates only a few key messages that you want to display to users, such as greetings in different languages, then this approach will not be unwieldy. Flickr (*http://www.flickr .com*) is one example of this approach; it gives users greeting messages such as:

```
Labas Jonathan C LeBlanc!
Now you know how to greet people in Lithuanian!
```

or:

```
Bună Ziua Jonathan C LeBlanc!
Now you know how to greet people in Romanian!
```

These are good examples of a manageable localization approach. If we are trying to support a message bundle with dozens or hundreds of messages, however, using inline message bundles makes for a poor development experience.

No matter which method you choose to include your message bundles, messages will be available through the `${Msg}` variable:

```
${Msg.greeting}
Welcome to our service
```

This code displays the greeting for the current locale. The greeting in our bundle contains a reference to `${viewer.name}`, which will be evaluated at the time that the message bundle is rendered.

Localization support such as message bundles can help you deliver key content across multiple countries and languages. It is an important factor to think about *before* you begin the construction of an application, since supporting it early will spare you the future time and engineering effort required to integrate support into an existing project.

The OpenSocial REST API Libraries

Complementing the OpenSocial client-side JavaScript API are the OpenSocial REST client libraries for server-to-server communication. These are a series of server-side APIs for accessing a user's social data much like we would from the JavaScript layer.

 Even though we are talking about the OpenSocial REST APIs for the sake of completeness, it's important to note that their support on current providers that allow their use is divided and may not be entirely implemented. New providers may wish to use these libraries as a means of building quick APIs for their platforms, but application developers should use APIs set up by the provider, OpenSocial JavaScript, or OAuth for implementations.

Although many provider implementations of these APIs are not complete (if implemented), they are a great starting point for those who wish to set up their own Open-Social container. Instead of expending the effort to design and develop custom APIs for your platform, consider these libraries, which are available in many popular languages and are a great way to build a quick implementation with community support.

Which Libraries Are Available

OpenSocial defines a series of languages with corresponding libraries that developers may use for their websites or services. These include:

- .NET: *http://code.google.com/p/opensocial-net-client/*
- ActionScript: *http://code.google.com/p/opensocial-actionscript-client/*
- Java: *http://code.google.com/p/opensocial-java-client/*
- Objective-C: *http://code.google.com/p/opensocial-objc-client/*
- Perl: *http://search.cpan.org/~lyokato/Net-OpenSocial-Client-0.01_05/lib/Net/Open Social/Client.pm*
- PHP: *http://code.google.com/p/opensocial-php-client/*
- Python: *http://code.google.com/p/opensocial-python-client/*
- Ruby: *http://code.google.com/p/opensocial-ruby-client/*
- Smalltalk: *http://code.google.com/p/opensocial-pharo-client/*

More information about the client libraries is available on the OpenSocial wiki: *http://wiki.opensocial.org/index.php?title=Client_Libraries*.

OpenSocial Next: Areas of Exploration

As we explore the inner workings of an OpenSocial container system and the social aspects behind these containers, we can see the rich network of relationships developing around the online lives of individuals. OpenSocial is taking the first steps toward truly understanding and defining who a person is on the Web—what he does and what's important to him. We all have different personalities, needs, and wants, so why can't we map a personality profile to a user and extend that to everything he does on the Web? Why must we limit our interaction with our profiles to only the social networking containers that host them?

These are difficult questions to try to answer. In a traditional business model, any information that the company and users shared was tightly protected. Technologies and advancements were not shared between companies, which led to many proprietary solutions for similar products.

The open source movement helped to change these viewpoints, but we are a long way from truly being an open web society—where a single profile, a single activity stream, and a single relationship graph defines our online lives.

OpenSocial is moving in the right direction by embracing open web technologies and exploring the tools that people use online. This exploration has uncovered several areas where individuals interact on a regular basis and tools to help share the social state among the containers.

Enterprise Containers

Normally, when you talk about enterprise-level software approaches, you are not talking about open source in any form of the term. The OpenSocial foundation is working to change this approach by looking into providing a specification that is well defined enough to serve internal business models and still provide security.

In many workplaces, proprietary software governs our email, company profiles, and even our interaction with other members of the organization through messaging systems. There is no reason why a company profile cannot be driven by an OpenSocial container; why the tools you use to create expense reports, add vacation time, or even deliver presentations cannot be OpenSocial applications; or why messaging systems cannot be built using activity streams and messaging systems defined through Open-Social. This area of development has exciting implications for application developers, presenting them with the opportunity to build productivity tools for businesses in the same way they build applications on open social networks.

Mobile Transitions

It's no surprise to anyone that mobile interaction with social information on the Web is on the rise. The real question here is, do our mobile applications need to function in a silo, preventing us from using a standardized profile for our mobile experiences? The simple answer is no.

OpenSocial defines a series of RESTful URIs that allow any application developer to leverage a single social network of friendships, activities, and profile information from the mobile environment.

Mobile interactions with an OpenSocial framework are currently being explored, including the ability to deliver a container environment to the mobile web.

Distributed Web Frameworks

OpenSocial does a tremendous job of attempting to standardize the way that we interact with our online selves and the way that this social data is defined. At the same time, movements that complement these interactions are taking root within online communities. These distributed web frameworks can provide us with a standardization of activity data, a protocol for syndicating activities to sources outside a container, or even a means for linking our social selves with traditionally static entities.

Due to the incredible capabilities of these frameworks to define methods for expanding a container's reach and access to social data outside the container, the OpenSocial foundation is exploring methods for integrating them into the specification.

Distributed web technologies, and their benefits, are the subject of the next section.

OpenSocial and Distributed Web Frameworks

As OpenSocial matures into a comprehensive product offering, its architecture is starting to overlap that of many emerging distributed web frameworks. As a result, OpenSocial is exploring the frameworks' technologies and methodologies as possible alternatives to the ways in which it currently handles its data, requests, and content syndication.

There are several distributed web frameworks that overlap with the OpenSocial spec by defining alternative and standardized methods for accomplishing similar tasks. Before we fully dive into these technologies in Chapter 10, let's explore the core concepts behind a few of the frameworks that will change how OpenSocial defines its practices.

Activity Streams

The Activity Streams specification provides a unified, standard method for working with user activity data across any social container or other place where user commenting or updating may occur. It attempts to provide any possible verbs that an activity in any context may require. This may cover social sites, commenting widgets on news sites, or even enterprise-level software that takes advantages of user updates, interaction, or commenting.

Verbs, and the cordoning of content into logical blocks, are the basis for how Activity Streams works. A single activity stream may consist of several logical blocks, including sections such an *actor* (information about the person performing the activity), *object* (the thing being acted upon), or *target* (trackback information from the activity to the source). Verbs are used to define the type of activity that is being shared, such as whether the user "liked" something, "shared" something, "posted" something, and so on.

How would this change OpenSocial?

As we have seen in previous chapters, OpenSocial defines a standard method for how it outputs activity data for a user action. If Activity Streams were adopted into the OpenSocial specification, this method would be directly affected; the definition of an `opensocial.Activity` object would change dramatically, providing a much richer data set than is currently implemented.

PubSubHubbub

PubSubHubbub is a protocol that defines a method for updates, comments, or posts to be easily syndicated and shared between a root site and any subscriber sites that syndicate the content of articles, posts, or any other data from the root site.

PubSubHubbub accomplishes this through the use of relaying hubs. A topic site or feed URL declares the hub to be used within its RSS or ATOM feed file as a `link` element. This hub may be hosted by the feed publisher or on a community platform hub that provides services for anyone. A subscriber would then fetch the publisher feed, read the hub information, and then subscribe to the hub in order to get updates. This will allow the subscriber to subscribe to the particular feed that she is interested in seeing updates for. When the publisher updates or changes the feed content, it would ping the hub stating that there is a change. The hub then fetches the content and multicasts the new or changed content out to all subscribers.

In effect, this protocol enables syndication of activities, publications, articles, or any other piece of social data out of the hosted container. This can effectively widen the reach of the social network to a host of subscribers.

How would this change OpenSocial?

An OpenSocial container, for the most part, can be considered a social silo. A container defines its social information for only its site and, unless other means are built in, it may only allow off-site access to that information through the use of RESTful endpoints for the social data. This can be inefficient because the external service has to periodically poll the endpoints to check for updates to the data source.

PubSubHubbub can effectively eliminate the need for third-party services to do this. By subscribing to particular feeds from the social container, a service can be notified as changes occur. Building the ability to define update hubs for data would readily change the way in which activities or updates are managed through OpenSocial.

In addition, the capability to define a syndication hub could be integrated into the specification to make the process as seamless as possible.

Salmon Protocol

With services like PubSubHubbub, a publisher can ping a hub stating that a feed has changed. That hub would then fetch the updated content and aggregate it out to all hub subscribers. The Salmon protocol works on the upstream of this interaction. Let's say a hub subscriber makes a new comment on an article that was published. With the Salmon protocol in place, that comment can be pushed back up to the publisher site. The publisher then adds the comment to its version of the article. Once the article is updated, the publisher pings the hub, which then fetches the new comment and pushes the update to all subscriber sites.

The main benefit here is that there is no longer only a one-way relationship between a publisher and subscribers. You build, in effect, a link between all publishers and all subscribers, unifying the social experience among many different sites.

How would this change OpenSocial?

Much like with PubSubHubbub, the real benefits for OpenSocial to integrate the Salmon protocol come from expanding the social network far beyond the bounds of the root container. Not only can you push out new content and updates from the social container, but you can now also accept new updates from some third-party source. Basically, you would be able to create a social networking ecosystem composed of the root social network and numerous third-party sites and services.

To integrate such a service, OpenSocial would need to define the ability to push content and activities out to subscribers, such as through a protocol like PubSubHubbub. It would then need to be able to receive updates to that content from subscribers and verify the data. Finally, the updates would need to be pushed out to any feed subscribers.

The real challenge in this whole scenario is security and trust relationships. At some point in this process—either when subscribing to a hub or when validating updates from subscribers—the host container must ensure that the information coming back is from a trusted source, is not spam, and is a valid update. This may require the integration of permission levels for subscribers and proper authentication to work securely.

Open Graph Protocol

The Open Graph protocol is built upon the core precepts that a user's social graph can extend far beyond simple relationships with other people. As we interact on the social web, we leave our footprints wherever we go—on particular accounts, websites, or any other social linkage. These links, called *entity relationships*, can vastly enrich the user's social graph, delivering whole new unstructured content and user information that, just a few years ago, was really not available to us.

The Open Graph protocol seeks to give structure to those unstructured entities that are associated with a person, by providing an open, standard, and uniform method for working with these links to access an individual's social data. It accomplishes this standardization through the use of semantic-based metatagging, which provides basic to advanced customization options for a site. At a base level, the Open Graph protocol defines simple information like the page title, the type of object that is on the page, a standard image, or a trackback URL. It then builds upon that core data by defining geographically significant information (e.g., restaurant locations), contact information for the site, and numerous object types that help further refine categories for a site.

The Open Graph protocol aligns itself very readily with a user's existing social graph in an OpenSocial container.

How would this change OpenSocial?

If the Open Graph protocol is integrated within the OpenSocial specification, we may see an expansion of how a user's social graph functions. Currently, a user's social graph is viewed merely as a list of relationships with other people. This is basically a one-to-many mapping (i.e., between one OpenSocial `Person` object and many other `Person` objects).

To shift the paradigm defining what a social relationship is, the OpenSocial specification would need to provide different sources of relationship mapping. At minimum, the user's social graph should be able to return a mix of person-to-person relationships as well as person-to-object relationships.

Putting It All Together

 The full code for this sample is available at *https://github.com/jcleblanc/ programming-social-applications/blob/master/chapter_7/chapter_final .xml.*

Now that we've examined data pipelining and templating, one thing should be blatantly obvious: these two features of the OpenSocial specification can significantly reduce the amount of code that you need to write, create a highly modularized environment to promote multiuser development, and generally simplify debugging and data retrieval to allow you to focus on more important aspects of your gadget, such as monetization and social features.

Up until now, we've explored the individual specifications for accessing and working with data. Now we will put together a few of the lessons that we have learned into a fully functional example that showcases some of the major uses for templating and data pipelining.

In this example, we'll look at:

- Capturing data sources through data pipelining HTTP Requests
- Integrating data pipes into templates
- Using expressions
- Using loop structures
- Using special variables

Our sample code will use the data pipelining specification to pull in two RSS feeds, one from *www.reddit.com* and the other from the San Francisco local news section of *www .craigslist.org*. Following that, we'll create two separate pages that can be switched back and forth by tabs. These pages will use the templating specification to display the title, link, and date from these two feeds as styled, unordered lists. The general visual form that we will use for this application will mimic Figure 7-1.

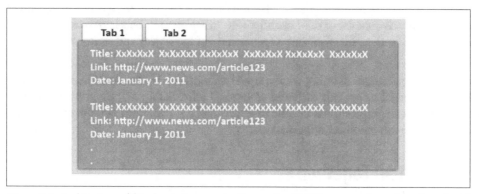

Figure 7-1. Architecture of this chapter's example, showcasing HTTP requests through an OpenSocial gadget

First, we have to look at the foundation of our gadget XML file and the requirements that we need to include:

```
<?xml version="1.0" encoding="utf-8s"?>
<Module>
    <ModulePrefs title="Chapter rollup example"
                 title_url="http://www.jcleblanc.com"
                 description="Displays templating and data pipelining
                              specifications"
                 author="Jonathan LeBlanc">
        <Require feature="opensocial-0.9"/>
        <Require feature="opensocial-data" />
        <Require feature="opensocial-templates" />
    </ModulePrefs>
```

Since the sample gadget that we are building will integrate functionality from data pipelining as well as templating, we need to require these features in our gadget:

- At the very minimum, we should include version 0.9 of the OpenSocial specification as opensocial-0.9. (This is the minimum version that is needed to run both the features from data pipelining and templating.)
- The data pipelining specification as opensocial-data.
- The templating specification as opensocial-templates.

Now that our JavaScript feature requirements are in place in our core gadget, we can focus on the Content section that will house our gadget functionality:

```
<Content type="html">
  <![CDATA[
  <style type="text/css">
    #nav{ margin:5px 0 5px 15px;
          padding-top:10px; }
    #nav a{ background-color:#e8f0f4;
            border:1px solid #0c7099;
            border-bottom:0;
            color:#000;
            padding:6px 8px;
            margin-top:5px; }
    #nav a{ cursor:pointer;
            font-weight:bold; }
    #nav a.navOff{ background-color:#0c7099;
                   color:#fff; }
    #nav, .page{ font:12px arial,helvetica,sans-serif; }
    .page{ margin:5px 0;
           padding:5px;
           margin:0 10px 15px;
           background-color:#e8f0f4;
           border:1px solid #0c7099; }
    .page li{ list-style-type:none;
              padding:3px 10px 3px 0; }
    .textSmall{ font-size:10px; }
    .hide{ display:none; }
  </style>
```

We first need to specify the styles that will be used in the gadget. These styles will define the look of the anchor tags that are used for the page tabs, the layout for the pages, and the formatting of the data pipes as unordered lists.

Following the styles, we define the navigation of the gadget, which will allow us to switch between the two feed pages:

```
<div id="nav">
  <a id="linkCraigslist"
     onclick="switchNode('pageCraigslist', 'pageReddit', this)">
     Craigslist Local</a>
  <a id="linkReddit"
     onclick="switchNode('pageReddit', 'pageCraigslist', this)"
```

```
          class="navOff">Reddit</a>
  </div>
```

Our navigation system consists of a `div` wrapping two anchor tags that are styled to look like tabs. To visualize the tab's `off` state, we can set a class of `navOff`. Other than that, our anchor tags contain an `onclick` event that, when triggered, will call the `switch Node(...)` function to swap between the current page and the other page.

Our next task is to define the data pipe that will pull in the RSS feeds from *www.reddit.com* and *www.craigslist.org*:

```
<script type="text/os-data" xmlns:os="http://ns.opensocial.org/2008/markup">
  <os:HttpRequest key="feeds" href="http://query.yahooapis.com/v1/public/yql?
    q=select%20*%20from%20yql.query.multi%20where%20queries%3D%22select%20
    *%20from%20rss%20where%20url%3D'http%3A%2F%2Fwww.reddit.com%2F.rss'%3B
    select%20*%20from%20rss%20where%20url%3D'http%3A%2F%2Fsfbay.craigslist.
    org%2Fvnn%2Findex.rss'%22&format=json&debug=true"/>
  </script>
```

As with some of our previous examples, we use the `os:HttpRequest` element to pull in our data feeds, using the Yahoo! Query Language to aggregate the sources. The YQL URL makes the request to the service, which in turn makes two separate RESTful requests to the two RSS sources and then binds the results into a single data pipe in JSON format. Our pipe is set to a key of `feeds`.

Next we will cover the visualization of these data sources through the templating specification:

```
<script type="text/os-template" require="feeds">
  <div id="pageReddit" class="page hide">
    <ul>
      <li repeat="${feeds.content.query.results.results[0].item}">
        <b>${Cur.title[0]}</b><br />
        <a href="${Cur.link}">${Cur.link}</a><br />
        <span class="textSmall">${Cur.pubDate}</a>
      </li>
    </ul>
  </div>
  <div id="pageCraigslist" class="page">
    <ul>
      <li repeat="${feeds.content.query.results.results[1].item}">
        <b>${Cur.title[0]}</b><br />
        <a href="${Cur.link}">${Cur.link}</a><br />
        <span class="textSmall">${Cur.date}</a>
      </li>
    </ul>
  </div>
</script>
```

Our template `script` block contains the `require` attribute stating that if the `feeds` data pipe is not available, the template should not be rendered with the data.

If `feeds` is available, the template will set up two `div` nodes, one set as visible and the other as hidden. Within these `div` nodes, or pages, we set up an unordered list. Then we use the repeat attribute of the templating specification to create an <li> node in the unordered list for each object in the associated RSS feed. Within each list item, we create markup to display the title, link, and current date for the appropriate RSS feed item.

Our last task is to define our JavaScript functionality to enable us to swap between the two different pages that we have defined:

```
<script type="text/javascript">
    //swap the visibility of one page
    function switchNode(activate, deactivate, linkObj){
        //get page nodes to swap
        var showNode = document.getElementById(activate);
        var hideNode = document.getElementById(deactivate);

        //switch the display properties of the two pages
        hideNode.className = "page hide";
        showNode.className = "page";

        //swap link tab classes
        var linkAlt = (linkObj.id == "linkCraigslist") ?
                        document.getElementById("linkReddit") :
                        document.getElementById("linkCraigslist");
        linkObj.className = "";
        linkAlt.className = "navOff";
    };
</script>
]]>
    </Content>
</Module>
```

Our JavaScript functionality layer consists of a single function, switchNode(...), which accepts three parameters:

activate
:   The ID of the page to be switched to a display status.

deactivate
:   The ID of the page to be hidden.

linkObj
:   The DOM node object representing the tab that was clicked. This determines the tab visualization states.

This is a simple function that has two responsibilities: swap the state of the pages, and swap the state of the tabs. We start out by swapping the pages, removing the hide class from the page to be displayed and adding the class to the page to be hidden. We then determine the tab that was clicked and the one that wasn't, and swap the classes for those tabs as well.

When we render, we should be presented with a tabbed interface like Figure 7-2, which contains a basic application that allows you to read up on current news and topics.

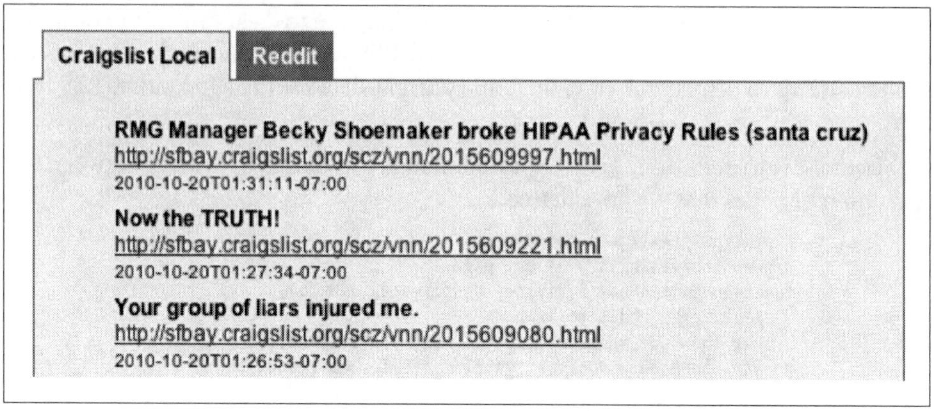

Figure 7-2. This chapter's example, showcasing HTTP requests in OpenSocial gadgets

CHAPTER 8

Social Application Security Concepts

When we start discussing applications that host and work with users' personal information, the conversation will naturally lead to user security. How do we protect users' personal data? Should the container hosting the applications be responsible for that information, or should the onus be on the application developers?

Besides the question of how to best protect end users, we must ask ourselves how strict we should be about content developed by third parties. How restrictive can we be before developers seriously consider not developing on the platform or site in question? How far can we go to protect end users before we begin to alienate our developers?

Finally, once we have a security model in place, how will it impact application performance? Will the overhead imposed by the security mechanism significantly slow down load times to the point where it causes timeouts or forces users to leave the platform?

These are the questions this chapter will address as we explore some of the available open source security technologies that allow us to host third-party code securely within a site or application container.

What You'll Learn

This chapter will focus on the development of secure models for hosting third-party code or applications on an existing site or container. We will explore currently available tools that provide a sandboxed environment in which to run third-party code on an existing site. Specifically, we will look into two technologies:

- Caja (pronounced "ka-ha")
- ADsafe

In addition to these two technologies, we will look at one of today's most used approaches for sandboxing code, iframes, and what security issues their use introduces.

Hosting Third-Party Code Through iframes

The current security strategy employed by many sites and services that allow third-party code is to contain the application content within an iframe. In the case of application development on a social networking site, many applications must first go through a review process to ensure that they're not malicious before being approved for use on the site. Application developers can then generally update their application as they see fit and have the changes appear in the live version immediately.

The iframe approach nullifies a number of different attacks that a malicious application developer may launch against the host site, but it does nothing to protect the user working in the application. The content of the iframe is not sanitized, which means that the same security issues that exist in any site on the Internet still exist in this context.

This is where other security implementations such as Caja and ADsafe come into play. They attempt to remove the majority of the attack vectors that an application developer may employ against a user. We will explore some of the specific attacks in the next section as part of our larger discussion of Caja.

A Secure Approach: The Caja Project

The Caja project has emerged as a means for securing third-party frontend code (HTML, CSS, and JavaScript) to protect both the container on which that code is hosted as well as the end user who is exposed to it.

In simple terms, Caja works by encasing the third-party code in a container, such as a `div` node, that provides a sanitized version of the DOM. When the third-party code then calls a DOM method, it is not accessing the true DOM of the root page. This means that the Caja sanitization system can control every DOM request that is being made and can either grant or deny access to certain functionality.

Taking that a step further, the project works by employing a two-part sanitization system. When the third-party code is first rendered on the page, it will go through the server-side *cajoler*, which will sanitize the code and remove anything that it deems malicious. Next, if new code is injected into the application via a JavaScript method (e.g., `innerHTML`), that code will be pushed through the client-side sanitizer. This client-side sanitizer is a much stricter system, usually allowing only approved HTML and CSS while removing JavaScript content.

This is the core functionality of the Caja project. We'll explore each component in more depth as we walk through the implementation of a Caja-protected application.

Why Use Caja?

Some readers may be wondering why to use Caja at all since it seems more restrictive for developers. And they're completely correct—Caja *does* restrict the actions and implementations of developers who are building code on top of an existing site or application container. Developers will have to go through extra steps and stick to a set of good programming practices when building out systems to run under Caja.

But the simple fact is that any developer worth his salt who *wants* to build something, *will*—especially in a stable rewriting environment such as the one Caja provides. And developers should not be the main concern for this implementation, anyway; rather, the focus should be on the people who are using the site or application, who don't have the background, knowledge, or inclination to protect themselves from malicious attacks from outside sources.

This is the main reason to implement Caja—to protect your end users from the potentially malicious code and sources that you are exposing them to by allowing third-party content to be hosted on your site or container. When it really comes down to it, the success of a product relies on the trust relationship between that product or company, and the people who use it on a regular basis. A user who doesn't trust a product will be far less inclined to use it.

Another clear advantage to Caja is that it enforces web standards. Sloppy development, corner cutting, and potentially malicious code that was employed to save time and effort will all be caught when the cajoler or sanitizer gets hold of it.

Attack Vectors: How Caja Protects

Browsers are powerful tools that enable a wide range of utilities for a user interacting with websites and web applications. Even with these powerful tools in place, browsers are still insecure beasts, full of security flaws and issues despite the extensive updates integrated within the HTML5 standard.

This is where Caja can help. There are numerous attack vectors that are exploitable in browsers that Caja aims to safeguard against. We will take a look at a few of these attack vectors to identify the exploitable browser components that Caja aims to protect against.

For a full list of attack vectors that Caja checks for, see *http://code.google.com/p/google -caja/wiki/AttackVectors*.

Redirecting Users Without Their Consent

One of the simplest attack vectors that may impact a user is an automatic redirection without her consent. The main issue here is that any frame can redirect any other named frame to another location automatically, meaning that the user may not be fully certain that the page that she is redirected to is the page she intended to view.

Let's look at a practical example of this issue. Say an application that we are running is intended to load third-party code in an iframe from *http://www.mybank.com*, allowing users to log in to their bank accounts, see their balances, and make transfers. Since the intended content of the iframe is known, the application could automatically redirect the user to another site—say, *http://www.attacker.com/stealbank*—without her knowledge or input, mimicking the view and functionality of *http://www.mybank .com* with the intention of stealing her bank account information:

```
window.top.location = "http://www.attacker.com/stealbank";
```

This is a major phishing concern for users, as that automatic redirection can happen without the user even being aware of it.

Mining a User's Browser History

Browsers natively integrate the ability to track the URLs that a user visits. They use this information to autocomplete links in the URL bar and to alter the color of clicked links. Malicious developers can take advantage of this native tracking functionality to help figure out which sites a user has visited, allowing them to launch more targeted phishing attacks against him.

In addition to the standard color of links within a web page, many sites implement link styles to change a link's appearance when the user has visited it:

```
<style type="text/css">
    a:visited{ color:#c0c0c0; }
    a:link{ color:#000; }
</style>
```

In this scenario, attackers can check the link's color to mine the browser history of the current user visiting the site. For instance, assume we have a few links defined on our site that link to other sources:

```
<a href="http://www.yahoo.com" id="link1">Yahoo!</a><br />
<a href="http://www.facebook.com" id="link2">Facebook</a>
```

Using the standard `getComputedStyle` JavaScript function, a developer can capture the color styling of those links to determine the user's visited status:

```
<script type="text/javascript">
    var compStyle = getComputedStyle(document.getElementById("link1"), "")
    var color = compStyle.getPropertyValue("color");
</script>
```

> The full code for this sample is available at *https://github.com/jcleblanc/ programming-social-applications/blob/master/chapter_8/attack_vector _history_miner.html*.

Using these simple techniques as a base, malicious developers can take advantage of link styles to mine a user's visited history.

Arbitrary Code Execution with document.createElement

If the third-party code has access to the page's root DOM but has restrictions on the scripts being loaded, it can execute arbitrary code blocks that have access to the page's global object.

The premise behind this attack vector is to create `script` blocks that can capture user information, such as site cookies:

```
var script = document.createElement("script");
script.appendChild(
    document.createTextNode(
        var userCookie = document.cookie;
        //use user cookies
    )
);
document.body.appendChild(script);
```

> The full code for this sample is available at *https://github.com/jcleblanc/ programming-social-applications/blob/master/chapter_8/attack_vector _code_execution.js*.

Using `document.getElement`, you can create a new `script` block, attach a block of code to hijack user information, and then attach that code to the body of the DOM to automatically render it, executing the malicious block within.

Logging the User's Keystrokes

If the third-party application has the ability to access the true DOM of a page, then it can log the user's keystrokes. The severity of this attack can range from a simple nuisance all the way to a major security issue if the root page contains password fields or user-specific information.

A probable attack vector for this type of code is to capture the user's username and password fields. Since a password field would prevent direct access to its value, logging the user's keystrokes can provide the attacker with all of the information he needs.

For instance, say we have a site that hosts third-party code. On this site, you have a username and password field to allow you to log in. Should this third-party code attach a keypress event on the body of the root page document, then it can log any keys that you press while you are on the page.

This type of attack can be perpetrated by any script that can essentially "phone home" by accessing the parent page that it is being presented on, much like the following sample:

```html
<!DOCTYPE HTML PUBLIC "-//W3C//DTD HTML 4.01//EN"
"http://www.w3.org/TR/html4/strict.dtd">
<html>
<head>
<title>Key Logger Attack</title>
</head>
<body>
<!-- username field -->
<label for="username">Username:</label>
<input type="text" name="username" /><br />

<!-- password field -->
<label for="password">Password:</label>
<input type="password" name="password" />

<!-- node to dump logged keys to -->
<div id="dumpNode"></div>

<script type="text/javascript">
var lastSend = Date.now();

//attach keypress event to the document body
document.body.onkeypress = function(event){
   //get current key pressed
   var keyCode = event.which || event.keyCode;
   var string = "";

   //was key pressed within 1 second of last press
   if (Date.now() - lastSend < 1000){
      string += String.fromCharCode(keyCode);
   } else {
      string = "<br />" + String.fromCharCode(keyCode);
   }

   //dump last key pressed and update time
   var dumpNode = document.getElementById("dumpNode");
   dumpNode.innerHTML += string;
   lastSend = Date.now();
};
</script>
</body>
</html>
```

The full code for this sample is available at *https://github.com/jcleblanc/ programming-social-applications/blob/master/chapter_8/attack_vector _keystroke_logger.html.*

In our document markup, we set up three fields: a username, a password, and a third node that we'll use to dump our logged keypresses.

As we get into the script, we first get the current time, which we will use to arbitrarily track when the user has moved on to a new word. We then attach an onkeypress event onto the body of the page. This will ensure that when the user presses a key anywhere within the page, her keys will be logged to our logger function.

When the event is triggered, we capture the key that was pressed. The if statement compares the last keypress event time to the current time. If the latest keypress event was less than a second after the last, then the key is assumed to be part of the same word and attached to the same line as the last key. One second is simply an arbitrary amount of time to wait; if the delay is longer than a second, we drop the new character to the next line.

Last, we dump the new character to our div node to display on screen.

The keys that are logged are based on the decimal representations outlined at *http://en .wikipedia.org/wiki/ASCII#ASCII_printable_characters*.

This attack is one representation of what can occur if a script has the ability to access the root DOM of the page that it exists on. The simplistic nature of this attack underscores the importance of building in at least some measure of security to prevent the third-party code from accessing the DOM, or having the third-party code running in a sandbox to prevent it from reaching outside its defined working area in the root page.

Setting Up Caja

Before we can test the Caja system against some actual files and gadgets, we need to obtain the Caja source from the project trunk and then build it.

First, we need to ensure that we have all of the prerequisites in place to download, build, and test the installation. Caja has the following minimum requirements:

- Subversion (SVN) to download the source files from the trunk and to keep the downloaded project files up to date.
- Java Development Kit (JDK) 6.
- Apache Ant 1.7 for the build system.
- JUnit for the testing framework. Once you've obtained it, simply place the *junit.jar* file in the *$ANT_HOME/lib* directory you set up for Ant.

Once we've met the prerequisites, we can start the process by obtaining the source code for the Caja project from the SVN trunk. Simply navigate to the folder location where you would like to load Caja and then run the following command:

```
svn checkout http://google-caja.googlecode.com/svn/trunk/ caja
```

This code issues an SVN checkout command against the Caja trunk and specifies our output directory to be the *caja* folder.

Next, we need to build the project using Ant. Simply navigate into the *caja* directory and run the ant command. This will initiate the Ant build process for the project:

```
cd caja
ant
```

After the *build.xml* script is loaded and the build process begins, you should be presented with the following output if the process is proceeding correctly:

```
Buildfile: build.xml

dirs:
.
.
.
BUILD SUCCESSFUL
Total time: 35 seconds
```

This series of build messages states what part of the build script is currently being processed, and gives you a BUILD SUCCESSFUL message to confirm that the process completed successfully.

Once the build has completed, you should see a series of new *ant-** directories in the root of the Caja project directory:

ant-docs
> The javadocs output

ant-jars
> All the jar files needed to run the cajoler

ant-lib
> The compiled classes and resources

ant-reports/tests/index.html
> Unit test status and logs

ant-reports/coverage/index.html
> Unit test coverage reports

ant-www
> Output of demos

You should be aware of a number of important directories within the Caja project. The folder structure that you will be integrating with is:

```
caja
|
+--bin : executable files for compiling from the command line
|
+--docs : documentation files.
|
+--src : source code (java and javascript)
```

```
|   |
|  +--com
|     |
|     +--google
|          |
|          +--caja
|               |
|               +--lexer : Tokenization and escaping
|               |
|               +--parser : Parsers and tree implementations
|               |    |
|               |    +--ParseTreeNode.java : Main parse tree interface
|               |    |
|               |    +--quasiliteral : Syntactic sugar for parse tree xforms
|               |
|               +--opensocial : Dealing with Gadget specs
|               |
|               +--plugin : Transformations
|               |    |
|               |    +--PluginCompilerMain.java : main class
|               |    |
|               |    +--stages : Parse tree transforms
|               |
|               +--reporting : Error and warning messaging.
|
+--tests : test files and resources
```

We will be working primarily with the contents of the *bin* directory at the root of the project. This is where we will compile mixed HTML/JavaScript files and OpenSocial gadgets from the command line—a topic we will explore next.

Cajoling Scripts from the Command Line

Caja secures your frontend code by sanitizing (or *cajoling*, in Caja terms) it through the command-line JavaScript compiler. In the sections that follow, we will explore how to take a mixed HTML/JavaScript file source and build out a cajoled, safe version of the code.

Once we see how to cajole our code, we will look at methods for reducing the weight of our JavaScript files.

Cajoling HTML and JavaScript

Before we begin compiling our mixed HTML and JavaScript documents into a safe code subset, we need to look at the tools that we will be using.

In the *caja* directory that we created for the project, you'll see a directory containing the scripts that we will use to compile our code. The *cajole_html* script is specific to the task of cajoling standard HTML and JavaScript, and it's the script we'll use here to cajole our standard code. After the cajoling process completes, we will have two output files:

- An HTML output file containing the markup of our script, divorced from any embedded JavaScript blocks. This HTML file will contain secure, directly embeddable markup that we can insert within a site. All unsafe markup tags, such as iframes, will be stripped from the final derived markup.
- The cajoled JavaScript file. The JavaScript will be a secured version of what we started with, stripping out any insecure script.

To run the mixed HTML/JavaScript command-line cajoler, we can simply go to the root of the *caja* directory from which we checked out the SVN source and run the appropriate cajole_html script with a few parameters:

```
cd caja
bin/cajole_html -i <htmlInputFile> -o <outputTarget>
```

cajole_html allows us to specify an input file to cajole (htmlInputFile) and an output filename to dump our two cajoled files to (outputTarget). htmlInputFile can be an absolute URL of a file to be cajoled or a direct reference to a file on the local system. outputTarget is simply the string name to call the output files, along with the file path to build them to. The two output files will be named:

- {outputTarget}.out.html
- {outputTarget}.out.js

These are the two files that you should expect to be generated when you run the cajoler against a source file with mixed HTML and JavaScript.

Running the cajoler

Let's look at an example of the cajoling process:

```
<!DOCTYPE html PUBLIC "-//W3C//DTD HTML 4.01//EN"
                      "http://www.w3.org/TR/html4/strict.dtd">
<html>
<head>
<title>Caja Sample HTML</title>
</head>
<body>

<h1>Sample Redirection Script</h1>
<a onclick="goRedirect()">Click to Redirect</a>

<script type="text/javascript">
//redirect user to new site
function goRedirect(){
   var redirects;
   with(redirects){
      var href = "http://www.yahoo.com"
      window.location = href;
   }
```

```
        }
    </script>

    </body>
    </html>
```

When we cajole this mixed HTML/JavaScript file via the command line, we get the following messages:

```
 1   notseveral-lm:caja jleblanc$ bin/cajole_html -i
     ../git/programming-social-applications/caja/ch9_caja_sample_html.html
     -o caja_sample
 2   LOG    : Checkpoint: LegacyNamespaceFixupStage at T+0.113971 seconds
 3   LOG    : Checkpoint: ResolveUriStage at T+0.12005 seconds
 4   LOG    : Checkpoint: RewriteHtmlStage at T+0.124126 seconds
 5   LINT   : ch9_caja_sample_html.html:16+42: Semicolon inserted
 6   LOG    : Checkpoint: InlineCssImportsStage at T+0.204033 seconds
 7   LOG    : Checkpoint: SanitizeHtmlStage at T+0.204083 seconds
 8   WARNING: ch9_caja_sample_html.html:2+1 - 23+8: folding element html into parent
 9   WARNING: ch9_caja_sample_html.html:3+1 - 5+8: folding element head into parent
10    WARNING: ch9_caja_sample_html.html:4+1 - 32: removing disallowed tag title
11    WARNING: ch9_caja_sample_html.html:6+1 - 22+8: folding element body into parent
12   LOG    : Checkpoint: ValidateCssStage at T+0.206399 seconds
13   LOG    : Checkpoint: RewriteCssStage at T+0.222766 seconds
14   LOG    : Checkpoint: HtmlToBundleStage at T+0.222807 seconds
15   LOG    : Checkpoint: OptimizeJavascriptStage at T+0.279367 seconds
16   LOG    : Checkpoint: ValidateJavascriptStage at T+0.279401 seconds
17   ERROR  : ch9_caja_sample_html.html:15+5 - 18+6: "with" blocks are not allowed
18   LOG    : Checkpoint: ConsolidateCodeStage at T+0.553624 seconds
19   LOG    : Checkpoint: CheckForErrorsStage at T+0.561566 seconds
```

For the sake of this example, we will ignore the LOG messages—they are just notifications at different stages of the cajoling process. We are, however, interested in the LINT, WARNING, and ERROR messages, as those are pertinent to our build process.

The LINT message on line 5 states that a semicolon was inserted. This message was generated because we forgot a semicolon at the end of the line when we defined our url parameter in our HTML sample code. By default, JavaScript tries to help developers by automatically inserting a semicolon if one was omitted. But because this process can sometimes insert semicolons where you do not want them—causing errors in the program flow—messages like this are produced.

Next, we have the WARNING messages on lines 8 through 11. Since Caja is building an HTML and JavaScript file to be inserted on an existing page (such as a gadget), the html, head, and body tags are all folded up into the parent and thus removed from the output in the HTML file. In addition, the title element is also removed because the code base is running in an existing container.

Last is the ERROR message on line 17, which tells us that with blocks in JavaScript are not allowed in compiling. This error will stop the cajoling process and not produce output files.

If we were to remove the `with` block in question from our code, we would be able to produce cajoled files. This involves changing our `script` block to the following:

```
<script type="text/javascript">
//redirect user to new site
function goRedirect(){
    var href = "http://www.yahoo.com";
    window.location = href;
}
</script>
```

If we were to then recajole the scripts:

```
notseveral-lm:caja jleblanc$ bin/cajole_html -i
../git/programming-social-applications/caja/ch9_caja_sample_html.html
-o caja_sample
```

We would get the following two output files:

caja_sample.out.html
> The sanitized HTML of our file

caja_sample.out.js
> The cajoled JavaScript of our original file, with the added layers of Caja security

Next, we'll explore these files to see what content is produced.

The cajoled HTML

When we look at the content of the *caja_sample_out.html* file, we see the following:

```
<h1>Sample Redirection Script</h1>
<a id="id_2___" target="_blank">Click to Redirect</a>
```

Our html, head, and body elements have all been removed from the output. Since the content of a cajoled file is meant to exist within the body of some container, it will exist in the same DOM as that container and thus must not include competing root nodes. The content of our HTML file is stripped down to our h1 and the redirect `<a>` tag. Within the `<a>` tag, our `onclick` event is silently stripped out of the HTML content. When Caja runs into tags that are not allowed and it can safely remove those tags without compromising valuable output, the cajoler will silently strip them out and output usable files.

 If you are embedding `onclick` handlers directly into your markup layer, Caja will most likely strip them from the returned HTML, depending on how strict your implementation is. To avoid this, you should attach JavaScript event handlers after the page content has loaded by using the traditional methods of working between `object.onclick`, `object.attachEvent`, or `object.addEventListener`.

The cajoled JavaScript

Next let's look at the JavaScript file compiled during the cajoling process, *caja_sample.out.js*. If we open this file, we see a much larger JavaScript construct than we defined in our functional `script` block:

```
{
    ___.loadModule({
        'instantiate': function (___, IMPORTS___) {
            return ___.prepareModule({
                'instantiate': function (___, IMPORTS___) {
                    var $v = ___.readImport(IMPORTS___, '$v', {
                        'getOuters': { '()': {} },
                        'initOuter': { '()': {} },
                        'cf': { '()': {} },
                        'ro': { '()': {} }
                    });
                    var moduleResult___, $dis, el___, emitter___, c_1___;
                    moduleResult___ = ___.NO_RESULT;
                    $dis = $v.getOuters();
                    $v.initOuter('onerror');
                    {
                        emitter___ = IMPORTS___.htmlEmitter___;
                        el___ = emitter___.byId('id_2___');
                        c_1___ = ___.markFuncFreeze(function (event, thisNode___) {
                            $v.cf($v.ro('goRedirect'), [ ]);
                        });
                        el___.onclick = function (event) {
                            return plugin_dispatchEvent___(this, event,
                            ___.getId(IMPORTS___), c_1___);
                        };
                        emitter___.setAttr(el___, 'id', 'redirect-' +
                        IMPORTS___.getIdClass___());
                        el___ = emitter___.finish();
                    }
                    return moduleResult___;
                },
                'cajolerName': 'com.google.caja',
                'cajolerVersion': '4319',
                'cajoledDate': 1288626955029
            })(IMPORTS___), ___.prepareModule({
                'instantiate': function (___, IMPORTS___) {
                    var $v = ___.readImport(IMPORTS___, '$v', {
                        'getOuters': { '()': {} },
                        'initOuter': { '()': {} },
                        'so': { '()': {} },
                        's': { '()': {} },
                        'ro': { '()': {} },
                        'dis': { '()': {} }
                    });
                    var moduleResult___, $dis;
                    moduleResult___ = ___.NO_RESULT;
                    $dis = $v.getOuters();
                    $v.initOuter('onerror');
                    try {
```

```
{
    {
        $v.so('goRedirect', ___.markFuncFreeze(function () {
            var goRedirect;
            function goRedirect$_caller($dis) {
                var href;
                href = 'http://www.yahoo.com';
                $v.s($v.ro('window'), 'location', href);
            }
            goRedirect$_caller.FUNC___ = 'goRedirect$_caller';
            goRedirect = $v.dis(___.primFreeze(goRedirect$_caller),
                'goRedirect');
            return goRedirect;
        }).CALL___());
    }
} catch (ex___) {
    ___.getNewModuleHandler().handleUncaughtException(ex___,
    $v.ro('onerror'), 'ch9_caja_sample_html.html', '13');
}
return moduleResult___;
},
'cajolerName': 'com.google.caja',
'cajolerVersion': '4319',
'cajoledDate': 1288626955094
})(IMPORTS___), ___.prepareModule({
    'instantiate': function (___, IMPORTS___) {
        var moduleResult___;
        moduleResult___ = ___.NO_RESULT;
        {
            IMPORTS___.htmlEmitter___.signalLoaded();
        }
        return moduleResult___;
    },
    'cajolerName': 'com.google.caja',
    'cajolerVersion': '4319',
    'cajoledDate': 1288626955121
})(IMPORTS___);
},
'cajolerName': 'com.google.caja',
'cajolerVersion': '4319',
'cajoledDate': 1288626955128
});
}
```

The reason this new JavaScript block is so much more extensive than the code we started with is that the cajoled code applies error checks and security layers on top of our original code. Our original functionality is highlighted in the preceding example, now with secured access to our redirection code.

Modifying the Cajoler Rendering Format

The cajoling script gives us the option to alter the cajoling output through a few rendering methods. In the following command, besides the input and output files that we have already talked about, you'll see an -r option at the end. This option allows us to specify the rendering method that we want to use during the cajoling process:

```
bin/cajole_html -i <htmlInputFile> -o <outputTarget> -r <rendererOption>
```

There are a number of attributes that we can set as our renderOption, as listed in Table 8-1.

Table 8-1. renderOption attributes

Attribute	Description
minify	Specifies whether to return the cajoled code as a minified file or not. It is best to output the cajoled code as a minified block if you are planning on displaying it in a production environment.
pretty	This option is the cajoler's default output. It will display the cajoled output in a human-readable format.
sidebyside	Displays the original source code in comments above the cajoled code. This is extremely helpful for identifying where in the final cajoled code base your original content was rewritten to.
debugger	Displays a series of debugging output at the bottom of the cajoled JavaScript file.

These rendering options will help you read and understand the code produced by the cajoling process.

Running Caja from a Web Application

 The full code for this sample is available at *https://github.com/jcleblanc/programming-social-applications/blob/master/chapter_8/caja_web_application.html*.

We've seen how to take a mixed HTML and JavaScript document and cajole it into two files made up of the sanitized markup and cajoled JavaScript of the original code. Taking that knowledge as our base, we'll now explore how to cajole content from a web source.

The SVN source that we obtained for Caja includes a sanitization JavaScript file that will allow us to run a cajoling function against some provided web content. The file is located at *src/com/google/caja/plugin/html-sanitizer.js* within the *caja* directory.

The other file we will need is a whitelist of all of the available HTML tags, which the sanitizer will use to determine which tags should be left alone, which should be sanitized, and which should be removed completely. A sample file (*html4-defs.js*) with this type of structure is available at *https://github.com/jcleblanc/programming-social-applications/tree/master/caja/web_sanitizer_simple/* and provides an aggressive parsing whitelist that we will use in our example.

With these two files in hand, we can begin building out the markup and JavaScript to create a simple parsing mechanism:

```
<!DOCTYPE html PUBLIC "-//W3C//DTD HTML 4.01//EN"
                      "http://www.w3.org/TR/html4/strict.dtd">
<html>
<head>
<title>Simple Web Application Cajoler</title>
</head>
<body>
<script src="html4-defs.js"></script>
<script src="../../src/com/google/caja/plugin/html-sanitizer.js"></script>

<h1>Original Content</h1>
<div id="original"></div>

<h1>Cajoled Content</h1>
<div id="cajoled"></div>

<script>
//build mixed HTML / JavaScript content string
var content = '<h2>Testing Web Cajoler</h2>\n'
            + '<a href="javascript:alert(0)">'
            + '<img src="http://code.google.com/p/google-caja/logo"></a>\n'
            + '<a href="http://code.google.com/p/google-caja">test</a>\n'
            + '<script src="http://attacker.com/snifftraffic.js"><\/script>';

//display original content before cajoling
document.getElementById("original").innerText = content;

//display cajoled content
document.getElementById("cajoled").innerText = html_sanitize(content);
</script>
</body>
</html>
```

The first elements that we set up in the body of our sample are the links to the two files just described. The *html-sanitizer.js* file contains the function html_sanitize(...), which we will use to sanitize code within our web application. The *html4-defs.js* file contains the HTML and script nodes, plus their associated attributes, that will help the cajoler understand how to parse the content that we will push through to the html_sanitize(...) function.

Next, we set up two div nodes to hold the output of our sample. The first, with an id of original, is the nonsanitized code that we will use for comparison. The second, with an id of cajoled, is the same code after being run through the cajoler.

As we start our script block, we first build the mixed HTML/JavaScript string that we want to use as our test content for the cajoler. In that test content, we embed a standard <h2> tag, an <img> tag that has an <a> link with an embedded JavaScript alert, a standard link, and finally a *script include* that attempts to load some undesirable content.

We then output the content of that string into the div node that we set up to hold the original code prior to cajoling.

In the last element, we output the cajoled content of the same code to our cajoled `div` node. This process uses the `html_sanitize(...)` function in the *html-sanitizer.js* file to cajole the content that we set up based on the whitelisted tags in the *html4-defs.js* file.

When we load the sample file in our browser, we are presented with the output that was loaded into both `div` nodes.

Our original content is a direct insertion of the content string that we set up. There is nothing special of note here, with the exception of being able to use the output in a direct comparison with the cajoled content:

```
Original Content
<h2>Testing Web Cajoler</h2>
<a href="javascript:alert(0)">
    <img src="http://code.google.com/p/google-caja/logo?cct=1282547901">
</a>
<a href="http://code.google.com/p/google-caja">
    test
</a>
<script src="http://www.attacker.com/snifftraffic.js"></script>
```

The cajoled content is much more interesting. It's the same content as the previous code, but it has been sanitized to remove anything that the whitelist deemed a potential security risk to a user viewing the content:

```
Cajoled Content
<h2>Testing Web Cajoler</h2>
<a><img></a>
<a>test</a>
```

The sanitization process performed the following actions:

1. Attribute removal: The `href` attributes have been removed from both anchor tags, as the whitelist deems them potentially harmful due to URI security concerns.

2. Attribute removal: The `src` of the `<img>` tag has been removed due to security concerns about the URI.

3. Element removal: Script `src` elements have been deemed harmful and have thus been removed.

You can manipulate the whitelist structure to allow additional tags through in this example. The whitelist object we've used in this case is a much more aggressive parsing mechanism than the one embedded in the standard cajoling process.

Running Caja with an OpenSocial Gadget

As we've seen, the command-line scripts in the Caja *bin* directory include a script to run the command-line cajoler on an input file. There used to be another option here for cajoling a gadget automatically, `cajole_gadget`, but that has been removed from Caja's base functionality and has instead been integrated into the Shindig core as a user-enabled extension. Thus, the `cajole_gadget` script is no longer an option for com-mand-line cajoling of OpenSocial gadgets.

So, in the next sections, we will explore other ways to integrate Caja into an existing gadget to secure the gadget rendering process.

Adding Caja to a Gadget

To add Caja capabilities into an OpenSocial gadget, we can leverage the feature to include abilities in the gadget XML specification. We do this by embedding a `Require` statement for the Caja feature within the `ModulePrefs` of an OpenSocial gadget.

```
<ModulePrefs>
 <Require feature="caja" />
</ModulePrefs>
```

This will include the Caja JavaScript libraries that provide the capability to cajole a gadget's views.

Caja is a standard feature available within Apache Shindig 1.1.

A Practical Example

The full code for this sample is available at *https://github.com/jcleblanc/ programming-social-applications/blob/master/chapter_8/caja_openso cial_gadget.xml.*

Now that we know how to initialize the cajoler within an OpenSocial gadget, let's explore a real gadget to see how this is implemented in practice.

Our gadget's function is to display a numeric value on the screen that defaults to 0. We will then offer a series of buttons to increment or decrement that value:

```
<?xml version="1.0" encoding="utf-8"?>
<Module>
    <ModulePrefs title="Caja Sample"
                 title_url="http://www.jcleblanc.com"
                 description="Displays a simple content section to cajole"
                 author="Jonathan LeBlanc">
        <Require feature="opensocial-0.9"/>
        <Require feature="caja" />
    </ModulePrefs>
    <Content type="html">
        <![CDATA[
        <div id="number">0</div>
```

```
        <button onclick="changeNum('+')">+</button>
        <button onclick="changeNum('-')">-</button>

        <script type="text/javascript">
        //increment or decrement the counter
        function changeNum(changeType){
            var num = document.getElementById("number");
            num.innerHTML = (changeType == "+") ?
                            parseInt(num.innerHTML) + 1 :
                            parseInt(num.innerHTML) - 1;
        }
        </script>
    ]]>
    </Content>
</Module>
```

Our gadget includes the Caja feature that makes the JavaScript libraries for the cajoling process available in the gadget. The gadget's Content section is what will be cajoled when the gadget is rendered in a container that supports Caja.

Once the container has cajoled our gadget's content, the Content section will likely remind you of the HTML/JavaScript cajoled scripts from earlier in the chapter:

```
try {
    {
        $v.so('changeNum', ___.markFuncFreeze(function () {
            var changeNum;
            function changeNum$_caller($dis, changeType) {
                var num;
                num = $v.cm($v.ro('document'), 'getElementById', [
                    'number' ]);
                $v.s(num, 'innerHTML', changeType == '+'?
                $v.cf($v.ro('parseInt'), [ $v.r(num, 'innerHTML') ]
                    ) + 1: $v.cf($v.ro('parseInt'), [ $v.r(num,
                    'innerHTML') ]) - 1);
            }
            changeNum$_caller.FUNC___ = 'changeNum$_caller';
            changeNum = $v.dis(___.primFreeze(changeNum$_caller),
                'changeNum');
            return changeNum;
        }).CALL___());
    }
} catch (ex___) {
    ___.getNewModuleHandler().handleUncaughtException(ex___,
    $v.ro('onerror'), 'redirection.html', '7');
}
```

The preceding snippet contains only the subset of the code output that directly relates to our original content, instead of the entire block of cajoled JavaScript as we saw previously in the HTML/JavaScript example.

Using JSLint to Spot JavaScript Issues Early

JSLint will hurt your feelings.

—Douglas Crockford

JSLint is a tool developed by Douglas Crockford[*] to compile source JavaScript and inform the user of any potential security and rendering issues that are present in the code. The compiler itself is written in JavaScript, so it's a fully encapsulated JavaScript environment.

 You can access the JSLint tool at *http://www.jslint.org*. The site lets you select what types of issues you would like to search for and report on.

For instance, take the following JavaScript code, which calculates a timestamp based on a provided year, month, and day:

```
function toTimestamp(year, month, day){
    var datum = new Date(Date.UTC(year,month-1,day));
    return datum.getTime()/1000
}

tstamp = toTimestamp(2011, 5, 15);
```

If we run this code block through the JSLint process, we will receive a series of messages listing all of the things that are wrong with our code:

```
Error:
 Problem at line 3 character 31: Missing semicolon.
 return datum.getTime()/1000
  Implied global: tstamp 6
```

In this message, we can see that we are missing a semicolon in our function's `return` statement. In addition, our `tstamp` variable is not specified with a `var` at any point, so it is referenced as an implied global.

Now, if we run the same code through the cajoling process instead, we can see that it reports similar issues:

```
LOG Checkpoint: InlineCssImportsStage at T+0.548912216 seconds:
LOG timestamp.html:4+31: Semicolon inserted:history.html:4:
    return datum.getTime()/1000
LOG Checkpoint: RewriteHtmlStage at T+0.096969253 seconds:
```

---

[*] Douglas Crockford is well known for his work with the JSON specification and his efforts to define a professional subset of JavaScript that engineers should use as a standard. If you'd like further information, his book *JavaScript: The Good Parts* (O'Reilly; *http://oreilly.com/catalog/9780596517748*) is an excellent resource.

The preceding portion of LOG messages shows that the semicolon insertion issue has been caught. The Caja sanitization process has silently handled the global variable reported by the JSLint process.

JSLint is an excellent tool for debugging JavaScript before passing it through the Caja cajoling process. It provides extensive details on potentially unsafe JavaScript practices and attempts to help developers process issues with their code prior to implementing it in any production-ready products.

 Before passing JavaScript through the Caja cajoler, you should resolve all errors reported in the JSLint process. If Caja is generating generic error messages, JSLint can also make an excellent debugging tool.

Playing in the Caja Playground

Caja Playground (Figure 8-1) was developed by Google to test the cajoling process for scripts in a sandboxed environment. It can be accessed at *http://caja.appspot.com/* and contains a number of predefined scripts and sites that can help a developer who's just getting started with Caja.

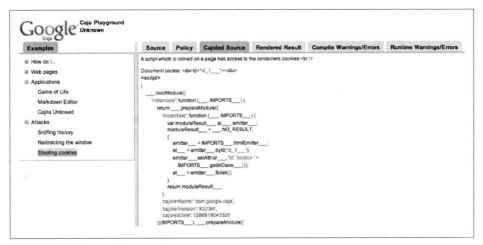

Figure 8-1. The Caja Playground

This utility is the perfect tool for testing out script blocks in a safe environment prior to migrating over to a fully cajoled environment. You will be able to test out modular blocks of code or entire sites by cajoling them, testing the rendered output, and noting any associated errors or warnings that crop up during the process.

Tips for Working in a Caja Environment

Developers who are working with Caja for the first time usually have one of two mindsets:

- *The JavaScript I write is secure and will pass through Caja without a problem.*
- *Caja is going to prevent any of my code from working.*

Caja can seem daunting, but with an understanding of working with JavaScript in an application environment and a few tips on building in this environment, you'll find the process much easier.

Implement Code Modularity: Don't Cajole an Entire Project

 Testing code often by passing it through the cajoling process can help eliminate issues early and give developers a good idea of their project's progress.

One of the worst things that a developer can do when cajoling a block of code is to attempt to cajole a large amount of JavaScript at once. (If you are new to Caja, doing this might traumatize you.) Most likely what will be produced is an extensive number of warnings and errors about issues with the code, many of which may be reported due to *other* errors or warnings in the code. This will tend to scare away many developers and may not be a very accurate representation of the code's issues.

Developing code in a modular fashion—e.g., building encapsulated reusable blocks in standard functions—is the first step in ensuring that it can be tested in blocks. The goal to this approach is the ability to integrate *function by function* into the script that is being cajoled, so you can deal with errors and warnings from the cajoling process in a much more manageable way.

When migrating an existing code base to an environment that runs Caja, you can use this approach as well. Working with small blocks of code instead of attempting to debug an entire code base can help you manage the output of the cajoling process.

Use Precajoled JavaScript Libraries

JavaScript libraries such as YUI, JQuery, Prototype, and Dojo have become core tools in website and application development. Numerous library developers have made strides in providing at least a subset of their libraries that can be cajoled without generating errors. The YUI, JQuery, and Prototype libraries currently have the most development work completed toward cajoling subsets of their functionality.

The YUI 2.8 (*http://developer.yahoo.com/yui/2/*) library has the most documentation on its availability within a cajoled environment. It marked the first attempt by the cross-functional YUI, Caja, and Developer Network teams at Yahoo! to provide a subset for use within Caja. As of YUI 2.8, any version 2 of the library can be cajoled if needed. YUI 3 is currently not tested within a Caja environment.

During development, the teams were able to release a large subset of 2.8's functionality, including the following components:

- YUI core
  - YAHOO global object (base requirement for all YUI components)
  - DOM collection (convenience methods for DOM interactions)
  - Event utility (event normalization and custom events)
- YUI library utilities
  - Animation utility
  - Connection manager (for XHR/AJAX)
  - DataSource utility
  - Drag and drop utility
  - Element utility
  - ImageLoader utility
  - Resize utility
  - Selector utility
- YUI library controls/widgets
  - AutoComplete
  - Button
  - Container (including Module, Overlay, Panel, Tooltip, Dialog, and SimpleDialog)
  - Menu
  - TabView
  - TreeView

The source and tests for the YUI 2.8 cajoling effort are available at *https://github.com/ jcleblanc/yui-caja* and can help provide a richer degree of functionality to an existing application in this type of environment.

Having the ability to use JavaScript libraries can help alleviate some of the tricky parts of working with Caja. To increase performance, the container may also provide pre-cajoled versions of the libraries so that the overhead of running the cajoler will not impact the third-party code each time it loads within the container or website.

Don't Rely on Firebug or the Cajoled JavaScript Source Code

As we've seen in the cajoled scripts we've built thus far, the cajoled JavaScript is not output in a very human-readable form. This means that traditional frontend engineering methods for parsing scripts, such as Firebug, are no longer very effective unless you're really familiar with the functionality of the cajoled code.

Some of the best methods available for working with the functionality of the JavaScript layer are those that we have already explored: JSLint and the Caja Playground. JSLint will allow you to test the viability of the JavaScript for the Caja process, and the Caja Playground will allow you to test the individual functions and features of a JavaScript block.

Don't Embed Events in Markup

Many newer developers (or those trying to cut corners) tend to embed the JavaScript event handler directly in the markup of their application or site, such as:

```
<a href="javascript:void(0)" onclick="processForm();">Process Form</a>
```

While this may work perfectly fine in an unprotected environment, adding event handlers like this may cause Caja to strip them out of the final output in many containers or sites. Although restrictions are imposed on the server-side cajoler that runs when the code first loads, the client-side sanitizer that runs against code inserted after the initial load—such as through an innerHTML call—is much stricter about what code it allows through.

The practice of not embedding events in markup is especially valuable when you are obtaining content from another source, such as through an AJAX request, where that source has embedded JavaScript events, and then you attempt to load it into the existing content through an innerHTML call. In most instances, the client-side sanitizer will strip all JavaScript from the AJAX return value, leaving you with a nonfunctional node structure. In this case, once an AJAX request returns, you can immediately file off a function to assign click handlers to required DOM nodes.

There are a few methods you can employ to attach event handlers to DOM nodes. In Caja's early days, when the onclick method was restricted, using addEventListener or attachEvent (depending on the browser) was one of the best options available. Both methods are now viable for adding events to nodes:

```
<div id="method1">Clicking here will do something!</div>
<div id="method2">Clicking here will do something too!</div>

<script type="text/javascript">
//method 1 click handler
function handler1(sender){
    document.getElementById('method1').innerHTML = "Method 1 Clicked";
}
```

```
//method 2 click handler
function handler2(sender){
    document.getElementById('method2').innerHTML = "Method 2 Clicked";
}

//attach click events for method 1
var myClickEl = document.getElementById('method1');
if(myClickEl.addEventListener){
    myClickEl.addEventListener('click', handler1, false);
} else if(myClickEl.attachEvent){
    myClickEl.attachEvent('click', handler1);
}

//attach click events for method 2
var myClickEl2 = document.getElementById('method2');
myClickEl2.onclick = handler2;
</script>
```

The full code for this sample is available at *https://github.com/jcleblanc/ programming-social-applications/blob/master/chapter_8/caja_working _event_handlers.html*.

We have a few pieces to look at in the preceding code. First, we set up the `div` nodes that we will add our events to. At the top of our `script` block, we then set up the two event handlers for each node, which will change the `innerHTML` content of the nodes when clicked.

We then get down to method 1, adding our first event handler. Using `addEvent Listener` and `attachEvent`, we bind a click event to our first `div` node. We have both methods in place to support all browsers, new and old. The second event handler uses the standard `onclick` approach to bind the event to a handler function.

Using this approach, you can bind any events in a cajoled environment, regardless of the security policy restrictions on where JavaScript events can be bound.

Centralize JavaScript: Request Data and Markup Only

Separating out your JavaScript, HTML, and CSS layers can help alleviate many of the issues that Caja introduces in a fully embedded system.

As we have touched on once or twice already, the Caja client-side sanitizer can be a much stricter system than the server-side cajoler. This client-side part of Caja tends to strip out all JavaScript and any potentially malicious HTML and CSS from the data being pushed on the site or application.

This issue will surface when the developers are trying to make HTTP requests—such as a standard AJAX request—to another source to obtain new content for the web application. The client-side sanitizer springs into action when the request completes and the content is about to be inserted into the application via an `innerHTML` call, through creating new DOM nodes and appending them to the application, or by way of any other similar insertion utility.

Let's say we have an application that has multiple pages. When a user clicks on a new page, an AJAX request fetches new markup for the page from the server and then replaces the current page when the request completes. Some developers might tend to encapsulate each page as a single unit, including the required JavaScript to run that particular page right in the markup that is returned to the application. This is where the trouble will arise, since the client-side sanitizer will strip all of that JavaScript from the return.

One of the best options for implementing this type of application structure is to centralize all JavaScript and load it when the application first loads, putting it under the less restrictive server-side cajoler parsing utility. When I say "centralize," I am referring to the load time, not a single file—JavaScript files should be broken up into logical sections, preferably minified.

Questions often arise from this discussion about attaching events to markup if inline JavaScript markup such as `onclick`, `onkeypress`, or the like is removed. Once the new markup is inserted into the application, events can be attached to their logical points. Our last tip, "Don't Embed Events in Markup," outlines the steps you should take to insert events into existing markup.

Many developers may argue that these are general best practices anyway, which should be followed even when they're not under the umbrella of Caja's cajoler and sanitizer.

A Lighter Alternative to Caja: ADsafe

ADsafe is a system that first gained popularity as a utility for cordoning off ads running on a page, since ads are simply one form of self-inflicted cross-site scripting (XSS) attack.

ADsafe's premise is to prevent a developer from using markup that is deemed unsafe, restrict access to the global page object, and limit access to variable types from the third-party code. Essentially, this creates a sandbox that protects the root site or container from third-party code by limiting the functionality that can exist within an application.

ADsafe removes the following features from JavaScript:

Global variables
> Variables that are defined in the global scope are not allowed within ADsafe. ADsafe does, however, permit limited access to the `Array`, `Boolean`, `Number`, `String`, and `Math` global objects of the page.

`this`

Since the use of `this` within a function request maintains a binding to the global object, it is restricted in ADsafe.

`eval`

`eval` provides access to the global scope, much like many of our other restricted tags, and also provides a mechanism for executing insecure code at runtime.

`arguments`

Access to the `arguments` pseudo array is restricted.

`with`

Since `with` modifies the scope chain, its use is restricted.

Dangerous methods and properties

Due to capability leakage in some browsers, `arguments`, `callee`, `caller`, `construc tor`, `prototype`, `stack`, `unwatch`, `valueOf`, and `watch` are not allowed in ADsafe when implemented using dot notation.

Names starting or ending with an underscore (_)

This is restricted due to dangerous properties or methods that may be defined with a dangling underscore in some browsers.

`Date` *and* `Math.random` *objects*

These objects are restricted to make it easier to determine the widget's behavior.

`[] subscript`

May be used only with a positive numeric value or a literal string.

Although the ADsafe service has a number of restrictions, it also provides numerous functions for accessing and working with the DOM safely. We will explore many of these functions in the following sections.

ADsafe Versus Caja: Which One Should You Use?

We have taken a thorough look at the Caja system for protecting a root site or container (and its associated users) from third-party code being hosted on it. Now that we are looking at a lighter solution to the same issue—ADsafe—we will inevitably need to answer the question of which one we should use. Let's look at our choices in a little more depth.

I categorize ADsafe into the *semitrust* bucket. What I mean by this is that ADsafe does a good job of removing many of the major tools that a malicious developer could use to attack a user. This does not mean that ADsafe takes into account and adjusts for *all* attack vectors; it just means ADsafe takes away a lot of the sharpest knives from the developer. When I say semitrust bucket, I am referring to the level of trust you have in the third-party code being hosted. ADsafe makes a great system if you *partially* trust the code that will be hosted, as you would in the case of ads. You trust that the source is a legitimate ad company, but you may not be entirely confident that it will never have an issue with its ads that affects your site (i.e., the site that the ads are hosted on). This is the perfect use case for ADsafe: when you have a limited trust relationship with the source of the content being hosted, and you know where the content may be coming from. The impact on developers building code to exist within an ADsafe object is minimal, and users are fairly well protected from malicious code.

On the other hand, I categorize Caja into a *no-trust* bucket. This means that Caja is a perfect tool for hosting code from sources that you don't know and developers that you have not built a trust relationship with. Since Caja's aim is to remove any malicious attack vectors from the third-party code being hosted and rewrite the entire code base into a secure version, it ensures that most of the malicious code that developers implement has been removed before the user ever interacts with it. This is a much more secure system for the user, but presents more challenges to the developer building out the code for the site or container.

Overall, ADsafe and Caja both have their target markets. Though they may overlap a bit, their primary developer audiences are quite different, which makes both ADsafe and Caja very acceptable solutions depending on the problem at hand.

How to Implement ADsafe

There are a few general guidelines and steps for wrapping third-party code, and thus adding in the protective checks, in the ADsafe container.

Our first task is to attach the ADsafe JavaScript library file into the page. This file can either link directly to a hosted version that is available in the Github ADsafe project (*adsafe.js* in *https://github.com/douglascrockford/ADsafe*), or it can be a local copy if you prefer:

```
<script src="http://www.ADsafe.org/adsafe.js"></script>
```

Once the script include is in place, we can make requests to create a new ADsafe object, encapsulating the application code from the third-party source:

```
"use strict";
ADSAFE.go("APPNAME_", function(dom){
    //application code
});
```

Let's explore this object in more depth to see the markup required around the go request.

Setting Up the ADSafe Object

To create the simplest ADsafe object we can use to encapsulate third-party code, we must follow this basic syntax:

```
<div id="APPNAME_">
    application markup
```

```
<script>
"use strict";
ADSAFE.go("APPNAME_", function(dom){
    //application functions and code
});
</script>
</div>
```

This code requirement starts with a `div` node that wraps the entire object. The `div` node has a few requirements itself:

- The `div` node must contain an `id`.
- The `id` must be made up of only uppercase ASCII letters.
- The `id` must have a trailing underscore (_) character.

At the root of the `div` node, we define the markup required to render the application:

```
<div id="APPNAME_">
    <span id="APPNAME_DATA"></span>
    ...
</div>
```

Any subnodes that are defined with an `id` property must follow the same `id` naming criteria as the root `div` node, but the `id` must be made up of the root `div` node's `id` and the name of the node itself. If the markup IDs do not follow this naming convention, you will be presented with the following log message if you try to collect the node via a query:

```
ADsafe error: ADsafe: Bad query:#test
```

Next, the `ADSAFE.go(...)` method provides the application with a DOM object that extends a limited subset of functionality to the main DOM.

The ADsafe object contains several methods that give developers additional functionality to allow DOM selection, event handling, and a number of other utilities. These are listed in Table 8-2.

Table 8-2. ADsafe object methods

Method	Description
create(*object*)	Creates a new object.
get(*object, name*)	Obtains the value of an object's name property.
go(*id, function*)	Starts the ADsafe widget. *id* must match the ID of the `div` node that it is contained within. *function* provides the access object for the DOM subset.
id(*id*)	Defines the widget. *id* must match the ID of the `div` node that it is contained within.
isArray(*value*)	If the value is an array, this method will return `true`.
later(*function, milli seconds*)	The `later` method functions like the `setTimeout` JavaScript function. It will call *func tion* at a defined time in the future, in milliseconds.
lib(*name, 23function*)	Creates an ADsafe library with a specified name. The function wraps the content of the library.

Method	Description
log(*string*)	Outputs a string to the browser log. In Firefox, this would be the Firebug console; in Chrome, this would be the console in the developer tools.
remove(*object*, *name*)	Removes a name property from an object.
set(*object*, *name*, *value*)	Sets a name property of an object with a specified value.

This is a simple implementation of the core ADsafe requirements for a basic application. We'll use this as a foundation to explore the features that can be implemented within the ADsafe object we've defined within the ADsafe.go(...) method.

The DOM Object

The DOM object has a series of methods through which you can obtain information about the document tree and manipulate it as you see fit. After capturing an object from the DOM, you will be able to run a series of methods on it. These methods are listed in Table 8-3.

Table 8-3. DOM object methods

Method	Description
.append(*bunch*)	Appends the objects in *bunch* to the end of the dom object. This method returns the concatenated dom object: ```var dom = dom.append(dom.q("#APPNAME_NODEID"));```

.combine(*array*)	Combines an array of bunches into a single bunch:
	
	 ```var bunch1 = dom.q("a");```
	```var bunch2 = dom.q("p");```
	```var combinedBunch = dom.combine([bunch1, bunch2]);```

.count()	The count method run against the DOM object will always return 1. ```var domCount = dom.count();```

.ephemeral(*bunch*)	Removes all nodes set as ephemeral when:
	
	 • The mouse button moves up.
	 • The escape key is pressed.
	 • Another bunch is set as ephemeral.
	
	 ```//set ephemeral state for all dom nodes```
	```var parentDiv = dom.ephemeral();```

.fragment()	Creates a new HTML document fragment with the intention of attaching it to the currently visible document tree. This object may be a container of nodes and will disappear once appended to the live document tree.
	
	 ```//create new document fragment```
	```var fragment = dom.fragment();```

.prepend(*bunch*)	Prepends the nodes in *bunch* before the first element in the DOM tree. The DOM will be provided back as the return value of the method request.

Method	Description
| | ```
//move all images to the top of the DOM tree
var moveBunch = dom.q("img");
var newDOM = dom.prepend(moveBunch);
``` |
| .q(query) | Allows you to search the DOM tree for specific nodes based on hunter and pecker selectors (described in the next section). The method will always return a bunch object containing 0 to many nodes. An exception will be thrown if the query is malformed or if a hunter selector is not the first selector.<br><br>```
//capture all paragraph nodes with a class of textNode
var bunch = dom.q("p.textNode");
``` |
| .remove() | Removes all nodes from the current DOM object, rendering the ADsafe widget useless.<br><br>```
//remove all nodes from dom
dom.remove();
``` |
| .row(array) | Creates a new HTML <tr> node. Each array item in the method call should be a text node. These text nodes will be inserted into the <tr> as <td> nodes, and a bunch containing the <tr> node will be returned. The row object will not be automatically attached to the document tree.<br><br>```
//create 2 text nodes and build row using them
var textNode1 = dom.text("My first td node");
var textNode2 = dom.text("My second td node");
var row = dom.row([textNode1, textNode2]);
``` |
| .tag(tagName, type, name) | Allows you to create a new HTML node that will not be attached automatically to the document tree. The tagName parameter is the node that you are trying to create. If tagName is set to button or input, you can supply the optional second type parameter to define the text for the object. The optional third parameter, user name, will allow you to supply a name for the new node, which is helpful for grouping radio buttons together.<br><br>```
//create new input text box node to hold a username
var node = dom.tag("input","text","username");
``` |
| .text(string) | Creates a new text node that will not be attached to the DOM tree. A bunch object will be returned with the newly created node. If an array of strings was provided to the method, then an array of nodes will be returned in the bunch.<br><br>```
//create new text node and attach to DOM
var textNode = dom.text("My new text node");
dom.prepend(textNode);
``` |

These DOM manipulation and targeting methods allow you to process large numbers of structures at once, instead of having to drill down to individual nodes or bunches of nodes.

Should you need to drill down to specific nodes in the DOM, there is a querying structure available for you to use, which we will explore next.

DOM Selection with the Query Method

One fantastic feature that ADsafe makes available for third-party code developers is a simple method, q, for performing DOM selection tasks. With this method, you can return one or more node elements and use `id` or `tagName` selectors with additional levels of criteria to filter that data into smaller subsets depending on your requirements.

Given that a new ADsafe widget has been instantiated with the go(...) method and uses a variable `dom` within the function that wraps the third-party code, providing limited access to the true DOM of the root page:

```
ADSAFE.go("APPNAME_", function(dom){ ... }
```

we can use the q method, made available through the `dom` variable, to perform DOM selection on elements within the third-party widget code:

```
dom.q("#APPNAME_NODEID");
```

The *hunter selector* `#APPNAME_NODEID` is just one way to capture an element within the DOM based on a provided ID. The q(...) method provides a number of other hunter selectors that we can use for the same task, as shown in Table 8-4.

Table 8-4. Query method hunter selectors

Selector	Description
#id	Return the node whose ID matches that located in the selector.
	`dom.q("#APPNAME_DATA");`
tagName	Return all nodes that match the tag name in the selector.
	`dom.q("span");`
+ tagName	Select all immediate sibling nodes with a matching tag name.
	`dom.q("+p");`
> tagName	Select all immediate child nodes with a matching tag name.
	`dom.q(">div");`
/	Select all immediate child nodes.
	`dom.q("/");`
*	Select all descendent nodes.
	`dom.q("*");`

DOM selection through the query method in ADsafe is the foundation for effectively working with the application or site's markup. It allows us to attach events to nodes, obtain values for properties and user-entered data, and set new values and properties dynamically.

The hunter selectors listed in Table 8-4 are just the start of what we can do with the query method. Concatenating query hunter selectors with specific *pecker selectors* will allow us to filter the query method to return a wide array of results, depending on the specific needs of the application or site.

Working with pecker selectors

Pecker selectors are additional search parameters that allow you to filter the query method to search for node properties, attributes, or even the state of the nodes themselves. Using these features, we can set up a network of advanced querying features to drill down to only the specific nodes that we are looking for.

Property selectors. Using *property selectors* allows us to filter a query and its resulting bunch object for a broad list of matching nodes based on the node class, name, and type. These selectors, shown in Table 8-5, will often come up in queries that are run against the markup of the ADsafe application or site.

Table 8-5. Property selectors

Selector	Description
.class	Keeps nodes with a specific class name.
| | ```
//keep all div nodes with a class of nodeClass
dom.q("div.nodeClass");
``` |
| &name | Keeps nodes with a specific name attribute. |
| | ```
//keep all input nodes with a name of username
dom.q("input&username");
``` |
| _type | Keeps nodes with a matching type. |
| | ```
//keep all radio input nodes
dom.q("input_radio");
``` |

Using these pecker selectors as our base, we can begin adding selector features to build up our advanced queries.

Attribute selectors. Getting into more specific pecker selectors now, we can use attribute selectors (Table 8-6) to search for nodes with attributes that do or do not contain specific values. These searches are much like using a regex search algorithm against a string in that they allow you to return a bunch containing only nodes that have a value, don't have a value, start or end with a value, contain a value, or meet a number of other search parameters.

Table 8-6. Attribute selectors

Selector	Description
[attribute]	Keeps nodes with the specified attribute.
| | ```
//keep all input nodes that have a type attribute
dom.q("input [type]");
``` |
| [attribute = value] | Keeps nodes with the specified attribute that matches a provided value. |
| | ```
//keep all input nodes that have a type of text
dom.q("input [type = text]");
``` |
| [attribute != value] | Keeps nodes with the specified attribute that does not match a provided value. |
| | ```
//keep all input nodes that do not have a type of radio
dom.q("input [type != radio]");
``` |

Selector	Description
[*attribute* *= *value*]	Keeps nodes with the specified attribute that contains a provided value.
	``//keep all image nodes that have alt text containing logo
dom.q("img [alt *= logo]");```
[*attribute* ^= *value*]	Keeps nodes with the specified attribute that starts with a provided value.
	``//keep all span nodes that have a class attribute starting with small
dom.q("span [class ^= small]");```
[*attribute* $= *value*]	Keeps nodes with the specified attribute that ends with a provided value.
	``//find all .gif format images
dom.q("img [src $= gif]");```
[*attribute* ~= *value*]	Keeps nodes with the specified attribute that contains a provided value as an element in a space-separated list. This is the same as using the .class pecker selector.
	``//keep all div nodes that contain the class of large
dom.q("div [class ~= large]");```
[*attribute* |= *value*]	Keeps nodes with the specified attribute that contains a provided value as an element in a hyphen-separated list.
	``//keep all div nodes with a margin style (inc. margin-left, etc.)
dom.q("div [style	= margin]");```

These highly targeted attribute search features will give you fine-grained control over the results returned in the bunch from your query.

State selectors. Our last group of pecker selector is state selectors (Table 8-7), which allow you to take your queries down to an even deeper level of specificity. The main types of searches you can perform using the state pecker selectors are those that need to return only a specific number of nodes in the bunch object; only nodes that have a specific enabled, visible, checked, or focused status; or only nodes of a specific type.

Table 8-7. State selectors

Selector	Description
: first	Keeps the first node in the bunch.
: rest	Keeps all nodes in the bunch except for the first one.
: even	Keeps half of the nodes in the bunch, starting with the second node.
: odd	Keeps half of the nodes in the bunch, starting with the first node.
: hidden	Keeps all nodes in the bunch that are currently hidden.
: visible	Keeps all nodes in the bunch that are currently visible.
: disabled	Keeps all nodes in the bunch that are in a disabled state.
: enabled	Keeps all nodes in the bunch that are in an enabled state.
: checked	Keeps all nodes in the bunch that are checked (e.g., checkbox).
: unchecked	Keeps all nodes in the bunch that are unchecked.
: focus	Keeps the node that currently has focus.

Selector	Description
: blur	Keeps all nodes that do not currently have focus.
: text	Keeps all text nodes.
: tag	Keeps all nontext nodes.
: trim	Keeps nontext nodes with no values.

State selectors offer you a deeper range of search utilities on top of the property and attribute searches described previously.

Now that we have covered the myriad of hunter and pecker selectors available to us for our searches, we can begin to build out advanced queries to return nodes using highly targeted algorithms.

Building advanced querying methods with hunter and pecker selectors

Even though the basic selectors we've discussed will allow you to capture the majority of the nodes that you want to work with in a page, you can also take advantage of some advanced selection options (Table 8-8) that are made available by concatenating several selectors together.

Table 8-8. Advanced selectors

Selector	Description
*_text	Select all nodes with their type parameter set to text (type=text).
*:text	Select all text nodes.
div + span * : text	Select the text that is within span tags that immediately follow div tags.
input [value*=profile]	Select all input tags that have a value containing the word "profile".
form input_hidden	Select all hidden fields in a form.
form input:hidden	Select all input fields that are hidden within a form.
input_radio&date:unchecked	Select any radio buttons that have a name property of date and are unchecked.
div.*container*.*color*	Select all div nodes that have a class containing both *container* and *color*.
#profileForm button_submit	Select the submit button within the form with the ID of profileForm.
ol//:enabled:hidden	Selects all hidden, enabled tags that are grandchildren within an ordered list.

Using advanced selection options will allow you to drill down to exactly the nodes that you want to work with.

Working with Bunch Objects

ADsafe uses a wrapper object on top of DOM nodes called a *bunch object*. Bunch objects allow the user to easily capture one or multiple DOM nodes under a single bunch and then manipulate all or some of it as needed.

Bunch objects are the cornerstone of all data fetching and manipulation that you will do through ADsafe. They increase code modularity, reduce code bloat, and improve overall application performance.

Within the bunch node wrapper are a series of methods that allow you to capture information about the nodes in the bunch, change and manipulate their attributes and values, and perform actions like cloning the nodes or stripping them from the bunch.

Bunch GET methods

Fetching data about the nodes that are contained within a bunch is the most-often used functionality for bunch objects, and ADsafe makes a series of GET methods available for developers to do this. Depending on the number of nodes contained within the bunch, the return values and structures from the GET method calls will differ, as outlined here:

- If a bunch contains no nodes, then the methods return undefined.
- If a bunch contains one node, a single value is returned (usually as a string).
- If a bunch contains more than one node, an array of values is returned.

There are a number of GET helper methods, described in Table 8-9, available for obtaining information about the bunch nodes returned from a query request.

Table 8-9. Bunch GET methods

Selector	Description
getCheck()	Obtains the checked value of the node.
	`var radioBtn = dom.q("input_radio");` `var isChecked = radioBtn.getCheck();`
getClass()	Obtains the class attribute of the node.
	`var divNode = dom.q("div.data");` `var class = divNode.getClass();`
getEnable()	Obtains the enable value of the node. The return value is a Boolean.
	`var btnSubmit = dom.q("input.submit");` `var submitEnabled = btnSubmit.getEnable();`
getMark()	Obtains the mark from the node.

	`//get a mark from a node with the id of CONTAINER_DATA`
	`var mark = dom.q("#CONTAINER_DATA").getMark();`
	`console.log(mark);`

getName()	Obtains the name attribute from the node.
	`var inputText = dom.q("input_text");` `var inputName = inputText.getName();`
getOffse tHeight()	Obtains the offsetHeight of the nodes. The offsetHeight is calculated by the actual height of the node including the node border but excluding the node margin. This is especially helpful for calculating the positioning nodes in an absolute-positioned environment.

Selector	Description
| | ```
var divNode = dom.q("#innerDiv");
var divHeight = divNode.getOffsetHeight();
``` |
| getOffset Width() | Obtains the offsetWidth of the nodes. The offsetWidth is calculated by the actual height of node including the node border but excluding the node margin. This is especially helpful for calculating the positioning nodes in an absolute-positioned environment. |
| | ```
var divNode = dom.q("#innerDiv");
var divWidth = divNode.getOffsetHeight();
``` |
| getParent() | Obtains the parent of the node, formatted as a bunch. This request will return duplicate entries if the parent of two sibling nodes is requested. If the node whose parent is being requested is the root node, getParent() will throw an exception. |
| | ```
try{
    var node = dom.q("#divWrapper");
    var nodeParent = node.getParent();
} catch(err) {
    //exception thrown - root node
}
``` |
| getSelec tion() | Obtains the text selected by the user in a textarea or input text node. |
| | ```
var input = dom.q("input_text");
var selected = input.getSelection();
``` |
| get Style(name) | Obtains the name CSS style of the node (i.e., where name is the CSS style type, such as position, float, or color). |
| | ```
var div = dom.q("div.positioned");
var divPosition = div.getStyle("position");
``` |
| getTagName() | Obtains the tag name of the node. |
| | ```
var node = dom.q("*.content");
var tags = node.getTagName();
``` |
| getTitle() | Obtains the title of the node. |
| | ```
//get title from node with an id of CONTAINER_DATA
var title = dom.q("#CONTAINER_DATA").getTitle();
console.log(title);
``` |
| getValue() | Obtains the value of the node. If the node requested doesn't have a value associated with it but has a child text node with a value, then that value will be used. If a password field is requested, undefined will be returned. |
| | ```
var input = dom.q("input.username").getValue();
var value = input.getValue();
``` |

By using these GET methods, you will greatly reduce the amount of code required to fetch data from DOM nodes within the ADsafe wrapper.

Bunch SET methods

ADsafe makes available a series of SET methods to allow you to manipulate markup, events, and text within your ADsafe application. These incredibly valuable helper methods are in place to make your life easier.

Many of these SET methods work in conjunction with the GET methods that we have just reviewed. Implementing a good mix of the two will allow you to take advantage of some of the advanced bunch manipulation features.

Using these methods combined with some advanced DOM queries executed through the q() method, you can develop highly targeted modules with a minimal amount of code.

Table 8-10 shows the full list of SET methods available to you.

Table 8-10. Bunch SET methods

Selector	Description

append(*appendees*)	Appends an appendees bunch as children to an existing bunch. If there is more than one appendee, they will be deeply cloned before insertion.
	
	```//append CONTAINER_TEXT node to CONTAINER_DATA node```
	```var data = dom.q("#CONTAINER_TEXT");```
	```var appended = dom.q("#CONTAINER_DATA").append(data);```

blur()	Removes the focus from a node.
	
	```//remove focus for input box with an id of CONTAINER_USER```
	```dom.q("#CONTAINER_USER").blur();```

check(*value*)	Sets the checked state (on or off) for radio or checkbox inputs.
	
	```//auto-check checkbox with a class name of checker```
	```var checkBtn = dom.q("input_checkbox.checker").check(true);```

each(*func*)	Allows you to loop through a series of nodes in a bunch. The *func* argument is a function that takes a bunch argument.
	
	```//loop through all <div> nodes in the application```
	```var dataNode = dom.q("div");```
	```dataNode.each(function(bunch){```
	``` console.log(bunch.getClass());```
	```});```

empty()	Removes all children from a node.
	
	```//remove all children of node with id of CONTAINER_PARENT```
	```var parentDiv = dom.q("#CONTAINER_PARENT");```
	```var emptyParent = parentDiv.empty();```

enable(*boolean*)	Sets the enabled status of a node. *boolean* is set to true for enabled or false for disabled.
	
	```//disable submit button```
	```var submitBtn = dom.q("input_submit").enable(false);```

ephemeral()	Removes all nodes when:
	
	• The mouse button moves up.
	• The escape key is pressed.
	• Another bunch is set as ephemeral.
	
	```//set ephemeral state for node with and id of CONTAINER_PARENT```
	```var parentDiv = dom.q("#CONTAINER_PARENT").ephemeral();```

fire(*event*)	Fires an event on the node. The *event* argument may be: • A string (e.g., click, keypress.)

Selector	Description
	• An object with an event property (e.g., {"*event*": "click"})
| | ```
//fire click event for button with an id of
CONTAINER_BUTTON
var button = dom.q("#CONTAINER_BUTTON");
button.fire("click");
``` |
| focus() | Sets focus to the selected node. |
| | ```
//set focus for input box with an id of CONTAINER_USER
dom.q("#CONTAINER_USER").focus();
``` |
| klass(*string*) | Sets the CSS class of a node to that added as the string argument to the method. |
| | ```
//set class for node with an id of CONTAINER_DATA to
"red"
var dataObj = dom.q("#CONTAINER_DATA").klass("red");
``` |
| mark(*value*) | Sets a mark on all nodes in a bunch. This essentially just allows you to tag nodes with data or notes, such as text or JSON structures. These marks can later be consumed with the getMark() bunch GET method. |
| | ```
//set mark on node with an id of CONTAINER_DATA
var mark = dom.q("#CONTAINER_DATA").mark("value123");
``` |
off(*even tName, func*)	Removes event handlers from provided nodes. The options for removing specific events are:
	• *bunch*.off() with no arguments will remove all event handlers from the nodes.
	• *bunch*.off("*eventName*") will remove all eventName events from the nodes.
	• *bunch*.off("*eventName*", *function*) will remove a specific eventName event from the bunch.
| | ```
//remove click event for node with an id of CONTAINER_BUTTON
var button = dom.q("#CONTAINER_BUTTON");
button.off("click");

//try to fire event - fire will cause exception
try{
    button.fire("click");
} catch(err) {
    console.log("click event failed: event
    removed");
}
``` |
| on(*eventName, func*) | Adds an event handler to a node. |
| | ```
//attach click event to button with an id of CONTAINER_BUTTON
var button = dom.q("#CONTAINER_BUTTON");
button.on("click", function(e){
    console.log("Button Clicked");
});
``` |
| prepend(*pre pendees*) | Prepends an appendees bunch to an existing bunch. If there is more than one appendee, they will be deeply cloned before insertion. |
| | ```
//prepend CONTAINER_TEXT node to CONTAINER_DATA node
var data = dom.q("#CONTAINER_TEXT");
var prepended = dom.q("#CONTAINER_DATA").prepend(data);
``` |
| protect() | Protects the provided nodes. When a node is protected, calls to getParent will throw an exception instead of providing access to the node's parent. In addition, events will not bubble up past a protected node. |
```

Selector	Description
	`//protect node with an the id of CONTAINER_PROTECT` `var node = dom.q("#CONTAINER_PROTECT").protect();`

select()	Sets focus and selects the text within a given input or `textarea` node. If the bunch provided does not contain exactly one node, an exception is thrown.
	
	`//when button clicked, select textarea`
	`var button = dom.q("#CONTAINER_TAREABTN");`
	`button.on("click", function(e){`
	`    var textarea = dom.q("#CONTAINER_TEXTAREA").select();`
	`});`

selec
tion(*string*)
	Swaps out the user-selected text from a text input or `textarea` node with the value of the `string` argument.
	
	`//attach click event to button with id of`
	`CONTAINER_MODIFY`
	`var button = dom.q("#CONTAINER_MODIFY");`
	`button.on("click", function(e){`
	`    //when button clicked, change selected text for input`
	`    //with an id of CONTAINER_SEL`
	`    var modInput = dom.q("#CONTAINER_SEL").selection("updated");`
	`});`

style(*name,*
value)
	Sets the CSS name style of a node to a particular value.
	
	`//set background color and font color for node`
	`var text = dom.q("#CONTAINER_TEXT");`
	`text.style("background-color",   "#000");`
	`text.style("color", "#fff");`

title(*value*)	Sets the title of a node.
	
	`//set title for node with an id of CONTAINER_DATA`
	`var title = dom.q("#CONTAINER_DATA").title("My data div");`

value(*value*)	Sets the value of a node.
	
	`//set default value text for all text input nodes`
	`var inputs = dom.q("input_text").value("default text");`

As we can see from this table, there is an extensive list of features that are available to you for manipulating the bunch objects that ADsafe uses as wrappers for DOM nodes.

Bunch miscellaneous methods

In addition to the standard GET and SET methods that are available for working with and manipulating bunch objects, ADsafe also makes available a number of miscellaneous methods (i.e., methods that don't specifically fit in one of the getter or setter blocks). Table 8-11 lists these methods.

Table 8-11. Bunch miscellaneous methods

Selector	Description
clone(*deep, num* *ber*)	Clones the nodes in the provided bunch. The new clone is not attached to the document tree. Should the deep argument be set to `true`, all child nodes will be cloned as well. If a numeric identifier is set as the number argument, then an array of *number* clones will be created and returned.

Selector	Description
	``//make three deep clones of node
var parentNode = dom.q("#CONTAINER_PARENT");
var clones = parentNode.clone(true, 3);```
count()	Returns the number of main nodes in a bunch, excluding the child nodes.
	``//get number of nodes in the bunch search for all div
//nodes
var numNodes = dom.q("div").count();```
explode()	Creates an array of bunches that each contain one node from an original bunch of nodes.
	``//break all div nodes into individual bunch objects
var node = dom.q("div");
var nodeArray = node.explode();```
fragment()	Creates a new HTML document fragment.
	``//create new fragment from bunch with id of
//CONTAINER_PARENT
var fragment = dom.q("#CONTAINER_PARENT").fragment();```
q(*query*)	Allows you to perform a subquery on the nodes within an already obtained bunch.
	``//find all div nodes located within a node with
//an id of CONTAINER_PARENT
var parentNode = dom.q("#CONTAINER_PARENT");
var childNode = parentNode.q("div");```
remove()	Removes the node and all children from the DOM. This call also removes all events of the node and its children.
	``//remove node with the id of CONTAINER_PARENT
var removedNode = dom.q("#CONTAINER_PARENT").remove();```
replace(*replacement*)	Replaces a node with a bunch object or an array of bunch objects. The replaced node must have a parent node; otherwise, it will not be replaced by the request. If *replacement* is empty, the node is removed.
	``//replace node with id of CONTAINER_OLD with all div

//nodes that have a class of replacement
var replaceNodes = dom.q("div.replacement");
dom.q("#CONTAINER_OLD").replace(replaceNodes);``` |
| tag(*tagName, type, name*) | Creates a new tagName. If the tag is an input field or button, you may specify the *type* field to be able to set the appropriate input type. If the input type requires a name, you should specify *name* to group the fields together. This method will return a bunch containing the text node, not attached to the document tree. |
| | ```//create new radio button and append to DOM
var insertNode = dom.q("#CONTAINER_PARENT");
var newNode = insertNode.tag("input", "radio", "optCheck");
        insertNode.append(newNode);``` |
| text(*string*) | Creates a new text node if a string was specified, or a series of text nodes if an array of strings was specified. This method returns a bunch with the text node(s), not attached to the document tree. |
| | ```//create two new text nodes and append to DOM
var insertNode = dom.q("#CONTAINER_PARENT");
var newNodes = insertNode.text(["text node 1",
                               "text node 2"]);
insertNode.append(newNodes);``` |

The purpose of the GET, SET, and miscellaneous methods is to provide an abstraction layer on top of the complexity of the secure ADsafe system object. Using their combined power, you can create complex manipulation utilities with simple code constructs.

Attaching Events

As we discussed briefly in the section "Bunch SET methods" on page 301, there are methods available to help you easily and quickly fetch a node, or series of nodes, and attach event handlers to the bunch object that is returned. These methods are the query method, q(), to fetch the nodes, and the event attach method, on(), to insert the events:

```
//get node through the query method
var bunch = dom.q("QUERY");

//attach event onto the returned bunch object
bunch.on("EVENT", function(e){ ... }
```

In this example, we can see how to attach a click handler to a submit button to pop up an alert message:

```
var objSubmit = dom.q("#btnSubmit");
objSubmit.on("click", function(e){
   alert("You have just clicked the button - you win a prize");
});
```

The click event is just one of many DOM events that are supported through the event attach method. If we explore the full list of available events shown in Table 8-12, we see that there are several user-initiated features that we can account for in our programs.

Table 8-12. DOM events supported through the event attach method

Event	Description
blur	The focus on the element has been lost.
change	The user has changed the value of an input, select, or textarea field.
click	The user has clicked on the object with her mouse.
doubleclick	The user has clicked on the object twice with her mouse.
enterkey	The user has pressed the Enter key while in a focused element.
escapekey	The user has pressed the Escape key while in a focused element.
focus	The user has given an object focus.
keypress	The object currently in focus has received keyboard input from the user.
mousedown	The mouse button has been pressed down while the mouse is over the element.
mouseout	The mouse has moved off the element.
mouseover	The mouse has moved over the element.
mouseup	The mouse button has been released while the mouse is over the element.
specialclick	The user has clicked the alternative mouse button while hovering her mouse over the element.

There are two instances in which the event handlers for these events may be triggered:

- The user has performed an action that has triggered the event.
- The developer has programmatically triggered the event without user interaction.

If the developer triggers the events without user interaction, the browser's default action will not be triggered. For the default browser action to be triggered when the event is triggered, the user must be the event initiator.

When the event is triggered, the function that is associated with the event will be triggered:

```
objSubmit.on("click", function(e){ ... }
```

The function that is triggered will contain one argument, the event object. This event object can contain a number of properties that allow you to determine information about the event programmatically once it has been triggered. This object will help you to modularize your event handler so that you have a single handler for all events that uses the information from the event object to determine what action it should take.

Table 8-13 lists all of the properties that may be set within an event object.

Table 8-13. Event object properties

Property	Description
altKey	The state of the Alt key (pressed or not), represented as a Boolean.
ctrlKey	The state of the Control key (pressed or not), represented as a Boolean.
key	If a key was pressed to trigger the event, key will contain the code of the key pressed.
shiftKey	The state of the Shift key (pressed or not), represented as a Boolean.
target	A bunch that contains the target of the event.
that	A bunch that contains the node that is handling the event. This value may be the same as the target, or it may be a parent if bubbling occurs.
type	The event type displayed as a string.
x	The horizontal position of the mouse cursor relative to the target container.
y	The vertical position of the mouse cursor relative to the target container.

As you can see, there are many event features available for us to work with. This extensive list will help us to build highly targeted applications and sites that allow specific handling for user events and actions.

Defining Libraries

Should you wish to create library files to reuse over multiple widgets, or even if you simply want to keep your code base modularized and neat, then ADsafe libraries are a good starting point.

Libraries are simply script includes with some ADsafe architecture pieces thrown in. If we take a look at a base-level widget, we can see where the library files may be included:

```
<div id="APPNAME_">
 application markup

 //library file includes by name
 <script src="library.js"></script>

 <script>
 "use strict";
 ADSAFE.go("APPNAME_", function(dom, lib){
     //application functions and code
 });
 </script>
</div>
```

The script include must be placed after any call to set the ID of the widget (e.g., `id` method: `ADSAFE.id("APPNAME_")`) but before the call to the go method.

To access the content of the return object from a library file, we include the `lib` parameter in the `ADSAFE.go(...)` method call. We can then access functions by making requests to `lib.name`.

The library files themselves follow a simple ADsafe syntax:

```
ADSAFE.lib("name", function (lib){
"use strict";
    //code for the library module

    return {
        //return object
    };
});
```

Within the library file, you include a call to `ADSAFE.lib(...)`, specifying the library name. The anonymous function that is defined as the second parameter includes two pieces:

The code for the module
> This is the base code and functionality for the library module. It will not have access to the document unless the widget code passes the `dom` parameter to its methods. Including the `lib` parameter gives it access to the currently loaded libraries.

The return object
> This is the object that allows the widget to access the library's privileged methods through the `lib.name` request.

By using the practices outlined here, you will build up comprehensive generic libraries that contain functionality that you can reuse throughout different widgets.

Putting It All Together

The full code for this sample is available at *https://github.com/jcleblanc/ programming-social-applications/tree/master/chapter_8/chapter_final/*.

Now that we've explored some of the technologies used to secure third-party code on a site or container, let's put them to good use and build out a tool to showcase how one of our tools, Caja, strips content from an original, mixed HTML/JavaScript file.

What we'll do is set up a script that utilizes Caja's web parsing mechanism to provide a side-by-side comparison of raw and rendered results from both the original content and the cajoled content. Our basic visual format will look like Figure 8-2.

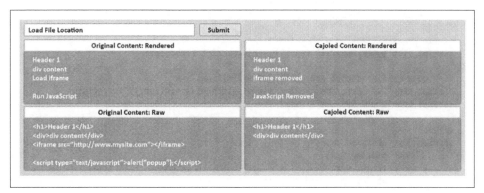

Figure 8-2. Architecture of our Caja rendering application

We will set up an input to allow you to specify a file location and then load the file. Once loaded, the file content will be dumped immediately into the original rendered and raw source boxes since it doesn't require any parsing. After that, the content will be run through the web cajoler script, and the resulting value will be dumped into the raw and rendered cajoled content boxes on the right.

The Data Source

First, we need to specify the source file that we will use to test our side-by-side comparison tool. For this example, we will load in this simple script as a proof of concept:

```
<h1>test 1 2 3</h1>
<div>this is a test</div>

<iframe src="http://www.yahoo.com" width="100%" height="200px">
   iframes not available
</iframe>
```

```
<script type="text/javascript">
    alert("I can alert to you!");
</script>
```

This mixed HTML/JavaScript markup will simply display a `header` and `div`, load an iframe, and then attempt to load an alert message to the user.

What we expect from the cajoled side of the content is the modification of this script to remove the iframe, which can load malicious pages, and display the alert message.

The Head: Script Includes and Styles

We start with the head of our document. This is where we will load in all of the script includes and styles that we'll use in the example:

```
<!DOCTYPE HTML PUBLIC "-//W3C//DTD HTML 4.01//EN"
    "http://www.w3.org/TR/html4/strict.dtd">
<html xmlns="http://www.w3.org/1999/xhtml" xml:lang="en-us" lang="en-us">
<head>
<title>Web sanitization with Caja</title>
<script src="jquery.min.js" type="text/javascript"></script>

<!-- caja cajoler script and whitelist definitions -->
<script src="../../src/com/google/caja/plugin/html-sanitizer.js"></script>
<script src="html4-defs.js"></script>

<style>
.contentBox{ width:400px;
             padding:5px;
             float:left;
             border:1px solid #868686;
             margin-right:10px; }
.contentRendered{ height:400px;
                  overflow:hidden; }
.contentRaw{ height:200px;
             overflow:auto; }
.contentBox *, form *{ font:12px arial,helvetica,sans-serif; }
.header{ background-color:#868686;
         color:#fff;
         font-size:16px;
         font-weight:bold;
         text-align:center;
         padding:5px; }
.clear{ clear:both;
        height:10px; }

#file{ width:300px; }
#errorMsg{ color:#d32424;
           font-weight:bold;
           display:none;   }
</style>
</head>
```

First, let's look at the script includes that we are adding:

jquery.min.js

This is the minified JQuery base file we're loading in. We will use the JQuery JavaScript library for DOM selection, for AJAX requests, and for inserting the text/ HTML into their appropriate boxes in the example. We're using a local file, but you could instead link to the CDN hosted file from *http://docs.jquery.com/Down loading_jQuery*.

html-sanitizer.js

This is the Caja web sanitization script that we are loading in from our local version of Caja. It provides the functionality to cajole the content that we will load in.

html4-defs.js

This is the HTML definitions file used by Caja to specify which nodes should be removed. This is a highly restrictive list and represents the client-side sanitizer technique imposed by a true Caja container.

Following those includes, we define the styles that will make the file markup look presentable for our needs.

The Body: Markup Layer

Now that we have our script includes and styles, let's take a quick look at the markup that we will be generating for this example:

```
<body>
<form action="javascript:void(0);">
    <div id="errorMsg"></div>
    <input type="text" name="file" id="file" />
    <input type="submit" value="Load File" onclick="getFile()">
</form>

<div class="contentBox contentRendered">
    <div class="header">Original Content: Rendered</div>
    <div id="original_rendered"></div>
</div>
<div class="contentBox contentRendered">
    <div class="header">Cajoled Content: Rendered</div>
    <div id="cajoled_rendered"></div>
</div>

<div class="clear"></div>

<div class="contentBox contentRaw">
    <div class="header">Original Content: Raw</div>
    <div id="original_raw"></div>
</div>
<div class="contentBox contentRaw">
    <div class="header">Cajoled Content: Raw</div>
    <div id="cajoled_raw"></div>
</div>
```

This content consists of two parts:

- The form that includes an input box to enter the file location from which we will load our example content. When the user clicks the submit button, the get File() function will be called to collect the file content. This form also includes an error messaging node that we'll use to display a basic message to the user if there is a problem loading the file.

- The div nodes that make up the four quadrants of our example:
  —The rendered original content (top left).
  —The raw original content (bottom left).
  —The rendered cajoled content (top right).
  —The raw cajoled content (bottom right).

Now that we have the markup layer defined, we can take a look at the JavaScript layer, which will provide our script with its file fetching and parsing functionality.

The Body: JavaScript Layer

Our final layer is the JavaScript content. This script block includes only the get File() function that will load and parse our content:

```
<script type="text/javascript">
function getFile(){
    var errorMsgNode = $('#errorMsg');
    errorMsgNode.css("display", "none");

    var filePath = $('#file').val();

    if (filePath.length > 1){
        $.ajax({
            url: filePath,
            success: function(data){
                //load unmodified code
                $('#original_raw').text(data);
                $('#original_rendered').html(data);

                //load cajoled content
                var cajoled_data = html_sanitize(data);
                $('#cajoled_raw').text(cajoled_data);
                $('#cajoled_rendered').html(cajoled_data);
            },
            error: function(request){
                var errorMsg = "Failed to load file"
                            + "<br />Status: " + request.status
                            + "<br />Error: " + request.statusText;

                errorMsgNode.css("display", "block");
                errorMsgNode.html(errorMsg);
            }
```

```
        });
    }
}
</script>
</body>
</html>
```

When the user enters a file location for the mixed HTML/JavaScript content that he would like to load and then clicks Submit, the getFile() function jumps into action.

Since we want to provide the user with some form of error messaging if something goes wrong, we first capture our error message node and ensure that it is hidden in case the previous attempt to load a file produced an error message that is still being displayed.

We then capture the file path that the user entered and, if it isn't blank, we make an AJAX request to get the content of that file. There are a few configuration options set up to handle different eventualities when we're running the request, including:

url

> The URL to which we are making the request.

success

> If the AJAX request succeeds and returns a valid HTTP response, we first load the unmodified return content into the original raw and rendered nodes by using the jQuery .text or .html methods on the respective nodes. We then take the raw data and run it through the html_sanitize method to strip out any nodes that may be malicious, as defined by the *html4-defs.js* include. Once the data is cajoled, we load that modified content into the respective raw and rendered nodes.

failure

> If the AJAX request failed with an invalid HTTP response, we create an error message string made up of a static error node, the HTTP status code, and the HTTP status text. We then place that string into our error message node and set it to a visible status.

That makes up the meat of our example, providing all of the functionality we need to run a side-by-side comparison that shows how Caja sanitizes an original source to prevent malicious attacks.

The Final Result

Once we render the load in the test file that we specified earlier in our example, we are presented with both a visual and source code comparison of the content, as shown in Figure 8-3.

The original content loads our iframe, header, div, and (when run) the script block that we included to display a pop up to the user. The original content raw dump is an unmodified version of the loaded file.

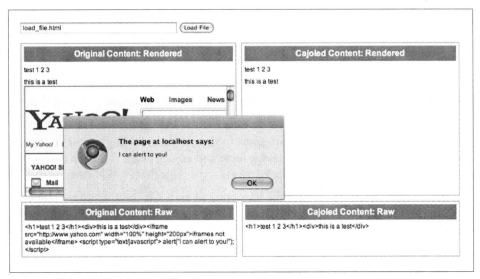

Figure 8-3. The Caja rendering application

The right column on the Caja side is a much different story. The `header` and `div` are preserved in the rendered version, but the iframe is stripped and a second alert is absent. When we look at the raw content of the cajoled file, we can see why. The iframe and `script` block have been removed from the file that we attempted to load.

This is just a simple sanitization script from Caja, so although it presents a useful peek into the Caja process, it's important to note that doesn't represent the server-side cajoler's full content manipulation capacity.

Conclusion

Throughout this chapter, we have explored a few different options that are currently available for securing social applications and third-party code within a container. We've looked at the implications of using iframes as a security model and have delved into iframe alternatives Caja and ADsafe.

Even if you do not implement these particular standards, working with them and understanding why a lot of code is filtered or disallowed within them has hopefully given you a better grasp of the security implications of allowing unmanaged, third-party code to exist on your site or service.

Preparing yourself for the eventuality of attacks from malicious developers or sloppy development practices will help you provide a safe experience for your end users. While these practices may require additional development work, they will help you achieve the ultimate goal: protecting those who use the services that you are hosting.

Securing Social Graph Access with OAuth

Open Authentication (OAuth) is an open standard for authorizing applications to access data on a user's behalf. Through OAuth, we can secure a user's personal and social graph information.

We will start this chapter by looking at a simple method that many provider sites employ to secure private resources: basic authentication. We will explore the pros and cons behind this type of implementation from the perspectives of the provider, the application, and the user.

With that exploration completed, we will jump into OAuth 1.0a, and the newer revision OAuth 2.0, which both offer a secure and open way to protect users' privileged profiles and data. We will look at how the authorization flows of these two standards work, and then dive into end-to-end examples to showcase the power behind the specifications.

By the end of this chapter, we will have a comprehensive understanding of how OAuth can be used to protect private data and resources.

Beyond Basic Auth

To start our exploration of OAuth, we'll first look into what *basic authentication* (*basic auth*, for short) is and how OAuth presents a more mature iteration of it. You may have seen basic auth being used by many companies, and you may have even worked with it before; if you have, you understand how easy it is to implement. But "easy" by no means implies "secure," and it certainly doesn't mean that basic auth should be employed just to increase the speed at which resources are returned.

Let's explore some basic auth fundamentals as well as a few of the potential pitfalls of using it, implementing it in an application, or providing it.

Basic Auth Implementation: How It Works

Basic auth is very simply implemented through traditional HTTP request methods. You just pass a username and password as login credentials through to the provider from which you are trying to obtain the privileged user information.

Let's say, for example, that we want to pull down some resources from a social URI endpoint that is designated by a provider site. We start out by making a simple HTTP GET request to the provider URI endpoint to capture that data:

```
GET /private/user/me HTTP/1.1
Host: server.example.com
```

Now let's say that the provider requires basic authentication (username and password for validation). Since we didn't include those login credentials with the request, the provider will return a simple HTTP error response stating that additional authorization is required:

```
HTTP/1.1 401 Authorization Required
Date: Fri, 17 Dec 2010 02:27:34 GMT
Server: Apache
Location: http://server.example.com/private/user/me
Cache-Control: max-age=300
Expires: Fri, 17 Dec 2010 02:32:34 GMT
Vary: Accept-Encoding
Content-Length: 148
Connection: close
Content-Type: text/html; charset=iso-8859-1

<!DOCTYPE HTML PUBLIC "-//IETF//DTD HTML 2.0//EN">
<html><head>
<title>Error: Unauthorized</title>
</head><body>
<h1>401 Unauthorized</h1>
</body></html>
```

Let's assume that this provider accepts basic authentication requests. We'll use an HTTP POST request including a username, password, and any arbitrary parameters that the URI endpoint requires to denote which resources to return. This POST request will look similar to the following:

```
POST /private/user/me HTTP/1.1
Host: server.example.com
Content-Type: application/x-www-form-urlencoded

username=joe_smith
&password=pass1234
&param1=myparameter1
&param2=myparameter2
```

The provider will then respond with the resources from the URI endpoint to which you made the request.

As you can see, you can get a good view of the basic auth process by simply tracking HTTP requests and responses. Even though the process is easy to implement, there is a whole range of reasons why you may want to avoid basic auth as a mechanism to protect your private resources. These include everything from the inconvenience of having to send the username and password with every request to concerns about security for storing that data.

The Reasons Against Using Basic Authentication

As we've covered, basic authentication is a very easy standard to understand and implement. Simply send the user's username and password as parameters in the HTTP request, and the provider site will verify the login credentials with every request, returning the requested resources if the credentials are authorized or an HTTP error response if not.

With any standard that is so easy to implement, you will invariably run into security or implementation concerns, and basic auth is no different. There are numerous reasons why you wouldn't want to implement basic auth as your sole mechanism for securing protected resources. Let's take a look at a few.

The client needs to store login information

The primary reason against using basic authentication for securing private resources is that the client application needs to somehow store the user's login information if it is to continue making requests on his behalf (i.e., without asking him for his username and password each time).

There are a few inherent concerns here:

- First and foremost, as I have mentioned, every company or application that requests user login credentials needs to store that information, either for the current session or permanently in its database. Users trust that the company is properly encoding those values and has extensive security procedures in place to protect their information. But, unfortunately, there have been numerous cases where companies storing usernames and passwords haven't used proper encoding practices (i.e., by storing login credentials as cleartext) and their databases have been hacked by malicious parties who then easily scanned the actual usernames and passwords stored within.

- If the user changes his password, he will have to reauthenticate with the client application so that it can acquire the new login credentials. This means that any headless actions performed by the client application in the meantime (that is, before reauthentication) will fail.

These are just a couple of the fundamental issues in an authentication system that works with a user's raw login credentials rather than a token-based, user abstraction system (which we'll cover shortly).

Having to send login information with every request

The next strike against basic auth is that with every request to the provider site, the client application needs to send along the login credentials. This may not be as much of an issue if a user has a secure HTTPS connection with the provider site, which means he's passing through encrypted versions of the credentials, but this is by no means the typical implementation.

It is often the case that the provider site with which the client application is communicating transfers data as unencrypted cleartext. This type of transfer system makes users vulnerable to malicious hackers, who can "sniff" the information being transferred to obtain a user's login credentials.

Users can't control or view which applications have their information

With a *token-based system*, the provider (Yahoo!, Twitter, Google, etc.) issues tokens to the client application instead of just validating a series of login credentials. What this means is that the provider itself can track what tokens have been issued and to whom they were issued.

This token-based process has two very clear benefits:

- The provider can display a list of all of the applications to which the user has granted access to his private information. This will allow the user to see where his information is being used and by whom.

- The provider can revoke the user permission that allows the application to access his private information. Since the tokens are controlled and maintained by the provider, it essentially controls which applications have access to private information.

These benefits are not available when you use basic auth as your security mechanism. There is no way for a user to see which client applications are storing his personal information, and there is no way to revoke that access and delete the information from the application systems, unless the client provides that ability itself. In any event, this information is not centralized, so the user will have to recall all of the applications to which he provided his login credentials and work with them individually if he wants to modify that relationship.

The OAuth 1.0a Standard

Before we discuss the newest OAuth standard, OAuth 2, we must do our due diligence and cover the version of the standard used by many of the top Internet-based companies (e.g., Yahoo!, Google): OAuth 1.0a.

The OAuth 1.0a standard was developed to give providers a way to implement a user authorization model, in which a user authorizes an application to access privileged information on her behalf from her profile and friends.

OAuth offers some major improvements over traditional models such as basic auth, including:

- Instead of having to send the user's username and password to the provider with every authentication request, you are working with abstract access tokens that do not share any of the user's passwords.

- Since tokens are issued from a provider site, they can be revoked at any time, putting more control into the user's hands. Several providers also implement a token expiration mechanism that requires an application to periodically renew the access token to continue making requests for user data.

- Users can see the tokens that they have active (i.e., which applications can access their data) on the provider site, meaning they can manually revoke access to an application. Since the application does not have a user's login credentials, it cannot make further requests for her data once she has revoked authorization.

Now that we've covered its benefits, let's continue our exploration of OAuth 1.0a by looking at how the token exchange process works for a user, an application, and a provider.

OAuth 1.0a Workflow

First, let's look at OAuth's general workflow behind the scenes as we get the authorization for a user and acquire a token so we can access her privileged information:

1. Obtain a consumer key and secret from the service provider that we are trying to access data from.

2. Make a request to the service provider to obtain a request token to permit us to seek permissions from the user.

3. Forward the user to the provider's login and permission screens in order to obtain her authorization to use her personal information.

4. Exchange the verified *request* token object for an *access* token, which allows us to make requests on the user's behalf.

Let's break down these steps further to see what is going on at a more granular level.

Obtain a consumer key and secret

To complete the OAuth workflow and start collecting a user's social information, the first thing we need to do is to obtain a consumer key and secret from the provider from which we are trying to access data (e.g., Yahoo!, Google, Twitter). These keys are normally issued when we're creating applications through the provider's developer programs, such as:

- The Yahoo! Application Platform: *http://developer.yahoo.com/yap*
- Twitter Applications: *http://developer.twitter.com/apps/new*

- FourSquare Applications: *http://foursquare.com/apps/*
- Google Apps: *http://www.google.com/apps/*

There is a simple, standard process that you will follow when creating these applications to obtain the secret and key, as shown in Figure 9-1.

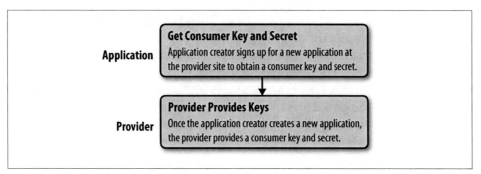

Figure 9-1. OAuth 1, step 1: Application owner obtains a consumer key and secret

 You should never expose your consumer key and secret publicly (such as within JavaScript code), as this information would allow an attacker to do things on your application's behalf, such as acquiring the personal information of any users who have given your application permission to access their data.

Once you've created an application, you should be provided with the consumer key and secret that will allow you to begin the programmatic aspects of your application development.

 If you are building a Flash application and embedding your consumer key and secret within the ActionScript code layer, keep in mind that Flash objects could be retrieved from their web source and decompiled by an unknown party. This would, in turn, expose your embedded consumer key and secret.

Many application providers, especially those associated with social networks, have numerous data types that can be collected for a user, such as her profile, friends, or recent activities. For this reason, the provider may display a permissions screen to allow you to select the type of information that you want to obtain from the user when she permits your application to access or set her personal information. These permissions are normally bound to the consumer key that you are issued.

When the user first uses your application, she will be presented with a screen asking her to accept these permissions prior to using the application. When she accepts, she will be returned to your application to complete the OAuth flow. The URI to which she is forwarded is defined during the call to fetch a request token. To preserve the security of the token exchange environment, the application provider will most likely have you preregister the callback URI that you intend to use when you're creating the application. This callback will be bound to the application, and when a call is made to fetch a request token, it will be verified against the callback URI specified in the object used to fetch the request token.

Get the request token

Now that we have the consumer key and secret for our application, we can initiate the first stage of our token exchange requests: capturing a request token.

We can break down this process into a simple handshake between the application and the provider. We will be using the consumer key and secret to make a request to the provider site to capture a request token. This process will validate where the request is coming from (your application) and set the callback URI for where to forward the user after she permits the application to access and set her protected information.

Once the provider validates the request, it will respond with a request token object containing all of the data that we will need in order to forward the user to the provider for verification, as shown in Figure 9-2.

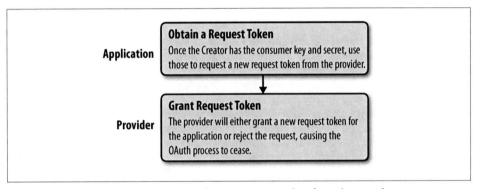

Figure 9-2. OAuth 1, step 2: Application obtains a request token from the provider

The HTTP request for making a request to capture a new request token will look something like the following:

```
GET /get_request_token?oauth_version=1.0
    &oauth_nonce=4f7cbc67b835fbe59920377f81cc3a53
    &oauth_timestamp=1291159360
    &oauth_consumer_key=djOyJHIzTWZmVXBmJmQ9WVdrOWFGZEhhMFozT...
    &oauth_callback=http%3A%2F%2Fwww.client.com%2Fcomplete.php
    &oauth_signature_method=HMAC-SHA1
    &oauth_signature=ItMr5tJNiobZX5iDIZj2%2FCJSkoI%3D
    HTTP/1.1
Host: server.example.com
```

If we break down the request object into its individual parameters (Table 9-1), we can see what each key brings to the overall request structure.

Table 9-1. Request parameters for the request token

Request parameter	Description
oauth_version	The OAuth version being used. This should be set to 1.0.
oauth_nonce	A random string to be used with the request.
oauth_timestamp	The current timestamp of the request. This will be validated when the request token is issued.
oauth_consumer_key	The consumer key that was issued when you created your OAuth-based application on the provider site, prior to implementation.
oauth_callback	The URI to return the user to once she has authorized your application to access her privileged information.
oauth_signa ture_method	The name of the signature method that should be used to sign the request to the provider.
oauth_signature	The secret key issued when you first created your OAuth application.

 The oauth_callback parameter you specify in the request URI sent to fetch the request token must match the one you set as the "return to" URI when you obtained the consumer key and secret. Otherwise, domain mismatch errors will be generated when the key provider performs domain verification checks.

After the request is initiated, the provider site will verify the submitted data, and if everything checks out, will issue a response containing the elements required to generate an unverified request token.

 An *unverified request token* has not gone through the user authorization process. Once the user authorizes the application with the request token, the provider will issue a verification code to turn that unverified request token into a verified one.

The response that comes back from the provider will look something like the following:

```
oauth_token=kced47h
&oauth_token_secret=eb086a06b3f11a52fe7
&oauth_expires_in=3600
&oauth_callback_confirmed=true
```

The provider is required to send back the oauth_token and oauth_token_secret parameters. These will allow you to build the request token object. There are some additional parameters that a provider may pass back in the response object, depending on its requirements (Table 9-2). Breaking down the key/value pairs in the preceding sample response, we can see the specific uses for each parameter in the OAuth token exchange flow.

Table 9-2. Response parameters for the request token

Response parameter	Description
`oauth_token`	The token to be used during the authorization phase to make an exchange request for an access token.
`oauth_token_secret`	The token secret to use in conjunction with the `oauth_token` to make an exchange for an access token.
`oauth_expires_in`	The lifetime of the request token. This value will be presented in seconds.
`oauth_callback_con firmed`	This value should always be set to `true`. It signifies that you are using OAuth Revision A (see the following note).

 Some background on the required `oauth_callback_confirmed` parameter: Revision A of the OAuth 1.0 specification included a security patch for a well-documented man-in-the-middle attack. This change also moved the `callback_url` parameter to the first token-exchange step (i.e., attempting to obtain a request token).

With our response object returned to us, we can now construct the request token object. This object is what we need to forward the user to the provider site so she can grant us access to her data, and to obtain a verified request token (which will in turn be used to acquire our access token).

So let's move on to obtaining that verified request token.

Get the user-verified request token

At this point, we have an unverified request token object available to us. What we will do now is to use this request token to forward the user to the authorization page on the provider site. From there, she can accept the permissions we've specified for our application to access her privileged information.

There are a few things that we need to do to forward the user to the provider site to begin the authorization process:

1. We have to obtain the provider site URL to which we will forward the user by extracting it from the request token object.
2. We need a way to pass the request token and secret through the authorization process to the callback URL. We'll use a cookie to accomplish this.

 We don't want to simply attach the token parameters in the query string as we forward the user through the authorization flow, because the custom parameters will likely be removed when the user is forwarded to the callback URL defined when we first made the request for a request token.

Once we have the redirect URL as well as the token and secret stored via a cookie (or some other method), we just need to send the user's browser to the redirect location.

After the user is redirected, she will be presented with a provider page, which prompts her to sign in (unless she's already signed in to the service) and accept the permissions of the application. The provider page will specify what privileged information the application will have access to. This may be something like the particular data from her profile the application wants to access, whether the application wants to set new updates for the user, or whether the application can leverage her connections to get friends' profiles.

Once the user has either accepted or denied the request for the application to use her information, she will be forwarded to the callback URL location that we specified when we created the request token in the first step of the OAuth process.

This entire process will look something like Figure 9-3.

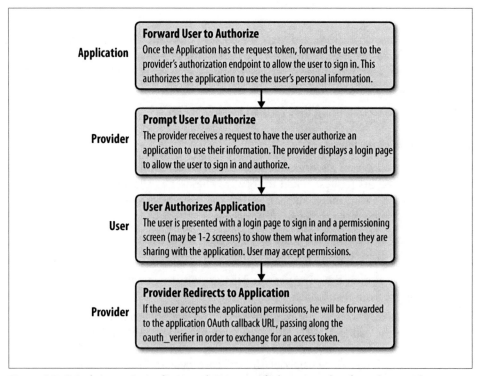

Figure 9-3. OAuth 1, step 3: Application obtains a verified request token from the provider

If the process was successful, once the user has been forwarded to the callback location on the application site, we should have a verified request token.

A verified request token object is constructed with the request token, request token secret, and a verification code that is passed to the callback once the user has accepted the application permissions.

Now that we have the verified request token, we can move to the next step: exchanging it for an access token.

Exchange the verified request token for an access token

For the last step in our authorization process, you will learn how to convert your verified request token to an access token and begin making authorized requests for data on behalf of the user who granted the application permission.

First, we extract the request token and token secret from the cookie (or whatever method you chose) that we created before we redirected the user to the provider's authorization page. Next, we extract the verifier parameter (verification code) that was passed to us from the provider (usually on the query string) and then use all three pieces to construct a verified request token object.

Next, we use that verified request token to make a request back to the provider to swap that request token for an access token that we can then use to make verified requests on the user's behalf. The provider site will either grant or deny the verified request token. If it grants the verified request token, the provider will return the access token information as the response object.

We will then use that return object to create an access token object, and in turn use that object to obtain the user's privileged information.

This process is illustrated in Figure 9-4.

When we make the request to exchange the verified request token for an access token—in this case, to Yahoo! as our provider—the request URI will look something like the following:

```
https://api.login.yahoo.com/oauth/v2/get_token
    ?oauth_consumer_key=drOWFGZE9Y29uc3VtZXJzZWNyZXQmeD1hYw...
    &oauth_signature_method=PLAINTEXT
    &oauth_version=1.0
    &oauth_verifier=svmhhd
    &oauth_token=gugucz&oauth_timestamp=1228169662
    &oauth_nonce=8B9SpF
    &oauth_signature=5f78507cf0acc38890cf5aa697210822e90c8b1c%261fa6
```

If we break down the individual parameters that are passed to the URI (shown in Table 9-3), we can see what purpose each one serves.

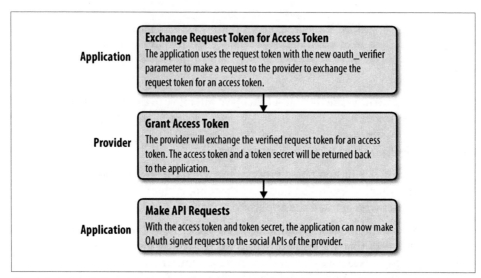

Application	**Exchange Request Token for Access Token** The application uses the request token with the new oauth_verifier parameter to make a request to the provider to exchange the request token for an access token.
Provider	**Grant Access Token** The provider will exchange the verified request token for an access token. The access token and a token secret will be returned back to the application.
Application	**Make API Requests** With the access token and token secret, the application can now make OAuth signed requests to the social APIs of the provider.

Figure 9-4. OAuth 1, step 4: Application exchanges verified request token for an access token

Table 9-3. Request parameters for the access token

Request parameter	Description
oauth_consumer_key	The consumer key provided when you first created your OAuth application on the provider site.
oauth_signa ture_method	The name of the signature method to be used with the request.
oauth_version	The OAuth version being used. This should be set to 1.0.
oauth_verifier	The verifier parameter that was sent to the callback URL, denoting that the user has authorized the application to use her private information.
oauth_token	The request token.
oauth_nonce	A random string.
oauth_signature	A concatenated string consisting of the consumer secret and token secret parameters.

Once the provider sends back a response object, if the exchange succeeded, it should look something like the following:

```
oauth_token=A%3DxiraOmPvtwHafRZOUOepGHTkBJhh63fh4crKlGJc57JBD...
&oauth_token_secret=a8f1fb99c205104af72f6ba45896d33c5b3b9949
&oauth_expires_in=3600
```

The oauth_token and oauth_token_secret parameters are required in the successful response object, and are the parameters we really need to be concerned with. But the provider may also send back additional parameters, as is the case in the preceding string. For example, although many providers do not implement an expiration time on their access tokens, some do. In such cases, the provider may attach an additional oauth_expires_in parameter containing the access token's expiration time in seconds.

Providers may also send another parameter with this object, `oauth_authorization_expires_in`, as shown in Table 9-4.

Table 9-4. Response parameters for the access token

Response parameter	Description
oauth_authorization_expires_in	The lifetime of the oauth_session_handle in seconds
oauth_expires_in	The lifetime of the token in seconds

Once we've created an access token object out of the provider's response, our application can start making signed requests to the provider to leverage the user's privileged information.

The End-User Experience

When OAuth is being used within an application, the experience for the end user who's interacting with the application is far less intrusive and complicated than the process that the developer has to go through to implement it.

Implementations of the permission screen, where users accept that the application will perform actions on their behalf, can vary widely depending on the platform on which it is implemented, but the basic principle is the same. The platform displays a page containing basic information about the application and providing a means by which users can permit or deny that application to use their personal data.

Let's explore what this screen looks like on some of the platforms that currently use OAuth. Twitter's implementation is as simple as it gets: it presents information about the application requesting access to the user's profile and provides a simple allow or deny option, as shown in Figure 9-5.

Figure 9-5. The Twitter OAuth authorization screen

Now let's take a look at an OAuth implementation that is more descriptive. The Yahoo! OAuth process first has the user log in to his Yahoo! account to verify his identity—before even presenting a permission screen to prompt him to accept or decline the application information requirements. This can be a good practice if, for example, a user has set his Yahoo! session to expire every two weeks and someone else uses his computer during that time. Without the Yahoo! verification login screen, that other person would be able to authorize applications to access the already logged-in user's personal information.

 Although there is a clear security benefit to adding a login feature to the OAuth process, every authorization page that the user is presented with will increase the drop-off rate (sometimes as much as 20%). This means that fewer users who start the OAuth process will actually finish and authenticate the application.

When the user signs in, he will be forwarded to the permission screen. This screen displays the application's title and breaks down the permissions that the application is requesting, including personal information like the user's address book (Yahoo! Contacts), his *http://pulse.yahoo.com* profile (Profiles), his activities (Yahoo! Updates), as well as numerous other options that the developer might have set when creating the application. The application will also display where application activities (i.e., news feeds items posted from the application) will be displayed. Depending on the application, this may include Yahoo! activity stream feeds, Facebook, or Twitter. Once the user accepts these permissions (shown in Figure 9-6), he will be forwarded to the application that he just authorized.

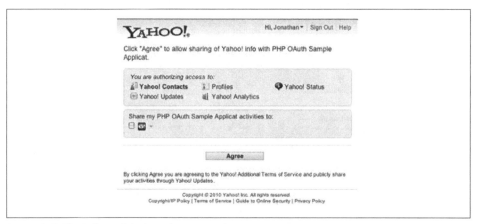

Figure 9-6. The Yahoo! OAuth application authorization screen

Even though the OAuth process is complex to implement from the developer's perspective, the OAuth permission screens that the end user sees are normally kept as simple as possible. The fact that users have to manually allow an application to do something on their behalf can sometimes scare them away, increasing the drop-off rate. Keeping the flow easy and mimicking simple acceptance screens that the user may see on a regular basis can help to minimize drop-off.

Two-Legged Versus Three-Legged OAuth

We've already explored the standard, three-legged (application, provider, user) method for using OAuth 1.0a, stepping through the token-exchange workflow to gain an access token. Although this is how OAuth was originally intended to be used, some providers employ another method, two-legged OAuth, to allow application developers to collect private data with aggregated sources such as firehose feeds.

The implementation of two-legged OAuth mimics typical client-server communication relationships and removes the need to involve users in the process. This is a good way for providers to allow applications to access data on their systems while being able to track the amount of data that the application is requesting, mostly for rate-limiting and abuse-prevention purposes.

A good way to think about two-legged OAuth is as the first and last steps of the three-legged OAuth process (getting the request token and exchanging that for an access token), eliminating the middle pieces in which the user authorizes the application.

The workflow for the two-legged OAuth process is:

1. The application owner creates a new OAuth application on the provider site to obtain a consumer key and secret.
2. The application will make requests to the provider site to access private data.

This process is much easier, but doesn't fulfill the need for an intermediary user authorization step when you're requesting privileged user information.

Now let's take a look at a practical example of the two-legged OAuth scenario.

Implementing two-legged OAuth in JavaScript

The full code for this sample is available at *https://github.com/jcleblanc/ programming-social-applications/blob/master/chapter_9/oauth1-java script-2legged.html*.

Let's see what a two-legged OAuth example looks like when being used to make an actual request to a provider site. There are a few things that I need to spell out about this example before we begin:

- We will be making a request through the Yahoo! Query Language (YQL) service to access a firehose feed from the Yahoo! update stream. These updates will contain notifications of any and all actions that are taken on the sites or services around Yahoo!.

- We will need to create an OAuth application through the Yahoo! Developer Network dashboard at *http://developer.yahoo.com/dashboard* to obtain our OAuth consumer key and consumer secret to sign the request.

- We will be making our cross-domain AJAX request using JQuery.

 There are not many end-to-end samples available in JavaScript because of the security issues behind embedding your OAuth keys in the JavaScript layer. Be aware that if you employ a JavaScript implementation, you'll need to protect your keys to prevent others from using them without your knowledge.

With those preliminaries out of the way, let's jump right into this short example.

The includes. The first thing to do, besides setting up the top of the HTML document, is specify the following includes:

oauth.js
> The OAuth library for generating our signature

sha1.js
> The signing library

jquery.min.js
> The minified JQuery base object

This will be the base of our example:

```
<!DOCTYPE html PUBLIC "-//W3C//DTD XHTML 1.0 Transitional//EN"
    "http://www.w3.org/TR/xhtml1/DTD/xhtml1-transitional.dtd">
<html xmlns="http://www.w3.org/1999/xhtml">
<head>
<meta http-equiv="Content-Type" content="text/html; charset=utf-8" />
<title>OAuth JavaScript Sample Application</title>
</head>
<body>

<!-- OAuth libraries and JQuery base -->
<script src="http://oauth.googlecode.com/svn/code/javascript/oauth.js"></script>
<script src="http://oauth.googlecode.com/svn/code/javascript/sha1.js"></script>
<script src="http://ajax.googleapis.com/ajax/libs/jquery/1.5/jquery.min.js"></script>
```

Next let's look at the function that will generate the OAuth request URI.

Constructing the OAuth request URI. The function to generate the OAuth request URI will accept three parameters: the OAuth consumer key and secret, and the URI endpoint to which we will make our two-legged OAuth requests. We will use those parameters to build a signed URL request:

```
<script type="text/javascript">
/**************************************************************************
 * Function: Build OAuth Request
 * Description: Builds a 2-legged OAuth signed request URI using a given OAuth
 *              key and secret with a specified URI endpoint
 **************************************************************************/
var buildOAuthRequest = function(key, secret, url){
   //create accessor and message objects
   var accessor = { consumerSecret:secret, tokenSecret:"" };
   var message = { action:url, method:"GET",
                   parameters:[["oauth_version", "1.0"],
                               ["oauth_consumer_key", key]]};

   //set timestamp, nonce and signature method
   OAuth.setTimestampAndNonce(message);
   OAuth.SignatureMethod.sign(message, accessor);

   //build signature URL
   var baseString =
      OAuth.decodeForm(OAuth.SignatureMethod.getBaseString(message));
   var signature =
      OAuth.getParameter(message.parameters, "oauth_signature");
   var signatureURL = baseString[1][0] + "?" + baseString[2][0]
                      + "&oauth_signature=" + encodeURIComponent(signature);

   return signatureURL;
};
```

We start by creating two objects to build the request. The first is an **accessor** object that will contain the consumer secret from the OAuth application and a blank token secret value. The second is the **message** object that acts as our request object and contains the URI endpoint to which we're making a request, the method type, and the OAuth consumer key and version as parameters.

Once we've created these objects, we generate a new OAuth timestamp and nonce using the message, and then sign the message using the **accessor** object.

Next, we build our base string and signature variables. Using those variables, we then generate the signature URI that will contain all of the necessary OAuth parameters to make a two-legged OAuth request. That final URI is returned from the function.

We can then use this function to make our request to YQL.

Making and parsing the request. We start out by storing the OAuth key and secret that we obtained when creating the OAuth application with the provider (in this case, Yahoo!). In addition, we store the URI to the firehose feed in YQL. This search query will look for any updates about hockey.

Once we have the variables in place, we generate the OAuth signed URI by making a request to our **buildOAuthRequest(...)** function that we covered earlier. With that in place, we can make our request and parse the returned data:

```
//OAuth keys and YQL query URI
var key = 'djOyJmk9bTBDQzlLQUZ5NGpEVdHbzlNVEUyTmpRek5EazJNZyOtJnM9jZQ--';
```

```
var secret = 'c74a018f7db1d8de5ab2664ef5ab';
var url = 'http://query.yahooapis.com/v1/yql
            ?q=select%20*%20from%20social.updates.search%20
            where%20query%3D%22hockey%22&format=json';

//obtain 2-legged OAuth request URL using key, secret and YQL URL
var yqlURL = buildOAuthRequest(key, secret, url);

//make cross-domain AJAX request against OAuth signed URI
$.getJSON(yqlURL, function(data){
    response = '';

    //check if there are any results available
    if (data.query.count > 0){
        results = data.query.results.update;

        //loop through all results and display poster and title with links
        for (var i = 0; i < results.length; i++){
            response += '<p>From: <a href="'
                        + results[i].profile_profileUrl + '">'
                        + results[i].profile_nickname + '</a><br /><a href="'
                        + results[i].link + '">'
                        + results[i].loc_longForm + '</a></p>'
        }
    //if no response is present, display appropriate message
    } else {
        response = 'No results were found';
    }

    //print message to screen
    document.write(response);
});
</script>

</body>
</html>
```

We use the getJSON(...) JQuery method to make our cross-domain request to YQL. Once the request completes, we should get a response object containing the result set that we searched for.

If there are results available, we loop through all update elements and display who the update is from, linked to their profiles, followed by the title of the update, linked to the update source. If there are no results, we display an appropriate message.

Using this basic practice, we can generate two-legged OAuth requests to any provider or service.

Three-Legged OAuth Implementation Example

Now that we have examined the particulars of the OAuth 1.0a process, let's look at a practical implementation of what we've learned to see how to build out an end-to-end project using OAuth.

In this example, we'll use OAuth to connect to Yahoo! on a user's behalf and then post out an activity to that user's update stream. This update stream will be available throughout the site—most notably, on *http://mail.yahoo.com*, *http://pulse.yahoo.com*, and through Yahoo! Messenger. This process will display that we have authenticated on a user's behalf and used read/write access permissions to push our new data to the user's private stream.

To start out this process, we need to create a new application on the Yahoo! system. Follow these steps to create the base application:

1. Go to *https://developer.apps.yahoo.com/projects* to load the application dashboard.

2. Click New Project at the top of the page that opens. When prompted, select a Standard application (not a YAP application, as those are applications that run on Yahoo-specific dropzones like *http://my.yahoo.com*).

3. Once you've selected the preceding options and the domain has been verified (if needed), you will be presented with a new, blank application.

Within the application window, you'll see a section under a Permissions header. This is where we will select the type of personal data access we want to bind to our application. For our needs, since we will simply be outputting a new activity to a user's update stream, we just need to set read/write access for the Yahoo! Updates permission set, as shown in Figure 9-7.

Figure 9-7. Yahoo! OAuth application permissions, bound to the application

Once you've saved the changes, a new consumer key and secret will be generated for your application. These keys are what we need to initiate development of our OAuth code.

At the top of the application page, you will see a page like the one in Figure 9-8, showing some direct information about the current application.

Figure 9-8. OAuth information for your Yahoo! application

We are specifically interested in three pieces of information here:

- The consumer key
- The consumer secret
- The application ID below the title of the application. We will use this ID in the Yahoo! process to identify the calling application.

Implementing OAuth 1.0a in PHP

 The full code for this sample is available at *https://github.com/jcleblanc/ programming-social-applications/tree/master/chapter_9/oauth1-php -3legged*.

Now that we have the application set up, our keys obtained, and a good understanding about how the process should work, let's explore how to implement this programmatically by looking at an example written in PHP using the associated PHP OAuth library.

We're going to take a full end-to-end example in PHP and split it up into its individual files and sections to see how we can apply the abstract steps from the OAuth process we walked through earlier in a program implementation.

Common variables and functions. Let's start with our file that will store all of the required URI endpoints, keys, and common methods. We'll call this one *common.php*:

```php
<?php
$key = 'drOWFGZEhhMFozTldNbWNHbzlNQSOtJnM9Y29uc3VtZXJfZWNyZXQQmeD1hYw--';
$secret = 'f803bc90f1b4b1086158d1b3c4f';
$appid = 'hWGkw5';

$debug = true;
$base_url = "http://www.jcleblanc.com/projects/oauth/complete.php";
$request_token_endpoint = 'https://api.login.yahoo.com/oauth/v2/get_request_token';
$authorize_endpoint = 'https://api.login.yahoo.com/oauth/v2/request_auth';
$oauth_access_token_endpoint = 'https://api.login.yahoo.com/oauth/v2/get_token';

/***************************************************************************
 * Function: Run CURL
 * Description: Executes a CURL request
 * Parameters: url (string) - URL to make request to
 *             method (string) - HTTP transfer method
 *             headers - HTTP transfer headers
 *             postvals - post values
 ***************************************************************************/
function run_curl($url, $method = 'GET', $headers = null, $postvals = null){
    $ch = curl_init($url);

    if ($method == 'GET'){
        curl_setopt($ch, CURLOPT_URL, $url);
        curl_setopt($ch, CURLOPT_RETURNTRANSFER, true);
    } else {
```

```
        $options = array(
            CURLOPT_HEADER => true,
            CURLINFO_HEADER_OUT => true,
            CURLOPT_VERBOSE => true,
            CURLOPT_HTTPHEADER => $headers,
            CURLOPT_RETURNTRANSFER => true,
            CURLOPT_POSTFIELDS => $postvals,
            CURLOPT_CUSTOMREQUEST => $method,
            CURLOPT_TIMEOUT => 3
        );
        curl_setopt_array($ch, $options);
    }

    $response = curl_exec($ch);
    curl_close($ch);

    return $response;
}
?>
```

In our *common.php* file, we store a number of values. First, we're storing the consumer key, secret, and application ID to variables so that we can use them in our OAuth process. We also set a debug flag, which we will use to output some debugging data at the end of the OAuth process. The next stored set of variables comprises the endpoints we'll need to make requests to during the process, including:

base_url

> The URL to return the user to after she accepts the application permissions. This is the step that completes the OAuth process.

request_token_endpoint

> The Yahoo! endpoint to which we will make a request to obtain a request token.

authorize_endpoint

> The Yahoo! endpoint to which the user is forwarded to sign in and accept the application permissions so that we can post updates on her behalf.

oauth_access_token_endpoint

> The Yahoo! endpoint that we will call in order to exchange the request token and oauth_verifier for an access token.

Last, we have our cURL function, which will make the majority of our data and token exchange requests. This function will be used to process simple GET requests as well as POST/PUT requests that we'll need to set headers and POST data.

Request token fetch and authorization forwarding. Now that we have our common variables and functions in place, let's get started with the actual OAuth token fetch requests. This is the file that starts the entire OAuth process, so we'll name it *index.php* for this example.

Let's break down the file into its major sections, starting with the first request to fetch the request token from Yahoo!:

```php
<?php
require_once "OAuth.php";        //oauth library
require_once "common.php";       //common functions and variables

//initialize consumer
$consumer = new OAuthConsumer($key, $secret, NULL);

//prepare to get request token
$sig_method = new OAuthSignatureMethod_HMAC_SHA1();
$params = array('oauth_callback' => $base_url);

//sign request and get request token
$req_req = OAuthRequest::from_consumer_and_token($consumer, NULL, 'GET',
                                                 $request_token_endpoint,
                                                 $params);
$req_req->sign_request($sig_method, $consumer, NULL);
$req_token = run_curl($req_req->to_url(), 'GET');
```

The first item on our list is to attach the required files for the process:

OAuth.php

> The OAuth library for signature generation and processing. For this example, we're using a standard library created by Andy Smith. The *OAuth.php* file is available from the Google code repository at *http://oauth.googlecode.com/svn/code/php/*.

common.php

> Our common variable and function file that we defined earlier in the section "Common variables and functions" on page 334.

Now we have to build the objects that will be used to fetch our request token. We start by creating a new OAuth Consumer, passing in our consumer key and secret. This basically creates a hash of the values that can be passed along with the request.

Next, we prepare some of the other elements that will be part of the request token fetch. We create a new instance of OAuthSignatureMethod_HMAC_SHA1 to store the signature method that we will use for the request. (This can be an HMAC-SHA1 signature or plain text, but for our example we'll use HMAC-SHA1.)

We then create the parameter set that will be attached to the request token. We create this associative array containing the oauth_callback, which is the URL to which the user is forwarded after she authenticates and accepts the application permissions.

 As mentioned previously, to safeguard against a known man-in-the-middle security vulnerability, Revision A of OAuth 1.0 requires that the oauth_callback parameter be attached at the RequestToken endpoint.

With our data structures in place, we build the request structure that will be used as the base for fetching our request token (OAuthRequest::from_consumer_and_token

$(...))$. We then sign the request with the `sign_request(...)` method, using the signature method we specified.

Last, we initiate a cURL GET request to the URI specified in our request object. The response from this request will either be the request token or an error.

Once we have the request token in hand, we can extract the pieces that we need and forward the user to the Yahoo! login page, where she can sign in to her account and accept the application permissions.

```
//if fetching request token was successful we should
//have oauth_token and oauth_token_secret
parse_str($req_token, $tokens);
$oauth_token = $tokens['oauth_token'];
$oauth_token_secret = $tokens['oauth_token_secret'];

//store key and token details in cookie to pass to complete stage
setcookie("requestToken",
          "token=$oauth_token&token_secret=$oauth_token_secret");

//build authentication url following sign-in and redirect user
$auth_url = $authorize_endpoint . "?oauth_token=$oauth_token";
header("Location: $auth_url");
?>
```

There are two pieces of information that we need to extract from the request token and store when forwarding the user off-site to Yahoo: the `oauth_token` and `oauth_token_secret`. Once the user has accepted the application permissions, we will be using these, along with the `oauth_verifier`, to exchange our request token for an access token.

We start by parsing the request token return object into an associative array. We then store the `oauth_token` and `oauth_token_secret` values into variables.

Next, we create a new cookie called `requestToken` and set its value to the `token` and `token_secret`. We are using a cookie simply as a mechanism for passing these values from the originating site, through the Yahoo! authorization page, and back to the originating site. This feature may be implemented in many different ways.

Once the cookie is set, we forward the user to the authorization URL on the Yahoo! site to sign in and accept the permissions of the application.

After the user has accepted the permissions, she will be forwarded to the complete URL, where we can obtain and use the access token.

Request token exchange and data requests. Let's summarize where we are at this point in the process:

- We have obtained a request token and stored the token information within a cookie titled `requestToken`.
- The user has completed the sign-in and authorization steps to allow our application to access and set her personal information.

- The user has been forwarded to the callback URL we specified when obtaining the request token. In addition, an `oauth_verifier` param has been passed along to allow us to exchange our request token for an access token.

Now we can take our last few steps to exchange the verified request token for an access token and make a request with that token. Let's start by looking at the exchange step:

```php
<?php
require_once "OAuth.php";        //oauth library
require_once "common.php";       //common functions and variables

//get request token params from cookie and parse values
$request_cookie = $_COOKIE['requestToken'];
parse_str($request_cookie);

//create required consumer variables
$test_consumer = new OAuthConsumer($key, $secret, NULL);
$req_token = new OAuthConsumer($token, $token_secret, NULL);
$sig_method = new OAuthSignatureMethod_HMAC_SHA1();

//exchange authenticated request token for access token
$params = array('oauth_verifier' => $_GET['oauth_verifier']);
$acc_req = OAuthRequest::from_consumer_and_token($test_consumer, $req_token, 'GET',
                                                 $oauth_access_token_endpoint,
                                                 $params);
$acc_req->sign_request($sig_method, $test_consumer, $req_token);
$access_ret = run_curl($acc_req->to_url(), 'GET');

//if access token fetch succeeded, we should have oauth_token and
//oauth_token_secret parse and generate access consumer from values
$access_token = array();
parse_str($access_ret, $access_token);
$access_consumer = new OAuthConsumer($access_token['oauth_token'],
    $access_token['oauth_token_secret'], NULL);
```

We begin by including the OAuth library, our common variables, and our cURL function, as we did previously.

With those in place, we extract the value of the request token from our `requestToken` cookie and parse it out into the individual variables. With this done, we now have the `$token` and `$token_secret` variables available to us.

Now we have to create the objects needed to exchange our request token for an access token. We start by creating a hash of the standard key and secret of our application (`$test_consumer`). We then create another one for the request token that we passed through. Finally, we set the signature method that we want to use.

We now have all of the pieces in place to do the exchange. The next step mimics the procedure that we used to obtain the request token, but with different parameters. We create an extra parameter object containing the `oauth_verifier` that signifies that the user accepted the application permissions.

Next, we call the `from_consumer_and_token(...)` method to generate our request object, passing in the standard consumer object, our request token object, the request token–to–access token URI endpoint on Yahoo, and the `oauth_verifier` parameter object. Once it's constructed, we sign the request using our signature method, standard consumer object, and request token object.

Last, we make a cURL request to the exchange endpoint. If all succeeded, `$access _ret` should now contain the access token values we need to make requests.

Now we just need to make a consumer object out of the access token return values, and we're done with the exchange. We parse out the return values from the cURL request to get the access token object and store them in `$access_token`. We then create a new `OAuthConsumer` instance, passing in the `oauth_token` and `oauth_token_secret` from the access token object. We now have the access consumer.

Now we can take a look at making that activity stream update request to Yahoo! using our newfound access consumer:

```php
//build update PUT request payload
$guid = $access_token['xoauth_yahoo_guid'];
$title = ': Visit my site';                               //activity title
$description = 'Current articles, updates and events'; //activity description
$link = 'http://www.jcleblanc.com';                       //title link
$source = 'APP.'.$appid;                                   //source of the update
$date = time();                                           //activity timestamp
$suid = $appid.time();                                    //unique activity ID
$body = array(
    'updates' => array(
        array(
            'collectionID' => $guid,
            'collectionType' => 'guid',
            'class' => 'app',
            'source' => $source,
            'type' => 'appActivity',
            'imgURL' => 'http://jcleblanc.com/images/page.png',
            'imgHeight' => '80',
            'imgWidth' => '80',
            'suid' => $suid,
            'title' => $title,
            'description' => $description,
            'link' => $link,
            'pubDate' => (string)$date
        )
    )
);

//build update PUT request URL
$url = sprintf("http://%s/v1/user/%s/updates/%s/%s",
    'social.yahooapis.com',
    $guid,
    $source,
    urlencode($suid)
);
```

```
//build and sign request
$request = OAuthRequest::from_consumer_and_token($test_consumer,
    $access_consumer,
    'PUT',
    $url,
    array());

$request->sign_request(new OAuthSignatureMethod_HMAC_SHA1(),
    $test_consumer,
    $access_consumer
);

//define request headers
$headers = array("Accept: application/json");
$headers[] = $request->to_header();
$headers[] = "Content-type: application/json";

//json encode request payload and make PUT request
$content = json_encode($body);
$resp = run_curl($url, 'PUT', $headers, $content);
```

There are a few elements in play within this section of the code. Let's go through each of the major sections to assess its significance.

The first large block being generated is the object that we will send to Yahoo! to define what the activity's content and background are. We won't go through all of the parameters being added here; there are a few standard parameters required for the update, as listed here: *http://developer.yahoo.com/social/rest_api_guide/Single-update-resource .html*. The one item of note is that the Yahoo! access token object embeds an xoauth_yahoo_guid parameter, which is the unique identifier for the user that has currently authenticated. This is what we use to target the activity to a specific user.

With our object built out, we can now generate the PUT request URI that we will be calling to send the new activity through. Yahoo! defines the following URI structure for making PUT requests to its Updates API:

```
http://social.yahooapis.com/v1/user/{guid}/updates/{source}/{suid}
```

This URI contains a few custom values, including the unique identifier for the user (guid), the source of the update in the format APP.{appid}, and any unique identifier for the update (suid). We generate this URI based on the values that we have already processed when building out the payload that will be sent with the request.

We now take a familiar step: we generate the OAuth request object using the from_con sumer_and_token(...) method, passing in our application consumer object, the access token consumer object, and the URI that we will be making the request to. Once we have built it, we sign the request object using the same HMAC-SHA1 signature method that we have employed previously.

Our next step is to define the headers that will be sent with the request. Here we state that JSON will be the content type that is accepted and sent, and will pass in the request headers.

Last, we JSON-encode the request payload and initiate an OAuth signed PUT request to the Yahoo! Updates API in order to insert a new activity in the user's stream.

Now that our payload is sent and the new activity has been generated on the Yahoo! side, we may want to dump some debugging information (remember that debug flag we set way back in the *common.php* file?):

```
//if debug mode, dump signatures & headers
if ($debug){
    $debug_out = array('Access token' => $access_token,
                       'PUT URL'      => $url,
                       'PUT headers'  => $headers,
                       'PUT content'  => $content,
                       'PUT response' => $resp);

    print_r($debug_out);
}
?>
```

If the debug flag was set to `true`, we'll be dumping out some data about the last request we made. We will print out:

- The content of the access token.
- The URI that was called to make the PUT request.
- The headers that were sent with the PUT request.
- The JSON-encoded body that was sent with the PUT request.
- The response from the PUT request.

Dumping out signatures and responses, and being able to validate the content of a request object, are incredibly important debugging tools when you're working with OAuth. They help you identify the problem areas when trouble arises, and the output signatures will allow you to see if there are missing parameters or improperly encoded structures.

Once the OAuth process completes and the activity PUT request succeeds, we can see our new update at *http://pulse.yahoo.com* by going to the activity stream for the user we set the activity for (*http://pulse.yahoo.com/y* for your own profile). You should see a new activity posted for the user, with the content that we sent to be posted. It should look something like Figure 9-9.

Once you have your access token available, you can make any number of requests to a service, depending on its APIs and offerings.

Figure 9-9. Example activity output from our Yahoo! OAuth 1 application

Implementing OAuth 1.0a in Python

 The full code for this sample is available at *https://github.com/jcleblanc/ programming-social-applications/tree/master/chapter_9/oauth1-python -3legged.*

Now that we have gone through the PHP implementation of OAuth 1.0a, let's look at a Python version. In this example, we will walk through the same type of implementation as the one from the PHP example, following these steps in the OAuth authorization token exchange:

1. Capture a request token object.
2. Forward the user to the authorization page on the provider site to grant the application access to her privileged information.
3. Exchange the verified request token for an access token.
4. Make signed requests to the provider for the user's profile information.

Now let's start breaking down the files that we will use for this request, starting with our application configuration file.

Configuration file. Since this example uses Google App Engine, we will use a YAML configuration file to load it. This file looks like the following:

```
application: oauth-python
version: 1
runtime: python
api_version: 1

handlers:
- url: /index.py
  script: index.py
- url: /complete.py
  script: complete.py
```

In this example, we have only a few endpoints that we will be worrying about for implementation:

index.py

> Begins the authorization process by requesting a new request token, then forwarding the user to the authorization page on the provider site to accept the application permissions.

complete.py

> Completes the authorization process by taking the verified request token and exchanging it for an access token that is used to make requests for privileged user information on the provider site.

Now that we understand the makeup of the example and how it flows, let's dig in to the common variable file that both *index.py* and *complete.py* will be using: *common.py*.

Common variables. The common variables file will hold the OAuth credentials that we obtained when we first created our application on the provider site, as well as several links that we will need throughout the OAuth process. In our case, this file is called *common.py*:

```
import os

#set oauth consumer / secret keys and application id
consumer_key = 'djJmQ9WVdrOVFqRjBZMEpOTjJzbWNM9Y29uc3VtZXJjZWNyZXQmeD1kYg--'
consumer_secret = '2308040af65e07fa0a9b9727e01a06e0d'
appid = 'B1reBR7k'

#application urls
callback_url = 'http://%s/complete.py' % (os.environ['HTTP_HOST'])

#oauth access token endpoints (Yahoo!)
request_token_endpoint = 'https://api.login.yahoo.com/oauth/v2/get_request_token'
authorize_endpoint = 'https://api.login.yahoo.com/oauth/v2/request_auth'
oauth_access_token_endpoint = 'https://api.login.yahoo.com/oauth/v2/get_token'
```

At the top, we have our required consumer key and secret. Additionally, we store the application ID (also generated by the provider when the application was created), as we need it to identify certain PUT/POST requests to the provider.

We then store the absolute URL to the callback file. This is where the user will be redirected once she has authorized the application.

Last, we have the OAuth token exchange endpoints that we will need throughout the process:

- The endpoint from which we obtain a request token.
- The authorization endpoint to which we forward the user to have her authorize the application.
- The access token endpoint where we exchange the verified request token for an access token.

We'll use all of these pieces at different intervals throughout the application. With those in place, we can take the first steps in the token exchange process.

Fetching the request token and forwarding the user for authorization. Our next task is to focus on acquiring the OAuth request token that we'll use, along with the provider's authorization endpoint, to have the user authorize the application to perform actions and obtain information on her behalf. This file is stored as *index.py*.

Besides the standard libraries, we are importing the OAuth library that we installed and our common variables file. We then get into the crux of the program through main():

```python
import os
import cgi
import time
import urllib
import oauth.oauth as oauth
import common
import Cookie


'''
' Function: Main
' Description:
'''
def main():
    #build base consumer object with oauth keys and sign using HMAC-SHA1
    base_consumer = oauth.OAuthConsumer(common.consumer_key,
        common.consumer_secret)
    signature_method_hmac_sha1 = oauth.OAuthSignatureMethod_HMAC_SHA1()

    #create and sign request token fetch request object
    request_rt = oauth.OAuthRequest.from_consumer_and_token(base_consumer,
        callback=common.callback_url, http_url=common.request_token_endpoint)
    request_rt.sign_request(signature_method_hmac_sha1, base_consumer, None)

    #obtain request token
    token_read = urllib.urlopen(request_rt.to_url())
    token_string = token_read.read()

    #parse request token into individual parameters
    token_params = cgi.parse_qs(token_string)
    oauth_token = token_params['oauth_token'][0]
    oauth_token_secret = token_params['oauth_token_secret'][0]

    #generate cookie with request token key and secret to pass through
    #authorization process
    cookie = Cookie.Cookie()
    cookie_token = 'token=%s&token_secret=%s' % (oauth_token, oauth_token_secret)
    cookie['request_token'] = cookie_token
    cookie['timestamp'] = time.time()
    print cookie

    #redirect user to authorization endpoint
    print "Location: %s?oauth_token=%s" % (common.authorize_endpoint, oauth_token)

if __name__ == '__main__':
    main()
```

We start out by creating the base-level OAuth objects that will be used for our requests. These are our base consumer (a consumer object containing the OAuth consumer key and secret for our application) and the signature method (HMAC-SHA1) that we will be using.

Next, we create the request object to obtain the request token. We make a request to the `from_consumer_and_token(...)` method to do this, passing in the base consumer object, the callback URL that we want to forward the user to after she authorizes the application, and the `http_url` that contains the request token URI on the provider site that we will need to contact. We then call `sign_request(...)` to sign the request object using our signature method object and base consumer.

We then make a request to the request token URI and read back the response from the provider site. This should be a string containing our request token and all associated parameters. We take this response string and split it into its individual parameters. From the token parameters, we then extract the request token and request token secret.

Now we need to find a way of passing the request token and request token secret parameters through the authorization process. For our needs, we will use a cookie. We create a new cookie object and store the token, secret, and timestamp as parameters for the cookie.

Last, we redirect the user to the authorization endpoint with the `oauth_token` parameter in order to have her authorize the application to access and set information on her behalf.

Once the user authorizes the application, she is forwarded to the callback URL that was defined in our request token object.

Token exchange and making authenticated private data requests. The user should now be forwarded to our *complete.py* file following authorization. This is where we will take the request token and validation code (validated request token) and exchange it for an access token to request the user's privileged information. Much like our previous file, we are including a number of standard libraries as well as the Python OAuth library and *common.py* file that holds our common variables and endpoints.

Before we jump into the final token exchange process, notice that at the top of the file there is a `dotdict` class, which accepts a dictionary object. We are using this class so we can refer to dictionary objects using dot notation (e.g., *object1.object2*), which is functionality required by the Python OAuth library we are using.

Now let's take a closer look at `main()` to see the token exchange process:

```
import os
import cgi
import sys
import Cookie
import urllib
import oauth.oauth as oauth
import common
```

```
'''
' Class: Dot Notation Insertion
' Description: Adds dot notation capabilities to a dictionary
'''
class dotdict(dict):
    def __getattr__(self, attr):
        return self.get(attr, None)
    __setattr__ = dict.__setitem__
    __delattr__ = dict.__delitem__


'''
' Function: Main
' Description:
'''
def main():
    #create new smart cookie to extract request token
    cookie = Cookie.SmartCookie()

    #if a cookie is available, load it
    if os.environ.has_key('HTTP_COOKIE'):
        cookie.load(os.environ['HTTP_COOKIE'])

        #if the request token cookie is available, load and parse it
        if cookie.has_key('request_token'):
            request_token = cookie.get('request_token').value
            rt_params = cgi.parse_qs(request_token)

            #parse query string parameters into dictionary
            qs_params = {}
            string_split = [s for s in os.environ['QUERY_STRING'].split('&') if s]
            for item in string_split:
                key,value = item.split('=')
                qs_params[key] = value

            #create base consumer and signature method objects
            base_consumer = oauth.OAuthConsumer(common.consumer_key,
                common.consumer_secret)
            signature_method_hmac_sha1 = oauth.OAuthSignatureMethod_HMAC_SHA1()

            #build dictionary of request token and secret to exchange for
            #access token
            req_token = dotdict({'key': rt_params['token'][0], 'secret':
                rt_params['token_secret'][0]})

            #build request token to access token exchange request object and sign it
            oauth_request = oauth.OAuthRequest.from_consumer_and_token(
                base_consumer, token=req_token,
                verifier=qs_params['oauth_verifier'],
                http_url=common.oauth_access_token_endpoint)
            oauth_request.sign_request(signature_method_hmac_sha1, base_consumer,
                req_token)

            #obtain request token as string and dictionary objects
            token_read = urllib.urlopen(oauth_request.to_url())
```

```
        token_string = token_read.read()
        token_params = cgi.parse_qs(token_string)

        #create access token object out of access token string
        access_token = oauth.OAuthToken.from_string(token_string)

        #create url to Yahoo! servers to access user profile
        guid = token_params['xoauth_yahoo_guid'][0]
        url = 'http://%s/v1/user/%s/profile' % ('social.yahooapis.com', guid)

        #create new oauth request and sign using HMAC-SHA1 to get profile of
        #authorized user
        oauth_request = oauth.OAuthRequest.from_consumer_and_token(
            base_consumer, token=access_token, http_method='GET', http_url=url)
        oauth_request.sign_request(signature_method_hmac_sha1, base_consumer,
            access_token)

        #make request to get profile of user
        profile_read = urllib.urlopen(oauth_request.to_url())
        profile_string = profile_read.read()
        print 'Content-Type: text/plain'
        print ''
        print profile_string
    else:
        #if request token cookie was not available, end
        print 'Request token cookie not found - exiting'
        sys.exit()
    else:
        #if cookies were not available, end
        print 'Request token cookie not found - exiting'
        sys.exit()

if __name__ == '__main__':
    main()
```

We start by checking whether HTTP_COOKIE can be obtained. If not, we display an appropriate error message and stop program execution. If so, we check for the existence of the cookie that we set in the *index.py* file containing our request token. If that cookie is absent, we display an appropriate error and stop program execution. If the cookie is present, we capture it and parse it into its individual parameters.

We then go through the step of obtaining all parameters from the query string, splitting them into their keys and values, and then placing them into a dictionary object.

We continue in a way similar to how the last file started, by defining our base_consumer and signature_method_hmac_sha1 variables, which are objects to hold our application's consumer key and secret and the signing method that we will be using, respectively.

Now we need to create a request token dictionary object out of the request token and secret that we extract from the cookie we set in *index.py*. Through our dotdict class, we also specify that this dictionary can be referenced using dot notation.

Next we need to construct an OAuth request object that we will use to request that the provider site exchange the validated request token for an access token. We do this by making a request to `from_consumer_and_token(...)`, passing in our base consumer, the request token, verifier parameter from the query string signifying that the user has authorized the application, and finally the access token exchange URI endpoint on the provider site. Once we've created it, we sign the request with the signature method we set up, the base consumer object, and the request token object.

We can now exchange the validated request token for an access token. We make a request to the access token endpoint and read back the access token response. This should be a series of parameters, so we parse those into a lookup object. We then create the access token object by calling `from_string(...)`, passing in the token string that was returned. Now we can start making requests for privileged user data.

 We may want to create a `token_params` lookup object out of the access token string, because some providers might send back additional parameters in the token exchange request. These parameters may be ignored and removed from the access token object when it's created. These additional parameters could be only informational, or they might contain elements such as a unique user identifier that can be used to make specific data requests to the provider site.

We can accomplish this type of request by first generating the URI to which we will be making the signed request. We extract the globally unique identifier (GUID) for the user from the access token object that we created. From that, we create the URI to Yahoo! in order to obtain the user's profile.

When we have the URI, we construct a new OAuth request using `from_consumer _and_token(...)`. We pass in the base consumer object, access token, HTTP method (in this case, GET), and the URI to obtain the profile that we just created. We then sign the request with the base consumer and access token objects.

Once ready, we simply make another request to the profile URI on the provider, read the response, and dump it to the screen.

This completes the steps needed to make an OAuth 1.0a signed request to a provider for privileged user resources.

Tools and Tips for Debugging Signature Issues

In this section, we'll dive into the most common OAuth issues and go over tips and tricks to address them.

Missing or duplicate parameters

One of the single most frustrating experiences you'll run into when working with OAuth is to see a "signature mismatch" or "signature invalid" response sent back from a request. If you haven't encountered this error very often, you might end up spending hours trying to debug signatures to figure out where the problem lies.

In most cases, invalid signature errors are produced for two reasons:

- You have forgotten a parameter in the request.
- You have duplicated a parameter in the request.

In the case of forgotten parameters, there are two techniques that work well to help you debug the signature issues. The first, and easiest, is to compare the invalid signature parameters against those expected at the OAuth stage where the error was produced. You can compare these parameters against those listed earlier in this chapter in the section "OAuth 1.0a Workflow" on page 319. You should be able to determine fairly quickly whether a missing parameter is the cause.

The other method involves comparing exact signatures. If you have access to valid signatures from the same platform (either through docs or another application), you can compare them to your invalid signatures to pinpoint discrepancies. This method comes in handy if you are aiding a development team that's encountering issues when you have an existing, functional application.

Double encoding the signature parameters

Another issue that developers who are new to authentication systems like OAuth often face is double-encoding parameter sets in the OAuth signatures.

Many people may say that this would never happen to them, that they're careful in their development. The truth of the matter is that this happens quite a bit. When you're working with complex signature generation, you may inadvertently URL-encode an entire list of parameters instead of just the values of those parameters. This will invalidate the signature because the individual signature parameters cannot be parsed (since the ampersands separating the parameters are encoded).

Most issues involving double encoding usually surface when the developer is constructing his own OAuth libraries, which he might do when a language he's using does not have a supported library or if the library requires editing for use (such as when OAuth 1.0 was upgraded to OAuth 1.0a).

Whenever possible, use standard OAuth libraries from *http://oauth.net/code/*.

Incorrect URI endpoints

One issue that comes up quite often when you're working with a new service is specifying an incorrect or incomplete URI for either the signature stages when capturing the request or access tokens, or when using the access token to make a signed request to a URI endpoint on the provider to obtain privileged information.

When it comes to the OAuth token exchange, remember that you will need to specify several URIs for each stage, including URIs for:

- Fetching the request token.
- Forwarding the user to the provider site to log in and go through the permission screen.
- Forwarding the user back to your site or application after he has signed in and given the application permission to access his personal information.
- Exchanging the verified request token for an access token.

The potential problems around using endpoints don't stop as soon as you obtain the access token. When you make OAuth requests to a URI endpoint defined by the provider as a means to access social data, there are a couple of things that can generally go awry.

The first is the incorrect URI endpoint. When large amounts of social documentation are available for obtaining a user's personal information, or when providers use a single URI with slightly different parameters to access the majority of their social information, this issue may come up. Dump out the URI that you are attempting to call and match it up against the documentation for the service that you want to use. This is the easiest way to verify that your URI endpoint is correct.

The second is the incomplete URI endpoint. When working with large amounts of data exchange, such as through the OAuth process, it is common for parameters to get left off the fully qualified URI. This can happen due to parameter overwriting, incorrect variable naming, or a host of other causes that may generate a bad URI response from the provider.

For instance, Yahoo! defines a URI for setting a user update (activities) that contains a number of dynamic attributes that you need to add before making a request:

http://social.yahooapis.com/v1/user/{guid}/updates/{source}/{suid}

Besides the static attributes in the URI, there are a few pieces of custom data that are required:

guid
:   The globally unique identifier of a user

source
:   The application source that the request originates from

suid
:   A unique identifier for the update

Let's say that we have just made some changes to our OAuth flow for passing the GUID of a user and are suddenly seeing provider responses stating that the incorrect URI endpoint was used. This can be due to a single parameter missing from the URI:

http://social.yahooapis.com/v1/user//updates/APP.1234/app1043324

If we look closely, we can see the double slashes and a missing GUID parameter. This is a common cause of errors in the OAuth flow and also one of the easiest to diagnose.

Invalid signature method

Another common occurrence in the world of OAuth signatures is receiving a message stating that the signature method you are using is not valid.

If you think back to the practical OAuth example we went through, where we inserted a new activity to the user's stream, you may remember that right before making requests to fetch the request token, or exchange the verified request token for an access token, we had to sign the request using our chosen signature method (in our case, it was HMAC-SHA1).

If you see this type of an error, it is often due to using a signature method that is not accepted by the provider, such as plain text in many cases. You can easily remedy this issue by checking to ensure that the signature method that you are using is valid.

 When in doubt, use HMAC-SHA1.

Token expiration

While the majority of providers do not expire their tokens—meaning that you can use a single access token until it is revoked—some do add an expiration extension on top of their OAuth 1.0a implementations. The expiration timeframe in these cases is usually a few weeks.

If, after you've used an access token for a period of time, you get errors that say something along the lines of "token expired" or "token rejected," it could be that the token has expired.

When you're obtaining an access token, if the token has an expiration attached to it, the expiration time will generally be embedded in the token string response. It may look something like the following:

```
{
  'oauth_token_secret': ['1ce460d4d5f8c10883b0e60e3d4a2d0d45'],
  'oauth_expires_in': ['3600'],
  'oauth_session_handle': ['AKXOoEw_Qns9ToVxJMsdcm3eYlqc_q4Zdm5yk-'],
  'oauth_authorization_expires_in': ['849662194'],
```

```
    'oauth_token': ['A=Qc9767HOtQMbzN8tbiAEVjJiLzbubnxN_...']
}
```

Parameters referring to expiration will give you an idea of how long you have until the token expires when you first obtain it.

If you are facing a token expiration, the provider will usually have documentation that explains the process through which you can exchange the expired access token. In most cases, you do this by making a new OAuth request to the same URI endpoint you used when exchanging the verified request token for the original access token, only passing in the expired access token instead of the request token.

OAuth 2

We have looked at the standard that has been employed by many of the top providers in the industry, OAuth 1.0a. Now it's time to look at the emerging revision to that standard, OAuth 2, which has already been implemented by companies such as Facebook (to secure its Graph API) and Gowalla (to access its check-in services).

 OAuth 2 is not compatible with the OAuth 1.0a workflow or token system. It is a complete revision to the specification.

There are a few major revisions to the specification that implementers should be aware of. Instead of having signing libraries such as those we used in the OAuth 1.0a examples, in OAuth 2, all requests are made via HTTPS requests. There is no longer any need to go through complex signing procedures in order to perform token exchange.

Another major difference has to do with the ease of implementation. Due to its reduced complexity, OAuth 2 will take far less time and effort to implement.

To understand this specification and how it works, let's start by going through the OAuth 2 workflow.

OAuth 2 Workflow

 While the OAuth 2 specification drafts are clear about the parameters that are required in the exchange requests and responses at each stage, implementers may have slight discrepancies in the parameter lists that they support, even going so far as to not request or provide required parameters or to change the expected values for given parameters. Be aware of the fields that are required and the responses provided by any service that you are using. You can find this information in the OAuth implementation docs for each service.

The OAuth 2 workflow is a rather simple set of back-and-forth requests between a client and the provider site. The user is still involved in the process to authorize the application to access his privileged information, but in general the interaction is between the client and provider, which exchange simple verification resources in order to issue (provider) and obtain (client) a final access token to make privileged requests. This entire flow is illustrated in Figure 9-10.

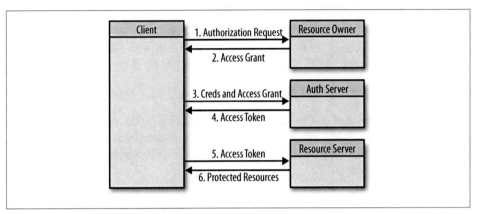

Figure 9-10. OAuth 2 authorization workflow

The OAuth 2 authorization flow consists of a few exchange requests. The flow depicted in Figure 9-10 contains the back-and-forth requests for obtaining the access token for a user and then making a request back to the provider's resource server to obtain some protected data.

In short, the OAuth 2 authorization flow consists of the following elements:

1. The client (your script) forwards the user to the resource owner (provider) in order to have him accept the permissions of the application, thereby allowing it to access his protected data.

2. Once the user accepts the permissions of the application, the resource owner forwards him to the callback location that was passed in with the original request to the resource owner. The resource owner also sends a verification code parameter (via the query string to the callback) denoting that the user has accepted the permissions.

3. Once the callback URL is called, the client then sends a request to the authorization server to get an access token for the user, passing along the verification code with the request.

4. The authorization server then sends back an access token object with an optional refresh token, depending on whether the service specifies a lifespan for the access token.

5. From this point, the client can make signed OAuth requests with the access token to the resource server in order to get protected resources about the user.

This is the general flow that the client (your application) will need to follow in order to begin accessing a user's private data.

Let's explore what requests and responses would look like for each stage of this process.

Steps 1–2: Client requests authorization, and provider grants access

 cURL is one of the best tools available for working with the OAuth 2 process, as it allows a high degree of customization in the requests.

The first request/response batch that is run in the OAuth 2 process is the authorization request in which the client forwards the user to the resource owner to accept the application permissions, followed by the resource owner responding with an access grant. This is shown in Figure 9-11.

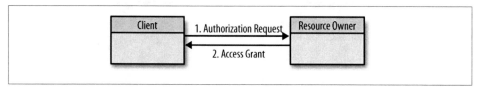

Figure 9-11. OAuth 2, steps 1–2: Client requests authorization from provider

When the client forwards the user to the resource server, it will also send a few additional parameters for identification and forwarding requirements. The structure of the URI request may look something like the following:

```
https://server.example.com
  ?response_type={type}
  &client_id={key}
  &redirect_uri={callback_uri}
```

which gives us an HTTP request similar to the following:

```
GET /authorize?response_type=code
      &client_id=s6BhdRkqt3
      &redirect_uri=https%3A%2F%2Fmysite%2Ecom%2Fcb
      HTTP/1.1
Host: server.example.com
```

The additional query parameters may include those listed in Table 9-5.

Table 9-5. Authorization request parameters

Parameter	Description

response_type (required)	The type of response that you are expecting. The value of this parameter *must* be either:
	
	token
	    Requesting access token
	
	code
	    Requesting an authorization code
	
	code_and_token
	    Both of the above
	
	In the case of this step—the authorization request—the appropriate response_type is code.

client_id (required)	The key that was issued when you first created your application.
redirect_uri (required)	The URI to which to forward the user after he has granted the application permission to access his protected information. The service that is being called should have required you to preregister your callback URI, so the preregistered value and the redirect_uri parameter should match.
scope (optional)	A list of space-delimited access scopes, defined by the authorization server. These scopes contain the type of protected data that a client can request from an end user (e.g., profiles or connections).
state (optional)	Used to maintain state between the request and callback stages. This value is passed along (usually as a query string parameter) when the end user is forwarded to the callback URI.

Once the user has been forwarded to the resource owner site, presented with a screen asking him to grant the application access to his protected data, and accepted those permissions, the resource owner will forward him to the callback URL with a verification code parameter on the query string:

```
http://www.mysite.com/oauth2/complete.php
  ?code=6e55f7019d56cb8bcd05c439890dacd6sdf
```

There are a few possible parameters available at this stage, listed in Table 9-6.

Table 9-6. Authorization response parameters

Parameter	Description
code (required)	The verification code that was generated by the authorization server. This will be used when making a request to fetch the access token.
state (required)	This parameter is required if a state parameter was sent in the authorization request for the user to accept the application permissions. If set, it is identical to the state that was sent in the request.

In short, the code parameter denotes that the user has accepted the client permissions and, thus, tells the provider's authorization server that it may grant an access token for the client.

Steps 3–4: Client requests access token, and provider grants access token

 Many services that implement OAuth 1.0a offer SDKs in different languages to mitigate the complexity of the OAuth process and provide an easy mechanism for accessing their data API endpoints. This is not as prevalent a practice with the OAuth 2 specification due to the ease of implementing the client. In many cases, though, services will offer SDKs to reduce the amount of code that you need to write. These are generally "kitchen sink" implementations that contain all the functionality you could ever want from the service.

Our next request/response step, outlined in Figure 9-12, consists of using the code parameter from our last step (along with a few other values) to make a request to an authorization server to fetch an access token, which we'll then use to make requests to access a user's protected data.

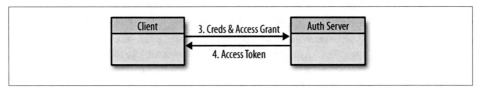

Figure 9-12. OAuth 2, steps 3–4: Client requests access token from provider

This is the simple method you should employ when making a request to receive an access token. You'll be making an HTTP POST request to the authorization server, passing in the code parameter and numerous client credentials as POST parameters. The response object that is returned will either be an error or the access token that you are looking for.

The URI you'll use to make this request depends on the service being used. If an SDK is not provided by the service, it will more than likely provide comprehensive OAuth request instructions within its developer documentation.

The POST request follows the general form of the following HTTP request:

```
POST /token HTTP/1.1
Host: server.example.com
Content-Type: application/x-www-form-urlencoded

grant_type=authorization_code
&client_id=5b14dbe141dfa7b8daa7601
&client_secret=4e624625c4b853c8f9eb41e
&code=6e55f7019d56cb8bcd05c439890dacd6sdf
&redirect_uri=https%3A%2F%2Fmysite%2Ecom%2Fcb
```

As we can see from this request, there are a number of POST fields that will be required at this step in order for us to obtain an access token. These are listed in Table 9-7.

Table 9-7. Access request parameters

Parameter	Description
grant_type (required)	The grant type that you are making a request for. The value must be one of the following: • authorization_code • password • refresh_token • client_credentials At this stage of the process, the appropriate value for grant_type is authorization_code.
client_id (required)	The key that was provided when you created your client (application) on the provider site.
client_secret (required)	The secret that was provided when you created your client (application) on the provider site.
code (required)	The authorization code that was passed to your callback_url as a GET parameter following the user's authentication of your client's permissions.
redirect_uri (required)	The URI to forward the user to after she has granted the application permission to access her protected information. The service that is being called should have required you to preregister your callback URI, so the preregistered value and the redirect_uri parameter should match.

If the authorization server responds successfully from the request, you'll be provided with an object containing the access token and all the data pieces you need to manage the access token and make requests for protected data.

The object will look something like the following:

```
object(stdClass)#1 (6) {
    ["expires_in"]=> int(1209474)
    ["expires_at"]=> string(31) "Wed, 22 Dec 2010 00:35:18 -0000"
    ["scope"]=> string(4) "read"
    ["access_token"]=> string(32) "4ced4e671b83f40a2e014c357ed7bad9"
    ["refresh_token"]=> string(32) "11ca1de7a26169963f2d6cdce3b4856b"
    ["username"]=> string(9) "jcleblanc"
}
```

There are a number of parameters that may be included in the access token object that is returned from the request. These are listed in Table 9-8.

Table 9-8. Access response parameters

Parameter	Description
access_token (required)	The access token that was issued by the authorization server. This is the value that you will use to make signed requests for protected end-user data.
expires_in (optional)	If the provider sets a lifetime (expiration) on the access token, the expires_in parameter will be set to the amount of time, in seconds, until the access token expires (e.g., 3600 = 1 hour).

Parameter	Description
refresh_token (optional)	Much like the expires_in parameter, if the provider has set an expiration time on the access_token, the refresh_token parameter should be present. This value can be used to request a new access token when the original expires.
scope (optional)	This parameter contains the scopes of the access token as a list of space-delimited strings, defining what protected data the client has access to. Authorization servers should set this value if the scopes of the access token are different from the scopes the client originally requested when forwarding the end user to the resource owner to accept the client application permissions.
token_type (required)	token_type contains the type of token that was issued. This provides the client with the details it needs to understand how to make requests for protected resources from the end user.

Once we've obtained the access token object and now that we understand what all of the pieces do, we can begin making requests for those prized end-user protected resources.

Steps 5–6: Client requests protected resources, and provider grants protected resources

The last step in the OAuth 2 process (which comprises the initial request up to obtaining protected resources) is to actually make a request that uses the access token to capture the end user's protected data.

Once the client sends a request to the resource server with the access token in tow, if the access token is valid and has the correct permissions set, the resource server will respond with an object containing the protected result set that was requested. Figure 9-13 shows this flow.

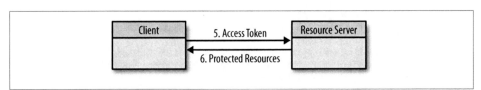

Figure 9-13. OAuth 2, steps 5–6: Client requests protected user resources from provider

The resource server will generally employ one of these three methods to pass the access token to a specific URI to make the protected resources accessible:

- Passing the access token through the query string as an HTTP GET parameter:

```
GET /user/jcleblanc?oauth_token=4ced4e671b83f40a2e014c357ed7bad9
```

- Passing the access token through the HTTP request header:

```
GET /user/jcleblanc
Authorization: Token oauth_token="4ced4e671b83f40a2e014c357ed7bad9"
```

- Passing the access token to the resource URI via an HTTP POST request:

```
POST /user/friends
oauth_token=4ced4e671b83f40a2e014c357ed7bad9
&user_id=jcleblanc
```

The resource server will validate the URI request and access token, then send back either the expected protected resource object or an error response if there was an issue processing the request or token. There are a number of HTTP error responses that might be returned from the resource server when it comes to OAuth 2 request. Some of the most common are listed in Table 9-9.

Table 9-9. Common access request error responses

Error	Description
insuffi cient_scope	The request for protected end-user resources requires a higher level of privileges than what has been granted to the access token. The provider should respond with a 403 (Forbidden) HTTP status code.
	If you receive this error, check to ensure that the scopes you initially set for your application are sufficient for accessing the data that you're requesting.
inva lid_request	This error is produced when the request is malformed in some way. The provider should respond with a 400 (Bad Request) HTTP status code.
	Some of the reasons for a malformed request may be:
	• The request is missing parameters that are required by the provider.
	• There are unsupported parameters or parameter values in the request. If the request includes a parameter or parameter value that the provider doesn't recognize, this error may result.
	• There are repeated parameters in the request object.
	Check the provider documentation to verify the parameters it expects when the request is being made.
invalid_token	This error is produced when the access token that has been provided (not the full request as with invalid_request) is malformed in some way. The provider should respond with a 401 (Unauthorized) HTTP status code.
	Some of the reasons for a malformed access token include:
	• The access token has expired. Check the expires_in parameter provided with the access token object to see if it has expired. If it has, used the refresh_token parameter to request a new access token.
	• The access token has been revoked by the provider. This may be due to some sort of abuse by the client. If you get this error, check the provider's terms of use to see if you have violated any of the terms.

If you plan your development for both an expected end-user protected resource as well as a host of potential error codes, you should be able to appropriately handle most of the situations that arise. In doing so, you can minimize the impact on the end user and reduce your application's drop-off rate.

Even though we now have a means of accessing protected resources, we still have one last aspect of the token and resource exchange to address. If the provider you're working with to extract the protected end-user resources has a lifespan set on its access tokens, you'll need to be able to determine when your access token expires and how to refresh it. We'll cover this final step next.

Optional steps 7–8: Refreshing the access token

 The `expires_in` parameter returned within an access token object should provide you with the means to verify whether the access token for a user has expired. When using the access token to request protected user resources, you should note any error messages stating that the access token has expired; this helps you appropriately handle the instance where an access token expires during regular use.

Depending on the security requirements of the provider that you are working with, the provider may expire the access token after a short period of time, such as a week or two. Once the token expires, your application client will receive errors stating that the access token is no longer valid. At this point, you'll need to refresh the access token with the provider for another one to two weeks (or however long the provider sets as the token's lifespan).

You can refresh the access token without involving the user. The user doesn't need to go through the authorization and permission acceptance step again, as she did when we fetched our initial access token. You will simply need to make another POST request to the provider with some information about the application and the refresh token. This request is very similar to the one we used to fetch the initial access token, and follows this general form:

```
POST /token HTTP/1.1
Host: server.example.com
Content-Type: application/x-www-form-urlencoded

grant_type=refresh_token
&client_id=5b14dbe141dfa7b8daa7601
&client_secret=4e624625c4b853c8f9eb41e
&code=6e55f7019d56cb8bcd05c439890dacd6sdf
&refresh_token= da2e3e192bf68f3656eafa87d8
&redirect_uri=https%3A%2F%2Fmysite%2Ecom%2Fcb
```

As I mentioned earlier, the main differences between a request to fetch an access token for the user and one to refresh the access token after it has expired are the new grant type and the new `refresh_token` POST parameter.

The response object that is returned after you send the refresh token HTTP POST request should look very familiar at this point:

```
object(stdClass)#2 (5) {
    ["expires_in"]=> int(1209599)
    ["expires_at"]=> string(31) "Thu, 23 Dec 2010 22:45:59 -0000"
    ["refresh_token"]=> string(32) "6437242c178efec9e36e1d74db2586e9"
    ["access_token"]=> string(32) "31d8412c11bcef9a973529029262b14f"
```

```
    ["username"]=> string(9) "jcleblanc"
}
```

It is simply an access token with another expiration time, refresh token string, and access token to allow us to make further protected-resource requests.

 A well-built application will require the end user to accept the application permissions only once. The access token can then be stored (securely, please!) for later use when the user logs in or uses the application again. Basically, as soon as you know who the end user is and can verify that you have an existing access token for her, you shouldn't need to involve her again.

Implementation Example: Facebook

Now that we understand how the OAuth 2 process works, let's take a look at a practical example of the specification: the Facebook OAuth 2 implementation. In this example, we'll step through the process again to capture an access token, use that access token to capture protected user resources, and refresh the access token if its lifespan is specified.

This process contains several steps, including:

1. Constructing our common variables and functions to use in the process.
2. Making a request to have the user authorize the application.
3. Exchanging the user authorization grant for an access token.
4. Making requests for protected user data using the access token.

These steps will give us a good overall view of how OAuth 2 functions.

Creating your application

Before we explore integrations of OAuth 2 using the Facebook platform and leveraging its Graph API, we need to start by creating a new application on Facebook to obtain the OAuth 2 keys we need to actually implement the example.

First, we'll go to the Facebook developer page to create our new application. In your browser, navigate to *http://www.facebook.com/developers/*. At the top of that page, you'll see a button to allow you to set up a new application, as shown in Figure 9-14. Click that button to begin. This should be in the same section that lists the applications that you have already created with Facebook (if any).

Figure 9-14. Facebook's Set Up New App button

Enter in the application name and any other essential information to begin creating the application. Once you've completed the initial step, you should see a full application page asking for further details and information about your application. Fill in all information that is pertinent to and required for the application.

Once you've done that, we need to get our OAuth 2 keys that will allow us to begin the actual development of our application. On the side of the application window, you should see a section labeled Web Site. Click on this label to display the OAuth 2 keys, as shown in Figure 9-15.

Figure 9-15. Facebook application OAuth 2 credentials

You will be given the application ID and secret, and asked for an application URL and domain. Fill out this information, ensuring that the domain and site URL match the location where the application will reside.

Once you've done this and saved the changes, copy the application ID and secret. This brings us to our next step—starting the implementation.

Let's begin by exploring a simple OAuth 2 integration to capture a user's friends from the Facebook Graph API.

Implementing OAuth 2 using PHP

 The full code for this sample is available at *https://github.com/jcleblanc/ programming-social-applications/tree/master/chapter_9/oauth2-php -facebook*.

The first integration example that we will look at is PHP. As we go through the example, I'll lay out the content of each file that we are working with to explain how the integration will capture our current user's friends.

The first file we need to look at is the one containing the common variables and functions that we will be using at each stage of this process.

Common variables and functions. We start by implementing the common variables and functions that we will be using throughout the program. We'll call this file *common.php*:

```php
<?php
$key = 'b719d03bfca6cd9a91aa41995a080f8e';
$secret = 'fce944cdab7de45ef03a2dee37733ee8';

$callback_url = "http://www.mysite.com/oauth2-php-facebook/complete.php";
$authorization_endpoint = "https://graph.facebook.com/oauth/authorize";
$access_token_endpoint = "https://graph.facebook.com/oauth/access_token";

/****************************************************************************
 * Function: Run CURL
 * Description: Executes a CURL request
 * Parameters: url (string) - URL to make request to
 *             method (string) - HTTP transfer method
 *             headers - HTTP transfer headers
 *             postvals - post values
 ****************************************************************************/
function run_curl($url, $method = 'GET', $postvals = null){
  $ch = curl_init($url);

  //GET request: send headers and return data transfer
  if ($method == 'GET'){
    $options = array(
      CURLOPT_URL => $url,
      CURLOPT_RETURNTRANSFER => 1
    );
    curl_setopt_array($ch, $options);
  //POST / PUT request: send post object and return data transfer
  } else {
    $options = array(
      CURLOPT_URL => $url,
      CURLOPT_POST => 1,
      CURLOPT_POSTFIELDS => $postvals,
      CURLOPT_RETURNTRANSFER => 1
    );
    curl_setopt_array($ch, $options);
  }

  $response = curl_exec($ch);
  curl_close($ch);

  return $response;
}
?>
```

Then we define the keys needed for the application, which were provided when we created the application.

The next block contains the URLs that we will use during the token exchange process. These are:

The callback URL
Where the user will be forwarded after he authorizes the application to access his personal information.

The authorization endpoint
The URL where the user will be forwarded on the Facebook site in order to authorize the application.

The access token endpoint
On the callback page, this is the endpoint that will be called to exchange the authorization code for an access token.

Last, we have a cURL function that will allow us to make GET, POST, and PUT requests to the authorization endpoints as needed.

Making the authorization request. Now that we have our common variables and functions file in place, we can begin the OAuth 2 process to get an access token for the user. As we begin this process, we first need to forward the user to the Facebook authorization endpoint so that he can accept the application permissions to access his protected account information. In this example, the file is saved as *index.php*:

```php
<?php
require_once "common.php";

//construct Facebook auth URI
$auth_url = $authorization_endpoint
        . "?redirect_uri=" . $callback_url
        . "&client_id=" . $key
        . "&scope=email,publish_stream,manage_pages,friends_about_me";

//forward user to Facebook auth page
header("Location: $auth_url");
?>
```

We include our *common.php* file for our standard variables and functions, and then construct the authorization URL and query parameters that we will need to forward the user to for him to authorize the application. The authorization URL is constructed of:

- The authorization endpoint.
- The redirect URL—the location to forward the user to once he has accepted the application permissions.
- The client ID—the key that was provided for the application when it was created.

- Scopes—an optional string of additional data that you would like to be able to access from a user, such as his email address, his news feed, or data about his friends. We will explore the extent of the information that we can obtain using scopes in the section "Implementation Example: Requesting More User Information in the Facebook OAuth Process" on page 372, later in this chapter.

Once the endpoint and query parameters are concatenated, we forward the user to that location so he can authorize our application. He will be presented with an accept screen telling him what the application will have access to.

Once the user clicks the Allow button, he will be redirected to the callback URL that we specified when forwarding the user to this authorization page.

If the user does not accept our application permissions, then the provider should forward him back to the application page designated when the application was created.

Obtaining the access token. Now that the user has authorized the application to access his protected information, we can take the verification code that was sent as a query string parameter to the callback page and exchange that for an access token. The callback file, for the purpose of this example, is stored as *complete.php*:

```php
<?php
require_once "common.php";

//capture code from auth
$code = $_GET["code"];

//build access token request URI
$token_url = $access_token_endpoint . "?client_id=$key&"
        . "redirect_uri=" . urlencode($callback_url) . "&"
        . "client_secret=$secret&"
        . "code=$code";

//get access token & expiration - parse individual params
$token_obj = explode('&', run_curl($token_url, 'GET'));
$token = explode('=', $token_obj[0]);
$token = $token[1];
```

After we insert our *common.php* file, we capture the verification code parameter that was sent to this callback file as a query string parameter. This code represents the user's authorization and is what we'll use to obtain an access token.

We then construct the URI that will contain the data to be sent along with the request to fetch the access token via the query string. This object will include several parameters, including:

- The verification code parameter that we obtained from the query string when the user was forwarded from the permissions screen.
- The redirect URI, which is a direct copy of the callback URL used to get us to this callback file.
- The client secret provided when we first created our application.

We now need to make a request to get the access token and parse the parameters returned. We make a cURL GET request to the URI we just built and then split the return value of that request on the ampersands (&). We now have an array of variables containing several parameters from the original string, which looked something like the following, including the access token and expires parameters:

```
access_token=120037154734088|2.XPJGiXHQdcOxarTZWnjxlg__.3600.1297213200-796545577|
    -qlKX1pcIPb9YQT9x2KnaimKq-Y&expires=6543
```

Our access token string will be available in the first array location, so we split the key and value based on the equals sign (=). We then obtain the access token value from that final split.

We now have our access token we'll use to make data requests on a user's behalf, accessing his protected data on the platform.

Making signed requests. With our access token in hand, now it's time to make some of those protected data requests that we have been talking about. To accomplish this, we use the access token that we have already obtained and make cURL requests to defined Facebook URI endpoints. For this example, we will make a request to capture the friends of the currently logged-in user:

```
//construct URI to fetch friend information for current user
$friends_uri = "https://graph.facebook.com/me/friends?access_token=" . $token;

//fetch friends of current user and decode
$friends = json_decode(run_curl($friends_uri, 'GET'));

//print friends
echo "<h1>CURRENT USER FRIENDS</h1>";
var_dump($friends)
?>
```

The first thing that we need to do is to construct the URI to the friends endpoint of the Facebook graph API, attaching the access token to the end as a parameter.

Next, we will issue the cURL request to the Facebook endpoint to get the required data. We issue a HTTP GET cURL request and then store the JSON-decoded return string into a new variable.

We now have the object containing all of the current user's friends. We simply display an appropriate header and dump out the friend object that was returned back to us. In a real implementation, the information acquired from the friend graph can be used to obtain and display profiles for the user's friends, thereby increasing the social element of the containing site or service.

In this implementation, the $friends variable should contain the response friend objects for the current user, which will look something like the following:

```
object(stdClass)#1 (1) {
  ["data"]=>
    array(160) {
```

```
[0]=>
   object(stdClass)#2 (2) {
      ["name"]=> string(13) "Eric Miraglia"
      ["id"]=>string(6) "212467"
   }
[1]=>
   object(stdClass)#3 (2) {
      ["name"]=> string(11) "Paul Tarjan"
      ["id"]=> string(6) "218471"
   }
[2]=>
   object(stdClass)#100 (2) {
      ["name"]=> string(13) "Erik Eldridge"
      ["id"]=> string(9) "668324387"
   }
      .
      .
      .
[159]=>
   object(stdClass)#161 (2) {
      ["name"]=> string(10) "Yvan Aubut"
      ["id"]=> string(15) "100002041133104"
   }
  }
}
```

You can mimic this process for any of the URIs that Facebook defines in its developer documentation for accessing a user's protected information.

Implementing OAuth 2 using Python

 The full code for this sample is available at *https://github.com/jcleblanc/ programming-social-applications/tree/master/chapter_9/oauth2-python -facebook*.

Now that we have covered a PHP example, let's look at the same type of OAuth 2 implementation in Python to show how easy it is to build out this process across different languages and development environments.

Let's dive right into the code to uncover the Python process for accessing an end user's protected resources on Facebook. I'll take our implementation script and break it down into logical pieces, describing the steps that we will take from beginning to end.

The App Engine configuration file. Before we jump into the code, let's look at the configuration file that we are using for Google App Engine:

```
application: oauth2-facebook
version: 1
runtime: python
api_version: 1
```

```
handlers:
- url: /.*
  script: index.py
```

Since we have only one file that handles the complete OAuth 2 flow, *index.py*, all our requests to the application will leverage that single file.

When running the application example, we deploy this script to the App Engine *project.appspot.com* location. We'll use this to register a callback URL with Facebook when we create the application to get our key and secret for the OAuth process.

Now let's jump into the *index.py* file.

Modules, common variables, and paths. The first section of our example code contains our `import` statements, common variables, and the Facebook and OAuth endpoints that we will use during the individual steps of the program flow:

```
import cgi
import urllib
import json

#client OAuth keys
key = 'e141c565a48ea5502714df288'
secret = '3df893c8c9c953a374fcb8'

#Facebook URIs and application callbacks
callback_url = "http://oauth2-facebook.appspot.com/index.py"
authorization_endpoint = "https://graph.facebook.com/oauth/authorize"
access_token_endpoint = "https://graph.facebook.com/oauth/access_token"
```

Our `import` statements provide us with a number of functions we'll use throughout the program flow:

cgi

The Common Gateway Interface (`cgi`) module provides a number of utilities for CGI scripts. For our sample code's requirements, we are using the `cgi` module to be able to parse the query string. This will help us determine what stage of the OAuth process we're currently in.

urllib

This module allows us to perform GET and POST requests to the Facebook APIs in order to obtain an access token and send a request to the provider for protected user resources.

json

The JSON module allows us to parse the JSON string that is sent back by Facebook from our access token request.

We then store our common variables—the key and secret that were provided when we created our application. These will allow the provider to identify our application.

Last, we define the callback URI to which we'll return the end user once he accepts the application permissions, as well as the authorization and access token endpoints that will allow us to make requests against the provider for the token exchange process.

Obtaining authorization, acquiring the access token, and making requests. Now that we have the common variables and endpoints set up, we can begin looking into the actual program flow. This flow comprises the initial forwarding of the end user to the Facebook authorization endpoint, capturing the access token once he has accepted the application permissions, and making OAuth signed requests to Facebook to capture his friends:

```
#get query string parameters
params = cgi.FieldStorage()

"""
" If a code parameter is available in the query string then the user
" has given the client permission to access their protected data.
" If not, the script should forward the user to log in and accept
" the application permissions.
"""
if params.has_key('code'):
    code = params['code'].value

    #build access token request URI
    token_url = "%s?client_id=%s&redirect_uri=%s&client_secret=%s&code=%s" %
        (access_token_endpoint, key, urllib.quote_plus(callback_url),
        secret, code)

    #make request to capture access token
    f = urllib.urlopen(token_url)
    token_string = f.read()

    #split token string to obtain the access token object
    token_obj = token_string.split('&')
    access_token_obj = token_obj[0].split('=')
    access_token = access_token_obj[1]

    #construct URI to fetch friend information for current user
    friends_uri = "https://graph.facebook.com/me/friends?access_token=%s" %
        (access_token)

    #fetch friends of current user and decode
    request = urllib.urlopen(friends_uri)
    friends = json.read(request.read())

    #display access token and friends
    print 'Content-Type: text/plain'
    print ''
    print "<h1>Access Token String</h1>"
    print token_string
    print "<h1>Friends</h1>"
    print friends
else:
    #construct Facebook authorization URI
    auth_url = "%s?redirect_uri=%s&client_id=%s&scope=email,publish_stream,
```

```
        manage_pages,friends_about_me,friends_status,friends_website,
        friends_likes" % (authorization_endpoint, callback_url, key)

    #redirect the user to the Facebook authorization URI
    print "Location: " + auth_url
```

The first thing we're doing in the preceding script is capturing the query parameters, if any, from the address bar. We do this because, as we've discussed, when the user is forwarded to the callback URI (this same file) once he has accepted the application permissions, the query string returned will include a verification code parameter that we'll need to acquire an access token.

We then have the if/else statement to handle the two states of the program:

- The initial forwarding of the user to the permissions endpoint.
- The callback URI after the user has accepted the application permissions.

Let's begin with the else part of the statement, as that will handle the first state that we are looking for. We start out by constructing the URI endpoint to the Facebook permissions page to allow the user to grant the application permission to access his protected information. Besides the base URI, there are a few parameters that we pass along:

redirect_uri

>   The URI to which the end user is forwarded once he has accepted the permissions of the application. This URI must match the URI that you designated as the redirect URI when you created the application.

client_id

>   The key that was provided when you first created the application. This will identify your application in the request.

scope

>   Besides the basic information, these scopes will enable your application to pull and set additional information on the user's behalf. We will explore Facebook scopes in more detail later in this chapter, in the section "Implementation Example: Requesting More User Information in the Facebook OAuth Process" on page 372.

Once the URI is constructed, we forward the user to the permissions page.

Now let's focus on the initial part of the if statement. Once the user is forwarded back to the script from the permissions page, the code parameter will be in the query string. This moves the script into the if statement. We start the if statement by capturing our code parameter. We then need to construct the request to capture the access token. This request will need to be made via HTTP GET, so we build our GET string with the fields required for capturing the access token:

`client_id`

> The key that was provided to you when you first created the application. This will identify your application in the request.

`client_secret`

> The secret that was provided to you when you first created the application.

`code`

> The verification parameter that was attached to the query string. It signifies that the user has accepted the application permissions.

`redirect_uri`

> The URI to which the end user is forwarded once he has accepted the application permissions. This URI must match the URI that you designated as the redirect URI when you created the application.

We then initiate our GET request to the access token fetch URI. The results from the request will include a string containing the access token and an expiration parameter, listed in key/value pairs separated by ampersands, so we simply need to parse that string.

We separate the string first by the ampersands, giving us the key/value pairs for the access token and expiration parameters. We then split the first key/value pair, the access token, by the equals sign.

The value of the access token is now available to us. It will allow us to make requests for the user's protected data. If you print out the access token object, it should look something like the following:

```
access_token=199195400097233|2.403o8hqlgtJirbF4NpllbQ__.3600.1297281600-796545577|
    XXPD1WUDwiy1wm2N8S5DAHRlFdY&expires=3962
```

Note that the access token format returned from the provider may differ from service to service. For instance, when we go through the OAuth 2 process to connect to Gowalla servers, Gowalla responds back with a JSON object similar to the following:

```
{
  'username': 'jcleblanc',
  'access_token': '79b256c764618d1b8260a10c0',
  'expires_in': 1209580,
  'expires_at': 'Fri, 31 Dec 2010 19:19:57 -0000',
  'scope': 'read',
  'refresh_token': 'b259f5d4fa280a9687b18dfa57b2'
}
```

Nevertheless, with the access token that we now have available, we can begin constructing requests to the Facebook Graph API for the user's social information.

We construct the URI to capture the current user's friends, attaching the access token to the end of the URI as a query string parameter. We then make an HTTP GET request to that URI and capture the JSON return value containing the friends.

The last part of the script simply dumps our access token object and the friend object returned to us.

You can mimic this request for the current user's friends to instead capture the user's profile, update his stream, modify his pages, or any number of other data sources that Facebook defines in its Graph API. You can find more information on the Facebook Graph API (and the data that may be obtained) at *http://developers.facebook.com/docs/reference/api.*

> This full example is available via Github at *https://github.com/jcleblanc/oauth/tree/master/oauth2-python-facebook.*

Implementation Example: Requesting More User Information in the Facebook OAuth Process

I mentioned at a few points throughout the OAuth 2 Facebook examples that we would dive deeper into the topic of scopes. You might remember that we used the `scope` parameter in the URI where the user was forwarded to go through the authorization flow:

```
//construct Facebook auth URI
$auth_url = $authorization_endpoint
          . "?redirect_uri=" . $callback_url
          . "&client_id=" . $key
          . "&scope=email,publish_stream,manage_pages,friends_about_me";
```

The purpose of the `scope` parameter is to allow an application to request certain social information from a user.

> Some providers bind these scopes directly to the application ID or key issued when you first create your application instead of dynamically in the initial OAuth request token request. This means that they do not require a `scope` parameter in that initial request. Providing the `scope` parameter, such as in this Facebook implementation, allows you to define scopes in a very dynamic manner.

Facebook includes an extensive number of scopes that we can include as a comma-separated list in the authorization request.

Data permissions

Data permissions will allow your application to access information about a user, or a user's friends (in the form of a friend request), as shown in Table 9-10.

Table 9-10. Data permissions

User permission	Friend permission	Description
ads_management	Not available	Enables your application to manage ads and call the Facebook Ads API on the user's behalf.
email	Not available	The user's primary email address.
read_friendlists	manage_friendlists	Gives your application read access to the user-created friend lists.
read_insights	Not available	Gives your application read access to the data insights for user-owned pages, applications, and domains.
read_mailbox	Not available	Gives your application read access to the user's mailbox.
read_requests	Not available	Gives your application read access to the user's friend requests.
read_stream	Not available	Gives your application read and search access to all posts in the user's news feed.
user_about_me	friends_about_me	The About Me section of the user's profile.
user_activities	friends_activities	Recent user news feed activities.
user_address	Not available	The address listed in the user's profile.
user_birthday	friends_birthday	The birthday listed in the user's profile.
user_checkins	friends_checkins	The user's checkins.
user_education_history	friends_education_history	Education information listed in the user's profile.
user_events	friends_events	List of events the user is attending.
user_groups	friends_groups	List of groups the user is involved in.
user_hometown	friends_hometown	The hometown listed in the user's profile.
user_interests	friends_interests	Interests listed in the user profile.
user_likes	friends_likes	Pages that the user has liked.
user_location	friends_location	The user's last known location.
user_mobile_phone	Not available	The user's mobile phone number.
user_notes	friends_notes	Any notes the user has added to her profile.
user_online_presence	friends_online_presence	The user's online/offline status.
user_photo_video_tags	friends_photo_video_tags	Photos/videos the user has been tagged in.
user_photos	friends_photos	The photos that the user has uploaded.
user_relation ship_details	friends_relation ship_details	The user's relationship preferences.

User permission	Friend permission	Description
user_relationships	friends_relationships	The user's family and personal relationships.
user_religion_politics	friends_religion_politics	The user's religious and political affiliations.
user_status	friends_status	The most recent user status message.
user_videos	friends_videos	Videos that the user has uploaded.
user_website	friends_website	The URLs listed in the user's profile.
user_work_history	friends_work_history	The work history listed in the user's profile.
xmpp_login	Not available	Enables applications that integrate Facebook chat to log in users.

Publishing permissions

Publishing permissions (Table 9-11) enable the application to push or modify content on the user's behalf. These permissions are important when you're attempting to use viral channels to promote your application to new users or to keep current users engaged.

Table 9-11. Publishing permissions

Permission	Description
create_event	Allows your application to create and modify events on the user's behalf.
offline_access	Allows your application to make requests for privileged user information at any time. This permission makes any access tokens long-lived, as opposed to the standard short-lived access token that is provided through OAuth.
publish_checkins	Enables your application to perform checkins on the user's behalf.
publish_stream	Enables your application to publish content, comments, and likes to the user's news feed at any time.
rsvp_event	Allows your application to RSVP to events on the user's behalf.
sms	Enables your application to send text messages to the user and allows it to respond to messages from the user via text messaging.

Page permissions

Page permissions (Table 9-12) have a simple task: to provide access tokens for pages. This will allow the application to capture and set data in that context.

Table 9-12. Page permissions

Permission	Description
manage_pages	Allows the application to obtain access tokens for pages that the user is the administrator of.

Implementation Example: End-User Experience

No matter which development implementation example you chose—PHP or Python—the experience for the end user is the same.

During the first phase of the OAuth 2 process, the end user is forwarded to the provider site, where she can log in (unless she is already signed in) and accept the application permissions, much like what we've seen in our Facebook examples and what is shown in Figure 9-16.

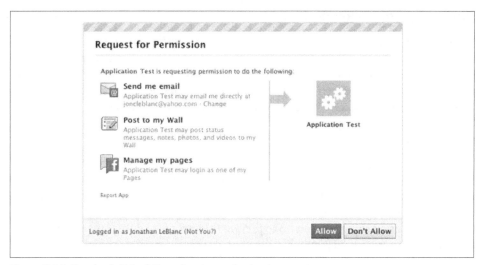

Figure 9-16. Facebook OAuth 2 application authorization screen

Generally, a provider will display any number of the following pieces of information on the permissions page:

- The application title, defined by the application creator.
- A description of what the application will do, defined by the application creator.
- A chosen thumbnail (usually, a company or product logo), defined by the application creator.
- Details on the type of protected information the application is requesting access to. The application creator generally selects the permissions, but the provider defines the specific text that is displayed to the end user.
- Links to a privacy policy or methods for revoking access for the application, defined by the provider.

On this permissions screen, the end user will generally have two options:

- She can allow the application to access her protected information and perform actions on her behalf. When she accepts these permissions, she will be forwarded to the `redirect_uri` defined by the application creator when he created the application.

- She can deny the application access to her protected information. This will immediately cease the OAuth process, and the user will typically be forwarded back to the main application or information site denoted by the application creator.

If the user accepts the permissions, she will then be presented with the application that she has just granted access.

Tips for Debugging Request Issues

While OAuth 2 provides a much simpler approach to authorization than its predecessor, OAuth 1.0a, you still might encounter signature issues and provider errors when going through the workflow to generate or work with an access token. Fortunately, there are some processes, tricks, and tips to help us develop scalable authorization flows that can appropriately handle most of the errors or use cases that come up.

Checking your request data

As with the OAuth 1.0a token exchange process, one of the best debugging methods that you can implement is simply to compare the data that you are sending via GET, POST, or the HTTP request header to the service provider. The solution to a signature mismatch issue can be as easy as dumping the payload that you are sending along, but the most important thing you can do to *prevent* this error is to ensure that the data that you are sending at each step matches the content that the provider requires.

There are several common payload issues to watch out for, including:

- Misspelling one or more of the required keys. This is a simple issue to resolve but comes up quite often.
- Implementers of the OAuth 2 specification may veer away from the specification requirements (and what is listed in this overview) by implementing a slightly different required key set or key naming convention, or even an older version of the draft specification. This can create situations where you send along the keys required for a particular step in the process, only to have the provider require different or additional information. Be aware of the requirements of the provider that you are working with before beginning integration.
- Inputting bad values for keys. Numerous keys in the payloads being sent to the provider require specific values to be set, such as the `grant_type` or `response_type` parameters that are required at different steps of the process. Ensure that the values that you are setting for your keys meet the specifications set forth by the provider.

The easiest way to protect yourself against such issues is to simply understand what's required by the provider you are working with. In the early stages of a specification, some implementers tend to pick and choose the features they want to integrate into their version of the core implementation. This doesn't mean that those features are incorrect, it simply means that they are nonstandard and will require some additional effort to implement.

Tracking access token expiration

The process through which we can refresh our access tokens has been mentioned a few times already in the OAuth 2 section. When working with a provider that imposes a lifespan on its access tokens, you must keep track of your access tokens' status in your client implementation.

There are a few things we need to check when determining whether to attempt to refresh the access token. First, when we exchange our `code` parameter for an access token, we are provided with an `expires_in` parameter that specifies the time until our token expires. If you're storing the access token for a user for later use (and you should be, to make the application easier to work with for repeat users), then you can use this parameter to extrapolate when the token will expire and store this value as well. When we next use the access token, we can check the expiration to see if it is time to refresh the token for the user.

The other aspects to watch for are the errors that are returned from the provider. If we check the expiration when we first use the access token, we can find out when it expires, but what if we've validated an access token and it expires *while* we are making requests to the provider for protected resources? That's where checking the errors produced by the provider comes into play. If you watch for an error stating that the access token is invalid, that's your cue to try to refresh it. This way, instead of sending back an error to the user saying that the request could not be processed, you can try to acquire a new token and make the request again. Since you do this without user interaction, she will never know that there was a problem.

Responding to error codes

 I cannot stress enough that you have to be precise when filling out your client details for a new OAuth application on a provider site, especially when registering a redirect URI. Some providers perform an exact match comparison between the details you've entered and what is being used in the program flow, so any discrepancy may generate client errors. For instance, exact URI checks for the redirect URI may produce an error if you've registered your redirect as *server.example.com* but you're forwarding the user to *http://server.example.com*. Be precise—it can save you a lot of headaches.

Generally, most providers will support a number of potential errors when you're making requests to the authorization server. Accounting for these errors and acting upon them with appropriate output or follow-up steps is key to building a well-rounded product:

```
HTTP/1.1 401 Unauthorized
Content-Type: application/json
Cache-Control: no-store
{
  "error":"invalid_grant",
  "error_description":"The access grant has expired"
}
```

There are a few defined fields for generating error messages, listed in Table 9-13.

Table 9-13. Error message parameters

Parameter	Description
error (required)	The error that was triggered. This parameter can contain only one error. Possible errors are available in Table 9-14.
error_description (optional)	Additional information about the error that was produced. The description should provide human-readable information on the cause and potential resolution of the error.
error_uri (optional)	Expanding on error_description, error_uri provides a URL to a site with additional human-readable information about the error that was produced.

There are a number of error parameters that may be generated by the provider. These are listed in Table 9-14.

Table 9-14. Provider error messages

Error	Description
access_denied	When the end user is forwarded to the resource owner (provider) site to authorize the client application, she has a choice of accepting or denying that request. In addition, users may revoke permission for your application to access their personal information at any time. These two events can be a root cause of an access_denied error.
	This error message can also be generated if the authorization server has denied the request. Although access_denied may be used as a generic server message for a multitude of errors, some providers may offer additional details on the error's nature. One common reason for the server denying a request involves *rate limiting*. Providers may limit the number of server requests that you can make to them within a certain span of time. A rate limiting error will usually have additional details to let you know that this is the problem.
invalid_client	This error is normally produced when the client that you are claiming to be does not exist from the provider's standpoint. One of the chief causes of this error is that the client_id parameter that was attached with the requests is not a valid ID with the provider (e.g., perhaps due to a copy/paste error). Check to ensure that the client_id parameter you're using matches the key you were issued when you set up your application on the provider site.
invalid_request	The invalid_request message is produced due to a malformed request from the client. There are a few reasons why a request may be deemed malformed:
	• The request is missing a required parameter. Check that you've included all of the parameters that the provider requires in your request.

Error	Description
	• The request contains an unsupported parameter or parameter value. If you are using a parameter (or a parameter value) that is not supported by the provider, the provider will produce this error response. Ensure that the parameters and values you've used are acceptable to the provider.
	• The request is somehow otherwise malformed. There may be issues with the request being double-encoded, having additional characters, or including some other element that it should not. Dump your request string and visually inspect it for such malformations.
	In short, this error means something is wrong with the parameters, values, or the request object that you have used. Check your provider's requirements and input *only* those parameters and parameter values that the provider deems acceptable.
invalid_scope	Many providers will allow you to pick from a number of scopes when you create your application (unless they just use a blanket scope for every implementation). These scopes relate to blocks of protected information that your client application may wish to access, such as profile details and friends.
	If the provider requires the scopes parameter when you're forwarding the user to its authorization site and this error is produced, one of the following is usually the culprit:
	• You chose the wrong scopes when setting up the client application (e.g., you chose the profile scope, but your client is trying to access user friends). This case sometimes comes up when scopes are preregistered with the provider rather than defined manually by the client. Ensure that the scopes you chose are adequate for the data that you're trying to access.
	• The scopes parameter is missing. Since the scopes parameter is optional according to the OAuth 2 specification, check the provider documentation to see if the provider requires it.
	• The scopes provided in the scopes parameter are incorrect or malformed; check to ensure that any scope entered is exactly what is required by the provider.
redirect_uri_mis match	This error is generated when the redirect_uri parameter that you specify in your requests does not match the redirect URI that you preregistered with the provider when creating your application. These two must match exactly, or you will see this type of error.
unauthorized_cli ent	This error is produced when the client does not have significant privileges to use the response_type that is being requested when the user is forwarded to the resource owner for an access grant.
	In many instances, this error will be produced if your client cannot access the token from the request (through either the token or code_and_token values for the response_type parameter).
	A client needs only the response_type of code to complete the flow and be granted an access token, so restrict what you are requesting in the response_type to only what you need.
unsuppor ted_response_type	When you're forwarding the end user to the resource owner for an access grant, one of the required parameters in your request is response_type, which may be code, token, or code_and_token. This error means that the provider does not support the response type that you used. Check to ensure that the response type you've used is correct and is supported by the provider.

Many providers also implement a number of error responses beyond those defined by the OAuth 2 specification. Understanding what these error responses mean and reacting to them appropriately can help you reduce the amount of debugging required when issues arise.

Conclusion

In this chapter, we have explored the simple process through which many providers traditionally allowed an application to access their services—the username and password login architecture of basic authentication. Although basic auth provided application developers with an incredibly easy, fast, and high-performance implementation backbone, it asked users to expose their personal login information through a username and password. When this type of architecture is mixed with external developers, there are bound to be security ramifications to exposing that data.

We then explored the two current OAuth implementations being used today, OAuth 1.0a and the emerging OAuth 2 standard. By examining workflow diagrams and sample implementations, we have seen firsthand the vast improvement these specifications represent over the basic authentication model. Working with tokens instead of user credentials puts control into the hands of the user—who can thus see who has access to their private data—and the provider that issued the tokens. Having this control means that if something malicious or unwanted happens in a client application, the user or provider can simply revoke the access token linking the user to the application.

The evolution of the OAuth standard demonstrates how open source authorization models are working to increase implementation and ease of use, encouraging adoption of the specification by reducing the complexity and effort required to implement it.

The Future of Social: Defining Social Entities Through Distributed Web Frameworks

Expanding upon our exploration of online social graphs, in this chapter we will look at several protocols that are trying to change the face of social media and sharing. With a constantly expanding user graph, sites employing these protocols are now using comment sharing, pulling social references from URLs or email addresses, and trying to standardize actions users perform on a site to derive rich reference data. In this chapter, you'll find out how.

What You'll Learn

This chapter will explore several specifications and protocols that are attempting to take what we currently know about user social graphs and expand it far beyond the bounds of any single site or container. These *distributed web frameworks* show us how leveraging user interactions with any content on the Web can help us build a rich network of customizations for a person. They allow for a much wider range of social graph development than is possible with traditional social networking containers such as Facebook, YAP, Orkut, and LinkedIn.

These are the topics that we will cover in our exploration:

- How to use the Open Graph protocol to turn any traditional website into a rich source of entity information.
- How the Activity Streams specification allows developers to create a unified format for broadcasting user activities to the rest of the Web, and how to determine what information should be displayed in these streams.
- WebFinger, which lets us use a simple email address to build out an extensive network of entity objects in a social graph.

- How OExchange defines methodologies that enable us to share any URL with any other service on the Web.
- PubSubHubbub, which leverages commenting and user feedback on a website and shows us how to build out a network of interconnected syndication sites for that feedback, pushing information from a parent source to a series of child listener sites.
- How the Salmon protocol expands upon the concepts of PubSubHubbub by enabling us not only to publish user comments and feedback downstream to a series of child listeners, but also to publish the content back upstream to the parent source.

Once we explore these social enhancement specifications, we will dive into some advanced social graphing examples and learn how to implement these technologies to extend a user's social graph beyond any single site or container.

The Open Graph Protocol: Defining Web Pages As Social Entities

In many of the previous chapters, we have discussed the fact that social graphs comprise two elements: relationships to people (your human social graph) and relationships to things (your entity social graph). The Open Graph protocol focuses on the latter, building web pages to become rich information entities in our social graph.

Entity relationships are vitally important in defining who a user is and what her interests are and help us determine, for example, products that she may be more inclined to purchase or other things she may be interested in. Entity relationships can help us target everything from applications to ads directly to the user's social profile—that is, to who she is on the Web. The more information that is available in a user graph, the more relevant our targeting can be for that user.

Let's explore how the Open Graph protocol works to define user entities, learn how to implement the metadata behind the protocol, and view some practical examples of the protocol being used in the wild.

The Rise and Fall of Metadata

When metadata programming was in its infancy over a decade ago, it had a noble goal—to bring cohesion to the Web so that someone could extract rich information about a website easily and in a standardized way. This lofty goal never really made it to fruition, due in large part to inadequate adoption of its practices and the lack of fully standardized implementations. Simply put, sites implementing rich data tags did so for their own goals, not to enrich the Web as a whole.

Since the Open Graph protocol has come on the scene, there's been a resurgence in the usefulness of site metatagging, chiefly due to the Facebook Like button.

 The Facebook Like button is a means by which third-party sites allow a user to "like" their page, which sends a message back through to the user's Facebook activity stream. The Open Graph protocol is the backbone of this technology in that it allows Facebook to extract title, description, media data, and more from the third-party site.

When a third-party site integrates the Facebook Like button, it needs to also integrate OpenLike protocol metatagging for Facebook to extract the most information about its page. Because application developers want to tap into Facebook's increasingly large audience, adoption rates of these metaprogramming standards have increased. The two elements metaprogramming lacked in its unsuccessful infancy were purpose and consistency, both of which are delivered by the Facebook Like button.

Even though the largest adoption of these standards comes through the Facebook implementation, the metadata derived from a page integrating the Open Graph protocol is open to anyone. There is no reason why you should not take advantage of the collateral benefits of the Facebook success story.

How the Open Graph Protocol Works

The Open Graph protocol uses `<meta>` tag markup to deliver a comprehensive view of a web entity within a user's social graph. These `<meta>` tags provide data about what is being described on a page or web source, such as a business, movie, actor, or sports team.

Besides the type of information that describes what is being displayed on the page, you can also include geographic information and contact details.

The Open Graph ecosystem comprises two main elements:

An Open Graph producer
This is the site that includes `<meta>` tag information about the entities being described.

An Open Graph consumer
This is a developer or site that consumes that `<meta>` tag information placed on a site—for example, the Facebook Like button integration.

These are the basics of the Open Graph protocol. The web application, or consumer, makes a request to the website for information about the site. The site, or producer, will respond with the metadata about itself. This process is depicted in Figure 10-1.

Next, we'll explore how to work with and implement the Open Graph protocol.

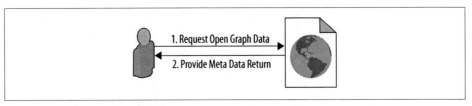

Figure 10-1. Open Graph protocol request/response workflow

Implementing the Open Graph Protocol

Since the Open Graph protocol uses a simple implementation based on metadata, incorporating it into your site is fairly straightforward and requires only some `<meta>` tags—the exact number depending on how much data you are looking to expose—in the `<head>` of your web pages.

Since this is a simple format, the main things we'll explore in this technology have to do with what information you can expose and how to expose it. The potential data you can expose can be broken up into page metadata, geographic information, contact information, and object types. Let's explore what these tags look like.

Defining page metadata

Page metadata is the foundation for transforming a web page into a rich data object in a user's social graph. The Open Graph protocol defines a number of metadata properties that are required for implementation. These are listed in Table 10-1.

Table 10-1. Required page metadata properties

Property	Description
og:image	An image to be associated with the object, such as a thumbnail or screenshot.
og:title	A title describing the site object, much like using the standard HTML `<title>` tag.
og:type	The type of object being represented on the page, such as a sports team or business.
og:url	The URL to the information page for the object.

Let's look at a practical example of how metadata is represented on a Yelp product review page for the Restaurant at Wente Vineyards in Livermore, CA:

```
<html xmlns:og="http://ogp.me/ns#">
<head>
<title>The Restaurant at Wente Vineyards - Livermore, CA</title>
<meta property="og:url" content="http://www.yelp.com/biz/gATFcGOL-qOtqm9HTaXJpg">
<meta property="og:type" content="restaurant">
<meta property="og:title" content="The Restaurant at Wente Vineyards">
<meta property="og:image"
        content="http://media2.px.yelpcdn.com/bphoto/iVSnIDCj-fWiPffHHkUVsQ/m">
...
</head>
```

```
...
</html>
```

In addition to the required tags, there are several tags whose implementation is optional but recommended for any site. These are listed in Table 10-2.

Table 10-2. Optional page metadata properties

Property	Description
og:description	An arbitrary description (which could be several sentences long) of the object being represented on the site.
og:site_name	The root site that the page is associated with. For instance, a single movie page on IMDb.com would set the content of the og:site_name <meta> tag to IMDb.

Let's go back to our previous Yelp example. Should Yelp wish to extend that review with the additional metadata properties from Table 10-2, it might look like this:

```
<meta property="og:site_name" content="Yelp">
<meta property="og:description" content="The award winning Restaurant at Wente
    Vineyards is truly a feast for the senses! The open architecture is inviting
    and the air alive with rich, savory aromas.">
```

Specifying Yelp as our site name indicates that this page is a small piece of the overall entity graph that is Yelp.com (*http://yelp.com*), comprising many reviews. The site_name offers a link to the richer social graph, and the description provides more detail about a page.

Specifying geolocation data

The Open Graph protocol supports the ability to define geographical information within the metadata tags. This is a valuable option for any site that is representing something with a real-world location, such as the restaurant we just looked at in the Yelp example.

There are a number of properties available for defining geographical information, from address information to latitude and longitude. These are specified in Table 10-3.

Table 10-3. Geolocation properties

Property	Description
og:country-name	The country name associated with the real-world object.
og:latitude	The geographical latitude of the real-world location represented on the page.
og:locality	The city/town/village associated with the real-world object.
og:longitude	The geographical longitude of the real-world location represented on the page.
og:postal-code	The postal or zip code associated with the real-world location.
og:region	The state or province associated with the real-world location.
og:street-address	A free-form text address associated with the real-world location.

Going back to our previous Yelp example, let's extend the page metadata tags with our new geographical information:

```
<html xmlns:og="http://ogp.me/ns#">
<head>
<!-- INSERT: Required OGP Tags -->
<meta property="og:latitude" content="37.6246361">
<meta property="og:longitude" content="-121.7567068">
<meta property="og:street-address" content="5050 Arroyo Rd" />
<meta property="og:locality" content="Livermore" />
<meta property="og:region" content="CA" />
<meta property="og:postal-code" content="94550" />
<meta property="og:country-name" content="USA" />
...
</head>
...
</html>
```

These tags are tremendously valuable for any site that represents a physical location, such as a business. It not only provides immediate address information, but it also integrates latitude and longitude coordinates that can be used to plot locations on mapping products or provide directions from a viewer's current location.

Specifying contact information

Taking the available metadata even further, let's assume that you are a business owner or that you provide some type of content where you want people to be able to contact you or your company. This is where contact `<meta>` tags come into play.

Using these tags (shown in Table 10-4), a site owner can include main contact information that people viewing the site can use.

Table 10-4. Contact properties

Property	Description
og:email	A contact email address for the business or site. Since this information is made publicly available, you should always use a dedicated email address for only the site in question.
og:fax_number	A contact fax number for the business or site.
og:phone_number	A contact phone number for the business or site.

If we expand even further on our previous Yelp restaurant review page to now include contact information, the new section may look something like this:

```
<html xmlns:og="http://ogp.me/ns#">
<head>
<!-- INSERT: Required OGP Tags -->
<meta property="og:email" content="restaurant@wente.com" />
<meta property="og:fax_number" content="925-456-2301" />
<meta property="og:phone_number" content="925-456-2300" />
...
</head>
```

```
...
</html>
```

Implementing contact information in conjunction with geographic data can provide enough data for any site to define a profile page for your business, such as how Yelp supplements its data with business contact information and an associated map to show the location.

Attaching video data

If you want to attach video data on your page and have it reflected in the Open Graph protocol metadata, you'll employ the `og:video` tag and its children.

There are a number of tags available for specifying a video file, as shown in Table 10-5.

Table 10-5. Video properties

Property	Description
og:video	The URL to the video file that you have embedded on the page.
og:video:height (optional)	The height of the video in pixels.
og:video:type (optional)	The MIME type for the video. If no type is specified, the parser should attempt to infer the type. The Open Graph protocol suggests using a default of application/x-shockwave-flash until HTML5 video is more common.
og:video:width (optional)	The width of the video, in pixels.

If we look at what these features look like as `<meta>` tags, we can see the implementation potential:

```
<html xmlns:og="http://ogp.me/ns#">
<head>
<!-- INSERT: Required OGP Tags -->
<meta property="og:video" content="http://www.example.com/keyboardcat.flv" />
<meta property="og:video:height" content="450" />
<meta property="og:video:width" content="550" />
<meta property="og:video:type" content="application/x-shockwave-flash" />
...
</head>
...
</html>
```

Using video metatagging for individual pages can help to surface videos underneath a root site, helping site viewers more easily discover its video content.

Attaching audio data

Much like the `og:video` tag, `og:audio` allows a site promoting audio content to tag information about the music being played on a particular page. Table 10-6 lists the available tags.

Table 10-6. Audio properties

Property	Description
og:audio	The absolute URL to the audio track being presented.
og:audio:album (optional)	The album name.
og:audio:artist (optional)	The artist name.
og:audio:title (optional)	The audio track title.
og:audio:type (optional)	The MIME type of the audio track. If no type is specified, the parser should attempt to infer the type.

Here's how these `<meta>` tags look in context:

```
<html xmlns:og="http://ogp.me/ns#">
<head>
<!-- INSERT: Required OGP Tags -->
<meta property="og:audio" content="http://www.example.com/song.mp3" />
<meta property="og:audio:album" content="My amazing album" />
<meta property="og:audio:title" content="The greatest song ever" />
<meta property="og:audio:artist" content="The best band" />
<meta property="og:audio:type" content="application/mp3" />
...
</head>
...
</html>
```

Implementing tagging for individual audio tracks on pages provides the same benefits as it does for video tags. You are able to surface individual pages more readily to individuals who are searching your content and provide them with the general information they need to get an idea of what is offered on your site.

Defining products using object types

Every element in an entity social graph is by definition a type of object. At a base level, that's all an entity is—an object describing the user interaction and any relevant information about it.

Defining an object type within the Open Graph protocol adds the entity to a specific section of the site (i.e., organizes the site by category). You define an object type using the following syntax:

```
<meta property="og:type" content="activity" />
```

The property value remains og:type, but you'll change the content value to whatever object type best defines the page. The types can be further grouped into individual categories. For example, the first category we'll look at, activities, should be used when the page content relates to sporting events, outings, physical activities, conferences, or the like.

activity   sport

The next category, businesses, encompasses sites that contain information about companies, such as restaurants, company websites, or any other business presence on the Web.

Businesses

bar	café	restaurant
company	hotel	

Use group types when delivering content to people who are interested in specific sporting information or certain causes. Pages that might include these object types are football, baseball, or hockey team or league sites; sites that are attempting to gain community support for causes or events, such as marches for cancer; and rally or protest sites.

Groups

cause   sports_league   sports_team

Organization object types are intended for groups that are not included under businesses, such as schools, nonprofits, and federal or local government sites.

Organizations

band	non_profit	university
government	school	

If the site content is devoted to a specific person, using the people object types will ensure that the site is placed in the appropriate category within the graph. This category may include fan pages, sites including biographical data for individuals, or campaign sites for political candidates.

People

actor	director	politician
athlete	musician	public_figure

Place objects target pages that contain geographical, map, or location-based data. This may include landmarks such as the Statue of Liberty, city informational websites, or sites that provide information on specific countries.

Places

city	country	landmark

Products and entertainment objects cover a number of the remaining page attributes and include items like books, movie sites, and TV shows. Should the product page include a UPC or ISBN, you may use the `og:upc` or `og:isbn` object types to better specify the page content.

Products and entertainment

album	food	product
book	game	song
drink	movie	tv_show

Finally, the websites group is used to denote many social media outreach channels that do not fit into the products and entertainment category. These include articles, blogs, and generic websites. The website type can be used as a generic attribute for sites that do not fit in above categories.

Websites

article	blog	website

Using this extensive list of object types, you can specify the kind of information contained within your page, properly categorizing the elements of a user's online entity graph and thus providing a rich extension to the standard definition of a social graph.

A Real-World Example: The Facebook Open Graph

The Facebook implementation of the Open Graph protocol (*http://developers.facebook.com/docs/opengraph*) allows a site owner to represent his site, business, or product page as if it were a Facebook page, without it actually residing in the social network.

The Facebook Open Graph consists of a few pieces, implemented by a site owner:

- The Open Graph protocol `<meta>` tags to define the site object
- A few Facebook administration tags
- The Facebook Like button

It currently only supports web pages that represent real-world things such as sports teams, movies, actors, restaurants, etc.

The Facebook Like button is a simple page implementation that displays a button with the word Like on it. When a user likes a page, his name and profile—as well as those of any of his friends who have liked the same page—is displayed, as shown in Figure 10-2.

Figure 10-2. The Facebook Like button on a website

Once the user clicks Like, he is connected to the page containing the Like button, and the like instance is subsequently published on his profile. The Like button is included on a page via either an iframe or the Facebook JavaScript API and the `<fb:like>` XFBML tag.

Under the likes and interests sections of the user's profile, the new like instance will be displayed, and under his news feed's recent activity, a like notice will be posted (Figure 10-3).

Figure 10-3. How a Facebook like instance appears on a Facebook profile

When a user likes a page, he enables the liked page source to publish updates, much as if it were a real Facebook page.

The markup

Now that we understand how the Facebook Open Graph works from start to end, let's take a look at what the code looks like within a website. We will use the Open Graph protocol website as the source of our markup: *http://opengraphprotocol.org/*.

The first pieces of markup information that we want to look at are the `<meta>` tags that will add the Like button so we can build an entity profile for the page. If we view the page source, we are presented with the following Open Graph tags:

```
<meta property="og:title" content="Open Graph Protocol" />
<meta property="og:type" content="website" />
<meta property="og:url" content="http://opengraphprotocol.org/" />
<meta property="og:image"
      content="http://opengraphprotocol.org/open_graph_protocol_logo.png" />
<meta property="og:description" content="The Open Graph protocol enables any
```

```
        web page to become a rich object in a social graph. " />
    <meta property="fb:admins" content="706023" />
```

We've already talked about the standard Open Graph tags, but the Facebook Open Graph adds a few administrative tags that we need to go over.

 You can create a Facebook application from its setup site at *http://devel opers.facebook.com/setup/*. This will allow you to associate a series of Open Graph–defined pages with a single umbrella application.

The `fb:admins` `<meta>` tag enables you to associate a Facebook Like button with an account or page that you own. This gives you access to Facebook's well-associated graph of entity information and allows for trackback to an internal Facebook page where users can collect more information about your page.

```
    <meta property="fb:admins" content="USER_ID1, USER_ID2, ..." />
```

The other administrative tag is the Facebook application ID, which provides a way for you to associate a series of pages with a single application. This allows you to treat all sources as if they were under the application umbrella.

For example, let's say that you have a news site with thousands of pages that all have Facebook Like buttons on them. With the `fb:app_id` tag, you can associate all of those pages with a single application ID, allowing you to programmatically publish updates to individuals who have liked any of the pages under that application ID umbrella.

```
    <meta property="fb:app_id" content="143306585343"/>
```

The last piece of markup required can either be the JavaScript API and the `<fb:like>` XFBML tag, or an iframe that loads the actual Like button. This markup allows you to create a direct link for already signed-in users to like a page without having to go through their Facebook accounts.

```
    <iframe src="http://www.facebook.com/plugins/like.php?href=http%3A%2F%2F
        opengraphprotocol.org%2F&amp;layout=standard&amp;show_faces=true&amp;
        width=450&amp;action=like&amp;colorscheme=light" scrolling="no"
        frameborder="0" allowtransparency="true" style="border:none; overflow:hidden;
        width:450px; height:80px;"></iframe>
```

The Facebook Open Graph is definitely the biggest implementation of the Open Graph protocol. As such, it is pushing adoption of the protocol, allowing developers who don't necessarily care about the Facebook implementation to take advantage of the same metadata tags that those who do use it have implemented on their sites.

Practical Implementation: Capturing Open Graph Data from a Web Source

We've discussed, at length, the topic of how you can make any site a *producer* of Open Graph information—that is, a rich provider of entity-based social data. Now that we understand that, let's look into the process of creating an Open Graph *consumer*.

We will explore similar implementations of this process in two languages: PHP and Python. The end product is the same, so you can use either one you prefer.

PHP implementation: Open Graph node

 The full code for this sample is available at *https://github.com/jcleblanc/programming-social-applications/tree/master/chapter_10/opengraph-php-parser*.

First, let's explore an Open Graph protocol parser implementation using PHP. In this example, we'll develop a class that contains all of the functionality we need to parse Open Graph tags from any web source that contains them.

So what do want to get out of this class structure? If we break it down into a few elements, at a base level our only requirements are that it:

- Includes a method for capturing and storing all `<meta>` tags with a property attribute starting with `og:` from a provided URL.
- Provides one method for returning a single Open Graph tag value, and another for returning the entire list of obtained tags.

Now let's see how these simple requirements play out when implemented in an actual PHP class structure:

```php
<?php
/*****************************************************************************
 * Class Name: Open Graph Parser
 * Description: Parses an HTML document to retrieve and store Open Graph
 *              tags from the meta data
 * Useage:
 *    $url = 'http://www.example.com/index.html';
 *    $graph = new OpenGraph($url);
 *    print_r($graph->get_one('title'));  //get only title element
 *    print_r($graph->get_all());         //return all Open Graph tags
 *****************************************************************************/
class OpenGraph{
   //the open graph associative array
   private static $og_content = array();

   /*****************************************************************************
    * Function: Class Constructor
    * Description: Initiates the request to fetch OG data
    * Params: $url (string) - URL of page to collect OG tags from
    *****************************************************************************/
   public function __construct($url){
      if ($url){
         self::$og_content = self::get_graph($url);
      }
   }
```

```
/**************************************************************************
 * Function: Get Open Graph
 * Description: Initiates the request to fetch OG data
 * Params: $url (string) - URL of page to collect OG tags from
 * Return: Object - associative array containing the OG data in format
 *                  property : content
 **************************************************************************/
private function get_graph($url){
    //fetch html content from web source and filter to meta data
    $dom = new DOMDocument();
    @$dom->loadHtmlFile($url);
    $tags = $dom->getElementsByTagName('meta');

    //set open graph search tag and return object
    $og_pattern = '/^og:/';
    $graph_content = array();

    //for each open graph tag, store in return object as property : content
    foreach ($tags as $element){
        if (preg_match($og_pattern, $element->getAttribute('property'))){
            $graph_content[preg_replace($og_pattern, '',
                $element->getAttribute('property'))] =
                $element->getAttribute('content');
        }
    }

    //store all open graph tags
    return $graph_content;
}

/**************************************************************************
 * Function: Get One Tag
 * Description: Fetches the content of one OG tag
 * Return: String - the content of one requested OG tag
 **************************************************************************/
public function get_one($element){
    return self::$og_content[$element];
}

/**************************************************************************
 * Function: Get All Tags
 * Description: Fetches the content of one OG tag
 * Return: Object - The entire OG associative array
 **************************************************************************/
public function get_all(){
    return self::$og_content;
}
}
?>
```

Analyzing our code by individual sections, we can see that within the class the following methods are available:

__construct

> This is the class constructor that is run when you create a new instance of the class using the code `new OpenGraph()`. The constructor accepts a URL string as the single parameter; this is the URL that the class will access to collect its Open Graph metadata. Once in the constructor, if a URL string was specified, the class `og_con tent` property will be set to the return value of the `get_graph` method—i.e., the associative array of Open Graph tags.

get_graph

> Once initiated, the `get_graph` method will capture the content of the URL as a DOM document, then further filter the resulting value to return only `<meta>` tags within the content. We then loop through each `<meta>` tag that was found. If the `<meta>` tag contains a property attribute that starts with og:, the tag is a valid Open Graph tag. The key of the return associative array is set to the property value (minus the og:, which is stripped out of the string), and the value is set to the content of the tag. Once all valid tags are stored within the return associative array, it is returned from the method.

get_one

> Provides a public method to allow you to return one Open Graph tag from the obtained graph data. The single argument that is allowed is a string representing the property value of the Open Graph tag. The method returns the string value of the content of that same tag.

get_all

> Provides a public method to allow you to return all Open Graph tags from the obtained graph data. This method does not take any arguments from the user and returns the entire associative array in the format of *property: content*.

Now that we have our class structure together, we can explore how to use it in a practical implementation use case. For this example, we are revisiting our old Yelp restaurant review example from earlier in the chapter. In a separate file, we can build out the requests:

```php
<?php
require_once('OpenGraph.php');

//set url to get OG data from and initialtize class
$url = 'http://www.yelp.com/biz/the-restaurant-at-wente-vineyards-livermore-2';
$graph = new OpenGraph($url);

//print title and then the entire meta graph
print_r($graph->get_one('title'));
print_r($graph->get_all());
?>
```

We first set the URL from which we want to scrape the Open Graph metadata. Following that, we create a new Open Graph class object, passing in that URL. The class constructor will scrape the Open Graph data from the provided URL (if available) and store it within that instance of the class.

We can then begin making public method requests against the class object to display some of the Open Graph data that we captured.

First, we make a request to the `get_one(...)` method, passing in the string `title` as the argument to the method call. This signifies that we want to return the Open Graph `<meta>` tag content whose property is `og:title`.

When we call the `get_one(...)` method, the following string will be printed on the page:

```
The Restaurant at Wente Vineyards
```

We then make a request to the public `get_all()` method. This method will fetch the entire associative array of Open Graph tags that we were able to pull from the specified page. Once we print out the return value from that method, we are presented with the following:

```
Array
(
    [url] => http://www.yelp.com/biz/gATFcGOL-qOtqm9HTaXJpg
    [longitude] => -121.7567068
    [type] => restaurant
    [description] =>
    [latitude] => 37.6246361
    [title] => The Restaurant at Wente Vineyards
    [image] => http://media2.px.yelpcdn.com/bphoto/iVSnIDCj-fWiPffHHkUVsQ/m
)
```

You can obtain the full class file and sample implementation from *https://github.com/ jcleblanc/programming-social-applications/tree/master/open-graph/php-parser/*.

You can use this simple implementation to scrape Open Graph data from any web source. It will allow you to access stored values to obtain rich entity information about a web page, extending the user social graph beyond the traditional confines of a social networking container or any single web page.

Python implementation: Open Graph node

The full code for this sample is available at *https://github.com/jcleblanc/ programming-social-applications/tree/master/chapter_10/opengraph-py thon-parser*.

Now let's look at the same Open Graph protocol tag-parsing class, but this time using Python. Much like the PHP example, we're going to be creating a class that contains the following functionality:

- Includes a method for capturing and storing all `<meta>` tags with a property attribute starting with `og:` from a provided URL.
- Provides one method for returning a single Open Graph tag value, and another for returning the entire list of obtained tags.

Let's take a look at how this implementation is built.

 The following Open Graph Python implementation uses an HTML/
XML parser called Beautiful Soup to capture <meta> tags from a provided
source. Beautiful Soup is a tremendously valuable parsing library for
Python and can be downloaded and installed from *http://www.crummy
.com/software/BeautifulSoup/*.

```python
import urllib
import re
from BeautifulSoup import BeautifulSoup

"""
" Class: Open Graph Parser
" Description: Parses an HTML document to retrieve and store Open Graph
"             tags from the meta data
" Useage:
"     url = 'http://www.nhl.com/ice/player.htm?id=8468482';
"     og_instance = OpenGraphParser(url)
"     print og_instance.get_one('og:title')
"     print og_instance.get_all()
"""
class OpenGraphParser:
    og_content = {}

    """
    " Method: Init
    " Description: Initializes the open graph fetch.  If url was provided,
    "             og_content will be set to return value of get_graph method
    " Arguments: url (string) - The URL from which to collect the OG data
    """
    def __init__(self, url):
        if url is not None:
            self.og_content = self.get_graph(url)

    """
    " Method: Get Open Graph
    " Description: Fetches HTML from provided url then filters to only meta tags.
    "             Goes through all meta tags and any starting with og: get
    "             stored and returned to the init method.
    " Arguments: url (string) - The URL from which to collect the OG data
    " Returns: dictionary - The matching OG tags
    """
    def get_graph(self, url):
        #fetch all meta tags from the url source
        sock = urllib.urlopen(url)
        htmlSource = sock.read()
        sock.close()
        soup = BeautifulSoup(htmlSource)
        meta = soup.findAll('meta')

        #get all og:* tags from meta data
        content = {}
```

```
        for tag in meta:
            if tag.has_key('property'):
                if re.search('og:', tag['property']) is not None:
                    content[re.sub('og:', '', tag['property'])] = tag['content']

        return content

    """
    " Method: Get One Tag
    " Description: Returns the content of one OG tag
    " Arguments: tag (string) - The OG tag whose content should be returned
    " Returns: string - the value of the OG tag
    """
    def get_one(self, tag):
        return self.og_content[tag]


    """
    " Method: Get All Tags
    " Description: Returns all found OG tags
    " Returns: dictionary - All OG tags
    """
    def get_all(self):
        return self.og_content
```

This class structure will make up the core functionality behind our parser. When instantiated, the class object will fetch and store all Open Graph <meta> tags from the provided source URL and will allow you to pull any of that data as needed.

The OpenGraphParser class consists of a number of methods to help us accomplish our goals:

__init__
: Initializes the class instance. The init method accepts a single argument, a string whose content is the URL from which we will attempt to obtain Open Graph <meta> tag data. If the URL exists, the class property og_content will be set to the return value of the get_graph(...) method—i.e., the Open Graph <meta> tag data.

get_graph
: The meat of the fetch request, get_graph accepts one argument—the URL from which we will obtain the Open Graph data. This method starts out by fetching the HTML document from the provided URL, then uses Beautiful Soup to fetch all <meta> tags that exist within the source. We then loop through all <meta> tags, and if they have a property value that begins with og: (signifying an Open Graph tag), we store the key and value in our dictionary variable. Once all tags are obtained, the dictionary is returned.

get_one
: Provides a means for obtaining the value of a single Open Graph tag from the stored dictionary property. This method accepts one argument, the key whose value should be returned, and returns the value of that key as a string.

---

get_all

> Provides a means for obtaining all Open Graph data stored within the class instance. This method does not accept any arguments and returns the dictionary object containing all Open Graph data.

Now that we have the class in place, we can begin to fetch Open Graph data from a given URL. If we implement our new class, we can see how this works:

```
from OpenGraph import OpenGraphParser

#initialize open graph parser class instance with url
url = 'http://www.nhl.com/ice/player.htm?id=8468482';
og_instance = OpenGraphParser(url)

#output since description and entire og tag dictionary
print og_instance.get_one('description')
print og_instance.get_all()
```

We first import the class into our Python script so that we can use it. Then we need to initialize an instance of the class object. We set the URL that we want to obtain (in this case, the NHL player page for Dany Heatley) and create a new class instance, passing through the URL to the class __init__ method.

Now that we have the Open Graph data locked in our class object, we can begin extracting the information as required. We first make a request to the get_once(...) method, passing in description as our argument. This will obtain the Open Graph tag for og:description, returning a string similar to the following:

```
Dany Heatley of the San Jose Sharks. 2010-2011 Stats:
19 Games Played, 7 Goals, 12 Assists
```

The next method that we call is a request to get_all(). When this method is called, it will return the entire dictionary of Open Graph tags. When we print this out, we should have something similar to the following:

```
{
  u'site_name': u'NHL.com',
  u'description': u'Dany Heatley of the San Jose Sharks. 2010-2011
          Stats: 19 Games Played, 7 Goals, 12 Assists',
  u'title': u'Dany Heatley',
  u'url': u'http://sharks.nhl.com/club/player.htm?id=8468482',
  u'image': u'http://cdn.nhl.com/photos/mugs/thumb/8468482.jpg',
  u'type': u'athlete'
}
```

You can obtain the full class file and sample implementation from *https://github.com/jcleblanc/programming-social-applications/tree/master/open-graph/python-parser/*.

Using this simple class structure and a few lines of setup code, we can obtain a set of Open Graph tags from a web source. We can then use this data to begin to define a valuable source of entity social graph information for users, companies, or organizations.

The Shortcomings of the Open Graph Protocol

The simplicity of the Open Graph protocol makes it incredibly easy to implement and parse. Unfortunately, this same simplicity can also translate to some shortcomings you'll likely encounter when you're working with the specification, ranging from implementation differences between sites to the risk of inaccurate generalizations made about entire pages since tiered object types are not provided. We'll discuss a couple of these inherent Open Graph issues next.

Inability to implement tiered definitions to differentiate similar objects

One issue that has surfaced within the Open Graph protocol is being unable to differentiate objects with similar characteristics.

With several objects that have a real-world location, this is not a problem. We can differentiate the objects by utilizing additional geographical information—for example, if we have reviewed the same chain restaurant at different locations around a city.

But say we're not looking at something with a real-world location—for example, a movie review for *Fight Club*. There are two movies with the same name in this case, one from 1999 and another from 2006. Therein lies the problem. When we enter in all of the Open Graph information for both movies, they will be almost identical, except perhaps the description. However, since the description is an arbitrary string with no defined structure, we can rule this out as a differentiator.

The inability to provide tiered or secondary object definitions can create confusion when you're building out your entity social graph. You need to take into account the lack of further layers of customization when implementing the Open Graph protocol. The good news is that, since the protocol is simple in nature, implementing a parser that can handle multiple object definitions is not a major feat.

Page versus object definitions

The Open Graph protocol works by defining metadata *at a page level*. For web pages that display only one type of defined data, this works perfectly fine, but what if you are displaying multiple objects on a single page?

This is the second shortcoming on our list. Since the Open Graph protocol does not provide a method to allow you to break down a page into multiple defined objects, the extent to which you can define objects on a page is limited.

Fortunately, as with the previous issue of differentiating like objects, the protocol is simple enough that it would not be a labor-intensive process to integrate functionality for this use case.

Activity Streams: Standardizing Social Activities

With so many different social sites pushing updates, activities, and status changes for users, developers and implementers of applications that consume these streams will naturally run into the challenge of attempting to consolidate them into a single product.

The premise behind the Activity Streams specification is to define a method for expressing activities. This specification was created because existing activity-producing sites (e.g., FourSquare, Gowalla) fulfill the requirements for their own services, but do not capture the rich, comprehensive view of the activity.

Thinking of an activity as a collection of objects and defined sections allows us to encapsulate its full breadth, including the people who are creating the activity and the target for which it is being generated.

Why Do We Need to Define a Standard for Activities?

The reason why a standard like Activity Streams not only exists, but is also absolutely necessary, is obvious when we consider the number of sources that produce some type of activity or update for users.

Let's say that we are the average social Internet citizens and use a number of sites to keep in contact with friends, family, coworkers, and users with interests similar to ours. This might mean that we use Facebook to keep in contact with friends and family, Twitter to quickly disseminate large amounts of activities from like-minded people and/or for business outreach, and Gowalla or Foursquare for location checkins.

Now let's say we want to build a site that shows all of this data, or we want to feed all of the data into a single source and have it make sense. If every site and service out there implements its own methods for creating activities, we'll have to go through a rigorous process to merge everything. Even when we do that, some sites may include a large amount of data in their activities, while others may include only a few minor strings to represent the activity.

This is the reason for the Activity Streams standard; it makes consuming data across many platforms and services a much easier process. Even though services may take the Activity Streams specification and enhance it to fit their particular needs and data (e.g., adding new verbs or object types in the response data), the core implementation and standards will still be in place to encapsulate the total picture of an activity. This activities standard can go a long way if implemented by many of the major activity-creation sources.

Implementing Activity Streams

An activity comprises a number of elements such as the person creating the activity, the object being acted upon, and the target of the activity. For instance, consider the following sentence:

```
Mary added to a new photo into her collection.
```

If we break this sentence down by Activity Stream standards, we can describe the following items:

Mary
> The *actor* of the activity. We may create an `actor` object for Mary that links back to her profile or provides additional information about her.

photo
> The *object* of the activity. The photo may be a structure that contains media information such as a URI, width, and height.

collection
> The *target* of the activity. This target may be composed of many different objects such as photos and videos. The collection can be expanded with additional information or objects.

The Activity Streams specification goes beyond defining just a few simple constructs, attempting to build out a comprehensive model for developers and companies to structure their updates and activities according to the data they contain:

```
{
    "items" : [
        {
            "verb": "post",
            "published": "2011-02-18T16:26:43Z",
            "generator": {
                "url": "http://example.com/activities-app"
            },
            "provider": {
                "url": "http://providersite.com/activity-stream"
            },
            "title": "Mary added a new photo to her album.",
            "actor": {
                "url": "http://providersite.com/mary",
                "objectType": "person",
                "id": "tag:provider.com,20110218,162643:mary",
                "image": {
                    "url": "http://providersite.com/mary/image",
                    "width": 125,
                    "height": 125
                },
                "displayName": "Mary Smith"
            },
            "object" : {
                "url": "http://providersite.com/mary/album/my_place.jpg",
                "objectType": "http://activitystrea.ms/schema/1.0/photo",
```

```
          "id": "tag:provider.com,20110218,162643:my_place",
          "image": {
            "url": "http://providersite.com/mary/album/my_place_thumb.jpg",
            "width": 100,
            "height": 100
          }
        },
        "target": {
          "url": "http://targetsite.com/mary/album/",
          "objectType": "http://activitystrea.ms/schema/1.0/photo-album",
          "id": "tag:example.org,20110218,162643:album4323",
          "displayName": "Mary's Photo Album",
          "image": {
            "url": "http://providersite.com/mary/album/thumbnail.jpg",
            "width": 100,
            "height": 100
          }
        }
      }
    }
  ]
}
```

This basic example shows how an activity (or stream of activities) may be presented on a platform. It contains our major activity sections and provides an extensive amount of information about each individual source.

Table 10-7 shows the main fields we can set within an activity.

Table 10-7. Main settable sections within an activity

Property	Type	Description
actor	object	A single object containing the person or entity that performed the activity. Each activity must contain one actor property.
content (optional)	string	A human-readable HTML string that describes the activity. Thumbnail images may also be included in the markup.
generator (optional)	object	An object that describes the application or provider that generated the activity.
icon (optional)	string	An *IRI* (Internationalized Resource Identifier) that identifies an image that represents the activity that is produced. The image should have an aspect ratio of height equal to width (e.g., 20×20 square) and should be legible at small sizes (i.e., for use as a small icon associated with the activity).
id (optional)	string	A permanent, universally unique identifier for the activity in the form of an absolute IRI. In the case where an id is not present, the URL may be used as a less reliable identifier.
object	object	The primary object that is being described in an activity. For example, in the sentence, "Erik just purchased a new phone on Amazon," the object of the activity is the phone. If this field is not present, the object may be inferred from the context of the activity.
published	date-time	The date and time at which the activity occurred. This may be different from the time that it was published on the associated site—for example, if there was a posting delay. This field must be present in an activity.

Property	Type	Description
provider (optional)	object	An object that describes the application or provider that published the activity. This may not be the same as the source that created the activity, but should be a single object in either case.
target (optional)	object	The object that is the target of the activity. For instance, if the activity is "Erik just added a new item to his Amazon wish list," the target of the activity is the "Amazon wish list." This should be a single direct target, not an indirect target source.
title (optional)	string	A human-readable string that may contain HTML and that is used as a title or headline for the activity.
updated (optional)	date-time	If an activity has been modified, this field should include the date and time at which the modification occurred.
url (optional)	string	An IRI that links to an HTML representation of the activity.
verb	string	The verb string that describes the type of action in the activity and is required for each activity posted. Relative string representations other than a simple name (e.g., `post`) are not allowed.

These are the main, top-level items that we can set. Some of them have specific types that may also be set, such as string or date-time; however, many of them have a type set to object. This means that the item in question (e.g., `actor` or `target`) represents a larger topic that may be expanded. Each item in Table 10-7 that has a type set to object may have alternate attributes defined by the JSON Activity Streams specification, as you can see in the following example of an object comprising the `actor` element:

```
"actor": {
    "url": "http://providersite.com/mary",
    "objectType": "person",
    "id": "tag:provider.com,20110218,162643:mary",
    "image": {
        "url": "http://providersite.com/mary/image",
        "width": 125,
        "height": 125
    },
    "displayName": "Mary Smith"
},
```

Table 10-8 provides more details on the optional JSON attributes that may comprise an object.

Table 10-8. Optional object attributes

Attribute	Type	Description
attachments	array of objects	One or more objects that are related or relevant to the activity being generated (similar to the concept of attaching files in an email message).
author	object	An entity representing the person who created or authored the object. The entity is itself represented as an object, and an object may include a single `author` object.
		The person who *authored* the object may differ from the person who *published* the object.
content	string	A description of the object, provided in natural languages. This field may introduce HTML elements, including image representations such as thumbnails.

Attribute	Type	Description
displayName	string	A human-readable, plain-text name for the object. This display name must not contain HTML markup.
downstreamDu plicates	array of strings	One or more absolute IRIs that reference duplicate objects in the activity. These may be duplicates in different systems (e.g., if the provider has multiple, separate places that display activities) and may prompt the implementer to launch an object deduplication effort.
id	string	Provides a permanent and universally unique identifier for the object. The id should be presented in the form of an IRI. If an id is not present in the object, the consumer of the object may use the URL as a less reliable identifier.
image	media link	A human-consumable visual representation of the object. (The media link type will be described further shortly.)
objectType	string	A string displaying the type of object that is being presented. This may be either the short form of the type or the full IRI representation of the type.
published	date-time	The date and time when the object was published.
summary	string	A human-readable string containing a summary of the object. This string may include HTML markup and images.
updated	date-time	If an update to an object is published, this field should include the date and time when the update occurred.
upstreamDupli cates	array of strings	Much like downstreamDuplicates, this contains objects that are duplicates of the current object. Instead of duplicates that already exist, however, these are objects that the provider knowingly duplicates after posting with a new id.
url	string	A string that contains an IRI pointing to an HTML-based page that provides more details about the object. For instance, if the object is a Facebook page, url would point to it.

Now we have a clearer definition of what an object is. All of the attributes listed in Table 10-8 break down into individual media types, such as string or additional objects. But there is also a new type introduced in the table—media link.

A media link type defines an object that is geared toward presenting image, audio, and video content. For example, if we return to our previous actor object, the image element contains the media link object that displays a photo of our actor:

```
"actor": {
    "url": "http://providersite.com/mary",
    "objectType": "person",
    "id": "tag:provider.com,20110218,162643:mary",
    "image": {
        "url": "http://providersite.com/mary/image",
        "width": 125,
        "height": 125
    },
    "displayName": "Mary Smith"
},
```

You can define any element that has a type of media link by using a series of predefined attributes in the Activity Streams specification, as listed in Table 10-9.

Table 10-9. Media link object attributes

Attribute	Type	Description
duration (optional)	int	The duration of the media object in seconds. This should be included where it makes sense (e.g., video and audio files).
height (optional)	int	The height of the media object in pixels. Height should be included where it makes sense (e.g., videos or images).
url	string	The IRI of the media link resource. This must be included within a media link object.
width (optional)	int	The width of the media object in pixels. Width should be included where it makes sense (e.g., videos or images).

All of these elements define a base-level activity via the Activity Streams JSON specification. Implementers of the specification will work from this foundation to define their applications and extend it with their own verbs, object types, and additional elements beyond the defaults shown here.

Object Types

Within each object construct is an `objectType` string value. This defines the type of data that is being presented in the object, which helps a consumer determine what to do with the data and how to process it. The Activity Streams specification includes several object types that you can insert as the value of the `objectType` parameter.

Objects types may be referenced using their type name (e.g., article, review, video, etc.) or by the absolute URI to the schema, which also uses the type name as the last part of the URI: *http://activitystrea.ms/schema/1.0/type*.

So, for instance, an object with the type of `person` may use either of the following strings for the verb:

* `person`
* *http://activitystrea.ms/schema/1.0/person*

There are many different type categories available in the specification. Let's look at them now.

General object types

The Activity Streams specification defines a number of basic types, as shown in Table 10-10. These general types make up the vast majority of the object types that you will be using or consuming when working with an activity.

Table 10-10. General object types

Type	Description
article	The object is an article such as a news article, blog entry, or publication. Objects of this type usually consist of paragraphs of text with optional images and links.
audio	The content of the object is some sort of audio content.
badge	Represents a badge or award granted to the object.
bookmark	The object is a pointer to some URL, usually a web page. You can think of this in the same context as bookmarking a page in a browser; the object isn't the site URL itself but rather a pointer to the URL.
collec tion	A collection contains an arbitrary number of generic objects of any type, such as photos in an album.
comment	This type of object represents a text response to some other object, such as a person commenting on the content of a blog article. This type must not be used for other types of replies, such as video replies or reviews.
event	The event type represents an object that refers to something happening at a particular place within a certain interval of time.
file	This type of object is a file or some other document with no additional machine-readable semantics.
group	The group type should be used to represent a collection of people, such as a Facebook group. The construct of a group should allow a person object to join and leave.
image	An image type represents a graphical image object.
note	The note type represents a short-form text message, such as in a microblogging platform like Tumblr. These are often plain-text messages that are shorter than an article and whose useful lifespan is shorter than that of a blog entry.
person	The person object represents the account of a real person or sometimes a company entity.
place	A place is a geographically traceable location on Earth, such as a point containing an address or latitude/longitude coordinates.
product	A commercial good or service.
question	This is generally a representation of a poll or question.
review	Unlike a comment, the review type contains objects that are straightforward responses to another article, written as critiques or commentaries.
service	A service type may represent some entity (e.g., company, website, blog, etc.) that either performs service or work for another object (e.g., person) or acts as a container for other objects.
video	The video type contains video content, usually consisting of a video and audio track.

Verbs

The JSON Activity Streams specification defines one base verb that is used to indicate the type of activity being produced: post. The specification permits implementers to define their own verbs or pull them from some of the other defined specifications, such as the standard Activity Streams specification or the Atom specification.

Before we look into some of the other potential verbs that implementers may use, let's go through the verbs that are defined within the base Activity Streams specification. These verbs provide a good starting point for working with an activity.

Verbs may be referenced using their verb name (e.g., post, follow, join, etc.) or by the absolute URI to the schema, which also uses the verb name as the last part of the URI: *http://activitystrea.ms/schema/1.0/verb*.

So, for instance, an object with the type of share may use either of the following strings for the verb:

- share
- *http://activitystrea.ms/schema/1.0/share*

As with the object types, verbs are defined into a few categories, ranging from general verbs to more specialized verb categories. Let's start with general verbs.

General verbs

The defined general verbs (Table 10-11) will deliver the vast majority of the functionality that you will need for an activity.

Table 10-11. General verbs

Verb	Description
add	Indicates that the actor has added the object to the target, such as adding a series of photo objects to an album target.
cancel	The actor has canceled the object, such as canceling an event.
checkin	The actor has checked in to the object—for example, checking in to a place object.
delete	The actor has deleted the object. The implication of this verb is that the object has been permanently destroyed, but this is not necessarily the case.
favorite	Also known as the "mark as favorite" verb, this indicates that the activity actor has marked the object as something that he is interested in and may wish to revisit at a later date. Activities containing this verb may contain a collection of objects that the actor has added to his favorites.
follow	Also known as the "start following" verb, this indicates that the actor has begun following the activities of the object, usually a person or entity that produces activities. This is a one-way, nonreciprocated follower relationship.
give	Indicates that the actor is giving the object to the target. For instance, this may indicate an action such as an actor giving a product object to another person (target).
ignore	Indicates that the actor has ignored the object, such as when a person ignores a friend request.
invite	Indicates that the actor has sent an invite to the object, such as when a person (actor) sends an invite (object) to another person (target).
join	Indicates that the actor has become a member of the object, usually a group.
leave	Indicates that the actor has left the object—for example, if a person leaves a group or membership.

Verb	Description
like	Operating similarly to a Facebook like, this "mark as liked" verb indicates that the actor likes the content of the object.
make-friend	Unlike the follow verb, the make-friend verb indicates a two-way, reciprocated friendship link between the actor and the object, usually another person. This is like adding a new friend on Facebook.
play	Indicates that the actor has interacted with the object for an interval of time, such as in the case of a person playing a song or watching a video.
receive	Indicates that the actor is receiving the object, such as if the actor receives a product object.
remove	Indicates that the actor has removed the object from the target.
remove-friend	Indicates that the actor has removed the object from the collection of friends.
request-friend	Indicates that a friendship has been created, but is not yet reciprocated by the object (alternate party).
rsvp-maybe	This "possible RSVP" verb indicates that the actor has made a tentative RSVP for the object, such as stating that he may or may not be attending an event. This has neither a positive or negative connotation.
rsvp-no	This "negative RSVP" verb indicates that the actor has made a negative RSVP for the object, such as stating that he will not be attending an event.
rsvp-yes	This "positive RSVP" verb indicates that the actor has made a positive RSVP for the object, such as stating that he will be attending an event.
save	When using the "save" verb, the actor is indicating that they are taking the action of indicating that they would like to store a reference to the object for a later date as it is of particular interest for the actor primarily.
share	Indicates that the actor is promoting the object to other readers, such as his followers or friends. This does not necessarily mean that the actor created the object; it may simply indicate that he is calling attention to the object.
stop-following	Denotes that the actor has stopped following the object that is being displayed.
tag	The action of adding a target inside another object, such as when tagging a friend in a photo. You are specifying additional link information about the object.
unfavorite	Indicates that the actor has removed the object in question from a collection of favorite items.
unlike	Indicates that the actor has removed the object in question from a collection of liked items.
unsave	Indicates that the actor has removed the object in question from a collection of saved items.
update	Indicates that the object referenced has been modified, such as in the case of a person updating his profile.

Using verbs beyond (and more specific than) the standard post verb defined within the JSON specification will allow implementers to create rich activities that consumers can easily parse based on the information that the activities contain.

WebFinger: Expanding the Social Graph Through Email Addresses

The WebFinger protocol has its basis in Unix, where someone can run a `finger` command on an email address identifier to gain information about a user. WebFinger has modernized this functionality for the Web 2.0 world, defining a standard for providers to associate metadata with a user's email address to access her profiles, activities, and much more.

Some examples of information providers might associate with a user's email addresses include:

- Links to public profiles for the user.
- Direct profile data, such as a nickname or profile photo.
- Other linked services for the email address, such as Facebook, Twitter, or Flickr accounts.

These are just a few of the possible links that a provider may implement for metadata, but WebFinger is more focused on building a specification simply to ensure that this metadata is available. The providers themselves determine the amount of information to tie to an email address.

Finger to WebFinger: The Origin of WebFinger

Back in 1971, the finger program was created with the intention of enabling people to obtain information about other users in the network. This information can be any data that people choose to make public. Users access data through email addresses, running a command similar to the following:

```
finger username@company.com
```

Unfortunately, finger did not last as an implementation standard for many of our Web 2.0 protocols. It did, however, inspire the initial concept for the WebFinger protocol. After all, using an email address as a means for easily extracting a user's public profile information is an interesting idea. On many of the most popular sites we interact with on a daily basis (e.g., Yahoo!, Google, Facebook), we associate our email addresses with our user accounts—that is, our email addresses are directly tied to our profiles on these sites.

Now, with protocols such as OpenID—which allow users to sign in on any site using their email addresses from a few root providers—email addresses are more valuable than ever in defining a user's public profile.

Implementing WebFinger

Working with the WebFinger protocol is actually very easy. You simply make a series of cURL requests to a provider that implements WebFinger, which subsequently returns all of the information we need, as shown in Figure 10-4.

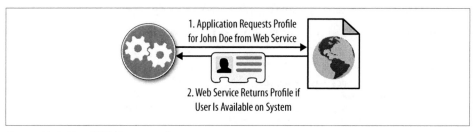

Figure 10-4. How WebFinger works

When a web application or service makes a request to a web source that uses WebFinger in order to obtain user information from that site, the web source will return either user record details or error information in the event that no user data was located.

As an example, let's take a look at extracting profile information using Google's Web-Finger implementation. First, we will make a request to the *.well-known/host-meta* file on Google to obtain more data about how Google's WebFinger implementation works to extract profile information based on users' email addresses. From a command prompt, we enter the following:

```
curl http://gmail.com/.well-known/host-meta
```

When implementing this procedure in a product or service, you can use the PHP cURL library (*http://php.net/manual/en/book.curl.php*) or PycURL for Python (*http://pycurl.sourceforge.net/*).

The response that is returned will contain data about the URI template format that Google uses to obtain the user's profile from her email address:

```
<?xml version='1.0' encoding='UTF-8'?>
<!-- NOTE: this host-meta end-point is a pre-alpha work in progress.
     Don't rely on it. -->
<!-- Please follow the list at http://groups.google.com/group/webfinger -->
<XRD xmlns='http://docs.oasis-open.org/ns/xri/xrd-1.0'
     xmlns:hm='http://host-meta.net/xrd/1.0'>
  <hm:Host xmlns='http://host-meta.net/xrd/1.0'>gmail.com</hm:Host>
  <Link rel='lrdd'
        template='http://www.google.com/s2/webfinger/?q={uri}'>
    <Title>Resource Descriptor</Title>
  </Link>
</XRD>
```

From the preceding response object, we can see that the URI format Google uses is *http://www.google.com/s2/webfinger/?q={uri}*. Now, if we make another request to Google using that URI, substituting the *uri* parameter with our email address, we should be able to get a user's profile data.

We make the following request from the command line:

```
curl http://www.google.com/s2/webfinger/?q=nakedtechnologist@gmail.com
```

When we run this, we'll get the profile response from Google that will deliver the user's public profile data:

```xml
<?xml version='1.0'?>
<XRD xmlns='http://docs.oasis-open.org/ns/xri/xrd-1.0'>
    <Subject>acct:nakedtechnologist@gmail.com</Subject>
    <Alias>http://www.google.com/profiles/nakedtechnologist</Alias>
    <Link rel='http://portablecontacts.net/spec/1.0'
        href='http://www-opensocial.googleusercontent.com/api/people/'/>
    <Link rel='http://portablecontacts.net/spec/1.0#me'
        href='http://www-opensocial.googleusercontent.com/api/
            people/118167121283215553793/'/>
    <Link rel='http://webfinger.net/rel/profile-page'
        href='http://www.google.com/profiles/nakedtechnologist'
        type='text/html'/>
    <Link rel='http://microformats.org/profile/hcard'
        href='http://www.google.com/profiles/nakedtechnologist'
        type='text/html'/>
    <Link rel='http://gmpg.org/xfn/11'
        href='http://www.google.com/profiles/nakedtechnologist'
        type='text/html'/>
    <Link rel='http://specs.openid.net/auth/2.0/provider'
        href='http://www.google.com/profiles/nakedtechnologist'/>
    <Link rel='describedby'
        href='http://www.google.com/profiles/nakedtechnologist'
        type='text/html'/>
    <Link rel='describedby'
        href='http://www.google.com/s2/webfinger/?
            q=nakedtechnologist%40gmail.com&amp;fmt=foaf'
        type='application/rdf+xml'/>
    <Link rel='http://schemas.google.com/g/2010#updates-from'
        href='https://www.googleapis.com/buzz/v1/activities/
            118167121283215553793/@public' type='application/atom+xml'/>
</XRD>
```

From the return object, we can extract some data about the user:

The user profile
   http://www.google.com/profiles/nakedtechnologist

The portable contacts link
   http://www-opensocial.googleusercontent.com/api/people/
   118167121283215553793/

The public Google Buzz feed
   https://www.googleapis.com/buzz/v1/activities/118167121283215553793/@public

We can continue this process for any users that may have a public profile.

We can use this same approach to access similar data from other implementers of the WebFinger protocol. For instance, to access data from Yahoo!, we would make cURL requests to the following URIs:

- Information on WebFinger URI template: *http://www.yahoo.com/.well-known/host-meta*
- Obtaining user public information: *http://webfinger.yahooapis.com/?id={%id}*

This process is standard among implementers.

The Shortcomings of the WebFinger Protocol

While the WebFinger protocol's simplicity and ease of use is a tremendous boon for developers who simply want to capture some public profile information about a user, the protocol also has a number of shortcomings that we should address.

Public data

The WebFinger protocol is built around the concept of consuming user public data that the provider has decided to give out.

> Think of this concept in the same way as viewing the Facebook profile of a user whom you are not friends with and who doesn't share his information with anyone but his friends. You might see a basic badge containing his nickname and profile picture, but you will not be provided with all the privileged data that you might if you were using a protocol such as OAuth.

This concept is perfectly fine if you're just looking for account links or some basic profile information about a user to provide additional data about him—this is specifically what WebFinger *should* be used for.

The shortcomings arise when you want to access information outside the public realm. Understanding the limits of the protocol—and the fact that it is not a back door into a user's profile—will help you avoid being frustrated by the type of data that is returned to you.

Provider implementation differences

As mentioned at the beginning of our WebFinger discussion, there are several types of data that providers may make available through the WebFinger protocol, but it doesn't enforce these within the specification itself. In other words, WebFinger's purpose is enabling consumers to access public social information through well-known provider channels, not in dictating the kind of information that the providers need to make available. What this means in practice is that each provider may return different information, links, and data when you call their service.

This is not a problem when you're working with a single provider and expecting certain information back from it, but it becomes an increasingly complex issue when you're collecting data from multiple providers, as the response objects may be different.

Simply being aware of the content that a provider returns, and understanding that there will be differences from provider to provider, will help alleviate the issue of nonmatching response structures.

OExchange: Building a Social Sharing Graph

OExchange is an open protocol that can be used to share any URL-based content with any service on the Web. Put simply, OExchange is trying to build a standard way to share content from a publisher site to many different service providers like Twitter, Yahoo!, and Google (among others).

In a traditional integration model, if you have a site that includes content that you would like your users to be able to share with other services, you would need to integrate with these services individually. Normally, this would mean implementing just the top sharing services, such as Twitter, and would likely involve many tedious integrations just to make those few services available to your users. The questions that OExchange seeks to answer are:

- Why are we still integrating with services individually?
- Why don't we have a standard way to send updates to a sharing source?
- Why can't we add new services dynamically?

OExchange attempts to address these questions by delivering a standardized mechanism for sharing among content systems, giving the service provider more content and the publisher new outlets for its content.

How Does OExchange Work?

There are a few steps we must complete to get the entire OExchange process in place. There are two main actors that we will be working with here:

Service provider
> This is the site or service that allows users to share content (e.g., Twitter's "Tweet this" button for sharing a story on its site).

Publisher
> This is the site or service that implements a way for its users to share content from it to a service provider (e.g., the site that integrates the "Tweet this" button).

Here are the steps (illustrated in Figure 10-5), from a high level, that each actor will need to take to implement an end-to-end OExchange solution:

1. The service provider (target) integrates discovery and publishing tools.

   The service provider opens up an endpoint on its system to allow content to be posted through the OExchange process. It also integrates a discovery file containing all the information that a publisher needs to implement the provider's service and add discovery mechanisms on its site.

2. The publisher (source) performs discovery on the service provider.

   The publisher uses a variety of discovery methods to obtain the discovery file from the service provider. This enables the publisher to implement the service provider's sharing mechanism.

3. The publisher sends a content offer to the service provider.

   Once a user chooses to share some content through the service provider, the publisher will forward the user's browser session to the offer endpoint on the server provider site.

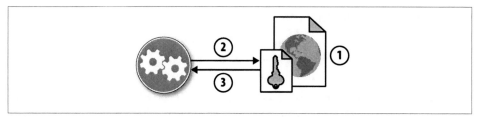

Figure 10-5. How OExchange works

At the end of the process, the user will be routed to the service provider site to share the offered content.

The Uses of OExchange

There are two primary uses for the OExchange protocol. For the service provider, it delivers a means of permitting other sites to push content to its site or service. When other sites integrate the service provider's sharing mechanism, they are sending more unique content to the service each time a user shares it.

For the publisher, it provides a simple means of offering its existing users new ways to share content with their favorite service providers and also attracts new users by pulling them from those services back to the publisher site—and it does all of this in a very standardized way, without the publisher having to integrate sharing methods for each service provider.

For instance, there are a number of "Share to [service]" widget systems currently available that implement the types of systems that OExchange seeks to standardize, such as AddThis (*http://www.addthis.com*; shown in Figure 10-6) and ShareThis (*http://www .sharethis.com*).

Figure 10-6. The AddThis sharing widget

While these are definitely extreme examples of service integrations, we can see how a publisher site could use the OExchange protocol to discover sharing information about a service provider in order to share its content with that service.

Using systems like OExchange, a site can generate many alternative outlets for its content, sharing out articles or documentation (or anything else it serves up) to many prime services, which may in turn deliver views and new users back to the site.

Implementing OExchange

Now that we have a broad understanding of how OExchange works and what its uses are, let's revisit the steps that we looked at in the section "How Does OExchange Work?" on page 414 and see how we can programmatically implement them.

We'll be looking at both the service provider and publisher implementations. While both sides provide a full overview of the steps, they may not both be required for every implementation—for example, if you're just consuming OExchange data from a service provider, or if you're the service provider yourself, providing the information to other publishers.

Let's start by looking at the service provider implementation.

1. Service provider (target) integrates discovery and publishing tools

 If you are using an existing service provider rather than implementing your own, there is no need to build your own OExchange service provider logic.

The service provider's first step in the OExchange process is to open up an endpoint on its service to which the publisher will forward the user's browser session via an HTTP GET request, passing through a number of different query string parameters.

This endpoint may look something similar to the following:

> *http://www.example.com/share.php?url={URI}*

The service provider can define its endpoint in any fashion it chooses (depending on factors such as whether the web stack uses file extensions), so it does not need to change its service architecture. This means that the endpoints may look like:

- *http://www.example.com/offer/share*
- *http://www.example.com/share.php?url={URI}*
- *http://www.example.com/share/?url={URI}*

or any number of other iterations, depending on what suits the service provider's web stack.

Next, the service provider needs to make its offer endpoint discoverable. We will use two methods to make this happen. First, we need to construct an eXtensible Resource Descriptor, or XRD, file (e.g., *oexchange.xrd*) that will allow a publisher to obtain icons, title, description, and a number of other values about a service.

This file will look something like the following:

```
<?xml version='1.0' encoding='UTF-8'?>
<XRD xmlns="http://docs.oasis-open.org/ns/xri/xrd-1.0">
    <Subject>http://www.oexchange.org/demo/linkeater</Subject>

    <Property type="http://www.oexchange.org/spec/0.8/prop/vendor">
        OExchange.org
    </Property>
    <Property type="http://www.oexchange.org/spec/0.8/prop/title">
        A Service that Eats Links
    </Property>
    <Property type="http://www.oexchange.org/spec/0.8/prop/name">
        LinkEater
    </Property>
    <Property type="http://www.oexchange.org/spec/0.8/prop/prompt">
        Send to LinkEater
    </Property>

    <Link rel= "icon"
        href="http://www.oexchange.org/images/linkeater_16x16.png"
        type="image/png" />
    <Link rel= "icon32"
        href="http://www.oexchange.org/images/linkeater_32x32.png"
        type="image/png" />

    <Link rel= "http://www.oexchange.org/spec/0.8/rel/offer"
        href="http://www.oexchange.org/demo/linkeater/offer.php"
        type="text/html" />
</XRD>
```

The first element and following property information will contain the subject of the service, vendor, title, name, and prompt for sending the user to the service. This will be followed by two link elements for the icons that a publisher may use on its sites to allow sharing to the service provider—one 16×16-pixel icon and one 32×32–pixel icon. The final link element contains the offer endpoint that the service provider has opened up on its service to allow a publisher to submit a content offer. This file may be stored anywhere on the service provider.

 To help you easily create an XRD file, OExchange has a discovery re-source generator tool available at *http://www.oexchange.org/tools/dis coverygen/*. You simply enter in the basic information about the service, and the XRD file is automatically generated.

To make this XRD file discoverable, you can add an HTML `<link>` tag to any page on your site or service that points to the specific XRD file:

```
<link rel="http://oexchange.org/spec/0.8/rel/related-target"
      type="application/xrd+xml"
      href="http://www.example.com/linkeater/oexchange.xrd" />
```

Finally, the service provider may add a link for the XRD file to the site's */.well-known/ host-meta* file. This will allow third-party services to retrieve a reference to the XRD file from the service provider's hostname. This *host-meta* file may look something like the following:

```
<?xml version='1.0' encoding='UTF-8'?>
<XRD xmlns='http://docs.oasis-open.org/ns/xri/xrd-1.0'
     xmlns:hm='http://host-meta.net/xrd/1.0'>
    <hm:Host>www.oexchange.org</hm:Host>

    <!--
        An OExchange Target is available on this host
    -->
    <Link
        rel="http://oexchange.org/spec/0.8/rel/resident-target"
        type="application/xrd+xml"
        href="http://www.oexchange.org/demo/linkeater/oexchange.xrd" >
    </Link>
</XRD>
```

Even though the discovery pieces are optional, it is recommended that you make the discovery services available to allow publishers and developers to locate and use your service.

2. Publisher (source) performs discovery on service provider

The next stage in the process takes place when a publisher wants to test whether a service provider that it is interested in extending a content offer to even supports the OExchange specification.

To allow you to easily discover whether a site or service implements OExchange and has an available XRD file, you can use the OExchange discovery test harness tool at *http://www.oexchange.org/tools/discovery harness/*. This tool also allows you to extract all data from an XRD file directly.

There are several defined methods for determining whether a service provider supports OExchange and for obtaining the title, icons, and offer endpoint that will be required in order to integrate it into another site or service.

Directly via the XRD file. The first method that a publisher can employ to gather information about the service provider's offer endpoint is directly through the XRD file that the provider has set up, assuming the publisher has the direct discovery link, such as *http://twitter.com/oexchange.xrd*.

Even though the XRD file may be placed at any location on its site, a provider should maintain that file at a consistent location, since it is the most direct method publishers can use to obtain the data required for the OExchange process.

Through hostname discovery. The second method a publisher may employ is using the *.well-known/host-meta* file on a site, such as *http://twitter.com/.well-known/host-meta*. This is an XRD file a service provider creates to describe the services that it makes available through simple HTTP requests on that host.

As we saw in the service provider setup section, the service provider may integrate a link to the OExchange XRD file, such as:

```
<Link rel="http://oexchange.org/spec/0.8/rel/resident-target"
      type="application/xrd+xml"
      href="http://www.oexchange.org/demo/linkeater/oexchange.xrd" >
</Link>
```

A publisher can thus obtain the XRD file and perform discovery to acquire all the information required to integrate a service provider in its offer listing.

Through individual page discovery. The final option we'll cover is for a service provider to integrate an HTML <link> within the pages on its site. This method would allow a publisher to poll a particular page on a site on which it would like to perform discovery, and obtain a link to the OExchange XRD file in the same way as with the *.well-known/host-meta* file option.

The <link> tag would look something like the following:

```
<link rel="http://oexchange.org/spec/0.8/rel/related-target"
      type="application/xrd+xml"
      href="http://www.example.com/linkeater/oexchange.xrd" />
```

3. Publisher sends content offer to service provider

Now that the publisher has performed discovery on the service provider that it would like its users to be able to share content with, it can enable its users to send content offers to the service provider. This allows the users to share the publisher's site-specific information with that service, such as how clicking a "Tweet this article" button on a news site may post the article's title and link out to Twitter.

Since we have already obtained the offer URL on the provider from the XRD file during discovery, we simply need to forward the user's browser session to the offer URL, passing along any parameters that may be needed to define the content offer.

Looking at this further, from the provider's XRD file we have obtained the following piece of information about the offer URL:

```
<Link rel= "http://www.oexchange.org/spec/0.8/rel/offer"
     href="http://www.oexchange.org/demo/linkeater/offer.php"
     type="text/html" />
```

Using the offer URL, *http://www.oexchange.org/demo/linkeater/offer.php*, we will build an HTTP GET URL string containing the parameters that define the content offer via the query string. Our final URL string will look similar to the following:

```
http://www.oexchange.org/demo/linkeater/offer.php?url=http://example.com/...
```

There are a number of parameters that we can apply to the URL string in order to define the content of the offer. These are listed in Table 10-12.

Table 10-12. Content offer parameters

Parameter	Description
url (required)	The URL that uniquely identifies the content being shared. This should be navigable from within a browser.
title (optional)	A human-readable string denoting the title of the content, much like the `<title>` meta tag of a web page.
description (optional)	A human-readable string denoting the description of the content, much like the `<description>` meta tag of a web page.
tags (optional)	A comma-delimited list of additional parameters that a target can use to further define the content being provided.
	Note that parameters containing a comma must be placed in double quotes (e.g., foo, bar, "San Francisco, CA").
ctype (optional)	Additional information on the type of the content being shared. The default is link.

The content type of an offer depends on the presence or absence of the ctype parameter. If this parameter is present, then the offer will accept additional parameters, which are dictated by the type being defined. These may additionally include other related URLs. If the ctype parameter is absent from the offer, then its value will default to link.

Even though the `ctype` parameter is optional, properly defining the type of content being shared will help the target site integrate it in a proper fashion (e.g., embedding shared image content within an `<img>` tag).

There are a number of types that may be defined for the `ctype` parameter, as listed in Table 10-13.

Table 10-13. Possible values for the ctype parameter

ctype	Description

flash	A Flash movie object that may be directly embedded by the target once received. This `ctype` definition supports the following additional parameters:
	
	`swfurl`
	The direct URL to the actual Flash resource, including any additional parameters required.
	
	`screenshot`
	A URI for an image representation of the Flash content. The image should be able to be rendered at the same size as the Flash object.
	
	`height`
	The preferred height of the Flash object.
	
	`width`
	The preferred width of the Flash object.

iframe	This `ctype` denotes that the content can be directly embedded within an iframe on the target side, such as an HTML source page. `iframe` supports the following additional parameters:
	
	`iframeurl`
	The URL that should be used as the source of the iframe.
	
	`screenshot`
	A screenshot representation of the iframe content. The image should be suitable for being displayed at the same size as the iframe.
	
	`height`
	The preferred height of the iframe.
	
	`width`
	The preferred width of the iframe.

image	The `image` ctype defines a simple web-renderable image. It supports the following additional parameters:
	
	`imageurl`
	The direct URL to the image resource.
	
	`height`
	The preferred height of the image.
	
	`width`
	The preferred width of the image.

link	Since this is the default value, its definition is not required. It denotes that the content is limited to the user-browsable URL defined in the content offer.

Once the full URL has been defined, the publisher will forward the user to the service provider URL via the browser. At this point, the service provider will have control over the browser session and can utilize the content as it sees fit. Generally, this will involve confirming that the user is logged in and having her verify the content of the post prior to publication.

 Even though the user must be forwarded to the service provider, the specification does not dictate how. The publisher may simply forward the user from its site to that of the service provider, launch a new tab or window through the use of a `_blank` link, open a pop-up window, or any number of other methods.

PubSubHubbub: Content Syndication

The PubSubHubbub (*Pub*lisher-*Sub*scriber *Hub*) protocol seeks to define how content systems syndicate user correspondence from a source site to a number of subdelivery sites. Using this method, sites can augment their comments with syndicated feeds from other sites, giving their users a much wider range of social interaction than they would experience from a single source.

Applying a distributed approach to server-to-server communication, a centralized hub between a provider and subscriber acts as a communication channel between the two. This makes it easier for a single provider to produce updates to content, as those updates will be syndicated out to many different subscribers at the same time, keeping each source in sync.

How Does PubSubHubbub Work?

The functional process outlined in the PubSubHubbub specification is fairly simple, involving only a series of requests and responses among these three parties:

Publisher
> The site or service that is publishing content that someone may want to syndicate at a different location.

Hub
> The middle layer between the publisher and subscriber. All communication between subscriber and publisher is routed through the hub.

Subscriber
> The site(s) that are interested in the content being produced or updated from the publisher.

The hub acts as a mechanism for syndicating content updates from a publisher out to one or more subscribers. Thus, the publisher avoids repeated polling for new or updated content.

With our players in place, we can look at how they interact with one another. The PubSubHubbub process comprising these parties is not time based, so it might take place over a long period of time. This subscription flow takes us through several steps, which we'll cover next.

1. Subscriber polls publisher's feed

Our starting point looks exactly like the traditional flow of a subscriber polling a publisher to obtain new or updated content, as shown in Figure 10-7.

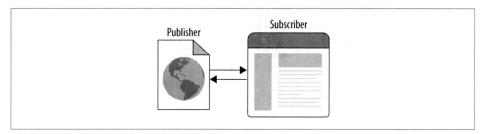

Figure 10-7. PubSubHubbub, step 1: Subscriber polls publisher's feed

The difference here is in the response object that the publisher sends back to the subscriber. This response will include a forward link to the hub—which the subscriber will use in the future to obtain updates from the publisher—in the Atom or RSS XML file. This link is in the form `<link rel="hub" ...>`.

2. Subscriber requests subscription to the publisher's feed updates from the hub

Now that the subscriber has the link to the hub, it issues an HTTP POST request to that URI. Figure 10-8 illustrates this transaction.

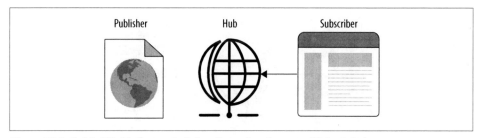

Figure 10-8. PubSubHubbub, step 2: Subscriber subscribes to publisher's hub

In this step, the subscriber requests a subscription to the publisher's updates. In the POST request, the subscriber specifies an endpoint URI indicating where the hub should POST new updates to.

3. Hub verifies subscriber and request

To protect itself against malicious requests, such as DoS (Denial of Service) attacks, the hub will first make a POST request back to the subscriber to verify its identity prior to processing the subscription. The subscriber sends a confirmation response back to the hub to prove that it is a valid subscriber party, demonstrated in Figure 10-9.

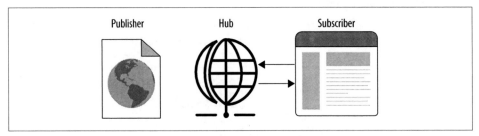

Figure 10-9. PubSubHubbub, step 3: Hub verifies subscriber's subscription request

At this point, the subscriber has subscribed to the hub and will be notified when there are new updates from the publisher. There may be many subscribers that go through this process, meaning that there is a one-to-many relationship between the publisher and its subscribers.

4. Publisher notifies hub of content updates

Once the publisher has some new content that it wants to syndicate out to all of its subscribers, it notifies the hub by issuing a POST request containing the updated feed URLs to the hub. The hub then makes a request back to the publisher requesting the content delivered at the feed URL locations. The publisher responds with the requested content. Figure 10-10 shows this flow.

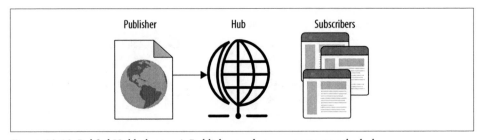

Figure 10-10. PubSubHubbub, step 4: Publisher pushes new content to the hub

If the publisher does not inform the hub when content changes have been made, the hub will periodically poll the publisher's feed for new updates. Either way, we now have the updated content on the hub.

5. Hub shares new content with subscribers

Once the hub receives the updates from the publisher, it can notify all subscribers that are subscribed to the feed for updates. Figure 10-11 shows this flow; the hub issues a POST request containing the update to the endpoint that the subscriber specified when it first subscribed.

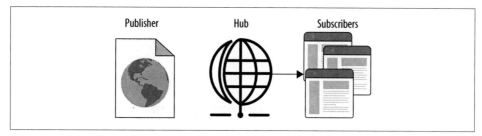

Figure 10-11. PubSubHubbub, step 5: Hub pushes updated content to subscribers

We now have updates pushed from the publisher to the subscriber.

The Benefits: From Publishers to Subscribers

The PubSubHubbub specification offers a number of benefits to both publishers and subscribers for using a distributed hub-based system. Let's take a look at a few.

Publisher: No repeated polling from multiple sources

The major benefit that publishers gain from this type of system is the fact that subscribers no longer need to periodically poll the publisher to check for updates to content they are interested in. A single subscriber making requests at regular intervals does not incur a lot of load, but if there are thousands of subscribers all continually requesting updated content from the publisher at regular intervals, it's easy to imagine how heavy the load can get on the publisher's side.

This burden on the publisher wouldn't be so bad if subscribers only made single requests once the content has changed, but the only way for subscribers to know that is to make a request to the provider, creating a Catch-22 situation. This is the point, and role, of the hub in this specification. Subscribers subscribe to the hub only once for a given feed, and when the publisher pushes updates to the hub, it will in turn notify the subscribers of the update. Although the hub may periodically poll the publisher's feeds if the publisher does not notify the hub of updates, this is only a single request source for a potentially large number of subscribers.

Subscriber: No need for repeated polling

On the other side of the fence, the largest benefit from the subscriber side is exactly the same as that of the publisher: there is no need to repeatedly poll the publisher for new updates.

In the past, if the subscriber wanted to get updated content from a publisher, it would need to periodically poll the publisher to obtain the content that it was interested in. In this polling request, the content may or may not have changed, so it was up to the subscriber to determine whether any update action was needed on its side. This is a highly inefficient system that wastes requests and processing resources for content that may not have even changed.

With the hub in place, however, the subscriber only needs to make a single request to subscribe to a publisher's feeds, specifying the update URI that the hub should POST updates to when the publisher updates any content. The subscriber simply waits for something to be POSTed to that endpoint and processes it once it arrives.

Publisher and subscriber: Identical content across multiple subscribers

Another core benefit to the distributed hub system stems from the fact that the hub will push out the same updated content to all subscribers. This means that any changes to the content will be viewed in the exact same way, no matter which source the user chooses to view that content with.

To put this in practical terms, let's say we have two subscribers subscribing to an article and comment thread on a provider site. Without a hub to control the flow of updates to all of the interested parties, it is up to the subscribers to manage how often they look for new comments on the article. This might mean that one of the parties is seeing vastly different comments from the other, creating individual silos out of each site.

With the hub in place, once new comments are posted or updates to the article are introduced, the provider can simply update the hub, which in turn updates all sub-scribers to that content.

This model creates a uniform series of sites that all reap the benefits of sharing identical content.

Hosted Hubs and Implementation Services

Implementers of the PubSubHubbub specification can create their own hosted hub solutions, but for those who would like to work off what is currently available in the market, there are a number of hubs and implementation services to choose from.

Anyone can create a PubSubHubbub server, and if an open hub is available, anyone can use it. Here are several of the implementation services and hosted hubs currently available:

- Google App Engine reference hub: *http://pubsubhubbub.appspot.com/*
- Superfeedr hosted hub: *http://superfeedr.com/hubbub*
- SubHub Django integrated hub: *https://code.launchpad.net/subhub*
- Ayup hosted hub: *http://ayup.us/*
- WordPress plug-in: *http://wordpress.org/extend/plugins/pushpress/*
- RabbitHub erlang implementation: *https://github.com/tonyg/rabbithub/#readme*
- Wolverine Twisted Python implementation: *https://github.com/progrium/wolverine#readme*
- WebGlue Ruby implementation: *https://github.com/zh/webglue#readme*
- Subfeedr Perl implementation: *https://github.com/miyagawa/Subfeedr#readme*
- PubSubHubbub: *https://github.com/barinek/pubsubhubbub-rb#readme*

These are excellent starting points for both leveraging hosted open hub solutions and utilizing current implementation examples of the project.

Workflow Libraries

There are a number of current libraries that allow you to quickly and easily build out the subscriber or publishers pieces of the PubSubHubbub workflow.

Subscriber clients

These subscriber clients will allow you to subscribe a site or service, via the hub, to a feed from the publisher:

- .NET: *http://code.google.com/p/npubsubhubbub/*
- Haskell: *http://hackage.haskell.org/package/pubsub-0.10*
- Java: *http://code.google.com/p/pubsubhubbub-java/downloads/*
- PHP: *http://github.com/lxbarth/PuSHSubscriber*
- Ruby on Rails: *http://github.com/empika/Superfeedr-PubSubHubbub-Rails-Plugin*
- Scala: *http://github.com/kafecho/scala-push*

For more information on the subscribers and alternative frameworks and CMS systems, visit *http://code.google.com/p/pubsubhubbub/wiki/SubscriberClients*.

Publisher clients

There are also a number of publisher clients available for use. These will allow you to implement feeds on a site that subscribers will be able to subscribe to via a hub. They will work to notify the hub of new updates from the publisher.

- C#: *http://code.google.com/p/pubsubhubbub-publisherclient-csharp/*
- Haskell: *http://hackage.haskell.org/package/pubsub-0.10*

- Java: *http://code.google.com/p/pubsubhubbub-java/*
- Perl: *http://search.cpan.org/~bradfitz/Net-PubSubHubbub-Publisher/*
- PHP: *http://code.google.com/p/pubsubhubbub/source/browse/#svn/trunk/publisher _clients/php*
- Python: *http://pypi.python.org/pypi/PubSubHubbub_Publisher/1.0*
- Ruby: *http://github.com/igrigorik/PubSubHubbub/tree/master*

For more information on the publisher clients and alternative plug-ins that are available, visit the publisher list at *http://code.google.com/p/pubsubhubbub/wiki/Publisher Clients*.

Building a Publisher in PHP

 The full code for this sample is available at *https://github.com/jcleblanc/ programming-social-applications/tree/master/chapter_10/pubsubhub bub-publisher-php*.

For a closer look at this specification, let's explore how to implement a publisher in the PubSubHubbub workflow using PHP.

We'll start with the Publisher class, which will provide us with all of the feed publishing functionality that we will need for this process. In this example, this file is stored as *publisher.php*:

```php
<?php
/*
 * Class: PubSubHubbub Publisher
 * Description: Allows for the publishing of new updates to the hub
 */
class Publisher{
    private $regex_url = '|^https?://|i';        //simple URL string validator
    private $hub = '';                           //hub URL

    //constructor that stores the hub and callback URLs for the subscriber
    public function __construct($hub){
        if (preg_match($this->regex_url, $hub)){ $this->hub = $hub; }
        else{ throw new Exception('Invalid hub URL supplied'); }
    }

    //makes request to hub to subscribe / unsubscribe
    public function publish($feeds){
        //set up POST string with mode
        $post_string = 'hub.mode=publish';

        //loop through each feed provided
        foreach ($feeds as $feed){
            //if feed is valid, add to POST string
            if (preg_match($this->regex_url, $feed)){
```

```
        $post_string .= '&hub.url=' . urlencode($feed);
    } else {
        throw new Exception('Invalid hub URL supplied');
    }
}

//set up cURL request
$ch = curl_init($this->hub);
$options = array(
    CURLOPT_HEADER => true,
    CURLINFO_HEADER_OUT => true,
    CURLOPT_VERBOSE => true,
    CURLOPT_RETURNTRANSFER => true,
    CURLOPT_POSTFIELDS => $post_string,
    CURLOPT_CUSTOMREQUEST => 'POST'
);
curl_setopt_array($ch, $options);

//make request to hub
$response = curl_exec($ch);
curl_close($ch);

//return response
return $response;
    }
}
?>
```

The Publisher class contains two methods: the constructor and the method to publish. When a new instance of the class is created and the constructor is called with a URL for the hub, it will simply check to ensure that the hub URL is valid and then store it.

When we call the publish method, we will start out by setting a base for our POST string that will be sent with the publish request to the hub. The hub expects a couple of parameters:

hub.mode
    This should be set to publish for the publishing action.

hub.url
    For each feed that should be updated, there should be a hub.url parameter.

We set the mode first, since it is a static value. We then loop through all feeds provided to the publish method, checking if each is a valid URL. If the URLs are valid, a new hub.mode parameter will be appended to the POST string; if invalid, an exception will be thrown.

We then make a cURL POST request, passing in the POST string, to the hub URL and return the response. A valid HTTP code response from the hub should be 204, but anything in the 2xx range will be accepted.

Now let's look at a quick implementation of this class:

```php
<?php
include("publisher.php");

//define hub and feeds
$hub = 'http://pubsubhubbub.appspot.com/';
$feeds = array('http://www.example.com/feed1.xml',
               'http://www.example.com/feed2.xml',
               'http://www.example.com/feed3.xml');

//create new subscriber
$publisher = new Publisher($hub);

//publish feeds
$response = $publisher->publish($feed);

//print response
var_dump($response);
?>
```

After including the Publisher class file, we define our hub URL and an array of the feeds that we would like to publish updates for. We then create a new instance of the Publisher class, passing in our hub URL variable. Once we've created this new instance, we can simply call the publish(...) method, passing in our feeds. The response from that method call should tell us the success state. For this example, we dump that response.

Building a Publisher in Python

 The full code for this sample is available at *https://github.com/jcleblanc/programming-social-applications/tree/master/chapter_10/pubsubhubbub-publisher-python*.

Now that we have looked at a publisher implementation in PHP, let's explore the same implementation using Python for an alternate vantage point.

For this example, the classes that make up the publisher are stored in a file named *publisher.py*:

```python
import re
import urllib
import urllib2

'''
' Class: Publishing Error
' Description: Custom error class for publishing exceptions
'''
class PublishError(Exception):
    def __init__(self, value):
        self.value = value
    def __str__(self):
```

```
        return repr(self.value)

'''
' Class: Publisher
' Description: Provides ability to publish updates for feeds
'''
class Publisher:
    regex_url = re.compile('^https?://')    #simple URL string validator

    #constructor that stores the hub for the publisher
    def __init__(self, hub):
        if self.regex_url.match(hub): self.hub = hub
        else: raise PublishError('Invalid hub URL supplied')

    #makes request to hub to update feeds
    def publish(self, feeds):
        #set the POST string mode
        post_string = 'hub.mode=publish'

        #add each feed as a URL in the POST string, unless invalid URL
        for feed in feeds:
            if self.regex_url.match(feed):
                post_string += '&hub.url=%s' % (urllib.quote(feed))
            else:
                raise PublishError('Invalid feed URL supplied: %s' % (feed))

        try:
            #make request to hub
            file = urllib2.urlopen(self.hub, post_string)
            return True
        except (IOError, urllib2.HTTPError), e:
            #process http conditions in 2xx range as valid
            if hasattr(e, 'code') and str(e.code)[0] == '2':
                return True

            #process alternative error conditions
            error = ''
            if hasattr(e, 'read'):
                error = e.read()
            raise PublishError('%s, Response: "%s"' % (e, error))
```

This file contains two classes, PublishError and Publisher. The purpose of Publish
Error is simply to provide a custom exception class to push out exceptions in the
publisher flow.

The Publisher class mirrors that of the PHP example, providing us with a constructor
and a method to publish our feeds. Once a new instance of the class is instantiated, the
constructor will simply check that the hub URL provided is valid. If it is, the URL will
be stored; otherwise, an exception is thrown.

When we call the publish method, we will start out by setting a base for the POST
string that will be sent with the publish request to the hub. The hub expects a couple
of parameters:

`hub.mode`

This should be set to `publish` for the publishing action.

`hub.url`

For each feed that should be updated, there should be a `hub.url` parameter.

We then loop through each feed provided in the feeds list. We check to ensure that the feed is valid and, if so, append a new `hub.url` parameter to the end of the POST string. If the feed is invalid, an exception is thrown.

Last, we try to make a POST request to the hub URL, passing in the POST string. If there were no errors produced, we simply return `True`. If errors are produced, we check whether the HTTP response was in the 2*xx* range. If so, we treat this as a valid response. If not, we throw an appropriate exception.

Now let's see how we can use the `Publisher` class:

```
from publisher import *

#define hub and feeds
hub = 'http://pubsubhubbub.appspot.com/'
feeds = ['http://www.example.com/feed1.xml',
         'http://www.example.com/feed2.xml',
         'http://www.example.com/feed3.xml']

#create new publisher
publisher = Publisher(hub)

#publish feed updates: response == True on success
response = publisher.publish(feeds)

#print message on success
if (response == True):
    print 'Content-Type: text/plain'
    print ''
    print 'Update successful'
```

We start the example by importing the class file and then defining the hub URL and the URLs for the feeds that we want to publish updates for. We then create a new instance of the `Publisher` class, passing in the hub URL, and then call the `publish` (...) method, passing in the feed list. If the response from that call is `True`, then the process completed successfully and we print out the appropriate message.

Building a Subscriber in PHP

 The full code for this sample is available at *https://github.com/jcleblanc/ programming-social-applications/tree/master/chapter_10/pubsubhub bub-subscriber-php*.

At this point, we've already explored how to set up publishers in both PHP and Python, so let's change gears now and build a subscriber in both languages. We'll start with PHP.

For this example, the subscriber file is stored as *subscriber.php*:

```php
<?php
/*
 * Class: Subscriber
 * Description: Provides ability to subscribe / unsubscribe from hub feeds
 */
class Subscriber{
    private $regex_url = '|^https?://|i';     //simple URL string validator
    private $hub = '';                        //hub URL
    private $callback = '';                   //callback URL

    //constructor that stores the hub and callback URLs for the subscriber
    public function __construct($hub, $callback){
        if (preg_match($this->regex_url, $hub)){ $this->hub = $hub; }
        else{ throw new Exception('Invalid hub URL supplied'); }

        if (preg_match($this->regex_url, $callback)){ $this->callback = $callback; }
        else{ throw new Exception('Invalid callback URL supplied'); }
    }

    //initiates a request to subscribe to a feed
    public function subscribe($feed){
        return $this->change_subscription('subscribe', $feed);
    }

    //initiates a request to unsubscribe from a feed
    public function unsubscribe($feed){
        return $this->change_subscription('unsubscribe', $feed);
    }

    //makes request to hub to subscribe / unsubscribe
    public function change_subscription($mode='subscribe', $feed){
        //check if provided feed is a valid URL
        if (preg_match($this->regex_url, $feed)){
            //set the post string for subscribe / unsubscribe
            $post_string = "hub.mode=$mode
                            &hub.callback={$this->callback}
                            &hub.verify=async
                            &hub.topic=$feed";

            //set up cURL request
            $ch = curl_init($this->hub);
            $options = array(
                CURLOPT_HEADER => true,
                CURLINFO_HEADER_OUT => true,
                CURLOPT_VERBOSE => true,
                CURLOPT_RETURNTRANSFER => true,
                CURLOPT_POSTFIELDS => $post_string,
                CURLOPT_CUSTOMREQUEST => 'POST'
            );
```

```
        curl_setopt_array($ch, $options);

        //make request to hub
        $response = curl_exec($ch);
        curl_close($ch);

        //return response
        return $response;
    } else {
        throw new Exception('Invalid feed URL supplied');
    }
  }
}
?>
```

The Subscriber class contains a number of methods that we will be using. When the class is first instantiated with a hub and callback URL, the constructor will be called. The purpose of the constructor is simply to check that the hub and callback are valid URLs. If they are valid, they are stored; otherwise, the appropriate exception message is thrown.

The purpose of both the subscribe(...) and unsubscribe(...) methods is simply to act as helper methods for an implementer. They will accept a feed on which the action should be taken and then call the change_subscription(...) method with the appropriate subscription mode, either subscribe or unsubscribe.

When unsubscribe is called, we ensure that the feed parameter is a valid URL. If it is, we start constructing the POST string that will be sent to the hub. This will consist of:

hub.mode
> The subscription mode to run, either subscribe or unsubscribe

hub.callback
> The callback URL on the subscriber site, to which new feed updates from the publisher should be POSTed

hub.verify
> The verify mode, either sync or async

hub.topic
> The feed URL

We then initiate a cURL POST request to the hub to perform the action against the hub. The response from the request is returned.

Now let's see this class in use:

```
<?php
include("subscriber.php");

//define hub, callback and feed
$hub = 'http://pubsubhubbub.appspot.com/';
$callback = 'http://www.example.com/publish';
$feed = 'http://www.example.com';
```

```
//create new subscriber
$subscriber = new Subscriber($hub, $callback);

//subscribe / unsubscribe methods
$response = $subscriber->subscribe($feed);
//$response = $subscriber->unsubscribe($feed);

//print response
var_dump($response);
?>
```

We include the class file and then define the URLs for the hub, callback, and feed. We then create a new Subscriber(...) object, passing in the hub and callback. Once the object is created, we can call either our subscribe or unsubscribe method, passing in the feed URL. The response from either method will be dumped out.

Building a Subscriber in Python

 The full code for this sample is available at *https://github.com/jcleblanc/ programming-social-applications/tree/master/chapter_10/pubsubhub bub-subscriber-python*.

Now let's explore the same subscriber implementation, but now using Python. For this example, the subscriber classes are stored in a file name *subscriber.py*:

```
import re
import urllib
import urllib2

'''
' Class: Subscription Error
' Description: Custom error class for subscription exceptions
'''
class SubscribeError(Exception):
    def __init__(self, value):
        self.value = value
    def __str__(self):
        return repr(self.value)

'''
' Class: Subscriber
' Description: Provides ability to subscribe / unsubscribe from hub feeds
'''
class Subscriber:
    regex_url = re.compile('^https?://')    #simple URL string validator

    #constructor that stores the hub and callback URLs for the subscriber
    def __init__(self, hub, callback):
        if self.regex_url.match(hub): self.hub = hub
        else: raise SubscribeError('Invalid hub URL supplied')
```

```
        if self.regex_url.match(callback): self.callback = callback
        else: raise SubscribeError('Invalid callback URL supplied')

    #initiates a request to subscribe to a feed
    def subscribe(self, feed):
        return self.change_subscription('subscribe', feed)

    #initiates a request to unsubscribe from a feed
    def unsubscribe(self, feed):
        return self.change_subscription('unsubscribe', feed)

    #makes request to hub to subscribe / unsubscribe
    def change_subscription(self, mode, feed):
        #check if provided feed is a valid URL
        if self.regex_url.match(feed):
            #set the post string for subscribe / unsubscribe
            post_string = 'hub.mode=%s&hub.callback=%s&hub.verify=async&hub.topic=%s'
                        % (mode, self.callback, urllib.quote(feed))

            try:
                #make return to hub
                file = urllib2.urlopen(self.hub, post_string)
                return True
            except (IOError, urllib2.HTTPError), e:
                #process http conditions in 2xx range as valid
                if hasattr(e, 'code') and str(e.code)[0] == '2':
                    return True

                #process alternative error conditions
                error = ''
                if hasattr(e, 'read'):
                    error = e.read()
                raise SubscribeError('%s, Response: "%s"' % (e, error))
        else:
            raise SubscribeError('Invalid feed URL supplied')
```

Just like with the Python publisher, the subscriber file has a custom exception class, SubscribeError, whose purpose is to output exceptions that are encountered during the execution of the subscription.

When a new instance of the Subscriber class is created, the constructor will be called. The constructor's purpose is to accept URLs for the hub and callback, check that they are valid, and store them if valid or display exceptions if they're not.

The subscribe(...) and unsubscribe(...) methods are helper methods that accept a feed URL and then call the change_subscription(...) method with the appropriate mode for the action to be taken, either subscribe or unsubscribe.

change_subscription(...) is used to make the request to the hub to subscribe to a feed. We start by checking if the feed URL provided is valid. If so, we start constructing the POST string that will be sent to the hub. It will consist of:

`hub.mode`
> The subscription mode to run, either `subscribe` or `unsubscribe`

`hub.callback`
> The callback URL on the subscriber site, to which new feed updates from the publisher should be POSTed

`hub.verify`
> The verify mode, either `sync` or `async`

`hub.topic`
> The feed URL

We then issue a POST request to the hub URL, passing in the POST string. If the request completes successfully, we return `True`. If an error is thrown, we handle it by first checking the HTTP response code. If the code is in the 2*xx* range, we treat it as a valid response and return `True`. A valid response should be an HTTP 202 code, but anything in the 2*xx* range is a success. If the code isn't in that range, we throw an exception with the appropriate error response.

Now let's see how we can use these classes to build a subscriber:

```
from subscriber import *

#define hub, callback and feed
hub = 'http://pubsubhubbub.appspot.com/'
callback = 'http://www.example.com/publish'
feed = 'http://www.example.com'

#create new subscriber
subscriber = Subscriber(hub, callback)

#subscribe / unsubscribe methods: response == True on success
response = subscriber.subscribe(feed)
#response = subscriber.unsubscribe(feed)

#print message on success
if (response == True):
    print 'Content-Type: text/plain'
    print ''
    print 'Request successful'
```

We start by importing the subscriber file that we created earlier and then define the URLs for our hub, callback, and the feed that we will be performing the action on. Next, we create a new `Subscriber` object, passing in the hub and callback. Using that new object, we call either the `subscribe(...)` or `unsubscribe(...)` methods, passing in the feed URL. Last, we check the response from the called method and, if `True`, display a message stating that the request was successful.

The Salmon Protocol: Unification of Conversation Entities

Aimed at extending the benefits while mitigating the shortcomings of social aggregation systems like PubSubHubbub, the Salmon protocol seeks to unify the conversation threads from source publishers through to distributed layers and subscribers.

Where publishers may use protocols like PubSubHubbub to easily and efficiently syndicate their content out to many different subscribers, Salmon seeks to further unify these sources by building a communications network where the conversations happening across many different networks can be synced.

The Salmon Protocol Workflow

The Salmon protocol itself simply defines methods for unifying conversations and updated content among a series of sites or services. Its workflow includes two main actors that will be communicating back and forth:

Publisher (source)
> The site or services containing the content and conversation entities that other sites subscribe to or aggregate

Subscriber (aggregator)
> The sites or services that aggregate the content and conversations from the publisher, syndicating out that content on their own sites

The communication between these two entities spans several different steps, which we'll cover next.

1. Publisher pushes updated content to subscriber

At the first stage of the process, the publisher updates its content or has updates to its discussion threads. It pushes these updates through to its subscribers via a communication method such as PubSubHubbub so that the subscribers may update their content. Figure 10-12 shows this full flow—from the publisher through the hub to the subscribers.

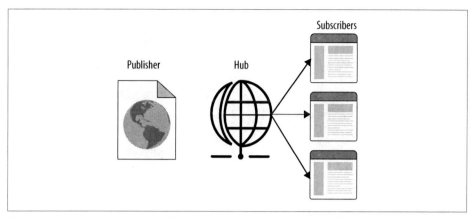

Figure 10-12. Salmon, step 1: Publisher pushes updated content to subscribers through hub (e.g., PubSubHubbub)

This step mirrors the communication step between publisher and subscriber that we saw in the PubSubHubbub protocol, where a centralized hub controls the flow of updates from publisher to subscriber.

When the content is pushed to the subscriber, it contains a link parameter with a callback URI on the publisher side that will be used to push content back upstream from subscriber to publisher.

The subscriber takes the new content and updates the version on its site or service so that it is in sync with the publisher. The callback URI provided in the update feed is stored for later use.

Subscriber pushes updated content back upstream to publisher

Once the content on the subscriber site or service is updated (e.g., new comments), the subscriber will retrieve the Salmon callback URI for the publisher and push its updated content back to the publisher via an HTTP POST request, as shown in Figure 10-13.

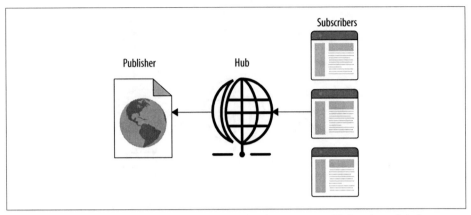

Figure 10-13. Salmon, step 2: Subscriber pushes updated content to publisher through hub

At this point, the publisher will need to implement a verification mechanism to ensure that the subscriber is a trusted source. If the subscriber is indeed trusted, then the publisher will integrate the changes back into its content.

Publisher pushes updated content to all subscribers

Once the new content is integrated back into the publisher site or service, that publisher will issue another call to all subscribers with the new updates so that they may all update their versions to the new unified content. Figure 10-14 shows this transaction.

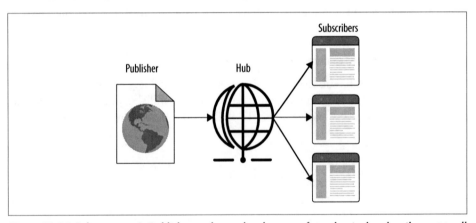

Figure 10-14. Salmon, step 3: Publisher pushes updated content from the single subscriber out to all subscribers

As with the first step, the publisher may use mechanisms such as PubSubHubbub to push content through to a series of subscribers.

Building on the Foundation of PubSubHubbub

We've already seen how the PubSubHubbub protocol can be used to easily push out updates from a publisher to a series of subscribers, but there is one piece missing in its flow.

Let's use a practical example to identify this issue. Say a news publisher has a comment widget placed on each news story to allow people to discuss the topic being displayed. This publisher uses a centralized PubSubHubbub hub to push out updates to the content and any recent comments on the article to all subscribers to its feed.

This process works perfectly well to ensure that all of the feed subscribers have the most up-to-date content from the publisher, but what happens if the subscriber site uses the updated comments to augment its existing comment flow? The subscriber may have users of its own that are continuing the conversation beyond what is reflected on the publisher site. If there are many subscribers, this equates to many different conversations seeded with comments from the feed of a publisher that isn't aware of what is being said in those conversations.

This is one such instance where the Salmon protocol can play a vital role. It can unify the conversation threads between the publisher and a series of trusted subscribers. In doing so, it aggregates these fragmented conversations into a single discussion within an interrelated network of sites.

Abuse and Spam Protection

One of the largest challenges with this protocol has to do with preventing abuse and spam when the subscribers communicate updates back to the publisher. There are a few concerns that we need to address here:

1. How can the publisher ensure that the updated content is coming from a trusted source?
2. How can the publisher prevent spam or abuse if it is accepting content from a number of subscribers?
3. How can the publisher ensure the quality of the updates?

The Salmon protocol seeks to solve these problems by providing information about the source of the update through the upstream request. Specifically, each Salmon request has a verifiable author and user agent that the publisher can use to determine trusted content sources.

At a basic level, a publisher can follow certain steps to determine if the source of the Salmon update is valid. Let's look at a simple example to showcase what this security flow may look like:

1. A subscriber site, *subscriber.example.com*, sends a Salmon request to the content publisher. The subscriber authors and signs the request with *acct:johndoe @subscriber.example.com*.

2. The publisher receives the Salmon request and uses protocols such as WebFinger, XRD, or LRDD (Link-based Resource Descriptor) to discover the *identity provider* (IdP) for *acct:johndoe@subscriber.example.com*. If the IdP turns out to be owned by *subscriber.example.com*, then the publisher will continue with the verification process.

3. The publisher then verifies the signature using retrieved public keys. If it checks out, the publisher may accept the Salmon request and integrate the updated content. The publisher should then return an HTTP 200 response back to the subscriber.

This is a simple example showcasing how a publisher may verify the source of a Salmon request. This can be extended even further to include any trusted third-party Salmon verification service, where the publisher would simply call the verifier to determine whether a source can be trusted.

Implementation Overview

We've explored the Salmon protocol from a few different angles at this point, including an overview of its stages and how to protect against abuse and spam. Now let's focus on what each stage of the protocol looks like from a programmatic view.

The Salmon protocol process starts when the publisher, or source, makes an update to its content and pushes the information out to all of its subscribers (through an RSS/ Atom-based HTTP POST request). Within the feed, the publisher includes a Salmon link with an href value pointing to some URI endpoint on its side where it can accept Salmon requests from subscribers:

```
<link rel="salmon" href="http://example.org/salmon-endpoint"/>
```

The subscriber will process the updates from the publisher as it normally would, and will store the Salmon endpoint on its side for future use.

Once an update (e.g., a comment) has been posted to that feed, the subscriber will store the comment on its side as usual, but will then send an HTTP POST request to the Salmon endpoint on the publisher containing a Salmon version of the update:

```
POST /salmon-endpoint HTTP/1.1
Host: example.org
Content-Type: application/atom+xml

<?xml version='1.0' encoding='UTF-8'?>
```

```
<me:env xmlns:me="http://salmon-protocol.org/ns/magic-env">
   <me:data type='application/atom+xml'>
```
```
   PD94bWwgdmVyc2lvbjOnMS4wJyBlbmNvZGluZzOnVVRGLTgnPz4KPGVudHJ5IHhtbG5zPS
   dodHRwOi8vd3d3LnczLm9yZy8yMDA1LOFOb20nPgogIDxpZD5OYWc6ZXhhbXBsBsZS5jb20s
   MjAwOTpjbXQtMC40ONDc3NTcxODwvaWQ-ICAKICA8YXVOaG9yPjxuYW1lPnRlc3RAZXhhbX
   BsZS5jb20L25hbWUPHVyaT5hY2NOOmpwYW56ZXJAZ29vZ2xlLmNvbTwvdXJpPjwvYXVOaW
   G9yPgogIDxOaHI6aW4tcmVwbHktdG8geG1sbnM6dGhyPSdodHRwOi8vcHVybC5vcmcvc3l
   uZGljYXRpb24vdGhyZWFkLzEuMCcKICAgICAggcmVmPSdOYWc6YmxvZ2dlci5jb20sMTk5O
   TpibG9nLTg5MzU5MTM3NDMxMxMjczNy5wb3NOLTM4NjE2NjMyNTg2NTNQnPnR
   hZzpibG9nZ2VyLmNvbSwxOTk5OmJsb2ctODkzNTkxMzcOMzEzMzEyNzM3LnBvc3QtMzg2M
   TY2MzI1ODUzODg1Nzk5NAogIDwvdGhyOmluLXJlcGx5LXRvPgogIDxjb250ZW50PlNhbG1
   vbiBzd2ltIHVwc3RyZWFtITwvY29udGVudD4KICA8dGlObGUbGUU2FsbW9uIHN3aW0gdXBzdH
   JlYWOhPC90aXRsZT4KICA8dXBkYXRlZD4yMDA5LTEyLTE4VDIwOjA0OjAzWjwvdXBkYXRl
   ZD4KPC9lbnRyeT4KICAgIA
```
```
   </me:data>
   <me:encoding>base64url</me:encoding>
   <me:alg>RSA-SHA256</me:alg>
   <me:sig>
```
```
   EvGSD2vi8qYcveHnb-rrlokO7qnCXjn8YSeCDDXlbhILSabgvNsPpbe76up8w63i2f
   WHvLKJzeGLKfyHg8ZomQ
```
```
   </me:sig>
</me:env>
```

The Salmon protocol utilizes the Magic Signatures specification to generate signatures for the request, as explained in the specification documentation at *http://salmon-proto col.googlecode.com/svn/trunk/draft-panzer-magicsig-01.html*.

Once the publisher has gone through the validation steps to ensure that the content is from a trusted source, it will respond back to the subscriber with standard HTTP response codes. These response codes will depend on the status of the update, as follows:

2xx

> Request was successful.

4xx

> There was an input problem.

5xx

> There was a source/server error.

If the Salmon request is valid, the publisher will publish the update (and syndicate it out to all other subscribers), moderate it, or discard it.

Conclusion

Whether you are seeking a standard way to publish and consume activities through the Activity Streams protocol or building an advanced provider/subscriber comment-sharing network via PubSubHubbub and the Salmon protocol, it's obvious that distributed web frameworks help us standardize the way we handle many of our regular social interactions.

Through our exploration of these protocols in this chapter, we have:

- Learned how we can turn a traditional website into a rich source of entity metadata by using the Open Graph protocol
- Explored how to standardize and consume activities through the use of Activity Streams, which enables us to pull detailed information about all parties involved in an activity
- Discovered how the WebFinger protocol turns a simple email address into a useful source of a user's social information
- Examined how we can build a standard method for sharing URL-based content with any other service on the Web
- Built complex provider/subscriber systems that allow for a rich network of cross-communication between numerous sites via PubSubHubbub and the Salmon protocol

These open protocols define methods that can help you increase your social influence on the Web and go a long way toward delivering truly engaging social networks between multiple sites and services.

Extending Your Social Graph with OpenID

When you're constructing a service that is intended for a base of users or provides a mechanism for giving people privileged access to certain resources, the issue of *authenticating* (allowing users to log in) naturally comes up.

Building an entire membership system and login infrastructure for this task can seem daunting, but it doesn't need to be. OpenID allows a website or service owner to quickly integrate a login system that builds off many of the top membership systems currently in use and is a great alternative to a traditional, home-brewed model.

This chapter will focus on OpenID's core features, covering examples and methods to show you how to leverage this standard to quickly integrate a user authentication system.

The OpenID Standard

OpenID provides sites and services with a decentralized protocol for authenticating users through a wide variety of providers. What this means is that a site integrating OpenID can allow its users to log in using, for example, their Yahoo!, Google, or AOL accounts. Not only can the consuming site avoid having to create a login system itself, but it can also take advantage of the accounts that its users already have, thereby increasing user registration and login rates.

In addition to simple authentication, OpenID also offers a series of extensions through which an OpenID provider can allow sites to obtain a user's profile information or integrate additional layers of security for the login procedure.

In the sections that follow, we'll take a closer look at these core elements of the OpenID standard.

Decentralization Is Key

What makes OpenID so intriguing is the fact that it offers a standard that is fully decentralized from the providers and consumers. This aspect is what allows a single consuming site to allow its users to log in via Yahoo! and Google, while another site may want to allow logins via Blogger or WordPress. Ultimately, it is up to the OpenID consumer (your site or service) to choose what login methods it would like to offer its user base.

Improvement over Traditional Login

We've touched on the differences between OpenID and a traditional login flow. In short, OpenID provides a number of advantages over a home-grown solution.

One of OpenID's greatest benefits over the traditional login flow is how accounts are created. With OpenID, since you are leveraging the user's existing account on a different site, you don't need to require her to create a new account when she first visits your site or service.

Using the login of another site as your base, you can create a default profile for the user with her linked account information and email address. With that, you can allow her to use your service and prompt her to flesh out the base profile with the rest of her details.

The topic of filling out the user profile brings us to our next point: using OpenID to build a rich social graph.

Accessing the Existing Membership Database and Social Graph

Many of the OpenID providers through which a user can log in to your site or service may have a large amount of existing data about the user and his linked account.

Using OpenID extensions, providers can permit an implementing site to pull profile information from their memberships systems, allowing the implementer to prepopulate its own user profile system. This is another important benefit of OpenID and increases the service's ease of use.

These extensions allow a consumer site to not only leverage a user's existing profile information, but the profile may also link to additional user accounts and interactions with other sites, services, or users. Having access to these sources will help you deliver a comprehensive social graph for the user right when he starts using your service.

Do I Already Have an OpenID? How Do I Sign Up for One?

Before we jump too far down the rabbit hole with OpenID specifics and implementations, let's start out by answering a very simple question: how do I know if I already have an OpenID account, and if I don't have one, how do I get one?

Let's tackle the first part of that question first: do you already have an OpenID? The answer is most likely yes. There are numerous companies, serving everything from social profiles to email, that already act as OpenID providers. For instance, if you have accounts with any of the following companies, you already have an OpenID account:

- Yahoo!
- Google
- Blogger
- AOL
- WordPress
- Hyves

There are many other providers also currently available. The OpenID website maintains a list of the most popular OpenID providers at *http://openid.net/get-an-openid/*.

Now let's address the second part of the question: if you don't already have an OpenID account, how can you get one? The answer to this is, again, very simple. Just pick your favorite site from the host of OpenID providers and create an account. You can now use that account login to authenticate through the OpenID process when an OpenID consumer prompts you to sign in to its service.

 If you don't already have an account with providers like Yahoo! or Google, it is a good idea to create an account with one of them for use with OpenID logins. They are two of the most popular providers that consumers integrate in their authentication process. After all, an OpenID provider is only useful if you can use it.

In addition to having an OpenID provider account, it is also a good idea to populate that profile with any information you would like to follow you from site to site, such as your name, email, location, etc. This will help prepopulate a profile for you when you sign in to a new service with an OpenID login.

The OpenID Authentication Flow

Much like OAuth (which we explored in Chapter 9), OpenID maintains a standardized flow by which a user can authenticate on a third-party relaying site to an OpenID provider such as Yahoo! or Google.

There are three participants in the OpenID authentication flow that we will be working with and describing in this chapter:

The user
> This is the end user who is attempting to sign in to a site or service using one of the OpenID providers.

The relaying party
> This is the OpenID consumer site that is implementing an OpenID provider login in order to allow users to authenticate their accounts.

The OpenID provider
> This is the site or service that has the membership database that the relaying party will authenticate against and through which the user will log in.

With that said, the OpenID authentication process will take us through four different steps, starting from when the user chooses which provider to use to sign in and ending with the authentication pass/fail returned by the provider when the user attempts to authenticate. These steps are:

1. Request user login by passing an OpenID identifier URI.
2. Perform discovery on the OpenID endpoint.
3. Require the user to authenticate his account.
4. Provide a pass/fail state based on the authentication.

Let's break these down to see what happens between the user, relaying party, and OpenID provider at each stage.

Step 1: Request Login with OpenID Identifier

At the first stage, we will focus on the initial steps that the user and relaying party need to take in order to begin the authentication process. Essentially, we need to pick an OpenID provider that we would like to authenticate with and ensure that it has a valid OpenID provider identifier. This process is illustrated in Figure 11-1.

First, the user will provide the relaying party with the OpenID identifier that she wants to use for authentication. This does not necessarily need to be the exact string URL for the provider; the relaying party should ideally offer the user a list with some visible identifiers, such as logos or links, from which the user can choose an OpenID provider.

 Making the initial choice as easy as possible for a user (such as through the use of a logo) will help to increase the sign-in rate on your site or service.

Once the user has selected an OpenID provider, the relaying party will begin performing discovery of the OpenID identifier URL. Before we do this, we need to normalize the

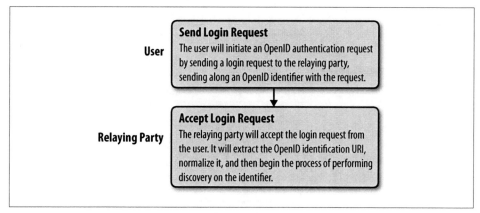

Figure 11-1. OpenID, step 1: User requests login with an OpenID identifier

supplied URL to ensure that discovery occurs correctly—that is, we need to transform the provided identifier into a canonical URL so that we can determine whether it matches the selected provider.

Once we complete the URL normalization process, we can move on to the discovery step.

Step 2: Perform Discovery to Establish the Endpoint URL

The process of performing discovery on an OpenID provider identifier will take us through a couple of substeps, both involving communication between the relaying party and the OpenID provider. Our goal in this stage is to perform discovery on the OpenID identifier to:

1. Determine whether the OpenID identifier is valid.
2. If it is valid, extract the endpoint URL to which the user will be forwarded for authentication.

This exchange is demonstrated in Figure 11-2.

Using the normalized URL from the last step, the relaying party will make a request to the provided OpenID identifier URL. If the identifier is valid, the provider will respond with the endpoint URL that is used either to redirect the user or to request the markup that sends the user through the authentication step.

Step 3: Request User Authentication

Depending on the version of OpenID being used (OpenID version 1 or 2), the request for user authentication will take one of two courses from a programmatic perspective. The code will either:

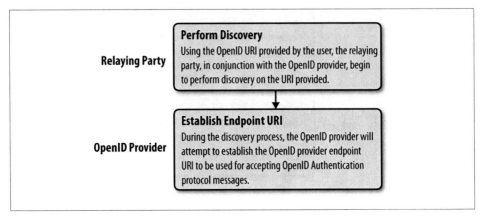

Figure 11-2. OpenID, step 2: Relaying party performs discovery on OpenID identifier

- Redirect the user to the endpoint established in the previous step (OpenID v1)

or:

- Obtain the authentication form markup from the provider endpoint and print it out to the screen for the user (OpenID v2)

In both cases, the process that occurs between the relaying party and the user looks the same, as shown in Figure 11-3.

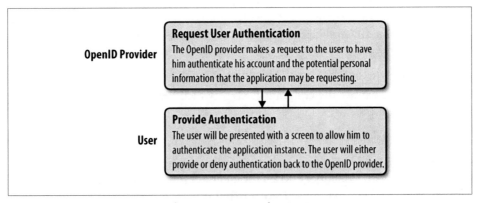

Figure 11-3. OpenID, step 3: Provider requests user authentication

In general terms, the relaying party will display the authentication form to the user to have him authenticate herself against the OpenID provider (through either the form or redirect method).

When the relaying party establishes the request between the user and provider for authentication, the request will include a number of OpenID parameters, including those listed in Table 11-1.

Table 11-1. *Authentication request parameters*

Request parameter	Description
openid.ns	The OpenID namespace URI to be used. For instance, this should be *http://specs.openid.net/auth/2.0* for OpenID 2.0 transactions.
openid.mode	The transaction mode to be used during the authentication process. The possible values are checkid_immediate or checkid_setup.
	If the user should be able to interact with the OpenID provider, then checkid_setup should be used.
openid.claimed_id (optional)	The claimed OpenID identifier, provided by the user.
openid.identity (optional)	The local OpenID provider identifier. If *http://specs.openid.net/auth/2.0/identifier_select* is used as the identity, then the provider should choose the correct identifier for the user.
openid.assoc_handle (optional)	A handle for an association between the relaying party (implementing site) and the OpenID provider that should be used to sign the request.
openid.return_to (optional)	The location where the user should be returned, with the OpenID response, after authentication has taken place.
	Many web-based providers require this field. If it is not included, it indicates that the relaying party does not want to return the user after authentication.
openid.realm (optional)	The URL pattern for the domain that the user should trust. For instance, **.mysite.com*.
	Note, if openid.return_to is omitted from the request, openid.realm is a required parameter.

The user, once presented with the form, will either authenticate or not. In either case, the user's response will be returned to the relaying party. This response object that is returned will include the parameters listed in Table 11-2.

Table 11-2. *Authentication response parameters*

Response parameter	Description
openid.ns	The OpenID namespace URI.
openid.mode	The current authentication mode. This value will be id_res at this point.
openid.op_endpoint	The endpoint URI of the OpenID provider to which the user was sent.
openid.claimed_id (optional)	The claimed OpenID identification URI for the user on the provider site.
	In the response object, openid.claimed_id and openid.identity will either both be present or absent.
openid.identity (optional)	The local identifier for the user on the provider site. For some providers, this value will usually be identical to the openid.claimed_id parameter.
openid.return_to	An exact copy of the return_to parameter provided in the original user authentication request.
openid.response_nonce	A unique string of 255 characters or fewer. The nonce will start with the current server time.

Response parameter	Description
openid.invalidate_handle (optional)	This will include an invalidation handle from the server if one was produced.
openid.assoc_handle	The handle for the association that was used to sign this assertion.
openid.signed	A comma-separated list of the fields that were signed with the request. This list must contain at least op_endpoint, return_to, response_nonce, assoc_handle, and, if present in the response, claimed_id and identity.
openid.sig	The base 64–encoded signature.

The relaying party and OpenID provider will then communicate with each other to complete the authentication process and provide the appropriate approval state.

Step 4: Provide Passed or Failed State

Once the user has interacted with the authentication form and submitted, he should be forwarded to the specified callback location. Everything should be in place at this point for the relaying party to communicate with the OpenID provider to complete the authentication process.

This step is outlined in Figure 11-4.

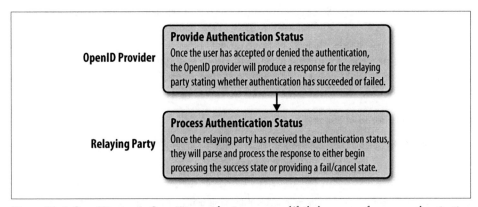

Figure 11-4. OpenID, step 4: OpenID provider issues passed/failed response for user authentication back to relaying party

Once the user is forwarded to the callback location, the relaying party will attempt to complete the authentication process. It will send a complete request to the OpenID provider with the variables passed to the callback location.

The OpenID provider will attempt to complete authentication with the provided data. It will issue either a fail state (authentication failed) or an approved state. If it provides an approved state, the response returned back to the relaying party will also hold the unique user identifier and any data requested from attached OpenID extensions.

At this point, the relaying party may use the returned data to process the user login.

OpenID Providers

Each OpenID provider has an OpenID URI associated with its authentication system to enable the discovery method required for the OpenID process.

When making an initial request to a provider in order to have a user authenticate her account, you will submit the URI of the provider. For instance, the following list details some of the more popular OpenID providers and their OpenID URIs:

- Yahoo: *https://me.yahoo.com*
- Flickr: *http://www.flickr.com*
- Google: *https://www.google.com/accounts/o8/id*
- WordPress: *https://username.wordpress.com/*
- MyOpenID: *https://www.myopenid.com/*
- MySpace: *http://www.myspace.com/username*
- AOL: *http://openid.aol.com/username*
- LiveJournal: *http://username.livejournal.com/*
- ClaimID: *https://claimid.com/username*
- Blogger: *http://blogname.blogspot.com*
- Hyves: *http://hyves.net*
- Orange: *http://orange.fr*
- Mixi: *http://mixi.com*

We'll explore how to use these in the OpenID authentication process later in this chapter.

Bypassing Domain Discovery Errors in OpenID

As part of their OpenID process, some providers require the relaying party to implement a domain discovery mechanism for when an end user transitions through the authentication screens. If this mechanism is not in place, these providers display warning messages to the user stating that they could not verify the relaying website. Figure 11-5 shows an example of this on Yahoo!.

 Displaying domain discovery warnings in your OpenID process can dramatically increase the drop-off rate of users logging in through your site.

Figure 11-5. Yahoo! OpenID authentication screen

Depending on the provider that you are working with for your OpenID implementation, you may be required to create an XRDS domain verification file, which allows you to define yourself as the site owner and in turn allows the provider to verify your site.

Creating one of these documents is a multistep process that requires you to have access to the root of your domain. The XRDS file itself will be a short XML document with a custom content-type header applied.

Before we go through these steps, let's look at what an XRDS file might look like. In this example, the XRDS file is saved as *xrds.php*.

```php
<?php
header('Content-Type: application/xrds+xml');

$xrd = '<?xml version="1.0" encoding="UTF-8"?><xrds:XRDS xmlns:xrds="xri://$xrds"
        xmlns:openid="http://openid.net/xmlns/1.0" xmlns:xri="xri://$xrd*($v*2.0)">' .
        '<XRD>' .
        '<Service xmlns="xri://$xrd*($v*2.0)">' .
        '<Type>http://specs.openid.net/auth/2.0/return_to</Type>' .
        '<URI>http://server.example.com/openid/complete.php</URI>' .
        '</Service>' .
        '</XRD>' .
```

```
            '</xrds:XRDS>';

   echo $xrd;
   ?>
```

In the preceding XRDS file, we are simply setting the content-type header as follows:

```
Content-Type: application/xrds+xml
```

We then create the XML part of the document and print it out. When implementing your own XRDS document, simply change the value within the `<URI>` node to point to the OpenID complete file on your server. This file is where the user should be forwarded after he has authenticated on the provider site in order to complete the OpenID process (we will explore this further in upcoming examples).

Once you have created that XRDS file, simply copy it to a location on the same server where the OpenID process will be initiated.

Next, on the root page of your domain (e.g., */index.html*), add a new `<meta>` tag in the `<head>` of the document that links to the XRDS file that you just put on the server. This `<meta>` tag will look something like the following, with a different content link:

```
<meta http-equiv="X-XRDS-Location"
      content="http://www.mysite.com/auth/xrds.php" />
```

The domain discovery process should now be implemented on your site, thus the provider can verify the domain and remove the warning message that end users see during the OpenID authentication process.

Most providers do not require the domain discovery mechanism, but if you are integrating one that displays warnings during the authentication process, it is a good idea to take the preceding steps to mitigate the drop-off issues that can result from having those warnings displayed to users.

OpenID Extensions

Many OpenID providers support extensions beyond the basic pass/fail state delivered through the standard OpenID implementation. These extensions allow an OpenID consumer to obtain some general information about the user authenticating through the service from her profile or to add levels of security to the authentication process.

 Before using an OpenID extension, you should ensure that your chosen provider supports the extension and full functionality that you are trying to implement. Even though many providers support the same extensions, some support different subsets of data within those extensions— meaning that you may not get all of the results you're expecting.

Besides the OAuth hybrid extension (which we will explore in much greater detail in the next chapter), the main OpenID extensions, and those that we will examine in this chapter, are:

Simple Registration (SREG)
Allows the relaying party to capture very basic personal information about a user, where available through her profile or the OpenID provider itself

Attribute Exchange (AX)
Enables the relaying party to capture more extensive personal information about a user, including the information delivered through Simple Registration

Provider Authentication Policy Extension (PAPE)
Allows the relaying party and provider to apply certain previously agreed-upon policies to the OpenID authentication process

Now that we have seen a brief overview of what each extension offers, let's drill down into them to learn what they are all about.

Simple Registration Extension

If your service requires only a small amount of information from an OpenID provider (such as a thumbnail, profile link, name, and some other basic public badge information), Simple Registration is a wonderful extension that delivers that information to the application after the user has logged in to the provider site.

The Simple Registration extension defines nine common user profile fields that a provider may be requested to supply through the OpenID authentication process. Note, however, that the Simple Registration specification does not require a provider to support all nine fields; the provider may support any number of them.

Many providers opt to support the Attribute Exchange extension in lieu of Simple Registration because Attribute Exchange defines not only the fields supported by the Simple Registration extension, but also a large number of others. This does not mean that no OpenID providers support Simple Registration; it simply means that some opt to support only the more comprehensive extension instead of both.

To this end, Table 11-3 shows the nine fields that Simple Registration supports and then, for comparison, ties in the matching supported field URIs for the Attribute Exchange extension.

Table 11-3. SREG supported fields and corresponding AX type URIs

Label	SREG property	AX type URI
Alias/Username	openid.sreg.nickname	http://axschema.org/namePerson/friendly
Country	openid.sreg.country	http://axschema.org/contact/country/home
Date of birth	openid.sreg.dob	http://axschema.org/birthDate
Email	openid.sreg.email	http://axschema.org/contact/email

Label	SREG property	AX type URI
Full name	`openid.sreg.fullname`	*http://axschema.org/namePerson*
Gender	`openid.sreg.gender`	*http://axschema.org/person/gender*
Postal code	`openid.sreg.postcode`	*http://axschema.org/contact/postalCode/home*
Primary language	`openid.sreg.language`	*http://axschema.org/pref/language*
Time zone	`openid.sreg.timezone`	*http://axschema.org/pref/timezone*

The Label column in Table 11-3 contains the fields that are supported through the Simple Registration process. The "SREG property" column includes that property names that you will use when integrating Simple Registration into your OpenID code base to denote the end-user fields that you want to capture. Finally, the "AX type URI" column contains the matching Attribute Exchange extension URIs that you would use to request those same fields through the Attribute Exchange extension code in your OpenID implementation.

Now that we have seen the base fields that are available through the Simple Registration extension, let's look at the additional fields offered through Attribute Exchange.

Attribute Exchange Extension

If your service requires more extensive user profile details than those provided by the Simple Registration process, Attribute Exchange may be the right mechanism for your needs. Support for the extension and (if it is supported) the specific attribute types available will depend on your particular provider. More details are available at the following websites:

Attribute Exchange 1.0
> *http://openid.net/specs/openid-attribute-exchange-1_0.html*

Types
> *http://www.axschema.org/types/*

In addition to the standard types, which we will discuss in the next few sections, there are several experimental types: *http://www.axschema.org/types/experimental/*.

Attribute exchange types: Addresses

The first category of Attribute Exchange types we will look at is address types. The AX extension defines a number of address identifiers for a default address (such as a home or personal shipping location) and a business address, as shown in Table 11-4.

Table 11-4. AX address types

Label	Type URI
Address	*http://axschema.org/contact/postalAddress/home*
Address line 2	*http://axschema.org/contact/postalAddressAdditional/home*
City	*http://axschema.org/contact/city/home*
Country	*http://axschema.org/contact/country/home*
State/Province	*http://axschema.org/contact/state/home*
Postal code	*http://axschema.org/contact/postalCode/home*
Business address	*http://axschema.org/contact/postalAddress/business*
Business address line 2	*http://axschema.org/contact/postalAddressAdditional/business*
Business city	*http://axschema.org/contact/city/business*
Business state/Province	*http://axschema.org/contact/state/business*
Business country	*http://axschema.org/contact/country/business*
Business postal code	*http://axschema.org/contact/postalCode/business*

These are great fields for companies to support or leverage if they need to store or request data from a user for shipping purposes. For instance, if an online merchant implemented OpenID for site sign-in using a provider that supported these AX attributes, it could prepopulate all of a user's shipping details.

Attribute exchange types: Audio and video greetings

The next category comprises audio and video greeting types. Depending on the service context in which they were created, these fields may include audio greetings, like those you set up on your phone, or short video greetings (Table 11-5).

Table 11-5. Audio and video greeting types

Label	Type URI
Audio greeting	*http://axschema.org/media/greeting/audio*
Spoken name	*http://axschema.org/media/spokenname*
Video greeting	*http://axschema.org/media/greeting/video*

A practical use case for this information is in the field of telephony, where someone might record audio and spoken name greetings—i.e., voice mail messages—for callers trying to reach him. Video greetings take this concept a step further, as in the case of video conferencing.

Attribute exchange types: Date of birth

The Attribute Exchange extension also provides definitions for the user's date of birth. Most providers that supply this information support only the full date of birth, but as you can see in Table 11-6, there are types defined for the individual components denoting the day, month, and year as well.

Table 11-6. Date of birth types

Label	Type URI
Birth day	*http://axschema.org/birthDate/birthday*
Birth month	*http://axschema.org/birthDate/birthMonth*
Birth year	*http://axschema.org/birthDate/birthYear*
Full birth date	*http://axschema.org/birthDate*

Date of birth information is perfect for sites that have certain age restrictions or those that require a user to certify that he is old enough to purchase a product (such as a game company). Even if the individual numeric values are not provided, the full birth date can be easily parsed into its individual components (just be aware of the short formats that other countries use, such as MM/DD/YYYY in the United States versus DD/MM/YYYY in Canada).

Attribute exchange types: Email

The next category, and our smallest by far, is email. The only field that is supported here is that of the user's email address (Table 11-7). This is probably one of the most popular requests for social data, however, and an area of contention among companies providing this data. It is a prime viral channel for social developers to reach out to their user base, but this potential benefit is tempered by the risk of a service using the data for malicious spamming or phishing attempts. OpenID providers that support this type try to make their users aware that they will be sharing this data with the third-party site or service, thereby putting the onus on the user to understand the potential harm in sharing this particular piece of information.

Table 11-7. Email type

Label	Type URI
Email	*http://axschema.org/contact/email*

The email field is a valuable resource for all developers. It provides a prime communication channel to the user who has authenticated your site or service. Many of the most popular OpenID providers support this field through the Attribute Exchange extension.

Attribute exchange types: Images

Images are a popular feature in any site or service that provides profile systems for its user base. These images are made available through the Attribute Exchange extension with a number of potential size fields, including the default user image, different aspect ratios, tiny favicons, and a square image that provides determinable sizes for the images. These are listed in Table 11-8.

Table 11-8. Image types

Label	Type URI
3:4 Aspect ratio image	http://axschema.org/media/image/aspect34
4:3 Aspect ration image	http://axschema.org/media/image/aspect43
Default image	http://axschema.org/media/image/default
Favicon image	http://axschema.org/media/image/favicon
Square image	http://axschema.org/media/image/aspect11

These fields are ideal for populating a user image in a profile without requiring the user to upload or link to an existing image. This method also syncs the user image between your site or service and the provider site through which the user logged in.

Attribute exchange types: Instant messaging

Another communication channel that the Attribute Exchange extension provides is that of the user's linked messenger accounts. The most popular messaging platforms are included in the specification (as shown in Table 11-9), providing the OpenID relaying site with a whole host of communication methods and account links about a user.

Table 11-9. Instant messaging types

Label	Type URI
AOL IM	http://axschema.org/contact/IM/AIM
ICQ IM	http://axschema.org/contact/IM/ICQ
Jabber IM	http://axschema.org/contact/IM/Jabber
MSN IM	http://axschema.org/contact/IM/MSN
Skype IM	http://axschema.org/contact/IM/Skype
Yahoo! IM	http://axschema.org/contact/IM/Yahoo

While most OpenID consumers may not want to use the user's messenger accounts as a direct means of communication (which could easily be construed as a form of spam or an invasion of user privacy), providing these account links in the user profile allows your users to link additional accounts to their profiles, helps you search for new connections to the user, and delivers a number of other social functions that give users an easy way to build up their profiles.

Attribute exchange types: Name

Along with the user's email address, the name provided through the AX extension is an excellent starting point for the construction of a user's profile. Many OpenID providers allow for some basic name information to be obtained during the authentication process—most commonly, the user alias or nickname because that is how the user has chosen to be identified and it is usually part of a user's public profile, which anyone can obtain without authentication.

Public profiles usually consist of a simple user badge comprising the user nickname, profile picture, direct profile link, and some sort of primary network. The public profile may also contain a primary URL defined by the user and a selection of the user connections. Figure 11-6 is an example of a simple public badge.

Jonathan LeBlanc
www.jcleblanc.com

Add Jonathan LeBlanc as Friend

Figure 11-6. Example of a Facebook public badge

There are a number of name fields available for us to use, listed in Table 11-10.

Table 11-10. Name types

Label	Type URI
Alias/Username	*http://axschema.org/namePerson/friendly*
Full name	*http://axschema.org/namePerson*
Name prefix	*http://axschema.org/namePerson/prefix*
First name	*http://axschema.org/namePerson/first*
Last name	*http://axschema.org/namePerson/last*
Middle name	*http://axschema.org/namePerson/middle*
Name suffix	*http://axschema.org/namePerson/suffix*

As mentioned earlier, the name information is the perfect starting point for developing a user profile. Since you are already having the user go through the process of authenticating her account, you should at least make it as easy as possible for her to create a user profile on your site. Prepopulating users' profiles for them with information such as their names will go a long way toward decreasing the drop-off rate that you may otherwise see during the user signup process.

Attribute exchange types: Telephone

Another set of fields that an OpenID provider may support through the AX extension is the user profile types for contact phone numbers (shown in Table 11-11), which deliver an alternate means of physical communication.

Table 11-11. Telephone types

Label	Type URI
Phone (preferred)	*http://axschema.org/contact/phone/default*
Phone (home)	*http://axschema.org/contact/phone/home*
Phone (work)	*http://axschema.org/contact/phone/business*
Phone (mobile)	*http://axschema.org/contact/phone/cell*
Phone (fax)	*http://axschema.org/contact/phone/fax*

Direct lines of communication are beneficial fields for companies with physical user support centers, or for those who may need to contact the user at some point in the future. If you have a service that ships physical goods or provides some sort of prolonged user service (such as an ISP), accessing alternate contact methods from the OpenID authentication process can come in very handy.

Attribute exchange types: Websites

The available website fields (Table 11-12) comprise a list of the more popular services that a user may link to his profile, including one default source for a custom site like a personal home page.

Table 11-12. Website types

Label	Type URI
Amazon	*http://axschema.org/contact/web/Amazon*
Blog	*http://axschema.org/contact/web/blog*
del.icio.us URL	*http://axschema.org/contact/web/Delicious*
Flickr URL	*http://axschema.org/contact/web/Flickr*
LinkedIn URL	*http://axschema.org/contact/web/Linkedin*
Personal web page	*http://axschema.org/contact/web/default*

Linking alternate sites for a user is always a good idea when creating a profile for him on your site. Many services that provide listings of user activities (and those of user connections) may also provide a method to aggregate feeds from other networks into that activity stream. These linked accounts are a vital piece of that process.

Attribute exchange types: Work

To provide a small amount of data about the work background of the person going through the authentication process, the company name and job title types are available (Table 11-13). These fields help you flesh out the user's profile—and the more information that you have about her, the easier it is to target offers, ads, and services specifically to her, increasing your monetization potential on a per-user basis.

Table 11-13. Work fields

Label	Type URI
Company name	*http://axschema.org/company/name*
Job title	*http://axschema.org/company/title*

If you cannot obtain the user's industry, being able to parse her company name and job title will help you determine the appropriate knowledge bucket to assign her to. This is especially valuable when you have no distinguishing interest indicators available for the user.

Attribute exchange types: Other personal details and preferences

Last but not least, the other personal details and preferences fields that are listed in Table 11-14 will allow the OpenID consumer to extract additional user information such as a short biography, gender, native language, and time zone.

Table 11-14. Other personal details and preferences types

Label	Type URI
Biography	*http://axschema.org/media/biography*
Gender	*http://axschema.org/person/gender*
Language	*http://axschema.org/pref/language*
Time zone	*http://axschema.org/pref/timezone*

Geography-, language-, and gender-based user targeting to invoke regionalized and personalized product interest is an excellent strategy for any consumer to employ.

Provider Authentication Policy Extension

The Provider Authentication Policy Extension defines a series of previously agreed-upon authentication policies that the OpenID provider applies when authenticating an end user through a relaying party (i.e., the site or service that is requesting the user authentication through something like a "Sign in with Yahoo" request). The PAPE mechanism also enables the OpenID provider to inform the relaying party of which authentication policies were used during the authentication process, which in turn enables the relaying party to determine how secure the authentication was. We will look at the methods for setting and obtaining this information in our upcoming OpenID example.

The PAPE policies that we will explore include:

- Phishing-resistant authentication
- Multifactor authentication
- Physical multifactor authentication

 These three authentication policies are being discussed only as starting points to cover the most common use cases—additional policies may be applied as needed.

In addition, PAPE provides a mechanism by which the relaying party may request that the OpenID provider inform it of the levels of authentication assurance (known as *NIST assurance levels*) that were used.

The three most common PAPE policies include numerous technologies that can be employed during the authentication process. Table 11-15 breaks these methods down by each policy in which they apply.

Table 11-15. Authentication methods available within each PAPE policy

Method	Phishing-resistant	Multifactor	Physical multifactor
Password via HTTPS			
Visual secret via HTTPS			
PIN and digital certificate via HTTPS	✓	✓	
PIN and "soft" OTP token via HTTPS		✓	
PIN and "hard" OTP token via HTTPS		✓	✓
PIN and "hard" crypto token via HTTPS	✓	✓	✓
Information card via HTTPS	✓	✓	

With all of that information in hand, now let's explore what the authentication policies and the NIST assurance levels actually mean in practice.

Phishing-resistant authentication

The phishing-resistant authentication works to prevent the relaying party from being able to capture enough information about the user to be able to authenticate to the user-selected OpenID provider as if it were the user himself. In basic terms, this authentication process prevents a site that you may not trust from pretending to be you when you are signing in using your OpenID account.

Multifactor authentication

Multifactor authentication means that the user will be authenticating the OpenID process using multiple authentication factors.

The authentication factors that are usually employed are:

- Something you know
- Something you have
- Something you are

For instance, passwords are a commonly used authentication factor (something you know). In the case of this policy type, multiple authentication factors may include the user password as well as a digital certificate.

Physical multifactor authentication

Much like the multifactor authentication policy, the physical multifactor authentication policy means that the user will need to authenticate using multiple authentication factors. The difference here is that one of those authentication factors must be a physical factor such as a hardware device or some piece of biometric data.

Also like the multifactor authentication policy, this policy usually employs the three common authentication factors (or some combination) listed previously—something you know, have, or are. For instance, the user may authenticate using his password and a hardware token.

NIST assurance levels

The National Institute of Standards and Technology (NIST) defines a series of guidelines for the levels of assurance protection that should be in place when services attempt to authenticate users over open networks. These recommendations indicate certain levels of protection that PAPE puts in place while authenticating users. In this section, we'll look into a few specific token types and protections that are employed at each defined NIST assurance level.

First, we'll look at the types of tokens that can be used at each authentication assurance level (Table 11-16). As we increase NIST assurance levels, we can see that the less secure token types (that is, the easiest to break) are removed.

Table 11-16. Token types for each NIST assurance level

Token type	Level 1	Level 2	Level 3	Level 4
Hard crypto token	✓	✓	✓	✓
One-time password device	✓	✓	✓	
Soft crypto token	✓	✓	✓	
Passwords and PINs	✓	✓		

So now we've outlined the token types that are applied, but what kind of protections will we receive at the different levels? It's especially important to understand this aspect of the NIST assurance levels, since this will help us determine which level is the most appropriate for what we are trying to accomplish. In many use cases, level 4 assurance contains a far higher degree of security than most common implementations will need. Table 11-17 details the attack protections offered at each level.

Table 11-17. Protections at each NIST assurance level

Protect against	Level 1	Level 2	Level 3	Level 4
Online guessing	✓	✓	✓	✓
Replay	✓	✓	✓	✓
Eavesdropper		✓	✓	✓
Verifier impersonation			✓	✓
Man-in-the-middle			✓	✓
Session hijacking				✓

Let's break down the assurance levels a little further by defining the attacks they protect against:

Online guessing
> This is an attack wherein the malicious party attempts to guess the user's password.

Replay
> In this type of attack, the malicious party (most likely the relaying party) purposely repeats or delays the user authentication process. A common attack vector for this is a spoofing attack whereby the relaying party may masquerade as the user who is attempting to authenticate.

Eavesdropper
> This is an attack in which the malicious party eavesdrops on two parties that use an anonymous key exchange protocol to secure their conversation.

Verifier impersonation
> In this attack, the malicious party impersonates the legitimate verifier in an effort to learn valuable information—for example, the user's password.

Man-in-the-middle
> This is a type of active eavesdropping attack wherein the malicious party makes a connection with the user and relays messages between the user and the attacker. In other words, the attacker impersonates the legitimate service to obtain the user's private information or attempts to hijack the user session to gain access to that information.

Session hijacking
> This attack involves the malicious party taking control (or impersonating) of a valid session between the user and the intended, valid web server source. These sessions

are usually controlled by a session token, which is what this attack uses. In one possible scenario, the malicious party sniffs a valid session to gain the session token, and then sends that token to the web server to open a new valid session, impersonating the user. Cross-site scripting is another possible method for the attacker to gain access to the session token.

Now that we understand the basics of the tokens and attack protections that are in place, let's take a quick look at the minimum number of authentication factors required at each NIST authentication level. Table 11-18 lists them.

Table 11-18. Minimum number of authentication factors required at each NIST level

Level	Factors
1	1
2	1
3	2
4	2

 Some OpenID providers do not support the NIST assurance protection levels in their implementation. In some of these cases, the provider may return a NIST level response of 0 to denote that the service should not be used for any secure transactions such as online payments. If you require a high level of security, you should always check the NIST level returned at the end of the OpenID authentication process before proceeding with secure transactions.

When we combine all of this information, we have the foundation for the NIST assurance-level security mechanisms employed within PAPE. Since we will always be dealing with user authentication within OpenID, it's important to be able to determine the current security level that we are authenticating into and to understand how we should be managing user privacy and security.

Extensions Currently Under Development

In addition to the OpenID extensions that we have already explored, there are several extensions that are currently under development and contain draft proposals for additional features that providers may make available within their OpenID authentication process. We'll cover a few of them now.

OpenID user interface work group proposal

The gist of the OpenID user interface work group proposal is to load the OpenID authentication process within a pop-up window instead of redirecting the entire browser window.

The main benefit here is the customization potential of the pop-up window itself. In the traditional OpenID model, the relaying party contacts the OpenID provider to handle the user authentication using a default authentication form and implementation; it's usually an entire login page that mimics its membership login system.

Using this proposed model, however, a provider site can determine that the authentication procedure should load in a pop-up window, meaning that it can display an authentication form of a certain size to best fit that window. The provider may want to resize the pop-up window as well in order to fit it to the required size of the authentication form. The onus here is on each provider, not on the relaying party, to pick a correct pop-up size. If the entire browser window is being taken up by the membership form, having a resize event just does not make sense.

The next benefit to the OpenID user interface work group proposal involves the failure state during the authentication process. Let's assume that the user is on the authentication page and hits the cancel button. Instead of sending a fail state back to the return URL of the relaying party, the provider site can simply close the window, giving the user a better experience.

For a final potential benefit to this proposal, let's now say that the user is visiting an English-based site and then tries to sign in via an OpenID provider. The provider will display its default authentication form based on the user's language preference—for this example, let's say this is set to Chinese. Pushing your user through language shifts just to authenticate makes for a poor user experience. Using this pop-up method, however, default language preferences can be set so that the language presented at each stage of the process is uniform.

Full information on this extension is available on the OpenID website at *http://wiki .openid.net/w/page/12995202/OpenID-User-Interface-Work-Group-Proposal*.

Contract exchange

The contract exchange extension proposal seeks to allow arbitrary parties to create and exchange a digitally signed "contract" during the authentication process.

This would introduce a new method of integrating additional security and accountability features into the authentication process, especially in the case of exchanging sensitive user information, such as banking information or credit card numbers, during authentication.

Full information on the contract exchange extension is available on the OpenID website at *http://wiki.openid.net/w/page/12995142/Contract-Exchange*.

OpenID and OAuth hybrid extension

The OpenID and OAuth hybrid extension combines the authentication flexibility of OpenID with the authorization capabilities of OAuth to allow an application to request a user's permission to access and set privileged resources.

We will explore this extension in depth in Chapter 12 (available online; see Preface for details), which includes extensive descriptions and examples to show you how to integrate these two technologies.

Full information on the hybrid extension is available on the OpenID website at *http://wiki.openid.net/w/page/12995194/OpenID-and-OAuth-Hybrid-Extension*.

Implementation Example: OpenID

Now that we understand how OpenID works to connect relaying sites to different provider companies so they can leverage those providers' user databases for their login flow, let's look at a practical example of an OpenID implementation. This example can be used to connect to different providers and uses the different extension capabilities that we have discussed: Simple Registration, Attribute Exchange, and PAPE policies.

This example will be broken down into a number of files, ranging from our initial HTML form that starts the process to our OpenID control files and those files that allow the service provider to perform site discovery on the domain in which they are being hosted.

To implement OpenID, you will need to either create your own OpenID library or utilize one of the many libraries already available from the developer site at *http://openid.net/developers/libraries/*. Unless you have a specific reason for creating your own library, I recommend that you not reinvent the wheel and instead use what is currently available.

When you are integrating OpenID on a new site, it is a good practice to have your XRDS domain discovery file in place to prevent certain providers, such as Yahoo!, from displaying domain verification errors to users during the OpenID process.

Implementing OpenID Using PHP

The full code for this sample is available at *https://github.com/jcleblanc/programming-social-applications/tree/master/chapter_11/openid-php*.

Our first practical OpenID implementation example will use PHP. Our intention is to build out an end-to-end implementation that will allow a user to input the OpenID provider that she wants to use, after which the program will allow her to log in with that provider service and deliver information about her at the end of the authentication process.

In addition to obtaining a pass/fail state for whether the user authenticated, we will acquire additional information and levels of security by implementing the previously discussed OpenID extensions:

- Simple Registration for acquiring basic user information
- Attribute Exchange for acquiring more extensive user information
- PAPE for providing additional security levels

At the end, we will have a solid understanding of how OpenID functions from a programmatic perspective.

The discovery form

Let's start off the process by building out the form that will allow the user to input the provider OpenID URL she wants to use and select some of the PAPE policies that she would like to send along as well.

 In a real-world implementation, you would not provide the user with a form field to have her input the OpenID provider URL or the policies that she would like to use. As mentioned earlier, you would add icons (or some other identifying marker) for each provider option in order to allow the user to initiate the login process by choosing one. When the user clicks an icon, you would then determine the corresponding OpenID URL for the selected provider and add in the policies that you need, without requiring further user interaction.

For the sake of this example, the following file will be named *index.html*:

```html
<!DOCTYPE html PUBLIC "-//W3C//DTD XHTML 1.0 Transitional//EN"
    "http://www.w3.org/TR/xhtml1/DTD/xhtml1-transitional.dtd">
<html xmlns="http://www.w3.org/1999/xhtml">
<head>
    <meta http-equiv="Content-Type" content="text/html; charset=utf-8" />
    <title>OpenID Sample Application</title>
</head>
<body>
<style type="text/css">
    form{ font:12px arial,helvetica,sans-serif; }
    #openid_url { background:#FFFFFF url(http://wiki.openid.net/f/openid-16x16.gif)
                             no-repeat scroll 5px 50%;
                             padding-left:25px; }
</style>

<form action="auth.php" method="GET">
    <input type="hidden" value="login" name="actionType">
    <h2>Sign in using OpenID</h2>
    <input type="text" style="font-size: 12px;" size="40" id="openid_url"
        name="openid_url">  
    <input type="submit" value="Sign in"><br />
    <small>(e.g. http://username.myopenid.com)</small>
```

```
    <br /><br />

    <b>PAPE Policies (Optional)</b><br />
    <input type="checkbox" name="policies[]" value="PAPE_AUTH_MULTI_FACTOR_PHYSICAL" />
    PAPE_AUTH_MULTI_FACTOR_PHYSICAL<br />
    <input type="checkbox" name="policies[]" value="PAPE_AUTH_MULTI_FACTOR" />
    PAPE_AUTH_MULTI_FACTOR<br />
    <input type="checkbox" name="policies[]" value="PAPE_AUTH_PHISHING_RESISTANT" />
    PAPE_AUTH_PHISHING_RESISTANT<br />
  </form>
  </body>
  </html>
```

The beginning of our file is quite standard and includes the styles that we will be using for the form, including an OpenID logo image.

The real piece that we will focus on is the form itself. First, when the user clicks the submit button to process the form, she will be forwarded to our *auth.php* file to generate the authentication requests for her to sign in to the provider.

Next, we have an input box to allow the user to enter the OpenID discovery URL for the provider that she would like to sign in to. In practice, this step usually includes a series of provider images (e.g., Yahoo!, Google, etc.) from which the user can select so that she does not have to know the discovery endpoint herself.

Last, we have a block of inputs to allow the user to select the different PAPE policies that she would like to use for the request.

Once the user fills out the form and submits it, she will be forwarded to our *auth.php* file.

The common includes, functions, and globals

All files involved in the discovery and processing of the OpenID functions and functionality in this example use a common set of includes, functions, and global definitions, which are stored in a file named *includes.php*.

Let's take a brief look at the common elements that we will use throughout this example:

```php
<?php
require_once "Auth/OpenID/Consumer.php";    //openid consumer code
require_once "Auth/OpenID/FileStore.php";   //file storage
require_once "Auth/OpenID/SReg.php";        //simple registration
require_once "Auth/OpenID/PAPE.php";        //pape policy
require_once "Auth/OpenID/AX.php";          //attribute exchange

define('FILE_COMPLETE', 'complete.php');
define('STORAGE_PATH', 'php_consumer');

/****************************************************************
 * Function: Get Consumer
 * Description: Creates consumer file storage and OpenID consumer
 ****************************************************************/
function get_consumer() {
```

```
    //ensure file storage path can be created
    if (!file_exists(STORAGE_PATH) && !mkdir(STORAGE_PATH)){
        print "Could not create FileStore directory '". STORAGE_PATH ."'.
            Please check permissions.";
        exit(0);
    }

    //create consumer file store
    $store = new Auth_OpenID_FileStore(STORAGE_PATH);

    //create and return consumer
    $consumer =& new Auth_OpenID_Consumer($store);
    return $consumer;
}
?>
```

There are three distinct blocks of functionality in our common includes file that we
need to go over.

First, the required file includes at the top introduce the OpenID files that we must have
to process the OpenID example. These are:

Consumer.php
> OpenID consumer code

FileStore.php
> The functionality to store

SReg.php
> The Simple Registration extension that enables us to obtain simple profile infor-
> mation about the user

PAPE.php
> The PAPE policy definition file that enables us to use the associated functionality

AX.php
> The Attribute Exchange file that enables us to obtain extended public profile in-
> formation about the user

The next block contains our global path definitions:

FILE_COMPLETE
> The filename (under the *APP_ROOT* folder) where the provider should forward
> the user once she has logged in to the provider

STORAGE_PATH
> The relative path to store the OpenID consumer objects

Finally, we have our get_consumer function, which allows us to obtain a new OpenID
consumer object and a consumer file storage mechanism that we will use later in the
program.

Now that we have an overview of the common file that we'll use throughout our program flow, let's jump into the authentication request file that the initial form forwards the user to.

The authentication request

 Support for extensions such as Attribute Exchange or Simple Registration fully depends on the provider that you are attempting to use. Each provider supports its own set of extensions and defines its own data sets that can be obtained. Be sure to check for support prior to using extensions.

The *auth.php* file contains a series of functions to initiate the authentication process and attach the three extensions that we are exploring in this example.

We'll first start a new PHP session and integrate our *includes.php* file that we just went over.

We can then jump into the make_request function, which will be the controller for this section of the authentication process:

```php
<?php
require_once "includes.php";  //configurations and common functions

/*******************************************************************
 * Function: Make Request
 * Description: Builds out the OpenID request using the defined
 *              request extensions
 *******************************************************************/
function make_request(){
    //get openid identifier URL
    if (empty($_GET['openid_url'])) {
        $error = "Expected an OpenID URL.";
        print $error;
        exit(0);
    }

    $openid = $_GET['openid_url'];
    $consumer = get_consumer();

    //begin openid authentication
    $auth_request = $consumer->begin($openid);

    //no authentication available
    if (!$auth_request) {
        echo "Authentication error; not a valid OpenID.";
    }

    //add openid extensions to the request
    $auth_request->addExtension(attach_ax());    //attribute exchange
    $auth_request->addExtension(attach_sreg());  //simple registration
    $auth_request->addExtension(attach_pape());  //pape policies
```

```php
$return_url = sprintf("http://%s%s/%s", $_SERVER['SERVER_NAME'],
                        dirname($_SERVER['PHP_SELF']),
                        FILE_COMPLETE);
$trust_root = sprintf("http://%s%s/", $_SERVER['SERVER_NAME'],
                        dirname($_SERVER['PHP_SELF']));

//openid v1 - send through redirect
if ($auth_request->shouldSendRedirect()){
    $redirect_url = $auth_request->redirectURL($trust_root, $return_url);

    //if no redirect available display error message, else redirect
    if (Auth_OpenID::isFailure($redirect_url)) {
        print "Could not redirect to server: " . $redirect_url->message;
    } else {
        header("Location: " . $redirect_url);
    }
//openid v2 - use javascript form to send POST to server
} else {
    //build form markup
    $form_id = 'openid_message';
    $form_html = $auth_request->htmlMarkup($trust_root, $return_url, false,
                                    array('id' => $form_id));

    //if markup cannot be built display error, else render form
    if (Auth_OpenID::isFailure($form_html)){
        print "Could not redirect to server: " . $form_html->message;
    } else {
        print $form_html;
    }
  }
}
```

At the top of the function, we first check to make sure that the user (or our program, for that matter) has defined an OpenID provider URL for us to initiate the authentication request against. Once we confirm that, we obtain the URL and create a new OpenID consumer object, as well as an OpenID consumer file storage mechanism.

We then call the authentication begin function against our OpenID consumer, passing along the OpenID URL. This step performs the URI discovery to validate that the specified URL is indeed a valid OpenID endpoint. If that succeeds, we can start attaching our extensions.

Calling the addExtension(...) method against our authentication request object for each extension, we pass in the return value of our extension generation functions as the attribute. These will simply be objects that define the type of data that we want or the process that we want to use. We'll look at these functions in more detail shortly.

Now we need to define a few URLs for the remainder of the process. The return_url variable is the absolute URL to the complete file that will be called once the user has logged in through the authentication process. The trust_root parameter is used to define a trusted location to validate that the authentication process is going through the expected channels.

Now, depending on the version of OpenID being employed, we will handle the request for authentication in different ways. We use the shouldSendRedirect() method against our authentication object to determine whether we should redirect the user (OpenID 1) or use a form POST (OpenID 2).

To redirect the user, we build a redirect URL with our trust_root and redirect_url, and then call Auth_OpenID::isFailure(...) to ensure that the redirect URL is valid. If so, we redirect the user.

To send a form POST request, we create a form ID and the form HTML markup using the htmlMarkup(...) method. We then call the Auth_OpenID::isFailure(...) method to ensure that the form markup can be displayed. If it can, we print it out for the user to authenticate with a login.

Now that you understand this process, let's take a closer look at the functions that generate the OpenID extension objects that we are sending along with our authentication request. We'll start by looking at the Attribute Exchange function:

```
/*****************************************************************
 * Function: Attach Attribute Exchange
 * Description: Creates attribute exchange OpenID extension request
 *              to allow capturing of extended profile attributes
 *****************************************************************/
function attach_ax(){
   //build attribute request list
   $attribute[] = Auth_OpenID_AX_AttrInfo::make(
                  'http://axschema.org/contact/email', 1, 1, 'email');
   $attribute[] = Auth_OpenID_AX_AttrInfo::make(
                  'http://axschema.org/namePerson', 1, 1, 'fullname');
   $attribute[] = Auth_OpenID_AX_AttrInfo::make(
                  'http://axschema.org/person/gender', 1, 1, 'gender');
   $attribute[] = Auth_OpenID_AX_AttrInfo::make(
                  'http://axschema.org/media/image/default', 1, 1, 'picture');

   //create attribute exchange request
   $ax = new Auth_OpenID_AX_FetchRequest;

   //add attributes to ax request
   foreach($attribute as $attr){
      $ax->add($attr);
   }

   //return ax request
   return $ax;
}
```

The AX function contains a fairly simple process for defining the user profile values that we want to obtain from the user once she has logged in to the provider site.

We first create an array of Attribute Exchange attribute information objects. We do so by making requests to `Auth_OpenID_AX_AttrInfo::make(...)` with several parameters to denote the piece of information that we are trying to obtain. These include:

type_uri *(string)*
> The URI for the OpenID type that defines the attribute.

count *(integer)*
> The number of values to request for the type. You might have a count greater than 1 if, for example, you are trying to obtain employment information from a user's profile when multiple jobs may be defined.

required *(Boolean)*
> Whether the type should be marked as required in the OpenID request, and is required to complete the request.

alias *(string)*
> The name alias to be attributed to the type in the request.

Now that we have defined the attributes we want to obtain, we create a new attribute exchange request object by calling the constructor for `Auth_OpenID_AX_FetchRequest`. We then loop through the array of attributes that we just created and add them to the new attribute exchange request object. Once this is complete, we return the object.

Next, let's look at attaching the functionality for the Simple Registration extension:

```
/*****************************************************************
 * Function: Attach Simple Registration
 * Description: Creates simple registration OpenID extension request
 *              to allow capturing of simple profile attributes
 *****************************************************************/
function attach_sreg(){
   //create simple registration request
   $sreg_request = Auth_OpenID_SRegRequest::build(
      array('nickname'),
      array('fullname', 'email'));

   //return sreg request
   return $sreg_request;
}
```

The Simple Registration extension process is even simpler than the Attribute Exchange process. We create the Simple Registration object at the same time that we define which user profile fields we'd like to obtain. We make a request to `Auth_OpenID_SRegRequest::build(...)`, passing in the fields that we would like to obtain as arrays of strings. Attributes that are passed in as the first array of strings are marked as required for the completion of the process, while attributes in the second array of strings are optional and may not be returned.

If you are unsure whether the provider you are working with makes available a certain user profile attribute that you are trying to obtain, then it is best to set its return requirement as optional and then be prepared to catch the case where the data may not be returned.

Now that we have set up our Simple Registration flow, let's define our PAPE policies for the request:

```
/*****************************************************************
 * Function: Attach PAPE
 * Description: Creates PAPE policy OpenID extension request to
 *              inform server of policy standards
 *****************************************************************/
function attach_pape(){
   //capture pape policies passed in via openid form
   $policy_uris = $_GET['policies'];

   //create pape policy request
   $pape_request = new Auth_OpenID_PAPE_Request($policy_uris);

   //return pape request
   return $pape_request;
}

//initiate the OpenID request
make_request();
?>
```

Our `attach_pape()` function follows the same type of flow as the SREG and AX extensions. We first obtain all selected PAPE policies from the query string that the user selected in the original form. These will be the authentication policies that we will use for the request.

We can then simply call the constructor for `Auth_OpenID_PAPE_Request()`, passing in the policies obtained from the form and return the object back. It's that simple.

Now that all of our functions are defined, we call `make_request()` to begin the authentication process.

The authentication callback

No matter which method we're using to authenticate the user (either forwarding the user on to the provider domain or printing out the authentication process as a form), the user will be presented with a login screen that allows her to log in to the service provider of her choice. Once she has entered in her username and password and has clicked to log in, she will be sent to the authentication callback location that is associated with the process. For our example, we have this file saved as *complete.php*. This file will allow us to complete the authentication process and pull out all of the data that we are requesting from our extensions.

Let's break down the callback into the logical blocks that we set up in the initial request, our primary OpenID authentication, and the extensions that we requested.

Checking the OpenID authentication state. The first thing that we are going to work with now is the OpenID response. We need to ensure that the user did not cancel the process and that there wasn't a failure at some point in the request:

```php
<?php
require_once("includes.php");

//get new OpenID consumer object
$consumer = get_consumer();

//complete openid process using current app root
$return_url = sprintf("http://%s%s/complete.php", $_SERVER['SERVER_NAME'],
                      dirname($_SERVER['PHP_SELF']));
$response = $consumer->complete($return_url);

//response state - authentication cancelled
if ($response->status == Auth_OpenID_CANCEL) {
    $response_state = 'OpenID authentication was cancelled';
//response state - authentication failed
} else if ($response->status == Auth_OpenID_FAILURE) {
    $response_state = "OpenID authentication failed: " . $response->message;
//response state - authentication succeeded
} else if ($response->status == Auth_OpenID_SUCCESS) {
    //get the identity url and capture success message
    $openid = htmlentities($response->getDisplayIdentifier());
    $response_state = sprintf('OpenID authentication succeeded:
        <a href="%s">%s</a>', $openid, $openid);

    if ($response->endpoint->canonicalID){
        $response_state .= '<br />XRI CanonicalID Included: '
                        . htmlentities($response->endpoint->canonicalID);
    }
}
```

We start the process by including our *includes.php* file that we detailed earlier. From this set of includes, we create a new OpenID consumer object that we can use to complete the OpenID process.

To complete the OpenID process, we need to do two things. We first construct the absolute URL to the *complete.php* file (where we currently are), which we will use to verify the complete state location. We then call the complete(...) method of our OpenID consumer, passing in the current URL. This method will interpret the server's response to our OpenID request. The absolute URL that we specified will be compared against the openid.current_url variable to confirm a match. If a match cannot be made, the OpenID complete(...) method will return a response of FAILURE. In any event, the response object returned from this method will provide us with all of the information that we need to process the OpenID server response.

We start that process by checking the string status of the OpenID complete(...) response object, $response->status. Depending on the response from this parameter, we will proceed in different ways:

Auth_OpenID_CANCEL
> The authentication process was cancelled. There is no information to obtain from the response.

Auth_OpenID_FAILURE
> The authentication process failed at some point. The message parameter in the response object will have more information about the failure, so we display the "Something went wrong" string with that message.

Auth_OpenID_SUCCESS
> The process completed successfully. We call getDisplayIdentifier() in the response object to obtain the profile URL of the user who authenticated, and then display that in a success message to the user.

The case that we will explore for the callback is the SUCCESS response. If there is a CANCEL or FAILURE instance, we'll need to handle those appropriately, but for the scope of this example we'll see how to pull our user information from an OpenID SUCCESS case.

After we have displayed the OpenID user identifier for the user in our SUCCESS case, we check the endpoint to see whether there is a CanonicalID field available. This field will be available if the verified identifier is an XRI (Extensible Resource Identifier). If available, the CanonicalID field that is discovered from the XRD (Extensible Resource Descriptor) should be used as the key lookup field when we're storing information about the end user.

Now that we have the simple OpenID information for the user, let's look at how we can extract further information from the extensions that we defined. We'll take a look at the Simple Registration extension first.

Capturing values returned by Simple Registration. Using the Simple Registration extension from our OpenID request, we can capture some profile, contact, and geographical information about a user through our existing OpenID process.

Within the SUCCESS instance of the OpenID response in our sample, we can display the information that the provider has returned from the Simple Registration extension:

```
//display sreg return data if available
$response_sreg =
    Auth_OpenID_SRegResponse::fromSuccessResponse($response)->contents();
foreach ($response_sreg as $item => $value){
    $response_state .= "<br />SReg returned <b>$item</b> with the value:
                        <b>$value</b>";
}
```

Using the Auth_OpenID_SRegResponse::fromSuccessResponse(...) method, we can capture the Simple Registration object from the OpenID response. Against that object, we can call the contents() helper method to return only the Simple Registration data.

(This method is really just returning the "data" structure inside the Simple Registration return object.)

The object that you are working with might look something like the following:

```
array(7) {
  ["openid.sreg.email"]=> array(1) {
    [0]=> string(17) "jontest@yahoo.com"
  }
  ["openid.sreg.nickname"]=> array(1) {
    [0]=> string(3) "Jon"
  }
  ["openid.sreg.gender"]=> array(1) {
    [0]=> string(1) "M"
  }
  ["openid.sreg.dob"]=> array(1) {
    [0]=> string(10) "1980-12-06"
  }
  ["openid.sreg.country"]=> array(1) {
    [0]=> string(2) "US"
  }
  ["openid.sreg.language"]=> array(1) {
    [0]=> string(2) "en"
  }
  ["openid.sreg.timezone"]=> array(1) {
    [0]=> string(18) "America/Los_Angeles"
  }
}
```

Once we have obtained that object, we then loop over each key and display the content from the process so that we can see what the provider has returned.

Now that we have processed the content from the Simple Registration extension, we can begin to look at the PAPE policy extension values.

Checking the PAPE policy states. Depending on the support the provider offers for PAPE policies and what we designated at the beginning of our OpenID example, we can display the PAPE policy responses from the provider to see how they affected the OpenID process:

```
//display pape policy return data if available
$response_pape = Auth_OpenID_PAPE_Response::fromSuccessResponse($response);
if ($response_pape){
    //pape policies affected by authentication
    if ($response_pape->auth_policies){
        $response_state .= "<br />PAPE returned policies which affected
                            the authentication:";

        foreach ($response_pape->auth_policies as $uri){
            $response_state .= '- ' . htmlentities($uri);
        }
    }

    //server authentication age
    if ($response_pape->auth_age){
```

```
        $response_state .= "<br />PAPE returned server authentication age with
                            the value: " . htmlentities($response_pape->auth_age);
    }

    //nist authentication level
    if ($response_pape->nist_auth_level) {
        $response_state .= "<br />PAPE returned server NIST auth level with the
                            value: " . htmlentities($response_pape->nist_auth_level);
    }
}
```

We first call the `Auth_OpenID_PAPE_Response::fromSuccessResponse(...)` method against our OpenID response object to return our PAPE data. If a PAPE response object exists, we can display the processing information.

We start by checking the policies that affected the authentication process. For each policy found, we display the URI.

Next, we tackle server authentication age. We display the age, if available, that was returned from the provider.

Last, we check the NIST authentication level that was used for the OpenID request. We return back the level that was used, if available.

The final extension that we will process is Attribute Exchange.

Capturing values returned by Attribute Exchange. If we specified that we wanted to use the Attribute Exchange extension in our request, we can easily process the data that is returned from the provider:

```
        //get attribute exchange return values
        $response_ax = new Auth_OpenID_AX_FetchResponse();
        $ax_return = $response_ax->fromSuccessResponse($response);
        foreach ($ax_return->data as $item => $value){
            $response_state .= "<br />AX returned <b>$item</b> with the value:
                                <b>{$value[0]}</b>";
        }
    }

    print $response_state;
    ?>
```

We fetch the Attribute Exchange structure from the OpenID response object by creating a new instance of `Auth_OpenID_AX_FetchResponse` and then calling the `fromSuc cessResponse(...)` method against the new instance, passing in the OpenID response object. We should now have an object that contains the Attribute Exchange information that we requested at the beginning of the OpenID process. This object should look something like the following:

```
array(4) {
  ["http://axschema.org/contact/email"]=> array(1) {
    [0]=> string(17) "jontest@yahoo.com"
  }
  ["http://axschema.org/namePerson"]=> array(1) {
```

```
  [0]=> string(16) "Jonathan LeBlanc"
}
["http://axschema.org/person/gender"]=> array(1) {
  [0]=> string(1) "M"
}
["http://axschema.org/media/image/default"]=> array(1) {
  [0]=> string(111) "https://a323.yahoofs.com/coreid/4ca0e24
          cibc9zws131sp2/VXtMnow7dKiKol09_NI9bAeW
          Ig--/7/tn48.jpeg?ciAgZ3NBvexVYA_D"
}
}
```

Once we've obtained this object, we loop through each returned element and add it to our response object to be displayed.

Once all OpenID elements and extension structures have been processed for the SUCCESS state, we print out the information to complete the example.

We should now have a functional example that will authenticate the user and capture some general profile information about her.

Implementing OpenID Using Python

 The full code for this sample is available at *https://github.com/jcleblanc/programming-social-applications/tree/master/chapter_11/openid-python*.

We've explored the OpenID implementation using PHP as the backing server-side language, so now let's see what shape the implementation takes when Python is used as the main delivery language. We will cover the same type of implementation as before—one that gives us a program that can perform discovery on a number of different OpenID providers and allow the user to sign in using their services. We will also integrate our same three OpenID extensions to provide additional security and user information during the process:

- Simple Registration for basic user information
- Attribute Exchange for more extensive user information
- PAPE for additional security levels

At the end of the example, we will have a complete end-to-end program that allows users to log in using a range of OpenID providers.

Getting the required OpenID library

For this example, we are using the Janrain OpenID Python library, which you can find in Janrain's list of libraries at *http://www.janrain.com/openid-enabled*. Before we begin implementing the code for this example, we first need to install the OpenID library.

Before running the `python setup.py install` command to install the OpenID library, you will need to have the `distutils` module installed. This is part of the Python standard library, but some distributions package it separately in a "python-dev" package.

To install this library, follow these steps:

1. Download the Janrain OpenID Python library from *https://github.com/openid/py thon-openid/downloads*. For this example, we use the "2.2.5.zip" download version.

2. Decompress the file that you just downloaded and then navigate into the directory via the command line.

3. From the root of the directory, run the command **python setup.py install**.

This should begin the installation of the OpenID Python library that we will use. Once it's installed, we can start building our OpenID sample.

The markup file

For this example, we are using Google App Engine to run the Python code against localhost. So, our first step is to create the YAML file that App Engine will use to set up the application. Our file, *app.yaml*, contains everything we need to successfully run the example:

```
application: openid
version: 1
runtime: python
api_version: 1

handlers:
- url: /index.py
  script: index.py
- url: /auth.py
  script: auth.py
- url: /complete.py
  script: complete.py
```

There are three file paths defined in the YAML file:

index.py
This prints out the initial form in which a user inputs the OpenID provider URI that he would like to use and then selects whether he also wants to use a PAPE phishing filter for the request.

auth.py
This file is where we will initiate the OpenID discovery and authentication processes based on the information input by the user in the aforementioned form.

complete.py
> This file will complete the OpenID authentication process and then display the information that was obtained through the process.

With that YAML file as our base, we can begin constructing the pieces that make up everything from the form to our completion script.

The discovery form

With our App Engine configuration file in place, let's turn our attention to the discovery form that a user interacts with before authenticating his user account for a given provider.

 As noted in the OpenID PHP example, this example requires that a user enter the OpenID provider discovery URI himself. While this is a good practice for testing, you should never require site users to know this information. In lieu of the form input, for each provider you should display an image or link that will automatically supply your scripts with the necessary information.

```
print '''\
Content-type: text/html; charset=UTF-8
<!DOCTYPE HTML PUBLIC "-//W3C//DTD HTML 4.01//EN"
    "http://www.w3.org/TR/html4/strict.dtd">
<html xmlns="http://www.w3.org/1999/xhtml">
<head>
<meta http-equiv="Content-Type" content="text/html; charset=utf-8" />
<title>OpenID Sample Application</title>
</head>
<body>
<style>
form{ font:12px arial,helvetica,sans-serif; }
#openid_url { background:#FFFFFF url(http://wiki.openid.net/f/openid-16x16.gif)
                        no-repeat scroll 5px 50%; padding-left:25px; }
</style>

<form action="auth.py" method="GET">
   <input type="hidden" value="login" name="actionType">
   <h2>Sign in using OpenID</h2>
   <input type="text" style="font-size: 12px;" value="" size="40" id="openid_url"
      name="openid_url">  
   <input type="submit" value="Sign in"><br />
   <small>(e.g. http://username.myopenid.com)</small><br /><br />

   <b>PAPE Policies (Optional)</b><br />
   <input type="checkbox" name="policy_phishing"
      value="PAPE_AUTH_PHISHING_RESISTANT" /> PAPE_AUTH_PHISHING_RESISTANT
   <br />
</form>
```

```
</body></html>
'''
```

The discovery form consists of a few pieces—besides the styling and layout—that we should focus on. The driver for this file is the form wrapping the contents. A user will interact with the form as follows:

1. He will input the OpenID provider discovery URI that he would like to use to authenticate himself with.

2. He will select from the optional PAPE options whether he wants to apply a phishing resistance filter on the provider side when the request is made.

3. He will submit the form to begin the authentication process.

Once those steps are taken, we will submit this form to the *auth.py* file, passing the parameters via the query string, to begin our form processing and authentication step.

The authentication request

Now that the form has been submitted, we are at the *auth.py* file endpoint to begin authentication. At this stage, the user should have submitted the discovery form specifying the provider endpoint URI he wants to use and whether he wants to have the PAPE phishing filter applied during the process.

The authentication request file will take those form results, perform discovery on the provider endpoint URI to ensure its validity, prepare an authentication request with our requested OpenID extensions, and finally, either print out the authentication form or forward the user to the form on the provider site (depending on the OpenID version).

To see how we will accomplish all of this, let's break apart the OpenID authentication request file into several logical steps, starting with the identifier discovery.

OpenID identifier discovery and request setup. Let's begin by importing the libraries that we will need for the request. We set up the imports for our standard libraries—sys, cgi, and os—and then import the OpenID library elements that we will need for this example.

Following this, we begin the authentication request file example by defining the main() function that will be the main element of our request:

```
import sys
import cgi
import openid
import os

from openid.consumer import consumer
from openid.extensions import pape, sreg, ax

'''
' Function: Main
' Description: Initiates the OpenID authentication process
'''
```

```
def main():
    #get query parameters
    params = cgi.FieldStorage()

    #check if an OpenID url was specified
    if not params.has_key('openid_url'):
        print_msg('Please enter an OpenID Identifier to verify.', 'text/plain')
    else:
        #capture OpenID url
        openid_url = params['openid_url'].value

        #create a base consumer object
        oidconsumer = consumer.Consumer({}, None)

        try:
            request = oidconsumer.begin(openid_url)
        except:
            print_msg('Error in discovery: ' + openid_url, 'text/plain')
        else:
            if request is None:
                print_msg('No OpenID services found', 'text/plain')
            else:
                #build trust root and url to return to
                trust_root = 'http://%s/' % (os.environ['HTTP_HOST'])
                return_to = 'http://%s/complete.py' % (os.environ['HTTP_HOST'])
```

Within our main() function, we first get the query string parameters that were passed to us from the previous form. These include the OpenID provider URI to use and the optional PAPE extension for protecting against phishing attacks.

We then check to see whether there was even an OpenID provider URI entered by the user. If not, we simply print an error to the user. If the URI was specified, we capture the string value to verify and then create an empty OpenID consumer object to perform discovery.

We then attempt to perform discovery on the OpenID provider URI. We display an error if an exception was thrown. If an exception was not thrown, we make sure that the request variable is not None; if it's not, we have a valid request object.

If the value is valid, we construct these two variables for later use:

The trust root URI
    The root of your OpenID sample from which the application is being run

The return to URL
    The absolute path to the file that the user will be forwarded to once he has authenticated his account

Now we can begin attaching our OpenID extensions on top of our request object.

Setting up the OpenID extension requests. As with our PHP example, we will attach these three extensions to our OpenID request:

- Simple Registration
- Attribute Exchange
- PAPE phishing policy

Let's break these down into the individual extensions:

```
#simple registration extension request
sreg_request = sreg.SRegRequest(required=['nickname'],
                                optional=['fullname', 'email'])
request.addExtension(sreg_request)

#attribute exchange extension request
ax_request = ax.FetchRequest()
ax_request.add(ax.AttrInfo('http://axschema.org/contact/email',
                           required=False, alias='email'))
ax_request.add(ax.AttrInfo('http://axschema.org/namePerson',
                           required=False, alias='fullname'))
ax_request.add(ax.AttrInfo('http://axschema.org/person/gender',
                           required=False, alias='gender'))
ax_request.add(ax.AttrInfo('http://axschema.org/media/image/default',
                           required=False, alias='picture'))
request.addExtension(ax_request)

#pape policy extension request
if params.has_key('policy_phishing'):
    pape_request = pape.Request([pape.AUTH_PHISHING_RESISTANT])
    request.addExtension(pape_request)
```

We start out with Simple Registration to attempt to capture a few pieces of information about the user. Using our Simple Registration library, we call the SRegRequest(...) method to create a new request object. To that function, we pass in the fields that are required for the request (the nickname) as well as those that are optional (the full name and email address). Once our request object is ready, we call the addExtension(...) method, passing in the Simple Registration request object that we just created in order to add the extension to the authentication request.

Next, we need to set up the Attribute Exchange request. We start by generating a new request object by calling the FetchRequest() method within our Attribute Exchange library. We then add to that request object (using the add(....) method) each piece of information that we hope to capture about the user, generated as an attribute info object. This information includes the user's email address, full name, gender, and default profile image. Once we've added every piece of information to the Attribute Exchange request object, we then add that object to the OpenID authentication request, again using the addExtension(...) method.

Last, we need to set up our PAPE request to apply the phishing resistance filter. If the user has chosen to include this option, we call the Request(...) method within our PAPE library to generate the request object, passing in an array of the filters that we would like to apply—in this case, just the phishing resistance filter. We then add that object to the overall OpenID request.

Now let's finalize the authentication build process and see how to generate the required page that the user will need to validate his user account.

Displaying the authentication login. We now have a fully qualified request object that we can use to authenticate the user session, but first we need to display the form through which this authentication takes place:

```
#openid v1 - send through redirect
if request.shouldSendRedirect():
    redirect_url = request.redirectURL(
        trust_root, return_to, immediate='immediate')
    print "Location: " + redirect_url
#openid v2 - use javascript form to send POST to server
else:
    form_html = request.htmlMarkup(
        trust_root, return_to,
        form_tag_attrs={'id':'openid_message'})

    print_msg(form_html, 'text/html')
```

In the preceding block of the code, we have two sections depending on the version of OpenID that is being used. We make a call to shouldSendRedirect() against the request object to determine whether the form should be printed out to screen or whether the user should be redirected to the provider site.

If we're using OpenID 1, we capture the redirect URL that we should send the user to, using the trust_root and return_to variables that we set up earlier. We then print out a location redirect to send the browser to the required page.

If we're using OpenID 2, we simply print out the authentication page. We make a request to htmlMarkup(...) against the request object, passing in the trust_root and return_to variables that we set up earlier. This will capture the markup that we need to display to the user. We then print out the content to the screen using a content type declaration of text/html.

That concludes the core of the sample, but there are still a few pieces that we need to look at for the authentication request component.

Printing messages and initiating program execution. Our last piece of this part of the script is the print helper function and the code that initiates the execution of the main() function:

```
'''
' Function: Print Message
' Description: Print a message with a provided content type
' Inputs: msg (string) - The message to be displayed
'         type (string) - The content type to use (e.g. text/plain)
'''
def print_msg(msg, type):
    if msg is not None:
        print 'Content-Type: %s' % (type)
        print ''
        print msg
```

```
#initiate load of main()
if __name__ == '__main__':
    main()
```

The `print_msg(...)` function is a simple tool to print messages to the screen with the correct content type applied. We pass in the message string that we want to print as the first parameter, and the content type that we want to use as the second parameter. As long as the message has some sort of content, it will be printed to the screen with the content type we've defined.

Now that all of our functions are defined, we set up a little code block at the end to initiate a request to the `main()` function once the program executes.

Once this file executes, either the user will be redirected to the provider for authentication or the authentication form will be printed out to screen. In either event, the user will be given the option to authenticate his user account. If he accepts the authentication step to verify himself, then we will be forwarded over to the authentication callback, defined by the `return_to` variable that we populated earlier in the program.

The authentication callback

At this point, the user should have authenticated his account and been redirected to the `return_to` callback URL. In the case of this example, that file is *complete.py*.

We will complete a number of tasks once the user reaches this page:

- Parsing the OpenID parameters passed along the query string
- Completing the authentication process using those parameters to provide us with a success or failure message
- Parsing the responses from each OpenID extension
- Printing out all obtained objects

We will be printing out the objects that are returned to us simply as a "getting started" end-to-end example of how OpenID works. Dumping out the end objects will allow you to work with different OpenID providers to see what type of information and which OpenID extensions are supported in their particular implementations. When working with a practical implementation to be used for actual end users—such as when prepopulating a form with the user information obtained from the Attribute Exchange extension request—you should always show only the base values of the results to the user.

With that disclaimer out of the way, let's jump into the code for the *complete.py* file. We'll split up the file into its logical pieces, just like we did with the *auth.py* file.

Let's start by capturing the OpenID parameters and using them to complete authentication.

Completing authentication. Our first tasks here are to capture the OpenID parameters that have been passed through to us via the query string, put them into a dictionary, and then complete the authentication process to get a success or failure message for the user authentication. After we import all of the required standard and OpenID libraries needed for this process, we begin by defining our `main()` function:

```
import sys
import cgi
import openid
import urllib
import os

from openid.consumer import consumer
from openid.extensions import pape, sreg, ax

'''
' Function: Main
' Description: Completes OpenID authentication process and prints results
'''
def main():
    #create a base consumer object
    oidconsumer = consumer.Consumer({}, None)

    #create return to url
    url = "http://%s/complete.py" % (os.environ['HTTP_HOST'])

    #print page content type
    print 'Content-Type: text/plain'
    print ''

    #parse query string parameters into dictionary
    params = {}
    string_split = [s for s in os.environ['QUERY_STRING'].split('&') if s]
    for item in string_split:
        key,value = item.split('=')
        params[key] = urllib.unquote(value)

    #complete OpenID authentication and get identifier
    info = oidconsumer.complete(params, url)
    display_identifier = info.getDisplayIdentifier()
```

The first thing we do within `main()` is to create a new base OpenID consumer object, from which we will be able to complete the authentication process. We then need to define the value of the `return_to` URL, which just so happens to be the absolute URL to the current file, *complete.py*. Since we will be printing all of our results to the current page, we also print out the content type that we will use for this page. In this case, that will be simply `text/plain` since there will be no associated HTML.

Now we need to build our dictionary of OpenID parameters. We create a new dictionary object, `params`, and then split all parameters in the query string into a new object based on the ampersand. For each entry found, we split the key and value apart based on the equals sign. We then store the parameters in the dictionary as unescaped strings.

Now that we have our dictionary of OpenID parameters, we complete the authentication process by calling `complete(...)` against the OpenID consumer object that we created, passing in the dictionary of OpenID parameters and the `return_to` absolute URL. If all goes well, we should get a response object filled with everything that was returned from the OpenID process.

The last piece of this part of the puzzle is to capture the OpenID identifier for the user. From the `info` variable, we call `getDisplayIdentifier()` to extract this information.

Now let's move on to extracting the OpenID extension responses that we requested during the user authentication.

Capturing the return values of the OpenID extension requests. At a base level, the OpenID extensions that we requested (Simple Registration, Attribute Exchange, and PAPE) are fairly easy to capture. The OpenID library includes a set of helper methods that allows us to extract the data we want from the OpenID return object:

```
#get simple registration extension response
sreg_resp = sreg.SRegResponse.fromSuccessResponse(info)

#get pape extension response
pape_obj = pape.Response.fromSuccessResponse(info)
pape_resp = '';
if pape_obj is not None:
    for policy_uri in pape_obj.auth_policies:
        pape_resp += cgi.escape(policy_uri) + ' | '

#build attribute exchange response object
ax_response = ax.FetchResponse.fromSuccessResponse(info)
if ax_response:
    ax_items = {
        'email': ax_response.get('http://axschema.org/contact/email'),
        'fullname': ax_response.get('http://axschema.org/namePerson'),
        'gender': ax_response.get('http://axschema.org/person/gender'),
        'picture': ax_response.get('http://axschema.org/media/image/default')
    }
```

Let's start by collecting the simple responses from Simple Registration and PAPE. To collect the Simple Registration response, we call `SRegResponse.fromSuccess` `Response(...)` against the `sreg` extension library, passing in the info object that holds the OpenID response.

 Responses from OpenID extensions are contingent upon the OpenID provider site supporting the fields that you are requesting. For instance, if you are requesting a user's email address through Simple Registration and the provider doesn't support either that field or the Simple Registration extension altogether, the response returned when we try to capture the object will be `None`.

For the data that we requested in the *auth.py* file, the Simple Registration response object will look something like the following:

```
{
  'openid.sreg.email': ['jbrown@yahoo.com'],
```

```
    'openid.sreg.nickname': ['John '],
    'openid.sreg.fullname': ['John Brown']
}
```

Now we turn our focus to the PAPE response object. Calling `Response.fromSuccess Response(...)` against the `pape` extension library, passing in the OpenID info object responses again, will return us the policies that were returned back by the provider (if supported). We loop through the policies by going through `pape_obj.auth_policies` and then add the values to the PAPE response object.

Finally, let's get our Attribute Exchange information. We call `FetchResponse.from SuccessResponse(...)` against the `ax` extension library, again passing in the OpenID info object response. If a response is available, we create a new dictionary filled with the individual values that we requested by calling `get(...)` and passing in the required schema value.

Once this process is complete, our dictionary should look something like the following:

```
{
  'gender': ['M'],
  'fullname': ['John Brown'],
  'email': ['jbrown@yahoo.com'],
  'picture': ['https://a323.yahoofs.com/coreid/4ca0e24cibc9zws131
        sp2/NI9bAeWIg--/7/tn48.jpeg']
}
```

Now that we have completed the OpenID authentication process and obtained the values from all our extensions, we just need to do one more thing—print it all out.

Printing out our response objects. This last step simply checks all of our responses and prints out the appropriate notification so that we can see whether our requests succeeded or not:

```
    print ax_items

#print all OpenID responses
print display_identifier

if sreg_resp is not None:
    print sreg_resp

if pape_resp is not None:
    print pape_resp

if info.status == consumer.FAILURE and display_identifier:
    message = "Verification failed"
elif info.status == consumer.SUCCESS:
    message = 'Success'
elif info.status == consumer.CANCEL:
    message = 'Verification cancelled'
elif info.status == consumer.SETUP_NEEDED:
    message = 'Setup needed'
else:
    message = 'Verification failed.'
```

```
    print message

if __name__ == '__main__':
    main()
```

We start by printing the response object we built from the Attribute Exchange response. This will be printed only if there was a response object built.

Next, we print the display identifier for the user. This is the unique absolute URI that is associated with the user who authenticated. This identifier will look something like the following:

https://me.yahoo.com/a/dV.URBo4t84y.G4v0jMmdeznx3OotpS4

If we navigate to that provided URI, we see a screen like the one shown in Figure 11-7.

Figure 11-7. Example of unique absolute URI contents on Yahoo

Now we check whether the responses from the Simple Registration and PAPE extensions were valid, and if so, print them out.

Last, we check the status of the OpenID authentication response by checking `info` `.status`. This value tells you whether the OpenID authentication process succeeded or failed, and is one of the following responses:

`consumer.FAILURE`
> The authentication process failed at some point.

`consumer.SUCCESS`
> The authentication process succeeded. At this point, we can begin processing all of the responses.

`consumer.CANCEL`
> The authentication process was cancelled and not completed.

`consumer.SETUP_NEEDED`
> Additional setup is required in the authentication request.

Any other response
> If any other response was returned, we should gracefully handle this with a "Something went wrong" message.

Once the message has been printed, all that remains is the `if` statement at the bottom of the file, which will initiate the `main()` function and start the process.

That completes the OpenID sample using Python. Using this as a base, you can create a comprehensive end-to-end product offering that allows users to sign in using their OpenID-enabled accounts.

Common Errors and Debugging Techniques

As is the case with any open protocol or service that allows you to leverage a large number of different provider companies, you may encounter issues during the discovery, authentication, or data retrieval phases. If the provider does not return clear error responses—other than "Something went wrong"—implementers may not know where the problem lies.

We'll explore some of the common issues that you may face when you're implementing and working with OpenID, as well as a few debugging steps that you can employ to resolve them.

Callback URL Mismatch

One common OpenID issue arises when you are attempting to perform discovery on an OpenID provider endpoint and have to construct a redirect URL (where to send the end user after she has authenticated) built off a trust root (the current root of the application) and the callback (where to send the end user).

The OpenID domain verification process is quite strict for most providers, requiring an exact match to the root domain. For instance, the following domains will not match:

- *http://jcleblanc.com*
- *http://www.jcleblanc.com*

If there is a callback URL mismatch, you will be presented with something along the lines of Figure 11-8.

You will need to ensure that there is a direct domain match when building your redirect URL (i.e., that the domain that you are constructing the callback from matches the current domain that the user is on).

While this is a common issue for new users of OpenID, it can be remedied quickly if you simply ensure that there is an exact domain match between the trust root and the callback to which you will forward the end user after authentication.

Undiscoverable OpenID Identifier

Another issue that you may encounter—and one that may cause you some frustration if you can't immediately determine what the problem is—has to do with the inability to complete the discovery process for a given OpenID identifier URL.

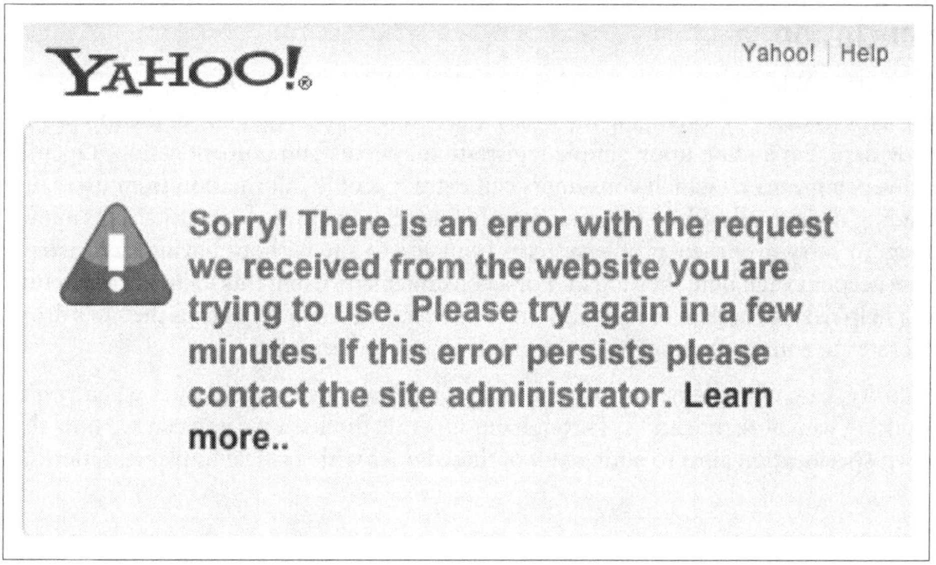

YAHOO!®

Sorry! There is an error with the request we received from the website you are trying to use. Please try again in a few minutes. If this error persists please contact the site administrator. Learn more..

Figure 11-8. Example of callback URL mismatch error screen

For instance, consider the following URLs:

- *http://www.jcleblanc.com*
- *http://jcleblanc.com/*
- *http://jcleblanc.com*
- *http://jcleblanc.com*

When entered into a browser, they would all load the same source site and would not present any challenge in determining what site we are looking for. However, when it comes to OpenID implementations, especially those of older specifications, these differences may create issues during the discovery process.

The problem of the undiscoverable OpenID identifier generally comes up with custom provider implementations of OpenID, where normalization is not being properly applied to a given identifier.

From the consumer point of view, there are two ways to resolve the issue:

- If you have control over the identifier URL that is being sent to the provider (that is, if the user doesn't enter it herself), then you can simply change the URL to exactly what the provider requires.
- You can also normalize the URL yourself prior to performing discovery.

Conclusion

OpenID enables any consumer site to quickly implement a membership login mechanism for its users by leveraging the massive account systems of many of the top profile providers. Expanding upon simple registration systems and authentication, OpenID delivers a means by which consumers can extract profile information from users, including their email addresses, general profile details, and linked accounts. This allows users to carry over their profile systems from site to site without having to register a new account each time they log in. For a consumer site, using this login infrastructure can help reduce the pain of registration for its users, which in turn keeps the site's dropoff rates to a minimum and its social graph robust and thriving.

Security, ease of implementation, and extensibility are always key issues when you're working with authentication. Through our OpenID discussions, you can see how this open specification aims to address all of these issues with a single implementation.

Index

Symbols

! (not) operator, 226
!= (not equals) operator, 226
&& (and) operator, 226
401 (Unauthorized) HTTP status code, 359
403 (Forbidden) HTTP status code, 212
< (less than) operator, 226
<= (less than or equal to) operator, 226
== (equals) operator, 226
> (greater than) operator, 226
>= (greater than or equal to) operator, 226
|| (or) operator, 226

A

access tokens
  exchanging for request tokens, 325–327,
      337–341, 345–348
  fetching, 356–358, 365
  granting protected resources, 358
  refreshing, 360
  request error responses
    insufficient_scope, 359
    invalid_request, 359
    invalid_token, 359
  request parameters
    client_id, 370
    client_secret, 371
    code, 371
    grant_type, 357
    oauth_consumer_key, 326
    oauth_nonce, 326
    oauth_signature, 326
    oauth_signature_method, 326
    oauth_token, 326, 339
    oauth_token_secret, 326, 339
    oauth_verifier, 326, 337, 338
    oauth_version, 326
    redirect_uri, 370
  response parameters
    access_token, 357
    expires_in, 357
    oauth_authorization_expires_in, 327
    oauth_expires_in, 327
    refresh_token, 358
    scope, 358, 370
    token_type, 358
  tracking expiration, 377
ActionScript libraries, 254
activities
  capturing user details, 179
  data requests for, 210
  defining standards for, 401
  general verbs
    add, 408
    cancel, 408
    checkin, 408
    delete, 408
    favorite, 408
    follow, 408
    give, 408
    ignore, 408
    invite, 408
    join, 408
    leave, 408
    like, 409
    make-friend, 409
    play, 409
    receive, 409
    remove, 409

We'd like to hear your suggestions for improving our indexes. Send email to *index@oreilly.com*.

JSON specification, 284, 404
    (see also Activity Streams specification)
JSP expression language, 226
JUnit testing framework, 271

K

keystrokes, logging, 269

L

large views
    about, 13
    canvas view, 15, 83, 122
    default view, 16, 83
    preview view, 16, 83
    as underdeveloped view, 22
leaderboards, 34
less than (<) operator, 226
less than or equal to (<=) operator, 226
libraries, defining, 307
like promotion, 35
Link element (ModulePrefs node)
    about, 79
    building gadget example, 92
    href attribute, 80, 92
    method attribute, 80
    rel attribute, 80
Link-based Resource Descriptor (LRDD), 442
LinkedIn site, 381
LiveJournal website, 453
Living Social (company), 30
Locale element (ModulePrefs node)
    about, 78
    country attribute, 78, 252
    lang attribute, 78, 252
    language_direction attribute, 78
    message bundles and, 252
    messages attribute, 79, 252
localization support with message bundles,
        251–253
location-based applications
    ad targeting, 35
    case study overview, 32
    local business promotions, 35
    meeting friends, 33
    offering competition, 34
    opt-in sharing model and, 43
    providing badges and points, 33
logging keystrokes, 269

login information
    sending with requests, 318
    storing, 317
    token-based systems and, 318
looping content
    about, 231
    escaped values method, 231–232
    looping with conditionals, 235
    looping with context, 235
    nested repeaters and, 233
    nonescaped values method, 233
    specifying index variable for repeater, 234
LRDD (Link-based Resource Descriptor), 442
lt (less than) operator, 226
lte (less than or equal to) operator, 226

M

Mac OS X (Leopard) environment
    installing Partuza, 67–69
    installing Shindig, 59–62
Mafia Wars game
    about, 27
    allowing user interaction, 28
    monetizing, 29
    social graph in, 28
malicious content
    drive-by downloads, 11
    iframes and, 133
man-in-the-middle attack, 323, 466
markup layer
    Caja considerations, 288, 311
    templating and, 19
mayorships, 34
message bundles
    about, 252
    localization support, 251–253
messages
    creating, 100–103
    displaying to users, 100
    positioning in windows, 103–105
    styling content, 105–108
<meta> tag
    about, 383
    fb:admins property, 392
    og:audio property, 388
    og:audio:album property, 388
    og:audio:artist property, 388
    og:audio:title property, 388
    og:audio:type property, 388

O

OAuth (Open Authentication)
  application permissions, 18
  combining OpenID with, 12
  iframes and, 134
  OpenID and, 468
  popularity of, 12
  signed requests and, 193–199
OAuth 1.0a standard
  about, 318
  debugging signature issues, 348–352
  end-user experience, 327–329
  three-legged implementation example, 332–348
  two-legged versus three-legged, 329–332
  workflow process
    about, 319
    exchanging request tokens for access tokens, 325–327
    getting request tokens, 321–323
    getting user-verified request token, 323–325
    obtaining consumer key and secret, 319
OAuth 2 standard
  about, 352
  debugging request issues, 376–380
  end-user experience, 375
  Facebook implementation example, 361–372
  Facebook support, 51
  requesting more social information, 372–374
  workflow process
    about, 353
    fetching access tokens, 356–358, 365
    granting protected resources, 358
    making signed requests, 366
    refreshing access tokens, 360
    requesting authorization, 354, 364
object attributes
  attachments, 404
  author, 404
  content, 404
  displayName, 405
  downstreamDuplicates, 405
  duration, 406
  height, 406
  id, 405
  image, 405

objectType, 405
  published, 405
  summary, 405
  updated, 405
  upsteramDuplicates, 405
  url, 405, 406
  width, 406
object types
  about, 406
  defining products using, 388–390
  general types
    article, 407
    audio, 407
    badge, 407
    bookmark, 407
    collection, 407
    comment, 407
    event, 407
    file, 407
    group, 407
    image, 407
    note, 407
    person, 407
    place, 407
    product, 407
    question, 407
    review, 407
    service, 407
    video, 407
Objective-C language, 254
OExchange protocol
  about, 382, 414
  implementing, 416–422
  primary uses for, 415
  process overview, 414
onclick event handler, 86
one-to-few cluster, 41, 48
onkeypress event, 271
Open Authentication (see OAuth)
Open Graph consumers, 383, 392
Open Graph producers, 383, 392
Open Graph protocol
  about, 258, 382
  capturing data from web sources, 392–399
  Facebook example, 390–392
  Facebook support, 51
  implementing, 384–390
  main elements, 383
  metadata and, 382

Ruby language, 254

S

Salmon protocol
    about, 258, 438
    abuse and spam protection, 441
    implementation overview, 442–443
    PubSubHubbub protocol and, 441
    workflow process, 438–441
same-origin policy, 10
<script> tag
    type attribute, 205, 219, 222
    xmlns:os attribute, 205
security, 11
    (see also ADsafe; Caja)
    clustering users and, 42
    cross-site scripting, 10
    drive-by downloads, 11
    embedded applications and, 9–11
    iframes and, 266, 268
    older browsers and, 10
    permission scopes and, 17
    same-origin policy, 10
    securing applications, 11
    signed requests and, 191–199
service providers
    content offers and, 420–422
    OpenID support, 453
    performing discovery on, 418
    publishers and, 416–418
services
    gifting, 32
    like promotion, 35
    quick-start tips, 37
    social graphs and, 40
    trust relationship with, 42
setprefs JavaScript library
    about, 96, 108–109
    building gadget XML file, 122
setTimeout function, 102, 293
settitle JavaScript library, 96, 110
ShareThis system, 416
sharing data
    balanced sharing, 186
    direct versus passive, 183–187
    opt-in sharing model, 43
    opt-out sharing model, 44
    oversharing applications, 24
Shindig

    about, 57
    Caja support, 282
    displaying gadgets, 125
    extending with JavaScript libraries, 117–121
    installation prerequisites, 58
    setting up, 58–64
    testing installation, 65
signature issues
    double encoding parameters, 349
    incorrect URI endpoints, 349
    invalid methods, 351
    token expiration, 351
    "signature invalid" response, 349
    "signature mismatch" response, 349
signed requests
    making, 194, 366
    oauth_consumer_key parameter, 193, 197
    oauth_nonce parameter, 193
    oauth_signature parameter, 193
    oauth_signature_method parameter, 193, 197
    oauth_timestamp parameter, 193
    oauth_token parameter, 193
    opensocial_app_id parameter, 193
    opensocial_app_url parameter, 193
    opensocial_instance_id parameter, 193
    opensocial_owner_id parameter, 193
    opensocial_viewer_id parameter, 193
    securing data connections with, 191–194
    validating on servers, 194–199
    xoauth_public_key parameter, 193
    xoauth_signature_publickey parameter, 197
Simple Registration (SREG) extension, 456
small views
    about, 12
    default view, 16, 83
    home view, 13, 83, 85, 122
    preview view, 16, 83
    profile view, 14, 83, 85, 122
    as underdeveloped view, 22
Smalltalk language, 254
social API server specification
    about, 130, 131
    implementation requirements, 131
social application containers
    about, 2
    additional code examples, 2

About the Author

Jonathan LeBlanc is a principal technology evangelist and Emmy award–winning software engineer. Specializing in open source initiatives around the implementation of social engagement services, Jonathan works with and promotes emerging technologies to aid in the adoption and utilization of new social development techniques. In this realm, he has worked on the OpenSocial foundation board. As a software engineer, Jonathan works extensively with social interaction development on the Web, engaging in new methods for targeting the social footprint of users to drive the ideal of an open Web.

Colophon

The animal on the cover of *Programming Social Applications* is a Diana monkey (*Cercopithecus diana*), an endangered monkey found in areas of West Africa, including Liberia, Sierra Leone, Ghana, and Côte d'Ivoire. Its name comes from the characteristic white stripe (or browband) across its forehead, which was thought to resemble the bow of Diana, the Roman goddess of the hunt. Its dark, sleek fur is contrasted by this telltale browband, as well as a white throat, underarms, and stripes on the thighs. It is considered one of the most beautiful of the Old World monkeys.

Diana monkeys dwell in primeval forests. They do not make nests, though they retreat to higher levels of the trees at night. They're rarely found on the ground, as they're able to sustain their diet of insects, fruit, invertebrates, young leaves, and flowers at all levels of the canopy. The monkeys' main predators include leopards, crowned hawk-eagles and other birds of prey, chimpanzees, and humans. To protect themselves from predators, Diana monkeys dwell in groups, usually consisting of one male and around 10 reproducing females and their offspring. In addition to alerting their fellow group members to danger, Diana monkeys sound distinct alarm calls for different predators. Their reproductive biology isn't very well understood, but it is known that their mating system is polygynous, breeding takes place year round, and females generally produce one offspring at a time.

Diana monkeys are classified as vulnerable by the International Union for Conservation of Nature (IUCN), mostly due to destruction of habitat and hunting. Like most primates, they can carry diseases like tuberculosis and yellow fever and spread them to humans; however, they're still hunted for food, medical research, and as pets.

The cover image is from Lydekker's *Royal Natural History*. The cover font is Adobe ITC Garamond. The text font is Linotype Birka; the heading font is Adobe Myriad Condensed; and the code font is LucasFont's TheSansMonoCondensed.

Get even more for your money.

Join the O'Reilly Community, and register the O'Reilly books you own. It's free, and you'll get:

- $4.99 ebook upgrade offer
- 40% upgrade offer on O'Reilly print books
- Membership discounts on books and events
- Free lifetime updates to ebooks and videos
- Multiple ebook formats, DRM FREE
- Participation in the O'Reilly community
- Newsletters
- Account management
- 100% Satisfaction Guarantee

Signing up is easy:

1. **Go to: oreilly.com/go/register**
2. **Create an O'Reilly login.**
3. **Provide your address.**
4. **Register your books.**

Note: English-language books only

To order books online:
oreilly.com/store

For questions about products or an order:
orders@oreilly.com

To sign up to get topic-specific email announcements and/or news about upcoming books, conferences, special offers, and new technologies:
elists@oreilly.com

For technical questions about book content:
booktech@oreilly.com

To submit new book proposals to our editors:
proposals@oreilly.com

O'Reilly books are available in multiple DRM-free ebook formats. For more information:
oreilly.com/ebooks

O'REILLY®

Spreading the knowledge of innovators   oreilly.com

Have it your way.

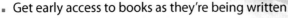

Lightning Source UK Ltd.
Milton Keynes UK
UKOW021324311012

201432UK00001B/15/P